Christian Egalitarian Leadership

The House of Prisca and Aquila

Our mission at the House of Prisca and Aquila is to produce quality books that expound accurately the word of God to empower women and men to minister together in a multicultural church. Our writers have a positive view of the Bible as God's revelation that affects both thoughts and words, so it is plenary, historically accurate, and consistent in itself; fully reliable; and authoritative as God's revelation. Because God is true, God's revelation is true, inclusive to men and women and speaking to a multiethnic church, wherein all the diversity of the church is represented within the parameters of egalitarianism and the Bible's inerrancy in its original autographs.

The word of God is what we are expounding, thereby empowering women and men to minister together in all levels of the church and home. The reason we say women and men together is because that is the model of Prisca and Aquila, ministering together to another member of the church—Apollos: "Having heard Apollos, Priscilla and Aquila took him aside and more accurately expounded to him the Way of God" (Acts 18:26). True exposition, like true religion, is by no means boring—it is fascinating. Books that reveal and expound God's true nature "burn within us" as they elucidate the Scripture and apply it to our lives.

This was the experience of the disciples who heard Jesus on the road to Emmaus: "Were not our hearts burning while Jesus was talking to us on the road, while he was opening the scriptures to us?" (Luke 24:32). Our goal is to create the classics of tomorrow: significant, accessible, pleasing to God, and lasting trade and academic books from an egalitarian inerrantist global perspective that "burn within us."

Our "house" is like the home to which Prisca and Aquila no doubt brought Apollos as they took him aside. It is like the home in Emmaus where Jesus stopped to break bread and reveal his presence. It is like the house built on the rock of obedience to Jesus (Matt 7:24). Our "house," as a euphemism for our publishing team, is a home where truth is shared and Jesus's Spirit breaks bread with us, nourishing all of us with his bounty of truth.

We are delighted to work together with Wipf and Stock in this series. For more information, visit www.houseofpriscaandaquila.com.

"Egalitarian leadership, as a biblical principle, has been the focus of numerous publications, events, and conversations for more than three decades. Global leaders continue to explore the impact of egalitarian leadership, marriages, businesses, and humanitarian endeavors. The editors of this volume have given us a vital resource—wisdom from leaders who have journeyed long as Christian egalitarians in all aspects of life. We thank you!"

—**Mimi Haddad**, President of CBE International

"I spend a lot of my time in the developing world doing missionary work. My life's goal has been to empower women to pursue ministry, and to help churches overcome gender discrimination so that men and women can learn to work together, both in the church and on the field. I am so grateful for Aída Spencer and her husband, David, for providing the theological tools I need to do my work. I can't write or study like they can, but their academic investment enables me to do my job. This book is not just one tool—it is a whole toolbox full of scholarship that I know will help many leaders cut through the obstacles so that we can empower every believer—male and female—to fulfill the Great Commission."

—**J. Lee Grady**, author of *10 Lies the Church Tells Women*

"This volume provides numerous resources through considered research and argumentation, along with stories and application to further the conversation toward living into Christian egalitarian leadership that is marked by service of the other. One hears in their many voices the helpful biblical, theological, philosophical, pastoral, familial, cross-cultural, and practical engagement and call to Christian egalitarian living. May the contributors' tribe ever increase."

—**Rick Wadholm Jr.**, author of *All The Gospel Into All The World*

"The crisis of our times is a dearth of biblical, egalitarian leadership. Spencer et al. effectively demonstrate the interrelationships between theory and practice as a framework for biblical egalitarian leadership. They provide fresh direction for Christian leaders on why and how to live out egalitarian kingdom diversity in the church, marketplace, in marriages, parenting, and across generations. The importance of this book cannot be overstated for such a time as this."

—**Deborah Fulthorp**, College of Theology Online Full Time Faculty, Grand Canyon University

Christian Egalitarian Leadership

*Empowering the Whole Church
according to the Scriptures*

Edited by
Aída Besançon Spencer
and
William David Spencer

WIPF & STOCK · Eugene, Oregon

CHRISTIAN EGALITARIAN LEADERSHIP
Empowering the Whole Church according to the Scriptures

House of Prisca and Aquila Series

Copyright © 2020 Wipf and Stock Publishers. All rights reserved. Except for brief quotations in critical publications or reviews, no part of this book may be reproduced in any manner without prior written permission from the publisher. Write: Permissions, Wipf and Stock Publishers, 199 W. 8th Ave., Suite 3, Eugene, OR 97401.

Wipf & Stock
An Imprint of Wipf and Stock Publishers
199 W. 8th Ave., Suite 3
Eugene, OR 97401

www.wipfandstock.com

PAPERBACK ISBN: 978-1-7252-7053-4
HARDCOVER ISBN: 978-1-7252-7054-1
EBOOK ISBN: 978-1-7252-7055-8

09/25/20

And, having called to himself [the Twelve], Jesus says to them: "You know that the ones being recognized to rule among the gentiles overpower them and their great ones tyrannize them. But, not so among you; but whoever may desire to become great among you will be your servant, and whoever may desire among you to be first will be slave of all; for even the Child of Humanity did not come to be served but to serve, and to give his life a ransom for many." (Mark 10:42–45 Aida's translation. See also Matt 20:25–28; Luke 22:25–27; 1 Pet 5:3)

Contents

List of Contributors ix
Acknowledgments xix
Introduction xxi
—William David Spencer

Part 1: Theory

1. An Overview of the New Testament Teachings on Christian Egalitarian Leadership 3
   —Aída Besançon Spencer and William David Spencer

2. Egalitarianism and Biblical Authority 26
   —John P. Lathrop

3. Women Discipling Men: A Biblical Pattern of Leadership 42
   —Grace Ying May

4. Equal Leadership: God's Intention at Creation 60
   —William David Spencer

5. Influence of Plato and Aristotle's Patriarchy on Christian Hierarchy Today 83
   —Jean A. Dimock

Part 2: Practice

6 The Multicultural Aspect of Egalitarian Leadership   117
   —Jeanne DeFazio

7 Egalitarian Multiethnic Leadership in the United States   129
   —Francois W. Augustin

8 Egalitarian Faith Nurturing in the African Context   152
   —Julius K. Kithinji

9 Our Egalitarian Marriage: Diverse yet United and Completing and Complementing Each Other   166
   —Benjamin Fung and Scarlet Tsao Fung

10 Rearing Egalitarian Children   180
   —Karen Sue Smith

11 Equipping Young People to Build Healthy Relationships: Consider It, Take Counsel, and Speak Up   194
   —Sandra Gatlin Whitley

12 God's People for All Seasons: Sharing Ministry with Laypeople   217
   —Lydia M. Sarandan

13 Gender Equality in the Church as a Model for the Neighborhood   233
   —Ralph A. Kee

14 Communal Decision Making and the Fate of Retiring Pastors   239
   —Lorraine Cleaves Anderson

15 Egalitarian Leadership in Global Mission   260
   —J. Creamer

   Conclusion   281
   —Aída Besançon Spencer

Subject Index   287

Scripture Index   293

Contributors

Lorraine Cleaves Anderson received her BA in special education: hearing impaired, and an MDiv with a concentration in urban ministry from Gordon-Conwell Theological Seminary. She is the retired founding pastor of International Community Church (American Baptist), Boston, where, under her leadership, the church developed a ministry of radical hospitality to churches from a variety of cultures. Rev. Anderson was student advisor and professor of theological education of the deaf at Gordon-Conwell's Center for Urban Ministerial Education, Boston. For five years, she was the founding director of a deaf-blind rubella program in the Midwest, and for two years, a teacher of the deaf-blind in the Boston area. Rev. Anderson was recipient of Christians for Biblical Equality's Priscilla and Aquila Award in 1995. In 2006, she completed Boston University's Sustaining Urban Pastoral Excellence Program and is listed in the Heritage Registry of Who's Who, 2007–2008. She is an ordained minister in the Conservative Baptist Association of America and The American Baptists Churches in the USA. She has been married for more than 40 years and is the mother of one married son. She has published "Legacy of Pain" with *Priscilla Papers* and *Under One Steeple: Multiple Congregations Sharing More Than Just Space* in the House of Prisca and Aquila Series (2012).

Francois W. Augustin is the planting pastor of The Livingstone Church—Boston (TLC), a multiethnic church that meets in the Jamaica Plain section of Boston. He was ordained at the Congregation Lion of Judah in 2017 by a multiethnic panel of pastors from four different Boston area churches. His church planting experience spans more than two decades. His multiethnic church leadership experience started at the Congregation Lion of Judah, Boston's largest Hispanic church, where he served on the Spanish ministry's worship team and helped launch a Saturday English service. Later, Rev. Augustin served on the planting team of a Haitian American church in Boston. After graduating from seminary, he spent two years belonging to and supporting Asian and Anglo-led churches prior to planting TLC. For the past three years, he has been leading global IT projects for a Fortune 500 corporation, primarily serving their European division. In addition to ministry practice, during his seminary years, he was a Byington research scholar who supported the initial research for *Reaching for the New Jerusalem: A Biblical and Theological Framework for the City* (Wipf and Stock, 2013). Following graduation, he served as an Athanasian teaching scholar with William David Spencer at Gordon-Conwell Theological Seminary and has been a regular contributor to the *Africanus Journal*. Rev. Augustin holds a BS with honors from UMass Amherst, where he also graduated as a member of the international scholars program. Later, he earned an ALM from Harvard University and an MDiv, *magna cum laude*, from Gordon-Conwell Theological Seminary.

J. Creamer has several decades of experience teaching in both multicultural classrooms and in global settings. She has taught on four continents: Asia, Africa, Australia, and North America. Her early training was in teaching elementary education, but she now teaches at the college and graduate level. She taught Greek and New Testament Survey as an adjunct professor with Gordon-Conwell Theological Seminary, Boston, for several years, and also served as a pastor at Pilgrim Church in Beverly, Massachusetts. She is currently a faculty member of the University of the Nations. She holds master's degrees in New Testament and in Old Testament from Gordon-Conwell Theological Seminary and a PhD in New Testament from North-West University in South Africa. She is ordained through the Cumberland Presbyterian Church. Rev. Dr. Creamer is author of *God as Creator in Acts 17:24: An Historical-Exegetical Study* (Wipf and Stock, 2017) and "Introduction" in *Empowering English Language Learners: Successful Strategies from Christian Educators* (Wipf and Stock, 2018), "Paul and the Philosophers in Athens: The Proclamation of God as Creator in Light of Stoic and Epicurean Cosmology," *Union Biblical Seminary Journal* (2018), "Who is Theophilus? Discovering the Original Reader of Luke–Acts," *In die Skriflig* 48:1 (June 2014), and "Making Known the Unknown God: An Exploration of Greco-Roman Backgrounds Related to Paul's Areopagus Speech," *Africanus Journal* 3:2 (Nov. 2011).

Jeanne DeFazio is a SAG/AFTRA (Screen Actors Guild – American Federation of Television and Radio Artists) actress of Spanish-Italian descent, who played supporting parts in theater, movies, and television series, then served the marginalized in the drama of real life. She became a teacher of second language-learner children in the barrios of San Diego. She completed a BA in history at the University of California, Davis, MAR in theology at Gordon-Conwell Theological Seminary, and a Cal State Teach English Language Learners program. From 2009 to the present, she has served as an Athanasian Teaching Scholar at Gordon-Conwell's multicultural Boston Center for Urban Ministerial Education. She is the co-editor of *Creative Ways to Build Christian Community, Redeeming the Screens, Berkeley Street Theatre,* and *Empowering English Language Learners*. She co-authored with Teresa Flowers: *How to Have an Attitude of Gratitude on the Night Shift* and edited *Keeping the Dream Alive: A Reflection on the Art of Harriet Lorence Nesbitt* and *Specialist Fourth Class John Joseph DeFazio: Advocating for Disabled American Veterans.*

Jean A. Dimock received her MA and DMin degrees from Gordon-Conwell Theological Seminary at its Boston Center for Urban Ministerial Education. Dr. Dimock's doctoral research and thesis concerned domestic violence. She is a domestic violence specialist who served as a New Hampshire guardian ad litem and works with women across the nation who find themselves in domestic violence homes. She also helps the children involved by giving the adults an understanding regarding what their children are experiencing and why certain behaviors exist. Jean also served as adjunct professor of both philosophy and psychology courses at Great Bay Community College in Portsmouth, New Hampshire. Professorial duties provided information that led to her chapter contribution for *Empowering English Language Learners: Successful Strategies for Christian Educators.* She exercises her love of painting and sketching whenever possible. Jean lives on the New Hampshire seacoast with her husband, and has two children, two grandchildren, and two felines.

Benjamin Wing Wo Fung is a certified public accountant in Hong Kong and the United States. He acquired his PhD from the North-West University in South Africa in 2017. Rev. Dr. Fung was an adjunct professor at Gordon-Conwell Theological Seminary and taught a Greek Head Start class and a New Testament Survey class at the Center for Urban Ministerial Education in Boston from 2008 to 2009. Currently, he is a visiting assistant professor (New Testament) of the Hong Kong Baptist Theological Seminary. He occasionally teaches for the Bethel Bible Seminary and Tung Fook Bible College and preaches and teaches at various churches in Hong Kong. He has written "What does *kathexēs* in Luke 1:3 mean? Discovering the writing order of the Gospel of Luke," *In die Skriflig* 51:1 (2017); "Do the writing methodologies of Greco-Roman historians have an impact on Luke's writing order?," *HTS Teologiese Studies/Theological Studies* 73:3 (2017); and *A Defense for the Chronological Order of Luke's Gospel: The Meaning of "Orderly" (Kathexēs) Account in Luke 1:3* in the Africanus Monograph Series (2019).

Scarlet Hai Yin Tsao Fung received legal education at the University of Hong Kong (LLB, PCLL) and holds a master of law from Yale University Law School. She is a solicitor in Hong Kong and the United Kingdom. She is also earning an MAR from Gordon-Conwell Theological Seminary. She practiced as a litigation lawyer at Baker & Mckenzie, an international law firm in Hong Kong, before becoming a law lecturer. Currently she is a consultant solicitor and an adjunct professor and director of the School of Law students' professional development and public service programme at the School of Law, City University of Hong Kong. Mrs. Fung has been doing public services both in Hong Kong and the United States, providing free legal services to the poor at the Community Legal Services Clinic at Yale Law School, helping domestic violence victims as a legal advocate at Help for Abused Women and Their Children (HAWC) in Massachusetts, and organizing and directing an outreach and mentoring program for underprivileged children and youths in Beverly, Salem, and Lynn, Massachusetts. In 2015, she founded the Children's Welfare Law and Services Network, mobilizing university students and alumni to do voluntary services for abused and underprivileged children in Hong Kong. She has published articles in legal journals as well as book chapters, including "The Legal System of the Hong Kong SAR," "Contract Law," and "Tort Law" in *Business Law in Hong Kong* (Sweet & Maxwell Asia). She has also written "Restoration of Adult Survivors of Child Sexual Abuse: How Can Caregivers Contribute to the Process?" (*Priscilla Papers* [Winter 2006]) and a book review of Steven R. Tracy's *Mending the Soul: Understanding and Healing Abuse*. Her ultimate goal is to help underprivileged children break the cycle of poverty and young people find their life vocations.

Ralph A. Kee, after pastoring youth, pastored in upstate New York from 1960–69 and, in 1971, was appointed by Missions Door to be a church planting missionary in Boston. His primary calling was to start neighborhood-focused churches and, when ready, pass on the pastoral leadership to someone else, maybe already part of that new church. He started South End Neighborhood Church of Emmanuel in Boston; restarted

Cambridgeport Baptist in Cambridge, Massachusetts; started New Life Fellowship in Allston that then joined a declining church to become the American Baptist International Community Church with Lorraine Anderson as its first pastor and Ralph's wife, Judith, as associate pastor; then started Quincy Street Missional Church in Dorchester, Massachusetts. He is a graduate of Moody Bible Institute and received his BA from the University of New Hampshire. He served as an adjunct professor at Gordon-Conwell Theological Seminary, Boston, teaching Clear Thinking for Effective Urban Ministry and Church Planting. For five years, Rev. Kee was eastern regional director for Missions Door, Washington D.C., New York City, and St. John, New Brunswick. He has written *Let's Do It! Multiplying Churches in Boston Now, Toward a More Adequate Mission-Speak, Awakening Your Inner City Planter . . . then putting it to work!, The Prophetic Task: Reconnecting the Four Original Schisms*, and *Diakonia: The Church at Work*. He is currently writing *Boston Church Planting Redescribed: Practice and Perceptions of Apostolic Ministry in the Hub*. He and his wife Judith, who served in Africa twenty years before they were married, in 1993 received the Christians for Biblical Equality Priscilla and Aquila Award.

Julius K. Kithinji is lecturer at St. Paul's University, Limuru, Kenya, and chair of the department of theology, philosophy, and biblical studies. He graduated in 2014 with a PhD from Kenyatta University, Kenya. He is a specialist in biblical studies, especially the New Testament. He currently lectures in New Testament Greek and hermeneutics. Rev. Dr. Kithinji is a minister ordained by the Methodist Church (Kenya). He has written articles and book chapters: "Agents of Wrath: Romans 13:1–15" in *Tamar Campaign: Contextual Bible Study Manual and Sermon Outlines on Gender-Based Violence* (2017); "Impunity and *Exousia* in Mark 1:21–28: Choices and Consequences for Kenyan Readers" in *The Postcolonial Church: Bible, Theology, and Mission* (2016), *Postcolonial Redaction of Social-Economic Parables in Luke's Gospel: Bible and the Poor in Kenya* (Lambert Academic, 2011), "Violent Men Consult Jesus: John 7:53–8:11" in *Tamar Campaign: Contextual Bible Study Manual and Sermon Outlines on Gender-Based Violence* (2017), "Decolonizing the Treatment of the Pharisees in 7:53–8:11," *International Journal of Development Research* 9:1 (2019), and coauthored (with Lydia Chemei) "Decolonizing and Reassembling the Voice of John's Gospel in a Time of Ecological Crisis," *African Multidisciplinary Journal* (2017).

John P. Lathrop graduated from Western Connecticut State College with a bachelor's degree in business administration, from Zion Bible Institute with a ministerial diploma, and from Gordon-Conwell Theological Seminary's Center for Urban Ministerial Education with an MA in urban ministry. He is an ordained minister with the International Fellowship of Christian Assemblies. He has written articles and book reviews that have been published by the *Africanus Journal, Berita Mujizat* ("Miracle News" in Indonesia), *Christian Trends Magazine* (in India), *Jurnal Jaffray* (Indonesia), Pentecostalpastor.com, *Priscilla Papers*, the *Pneuma Review*, and *Vista Magazine*. Rev. Lathrop has published four books: *Apostles, Prophets, Evangelists, Pastors and Teachers Then and Now* (Xulon, 2008), *The Power and Practice of the Church: God, Discipleship, and Ministry* (J. Timothy King, 2010), *Answer the Prayer of Jesus: A Call for Biblical Unity* (Wipf and Stock, 2011), and *Dreams and Visions: Divine Interventions in Human Experience* (J. Timothy King, 2012). He has contributed to *Some Men Are Our Heroes* (Wipf and Stock, 2010) and *The Foundations of Faith* (Pleasant Word, 2007). He also served with Jeanne DeFazio as coeditor of *Creative Ways to Build Christian Community* (Wipf and Stock, 2013).

Grace Ying May is associate professor of biblical studies at William Carey International University, Pasadena, California. She has a BA from Yale University, an MDiv from Gordon-Conwell Theological Seminary, and a ThD from Boston University. She is a minister ordained in the Presbyterian Church (USA) and founded Women of Wonder, Inc. (WOW!), a ministry to see sisters soar in their callings (www.womenofwonder.us). Rev. Dr. May has written "How the Apostle Paul Champions Women and Men in Church Leadership" in *The Quest for Gender Equity in Leadership* (2016), "The Way Forward: Men and Women in the Church" in *Seeking Harmony: The Intergenerational Theology of the Household of God* (2012), "Healthy Gender Relations" in *Growing Healthy Asian-American Churches* (2006), "The Family Table" in *Proclaiming the Scandal of the Cross* (2006), and "Viewing God through the Twin Lenses of Holiness and Mercy: A Chinese American Perspective" in *The Global God* (1998).

Lydia M. Sarandan is a retired pastor of the Presbyterian Church (USA) since 2009. She served twenty-eight years as minister of adult education with St. Andrew's Presbyterian Church, Newport Beach, California. Currently, she is a member and chair of The Salvation Army advisory board, Orange County, California. Rev. Dr. Sarandan has an MDiv and a DMin. Her training material, *How to Develop A Praying Church*, used for elder and deacon training at St. Andrew's Presbyterian Church, was developed for her DMin thesis for Gordon-Conwell Theological Seminary in 1992.

Karen Sue Smith is an author, life coach, and homeschool parent. She received an MDiv from Gordon-Conwell Theological Seminary and was ordained to pastoral ministry in Beverly, Massachusetts. She graduated with a BA in psychology from Taylor University. Rev. Smith wrote *Learning to Parent in the Light in a Dark World* (KDP, 2019). She has also written Sunday school curriculum. She received her life coach certification with Kingdom Builders Academy in 2019. She has homeschooled her three children for nineteen years. She served on the staff of Campus Crusade for Christ for five years. She has also served in several children's ministry positions. She is a certified structure of intelligence instructor and has completed brain gym training. She also completed training in catechesis of the Good Shepherd (levels 1 and 2) and godly play. She put this training into practice by leading a "Time with God" group for twelve years, giving time and space for children to develop their relationships with God.

Aída Besançon Spencer is senior professor of New Testament at Gordon-Conwell Theological Seminary, South Hamilton, Massachusetts. Born and reared in Santo Domingo, Dominican Republic, she earned a PhD in New Testament at Southern Baptist Theological Seminary and a ThM and MDiv at Princeton Theological Seminary. An ordained Presbyterian minister, Rev. Dr. Spencer has served as a social worker, college minister, and founding pastor of organization of Pilgrim Church in Beverly, Massachusetts. Listed in *Who's Who in the World*, *Contemporary Authors*, and *Who's Who of American Women*, she has authored numerous articles, chapters, and books, including *1 Timothy, 2 Timothy and Titus* in the New Covenant Commentary Series, *Beyond the Curse: Women Called to Ministry* (translated into Spanish and French), *Paul's Literary Style*, *2 Corinthians* in the Daily Bible Commentary and People's Bible Commentary series, *A Commentary on James* in the Kregel Exegetical Library, and cowritten or coedited *Reaching for the New Jerusalem: A Biblical and Theological Framework for the City*, *The Global God: Multicultural Evangelical Views of God*, *Global Voices on Biblical Equality*, *Joy through the Night: Biblical Resources on Suffering*, *The Goddess Revival: A Biblical Response to God(dess) Spirituality*, and *Marriage at the Crossroads*. The Spencers received the Christians for Biblical Equality Lifetime Achievement Award in 2005.

William David Spencer is distinguished adjunct professor of theology and the arts at Gordon-Conwell Theological Seminary's Boston Center for Urban Ministerial Education. Rev. Dr. Spencer's first experience in egalitarian Christian leadership began right after he accepted the lordship of Christ as a college student at Rutgers University in 1966, when he organized the first of two Jesus music bands, the Spheres, which performed for seven years along the USA's east coast. His first street ministry began the same year in his birth city Plainfield, New Jersey. After the riots of the late 1960s, he interned with Crosscounter, Inc., in Newark in 1970, helping city churches get back on their feet, also coleading another evangelistic Jesus band with opera singer Jerome Hines's music ministry. Earning his MDiv and ThM from Princeton Theological Seminary, he served as Protestant chaplain at Rider College (now university), then he and his wife, Aída, were called back to Newark by Crosscounter, Inc., and New York Theological Seminary to train seminarians in city ministry. Supporting Aída as she earned her doctorate in Louisville, Kentucky, he became adult literacy teaching coordinator for Jefferson County, setting up literacy and GED centers in Louisville and its environs. In Massachusetts, he earned his ThD in theology and ancient literature at Boston University School of Theology and has taught theology for Gordon-Conwell since 1983, from 1992 on at CUME. He also helped plant Pilgrim Church of Beverly, Massachusetts, where he has served as founding pastor of encouragement for more than thirty years. Winner of twenty writing and editing awards, he edited Christians for Biblical Equality's journal *Priscilla Papers* for ten years and for twelve has coedited *Africanus Journal*. He also coedits the Wipf and Stock book series *House of Prisca and Aquila*. He has authored about three hundred articles, chapters, editorials, poems, stories, and features, including authoring or editing seventeen books, including *The Prayer Life of Jesus, Dread Jesus, God through the Looking Glass*; two novels, *Cave of Little Faces* and the award-winning *Name in the Papers*; as well as a related CD of his original music: *Songs from the Cave, Ballads from the Papers* (2019). Two of his books, *Mysterium and Mystery* and *Chanting Down Babylon* have been declared by critics the definitive works in their fields. He and Aída's blog is *Applying Biblical Truths Today* at https://aandwspencer.blogspot.com.

Sandra Gatlin Whitley is an ordained elder in the African Methodist Episcopal Church. She has served since 2007 as the pastor of People's AME Church in Chelsea, Massachusetts. Pastor Whitley is a graduate of Alabama State University, Montgomery, earning a BS degree in business administration. Rev. Dr. Whitley also served in the United States Air Force for twenty-two years, earning the rank of lieutenant colonel, while in the meantime earning an MA degree in management from Webster University. Her military assignment took her to different parts of the world, including Massachusetts, where she accepted God's calling. She graduated from Gordon-Conwell Theological Seminary, earning an MDiv, MA in counseling, and a DMin. She also served as a Byington scholar and an Athanasian teaching scholar at Gordon-Conwell. She is the author of *Daughters,*

You Are Special: To Love and Be Loved by Our Heavenly Father (2020) and "Security in Christ: Attacked: Fear or Faith?" (*Journal for Advent Christian Thought*, spring 2004). She is the coauthor of "Gifted for Leadership: Gender Equality from an African American Perspective" in *Global Voices on Biblical Equality: Women and Men Serving Together in the Church* (Wipf and Stock, 2008), and authored the book review for *Tactics of Truth: Military Principles for Waging Spiritual War* by Ernest L. Vermont (*Africanus Journal*, April 2010). In addition to being an author and pastor/teacher, Rev. Whitley is a prayer warrior, preacher, biblical scholar, and marriage and family pastoral counselor. She is happily married to her friend and soul-mate, Rev. Kenneth Whitley, from Philadelphia, Pennsylvania. He also served in the United States Air Force for twenty-six years. Together, they serve in ministry, share a love of travel, photography, people, God's word, and spoiling their nieces, nephews, and godchildren. They both served on the ministerial staffs of Hanscom Air Force Base chapel, Bedford Massachusetts, and the Bethel AME Church, Boston, Massachusetts.

Acknowledgements

ALL OF US CONTRIBUTORS are thankful for the guidance of editors, institutions, church family, and blood family.

Two editorial assistants, JiHyung Kim and C.J. Gossage, helped with communication to the contributors and formatting. They were diligent, efficient, and always gracious. Miranda Kwon efficiently completed the Scripture Index. David Shorey and his staff at Gordon-Conwell Theological Seminary were as ever most efficient in printing the chapters when they were ready. Robert McFadden and Elizabeth Coffey were of great assistance locating books at Goddard Library and elsewhere. Once again, Deborah Beatty Mel finalized all the editing. The staff at Wipf and Stock were always gracious, helpful, and most competent.

Grace May thanks the administrators of William Carey International University for the time that they generously gave her to work on her chapter.

Lydia Sarandan is appreciative of many, including St. Andrew's Presbyterian Church, Newport Beach, and Dr. John A. Huffman, Jr., senior pastor, for providing her the opportunity to be a full-time minister of adult education and trusting her with the privilege of serving the congregation for twenty-eight years. She also acknowledges the faithful lay men and women whose hearts were open to study, to be equipped, and to use their talents, spiritual gifts, life experiences, and resources for ministry in the church, their community, and pursuing missional opportunities around the world. In addition, she appreciates The Salvation Army whose 150-year history has been a model of authentic servant leadership, spiritual integrity, encouragement, and living out the gospel in word and deed to benefit countless people and nations around the world. Of great joy to her has been the opportunity to serve on its Orange County Advisory Board. She is daily humbled by the Captains Nesan and Cheryl Kistan, the staff, officers, and volunteers whose commitment reflects the heart, hands, mind, and body of Jesus.

Lorraine Anderson thanks her two interviewers: Rev. Dr. Maung Maung Htwe, pastor of Overseas Burmese Christian Fellowship, Boston, Massachusetts, and Rev. Eric Nelson, retired pastor of Washington Street Baptist Church, Lynn, Massachusetts.

Julius Kithinji thanks Dr. Jewel Hyun and Elder Gene of Matthew 28 Ministries for their gracious support and specific motivation during the course of writing the chapter in this book, as well as Dr. Telesia Musili of Nairobi University (Kenya) and Meg Kithinji of Nakuru for helping him engage with relevant material on African family life and parenting.

Sandra Whitley is truly grateful for Dr. Jean Dimock keeping her to task, guiding, proofing, and supporting her in getting the chapter completed by deadline.

Jean Dimock is appreciative of her husband, Fred Dimock, for being genuinely interested, patient, and encouraging. Karen Smith appreciates her husband Dwight Smith's proofreading and editing her work. Francois Augustin is grateful for his wife, Stania Augustin, for her feedback. Sandra Whitley is thankful to God for her husband Ken's loving support and encouragement.

The contributors thank Aída and Bill for all the help they gave, with such gracious comments as: "thanks for all your hard work on this project," "thanks for inviting me to participate in this initiative and being the polite encouragers that you are," and "this chapter wouldn't be as good as it is without all the input, patience, and encouragement the two of you have given me consistently. I have been grateful for the two of you nearly every day since I started writing. You both make everyone you help look better!" and "Aída and her husband Bill have been a consistent spiritual presence in my heart and mind as I reflect on their direction and servant hearts as I earned my DMin at Gordon-Conwell Theological Seminary. Their caring, passion for ministry and excellent scholarship has enabled me to create practical, workable, life-skill training materials for the men and women in the church."

And, of course, most thanks go to the gracious, loving, and equipping, living triune God.

Introduction

William David Spencer

ARE EGALITARIAN OR HIERARCHICAL leaderships styles more successful? Stanford University Graduate School of Business's explorations into the question have sparked quite a controversy as commentators have drawn opposing answers from the data.

Dylan Walsh, in an article entitled "Rethinking Hierarchy in the Workplace" published under the school's "Insights by Stanford Business" heading, observes that "new research shows . . . egalitarian teams are able to work together" out of a sense of community that delivers an effective response to opposition encountered by their company. He cites Stanford professor of organizational behavior Lindred Greer: "When you look at real organizations, having a clear hierarchy within your firm actually makes people turn on each other when they face an outside threat." He also cites University of Amsterdam Professor Lisanne van Bunderen, who helped guide one of the studies, noting that the egalitarian team's sense of sharing a "common fate" contrasted with the hierarchical team's disintegration under outside pressure into individuals who "felt a need to fend for themselves, likely at the expense of others." As a result, the article notes, "Researchers found that the subset of hierarchical teams facing competition with rival firms struggled with infighting while the egalitarian teams cooperated on their work." Thus, author Walsh concludes, "Effective teamwork against threats requires not hierarchy, but egalitarianism; not centralized power, but a culture in which all voices count."[1]

---

1. Walsh, 'Rethinking Hierarchy.'

Not surprisingly, another article highlighted a different part of the findings: "According to a recent study conducted by the Stanford Business School, hierarchy isn't quite the modern demon that the tech sector would have us believe nor is egalitarianism the grand savior of modern business," author Adam Schell counters:

> As the Stanford study reveals, hierarchy is innate, it's in our DNA, while egalitarianism is a learned way of being. What the study suggests is human beings are hardwired to understand hierarchy. All children are born into a hierarchical state. Children have parents and grandparents and teachers and all of them give direction and guidance to the child. Egalitarianism, on the other hand, does not develop until late childhood and is contingent on the development of complex social processes that only begin to form around age seven.

According to the study, "Hierarchies are easier for people to grasp than egalitarian relationships because . . . they are predictable; and they are familiar, beginning with our very first social interaction—the parent-child relationship. Equality can be messy, and hierarchy is conceptually cleaner."[2]

However, in "Social Dominance in Childhood and Its Evolutionary Underpinnings: Why It Matters and What We Can Do," a carefully detailed article in *Pediatrics: Official Journal of the American Academy of Pediatrics*, author Patricia H. Hawley, a professor in the department of educational psychology and leadership at Texas Tech University, cautions, "not to endorse the naturalistic fallacy and conclude that because aggression and power hierarchies are natural, that they are therefore good. On the contrary, our efforts could be better spent striving to improve conditions under which children are raised and ameliorating the contingencies under which aggression is effectively operating."[3]

The point is well taken. This is a fallen world wherein our behavior from birth is conditioned by our fallen state. Original sin becomes actual sin for each of us and, as a result, our fate is to die and then be judged (Heb 9:27).

Still, how natural is hierarchy as a response is up to question in the view of anthropologists who study what are called "primitive," but we might term "original," cultures.

Writing for *Pyschology Today*, Boston College research professor Peter Gray begins his article, "How Hunter-Gatherers Maintained Their Egalitarian Ways: The important lessons from hunter-gatherers are about culture, not

---

2. Schell, "Hierarchical vs. Egalitarian."
3. Hawley, "Social Dominance in Childhood and Its Evolutionary Underpinnings."

genes," by assuring readers, "First . . . I must address this question: Is it true that hunter-gatherers were peaceful egalitarians? The answer is yes":

> During the twentieth century, anthropologists discovered and studied dozens of different hunter-gatherer societies, in various remote parts of the world, who had been nearly untouched by modern influences. Wherever they were found—in Africa, Asia, South America, or elsewhere; in deserts or in jungles—these societies had many characteristics in common. The people lived in small bands, of about 20 to 50 persons (including children) per band, who moved from camp to camp within a relatively circumscribed area to follow the available game and edible vegetation. The people had friends and relatives in neighboring bands and maintained peaceful relationships with neighboring bands. Warfare was unknown to most of these societies, and where it was known it was the result of interactions with warlike groups of people who were not hunter-gatherers. In each of these societies, the dominant cultural ethos was one that emphasized individual autonomy, non-directive childrearing methods, nonviolence, sharing, cooperation, and consensual decision-making. Their core value, which underlay all of the rest, was that of the equality of individuals.

Decrying that "we citizens of a modern democracy claim to believe in equality, but our sense of equality is not even close that of hunter-gatherers," Dr. Gray lists equal sharing of food and "material goods," no chief or boss ordering others around, parents practicing nondirective childrearing methods, causing all to live by intentional, active, and enforced cooperation.[4]

In a *New Scientist*'s "The Daily Newsletter" article entitled "Inequality: Why egalitarian societies died out," Deborah Rogers summarized research that she, Omkar Deshpande, and Marcus Feldman also did at Stanford University. She observed that "sharing and cooperation was the rule for millennia—but the very instability of unequal societies caused them to spread." After mentioning various theories of why egalitarian societies began to die out, she warned, "We cannot assume that because inequality exists, it is somehow beneficial." Her team's observation was that "equality—or inequality—is a cultural choice." Professor Rogers observes:

> Inequality did not spread from group to group because it is an inherently better system for survival, but because it creates demographic instability, which drives migration and conflict and leads to the cultural—or physical—extinction of egalitarian

---

4. Gray, "How Hunter-Gatherers Maintained Their Egalitarian Ways."

societies. Indeed, in our future research we aim to explore the very real possibility that natural selection itself operates differently under regimes of equality and inequality. Egalitarian societies may have fostered selection on a group level for cooperation, altruism and low fertility (which leads to a more stable population), while inequality might exacerbate selection on an individual level for high fertility, competition, aggression, social climbing and other selfish traits.[5]

In the controversy of whether hierarchical or egalitarian leadership is better for business, the data can be interpreted in either way. The scholars also cannot agree which structure is primal.

Of course, such a controversy is by no means a new phenomenon, nor does it confine itself to business, social science, pediatrics, anthropology. It is one Jesus faced among his own disciples. One of his biographers, Luke, the physician, records a dispute or argument (*philoneikia*) that broke out when his closest supporters began to fight over which one should be regarded by the others as the greatest (*meizōn*) among them (Luke 22:24). Jesus's triumphal entry into Jerusalem had just taken place and, apparently, this was his disciples' individual *response* to it—something to the effect of: "When you're clearly the boss of everybody, Lord, am I gonna be your five-star right-hand general?" Another biographer, Mark, tells us that this was not the first time the disciples jockeyed for power. While Jesus was still on the road, two of his disciples sidled up and asked him if they could be enthroned on his right and left hand when he came into his own rightful power. When the other ten disciples got wind of this request, they were furious (*aganakteō* in Mark 10:41). In each case Jesus gave the same reply: "Don't lord it over the others" (*katakurieuō* in Mark 10:42 and *kurieuō* in Luke 22:25). In this response, what Jesus was calling for was a non-hierarchical mutual leadership among his followers. As God-Among-Us and their real Lord, Jesus was teaching and demonstrating how he wanted them to act. Once the triumphal entry was over and he was reclining with them at the Passover meal, which would be his last supper with them, Jesus the Christ suddenly rose from the meal, shed his outer robe, wrapped a towel around himself, and washed each of their feet as a lowly servant would. His disciples were astonished—dismayed—and then he spelled it out for them, literally: "You call me 'The Teacher' and The Lord,' and correctly you speak, for I am. If, therefore, I have washed your feet—the Lord and the Teacher—also you owe one another to wash [their] feet. For, an example I have given to you in order that, just as I did to you, also you do" (John 13:13–15).

5. Rogers, "Inequality."

In summary, when Jesus's followers asked for places of privilege, he did not grant them authority over each other. He was outlining for them an egalitarian community nurtured by humble, others-oriented leadership. He wanted them operating as egalitarian, regarding every one of them as equal, no one of them being considered to have *ipso facto* authority by virtue of blood, gender, birthright, or any other artificial form of entitlement.

Therefore, when we see the community of believers described in chapter two of the Book of Acts, we see its members living out the example Jesus set. We are told they had leaders to whose teaching they held fast, persevering in it, as they practiced fellowship, communion, and prayer, and they shared all their resources in common (Acts 2:42–44). Their leaders did not exercise privilege over them, riding around in "Lear" chariots while everyone else walked. The community members retained their own possessions, which they voluntarily sold to share the profit when anyone (*tis*) was in need (*chreia*) (v. 45). They did not live in single-barracks communities where they were issued three sheets of papyri for the toilet each day and subsisted on beans as a cult. They had their own homes (*te kat' oikon*), where they practiced hospitality and even apparently had communion together (*klaō*, "break" *artos*, "bread," v. 46). They were happy; their neighbors liked them; and people were joining them (v. 47). And, as for their leaders, everyone was astonished at the wonders they could do (v. 43). This kind of mutually deferent fellowship impacted and stirred the greater community, and its impact spanned out over the world as each follower of Jesus exercised her or his individual gifting, according to how each had been called, equipped, and blessed by God's Holy Spirit.

In short, the Christian community described in the book of Acts was already living out the ideal envisioned in the wise words of Lindred Greer, the professor of organizational behavior at Stanford Graduate School of Business: "I've always said that if there were a Nobel Prize for management, it would go to the person who finds an organizational structure that's not based on vertical differentiation, on hierarchy, on leadership."[6] Jesus did that. And our hope is that this present book will help us all to move toward that goal.

Therefore, in our book that follows, our joint goal is to examine the superiority of the egalitarian Christian leadership's model of distributing power and responsibility to achieve Jesus's intentions for the structuring of his church in place of the all too rampant abuse-prone model of concentrating power in hierarchical leaders (while often distributing responsibility for such leaders' visions to work to everyone else) being practiced in Christian circles.

6. Walsh, "Rethinking Hierarchy."

Our book begins with a study of the Bible's teachings on Christian egalitarian leadership, while underscoring its high view of biblical authority. Next, we examine the leadership issues between women and men, going back to creation and the Bible's report of God's intention for how power was to be distributed, as opposed to the subverting influence of Platonic thought on Christian thinkers throughout history.

Then we move to a wide view of multicultural and multiethnic perspectives on this issue and its application. Since our goal in this book is to have a more theoretical section and a more practical section (although all chapters should have both components), we move next to applying egalitarian leadership to marriage, childrearing, the church, good neighboring, and even the care and empowering of the elderly. In brief, we take the concept of Christian egalitarian leadership from childhood through adolescence to adulthood and retirement. Our focus here is to empower 100 percent of the church to use its gifting, curtailing no member whom God has empowered to lead in a certain task that helps the church's mission to bring all under the leadership of Christ, the one true leader for all humanity.

Finally, we reflect on the church's global mission and end with a conclusion, gathering up the insights and their implications with suggestions for general application.

References

Gray, Peter. "How Hunter-Gatherers Maintained Their Egalitarian Ways: The important lessons from hunter-gatherers are about culture, not genes." *Psychology Today* (May 16, 2011). https://www.psychologytoday.com/us/blog/freedom-learn/201105/how-hunter-gatherers-maintained-their-egalitarian-ways. Accessed Dec. 24, 2019.

Hawley, Patricia H. "Social Dominance in Childhood and Its Evolutionary Underpinnings: Why It Matters and What We Can Do." *Pediatrics: Official Journal of the American Academy of Pediatrics* (March 2015). https://pediatrics.aappublications.org/content/135/Supplement_2/S31 March 2015, 135 (Supplement 2) S31-S38; DOI: https://doi.org/10.1542/peds.2014-3549D. Accessed Dec. 24, 2019.

Rogers, Deborah. "Inequality: Why egalitarian societies died out." *NewScientist* (July 25, 2012). https://www.newscientist.com/article/dn22071-inequality-why-egalitarian-societies-died-out/. Accessed Dec. 24, 2019.

Schell, Adam. "Hierarchical vs. Egalitarian: What's the best leadership style?" *Culturewizard by RW3, LLC* (May 9, 2016). https://www.rw-3.com/blog/hierarchical-vs.-egalitarian-whats-the-best-leadership-style. Accessed Oct. 31, 2019.

Walsh, Dylan. "Rethinking Hierarchy in the Workplace: Flat structures, research shows, can create more functional teams." *Insights by Stanford Business,* a website from The Stanford University Graduate School of Business (Sept. 5, 2017). https://www.gsb.stanford.edu/insights/rethinking-hierarchy-workplace. Accessed Oct. 31, 2019.

PART 1

Theory

1

An Overview of the New Testament Teachings on Christian Egalitarian Leadership

Aída Besançon Spencer and William David Spencer

Paul tells the Christians of the first century to remember the good news that he proclaimed to them. This good news has as of first importance that "Christ died for our sins . . . according to the Scriptures" and that he was buried and raised on the third day "according to the Scriptures" (1 Cor 15:3–4). Paul's good news has many ramifications for leadership. We propose that leadership, especially in the church, should be Christian egalitarian servant leadership. A leader is someone who guides, directs, advises, commands, or shows the way.[1] This leadership is also "according to the Scriptures." The ramifications are extensive. This volume is introductory, summarizing the scriptural teaching on the topic and suggesting some practical ramifications. This whole topic should be an obvious and basic one for all believers, but the church has sometimes become derailed, imitating its worldly culture. Our goal is to remind the church of its scriptural teachings about equality as shown by the themes of servant leadership, mutual submission, impartiality, spiritual gifts, the priesthood of all believers, and the New Covenant, and to urge the church to refocus on its scriptural roots, God's revelation.

---

1. *The American Heritage Dictionary*, 378, 482. Northouse, *Leadership*, defines leadership as "a process whereby an individual influences a group of individuals to achieve a common goal," 5.

What Is Christian Egalitarian Leadership and How Does It Relate to Servant Leadership?

Egalitarian leadership is an intrinsic aspect of servant leadership. Egalitarian leadership includes the equal leadership of men and women, Gentiles and Jews, rich and poor, slave and free, and the lack of permanent or/and innate human hierarchy except between God and humans. It is mutual service between partners in ministry for Christ's sake. As its opposite, hierarchy is an "arrangement of persons or things in a graded series, as by rank or ability" or "a body of persons having authority."[2] The definition of egalitarian Christian leadership begins with *Jesus's teachings*, especially to his twelve disciples in response to the Zebedee family wanting James and John to take the two most highly ranked positions: right and left of Jesus in glory. From Jesus's response, we learn what Christian leadership should be and should not be. It should be Christlike and sacrificial for others' good (Mark 10:37–45),[3] service-oriented (*diakonos, doulos*), humble, without hierarchy of rank except between humans and God. It is not ruling as the Gentiles did in an abusive and harmful use of power (Mark 10:40, 42–44). For instance, almost every Roman emperor, including Augustus, took over power, not by vote, but by overpowering their opponents. They did not rule to serve the people but to gain power, money, and prestige. Procurators in Judea became so oppressive that eventually they caused a revolt (AD 66–74). Pontius Pilate, for example, was considered by the Jews as unbending and callously hard, "a man of inflexible disposition, harsh and obdurate," greedy, vindictive, and cruel.[4]

In contrast, Christlike leadership is not self-centered nor self-seeking actions, competitive with others, pushing oneself forward or bossing others for one's own benefit only.[5] The sacrificial aspect of Christlike leadership, directly enjoined in Mark 10:45 ("the Son of Humanity did not come to be served but to serve and to give his life a ransom for many"),[6] includes the principles of mutual service and partnership, including the equal partnership and leadership between men and women, rich and poor, powerful and less

---

2. *American Heritage Dictionary*, s.v.

3. See also Matt 20:20–28; Luke 22:24–27.

4. Schürer, *History* 1, 384.

5. On the leader(s) as servant, see further Richards & Hoeldtke, *Theology of Church Leadership*, 103–12; Everist & Nessan, *Transforming Leadership*, 65–74; Ford, *Transforming Leadership*, 134–221; Greenleaf, *Servant Leadership*; Bilezikian, *Community*, 130–39; Ogden, *Reformation*, 173–78; Northouse, *Leadership*, ch. 10. The superapostles exemplify lording it over others (2 Cor 11:20). On the superapostles, see A. Spencer, *2 Corinthians*, 192–93.

6. All Bible quotations are translated from the Greek and Hebrew by Aída Besançon Spencer unless otherwise noted.

powerful, and old and young. For instance, welcoming a child is a model for affirmation. A child is a model for adults in God's kingdom.[7]

At the Last Supper, Jesus dramatically demonstrates and teaches sacrificial service when he washes his disciples' feet, just as a slave might do, and commands them to do likewise ("Therefore, if I myself wash your feet, the Lord and the Teacher, also you yourselves ought to wash one another's feet," John 13:14). Jesus has all power and authority (John 3:31–35; 13:13; Mark 1:7, 22). Jesus reiterates that the hierarchy between God-incarnate and humans is real. However, Jesus reverses that hierarchy by using his power for sacrificial humble service to others. This service is also mutual (for "one another"). He has reversed the position of master and slave.

Jesus shares his power by his appointment of human apostles who spread the good news and drive out demonic opposition (Mark 3:14–15; 6:7–13). Jesus underscores the equality between rich and poor, the more and less powerful, the honored and the ostracized several times, when he defends eating with tax collectors and sinners (Mark 2:15–17), feeds out of compassion all the people among his listeners (Mark 6:35–43; 8:1–9), and affirms the generous poor widow as opposed to the greedy leaders who seek their own honor (Mark 12:38–44). The right of equal access to education between men and women is affirmed when Mary's listening to Rabbi Jesus is preferred over her following ancient Jewish society's priority for women, household duties (Luke 10:38–42).[8]

While the twelve apostles symbolize the twelve tribes of the old covenant, the multinumbered women and men who were eyewitnesses of Jesus's resurrection look forward to the new covenant. Even though women were not considered valid witnesses in court, Jesus commissioned them as eyewitnesses of the resurrection.[9] In his teachings, Jesus emphasized not male-female distinctions in leadership, but, rather, humble, mutual service.

The disciples are all equal to one another. All must repent for forgiveness of sins and all must do God's will (e.g., Mark 1:4, 15; 3:33–34). Communion is given to all believers, symbolic of Jesus's death for all (Mark 14:22–24). Human equality on earth reflects Jesus's character and the nature of God. Jesus was renowned as being impartial and truthful with all ("for you do not see the outward appearance ["face"] of humans"). Jesus taught truthfully (Matt 22:16; Mark 12:14).[10] Since God the Trinity is one

7. Mark 9:33–37; 10:13–16; Matt 18:3–6. See also A. Spencer, "Biblical Equity," 110–17.

8. See also A. Spencer, *Beyond the Curse*, 57–68.

9. John 20:17; Matt 28:7, 10; Mark 16:7; Luke 24:5–10. See also A. Spencer, "Jesus' Treatment," 133–41.

10. See also A. Spencer, "Biblical Equity," 116.

(Mark 12:29–30), equality among people reflects God's own unity and love for all. Moreover, Jesus teaches that all humans are equal in honor because all humans have the same Teacher and Father (Matt 23:5–12). The "greatest" human is not the most honored, but the "servant" (Matt 23:11).

How Does the Apostle Paul Enact Jesus's Teachings on Egalitarian Servant Leadership?

Paul explicitly refers to Jesus's incarnation, death, resurrection, and ascension as models for Christian disciples. The attitude and practice of servant leadership are both commanded: "Do nothing according to selfish ambition nor according to empty glory, but in humility regarding others as better than yourselves, not each of you looking out for your own interests, but also to the interests of others" (Phil 2:3–4).[11] "Empty glory" (*kenodoxia*) is leadership simply to one's own benefit. It leads nowhere good. Mutual leadership is loving one another (Phil 2:2–4). Jesus's genuine glory showed his equality with God (Phil 2:6). Like Jesus, Christians are not to hang on to prominence and power when it conflicts with service in love. Jesus took the form of a slave not only when he washed his disciples' feet, but also when he became human. God the Father, in response, highly exalted Jesus back to his original hierarchy as Lord of all (Phil 2:7–11).

Mutual submission also relates to Christian egalitarian leadership and servant leadership. Servant leadership is Christlike. It is also demonstrated by God-the-Trinity. Paul enjoins the Ephesian Gentiles, "as beloved children," to imitate God's sacrificial love: "Walk in love, just as also Christ loved us and gave himself up for us as a fragrant offering and sacrifice to God" (Eph 5:2). Sacrificial service for others on God's behalf is the heart of Christian servant leadership. That love is summarized by a life of gratitude or thanksgiving. Christian leaders should be thankful for their spouses, if married; thankful for what possessions they have (satisfied and not greedy); and thankful to God by being pure.[12] Their words and actions should be true, good, and just or righteous (Eph 5:3–6, 20). These qualities are part of what makes their leadership Christian. They expose evil deeds of others, rescue the innocent, and try actively to please the Lord. Christians should edify each other and proactively awaken each other. They should use their time to obey God (Eph

---

11. Paul actualizes servant leadership in his "weakness" leadership style (2 Cor 11:7–33). See A. Spencer, *2 Corinthians*, 198–99.

12. See A. Spencer, "Toppling the Silent Idol," 32–37, 44.

5:7–17). Mutual submission is part of their godly Christlike lifestyle.[13] It is mutual, done to please Christ (Eph 5:18–21).

Each of the pairs cited in Ephesians 5 and 6 have mutual loving and caring relationships. Nowhere does Paul compare men with God the Father and women with God the Son. Rather, wives and husbands are to imitate Christ's love, beginning with the point of most weakness for each (lack of respect or lack of devotion). As Christ was submitted to the Father at the incarnation, so wives submit to their husbands with the same desire to please. The husband is not the decision maker or ruler (which in Greek most likely would be *archē*),[14] but rather the source ("head" or *kephalē*) of life. The "head" is defined by Paul as "Savior himself of the body," so the husband should protect rather than abuse the wife as a husband who does not love her would do (Eph 5:23).

There would be no "church" if Christ had not given himself up for it. In a similar way, the husband will be giving himself up for his wife to present her to Christ "in splendor" "without a spot or wrinkle" "holy and without blemish" (Eph 5:27). The wife should respond in cooperation and respect (Eph 5:21–24, 33). As Christ was a sacrificial offering and therefore Savior and source of the church, a husband should focus all his attention on his wife's growth, so she can become the perfect offering and the perfect priest in the priesthood of all believers. Love includes faithfulness and is devoted to the one spouse.[15]

In Ephesians 6, Paul changes his main verb to "obey" (*hupakouō*), instead of "submit" (*hupotassō*) for the relationships between children and parents and slaves and masters. These are temporary, not innate, relationships of hierarchy, arrangements by rank for age and social position. Children will grow up to be adults and, if married, will leave their parents and be joined to their spouses (Eph 5:31). Once children are brought up in the discipline of the Lord, they would be their parents' equal from a spiritual perspective (Eph 5:31; 6:4). Children honor their parents, while parents do not provoke or exasperate their children (Eph 6:2, 4). Slaves in Greco-Roman times had options for freedom. For example, Paul explains, if slaves can gain their freedom, they should do so (1 Cor 7:21).[16] They were not slaves because of race or gender. Slaves and masters are first of all related to Christ, pleasing Christ, doing God's will, as all Christians should do. Christ is master of all masters and is not partial to any class (Eph 6:5–9; 5:10, 17).

---

13. See also Padgett, *Christ*, 32, 34, 37–56, 127–31; Bilezikian, *Community*, 163.
14. E.g., ruler of the synagogue.
15. See also Spencer et al., *Marriage at the Crossroads*, 84–94.
16. For the many legal ways out of slavery, see Barth and Blanke, *Philemon*, 42–56.

There should be a mutual devotion between master and slave. Even in their temporary hierarchical relationships, the parties involved still have mutual, reciprocal, loving, cooperative partnerships.

All Christians should cooperate and respect each other (Eph 5:21). Mutual submission involves interdependence between equal people who are all submitted to Christ. Mutually submitted Christians are supportive to each other in actions and words out of respect for Christ. They encourage each other to use their gifts. Stephana(s)'s household demonstrates an example of such fluidity in ministry. They agreed as a household to "place themselves into ministry to the saints" (1 Cor 16:15). As a response, the Corinthian church is urged also to submit (*hupotassō*) themselves to believers such as they are and to all those working together with them (1 Cor 16:16). Paul concludes, urging the Corinthians to "give recognition to such persons" (1 Cor 16:18 NRSV; NIV 2011).[17] In effect, Stephanas's household and the Corinthians have a mutual partnership in ministry.[18]

The way we treat individuals in our relationships should reflect the way Christ has treated and continues to treat us. The way we lead should honor Christ and the church. Christ's commands should always be kept in the forefront. Moral failure of leaders dishonors Christ and Christ's devotion to the church. Therefore, our faith should not become an individual privatized affair, for it has communal effects. To ensure this does not happen, the Lord's power and mutual intercession are indispensable to be successful. Also, we should "wrestle not against flesh and blood," for other humans are not our real enemies (Eph 6:10–13, 18–19).

Christ's model of leadership becomes a snare to the Corinthians who admire the "strong" tyrannical leadership style of the superapostles, who "enslave," "consume," "take advantage," "act haughtily," and "strike their faces." They were rhetorically impressive but, in reality, arrogant and autocratic bullies who spiritually, economically, and physically abused the people they should serve. Instead, Paul advocates what appears to be a "weak" (*astheneō*) leadership style (2 Cor 11:20–21). Paul's model is the "meek" and "gentle" Christ (2 Cor 10:1; Matt 11:29), who may appear unimpressive from a worldly perspective. The "crucified" Messiah's costly victory came by way of suffering (1 Cor 2:2; Luke 14:26–27). Consequently, the authentic "weak" Christlike leadership, according to Paul, is one which entails the physical and mental difficulties or discomfort one has to endure from persecutions, arduous travel, hard work, and incessant concern for others because of a

---

17. Not "men" NIV 1984.
18. Further, see A. Spencer, "El Hogar," 72–77.

desire to communicate Christ's redemptive good news (2 Cor 11:21–33).[19] A Christlike leadership rejoices in truth, bearing and enduring all for the sake of those it serves (1 Cor 13:6–7).

Romans 16 is a list of Christian women and men, Jews and Gentiles, celebrated for their Christlike servant leadership. The list is also egalitarian in nature. Phoebe is a minister to and overseer of her church in Cenchreae (Rom 16:1–2). As opposed to James and John Zebedee who were self-serving (Mark 10:35–45), Phoebe serves and is served. She and the Romans model mutual cooperative service to each other. She is a mature mentor or discipler of Paul and many others (Rom 16:2). Phoebe waits for Paul's recommendation asking for help on her behalf as opposed to demanding and pushing for herself.[20]

Prisca and Aquila (Rom. 16:3–5a) are also mature church leaders who minister together as a couple and as equals. They give sacrificial, others-oriented service, risking their own lives for Paul. They persistently serve together the church, other churches, and coworker Paul. Their ministry promotes thanksgiving and gratitude. As Jews, they minister to Gentiles. Like Phoebe, they are missional.[21]

The ranking that Paul uses in Romans 16 is based on service and is not guided by a permanent hierarchy based on birth or sex or wealth or ethnicity.[22] Phoebe, Prisca, and Aquila serve the churches. Epaenetus is a "firstfruit" (a convert) of faith in Christ (16:5). Mary works hard (16:6). Andronicus and Junia live out sacrificial lives for Christ (16:7 "my fellow prisoners"). Paul celebrates them as believers and apostles who were in the faith earlier than himself (16:7). Paul's own humility is demonstrated by his calling other apostles "prominent." These are Paul's hardworking coworkers (16:6, 9, 12). Paul treats them as family (16:13). Many women (at least one-third)[23] and men work side by side, according to the list in Romans 16.[24]

---

19. See further Spencer, "2 Corinthians"; *2 Corinthians*, 164–201.

20. NTME translates the Greek appropriately describing Phoebe as "minister" and "overseer." See also A. Spencer, *Beyond the Curse*, 113–117.

21. See also A. Spencer, *2 Timothy & Titus*, 153–55.

22. Rebecca Groothuis explains that "functional" or temporary subordination can coexist with equality, but female permanent subordination cannot (Groothuis, *Good News*, 44–45).

23. Phoebe (16:1–2), Prisca (16:3–5), Mary (16:6), Junia (16:7), Tryphaena, Tryphosa, Persis (16:12), Rufus's mother (16:13), Julia, and Nereus's sister (16:15). See also Cohick, "Women as Leaders," 642–45.

24. See also Euodia and Syntyche, Paul's coworkers, who colabor with Paul (Phil. 4:2–3).

Do the Terms 'Equal' and 'Impartial' Even Occur in the Bible?

What other theological themes undergird Christian egalitarian leadership? Other than servant leadership and mutual submission, the biblical themes of equality or impartiality, spiritual gifts, the priesthood of all believers, and the new covenant undergird egalitarian leadership.

We have already seen how Christ Jesus's equality with God did not keep him from becoming human and dying on behalf of humans in the most demeaning form of ancient death: crucifixion (John 5:18; Phil 2:6–8). "Equality" (*isos, isotēs*) literally refers to the same size, testimony, or amount. For examples, the New Jerusalem is laid out like a square, each side having the *same* length and width (Rev. 21:16). Jesus taught that all who work in his vineyard receive the same reward. The same wage is given to those who labor all day and those who labor one hour. Workers should not compete with each other for higher recompense (Matt 20:1–16). However, the testimonies of the witnesses against Jesus before the Sanhedrin were not equal since they did not agree; their testimonies were not the *same*.[25]

Paul defines "equality" not as the same initial income, but the same final disbursement, so that all end with sufficient income. Consequently, the amounts requested for donations for ministry should not be the same for everyone. Charity depends on what someone has, not what someone does not have. Equality in practice signifies that when someone has abundance, they should share it with those in need, while needy persons receive what they require for existence. For, at a future time, the person who had been in need will be able to share with the person who once had abundance (2 Cor 8:12–14). Paul uses as his basis the Hebrews' experience with manna in the desert: "The one with much did not have too much, and the one with little did not have too little" (2 Cor 8:15 citing Exod 16:18). At the end of each day, each family gathered as much as they needed. No one was to store the manna overnight (Exod 16:18–20). In a similar fashion, Christians are to work so that all believers end up with the same amount of financial resources. This is economic interdependence so that the final proportions end up similar. Certainly, there is no basis for rank or status based on economics if all will be shared.

Spiritual equality must be demonstrated in social equality. Orthodoxy ("right doctrine") should be demonstrated by orthopraxy ("right practice"). Paul approves of Peter, a Jew, eating with Gentiles as a sign of Jewish and Gentile spiritual equality (Gal 2:12). However, when the circumcision

---

25. Mark 14:56, 59.

faction arrived, Peter and other Jews would eat no longer with their Gentile brothers and sisters. Paul reprimands them: "They were not acting consistently with the truth of the gospel" (Gal 2:14 NRSV).[26]

This theme of equality can also be seen in the teaching that God is *impartial* and therefore also believers should be impartial. God reveals to Peter in a vision that the laws of food purity should no longer separate Jew from Gentile (Acts 10:9–33).[27] Then Peter declares to Cornelius and his Gentile gathering: "Truly I understand that God is not partial (*prosōpolēmptēs*), but in every nation the one fearing him and doing righteous actions is acceptable to him" (Acts 10:34–35). The quality of impartiality is evident in the very essence of God. Even Jesus's enemies knew that Jesus was not partial to anyone.[28] Jesus welcomed and loved all who approached him.[29] That is because God is love (1 John 4:8, 16). This impartial nature of God is demonstrated in God's concern for those without power: the needy, orphan, widow, and stranger (Deut 10:17–18).

Jesus's concept of impartiality influenced early church values and leadership. Paul teaches how God both punishes and rewards Jew and Gentile, master and slave, those prominent and not prominent.[30] James reprimands the church for favoring the wealthy (Jas 2:1, 9). Therefore, a Gentile like Titus could become an important leader (Gal 2:3), a former slave like Onesimus could become a bishop (Phlm 10–18; Eusebius, *Hist. eccl.* 3.36), women could become apostles (e.g., Junia [Rom 16:7]) and ministers (e.g., Phoebe [Rom 16:1–2]). The Apostle Paul summarizes: "There is no longer Jew or Greek, there is no longer slave or free, there is no longer male and female; for all of you are one in Christ Jesus" (Gal 3:28 NRSV). All who are baptized "into Christ" are now clothed "with Christ" (Gal 3:27). It is Christ who is seen, not Jew, Gentile, slave, free, male, or female. All are Abraham's offspring, Abraham's heirs, and therefore privileged to have all the rights and benefits of any free Jewish male (Gal 3:29; Col 1:12). The powerless and foolish and poor were chosen by God so that no one might boast in God's presence. When "Christ crucified" is proclaimed, all power and wisdom on earth are nullified. We all have the same source of life in Christ Jesus (1 Cor 1:19–31). We can then boast only in the Lord, who acts with and delights in "steadfast love, justice, and righteousness" (1 Cor 1:31 citing Jer 9:23–24).

---

26. On the challenges of multicultural leadership, see Rogers, *Building a House*.
27. See also 1 Pet 1:17.
28. Matt 22:16; Mark 12:14; Luke 20:21.
29. See also Matt 18:10.
30. Rom 2:11; Gal 2:6; Eph 6:9; Col 3:25.

How Do Spiritual Gifts Relate to Christian Egalitarian Leadership?

A *leader* is someone who guides, directs, advises, commands, or shows the way to others. The study of spiritual gifts adds the principle that Christian leadership is a communal effort to cause the body of believers to grow into Christ. No gift is superior to another in this venture. Peter divides all spiritual gifts into two broad categories: gifts of the word and those of service (1 Pet 4:10–11). Paul isolates the gifts of the word in Ephesians: "And [Christ] himself gave some to be apostles, and some prophets, and some evangelists, and some pastors and teachers for the equipping of the saints for a work of ministry, for upbuilding of Christ's body, until all attain the unity of the faith and the personal knowledge of God's Son, for mature manhood,[31] for full maturity of the fullness of Christ" (Eph 4:11–13). These five gifts are especially verbal ones. They are foundational. Apostles testify to Christ's life and resurrection, prophets proclaim and thus reveal God's revelation for the times, evangelists reach new people and give them basic instruction in the faith, pastors protect and help people day by day, and teachers cause disciples to learn advanced knowledge.[32] Every gift here is indispensable, but the goal of these gifts is not self-serving; rather the gifts all work toward serving other believers, to train them for their own ministries, so that Christ's one body will be upbuilt and thus mature in faith, knowledge, and wisdom. In contrast, hierarchy may leave people as infants who do not mature, being stunted in growth, never advancing, and, as a result, subject to cults, superstition, and other deceitful teaching of aggressive, power-wielding pundits (4:14).

The body needs to become adequate to the head ("grow into Christ"). Paul clearly uses the "head" (*kephalē*) as an image of growth in Ephesians 4:15–16. Leadership has a goal: spiritual maturity ("growth of the body for upbuilding itself in love," 4:16b). The only clear hierarchy here is the "one God and Father of all" (4:6) who is ever present ("the one over all and through all and in all," 4:6).[33] Gifts are not achievements, but *gifts* from God's grace (4:7), which flourish with attitudes and behaviors such as humility and gentleness (4:2), which are aspects of mutual submission, exhibited by cooperating "ligaments" (4:16). Each part must do its work. The overseer is Christ who is the Giver and the gift, the means and the end (4:7–16). No human here is the ultimate decision maker or "mind" (*nous*) for all.

---

31. Here is one of the rare instances where the church is imaged as masculine, supplementing all those where the church is referred to as feminine.

32. See A. Spencer, *Beyond the Curse*, 99–109.

33. See A. Spencer et al., *Goddess Revival*, 136–39.

In 1 Peter 4:9–11, we learn that Christian leadership is a communal effort of love and service.[34] The context is the end times when danger and judgment are near. Therefore, believers need to keep that bigger picture in mind, get their heads together, and become self-controlled (as opposed to the wild living of the Gentiles, 4:3–7). While maintaining good communication with God ("prayers"), believers should be loving. Leadership is all about loving one another, which includes extending hospitality that serves others by using one's spiritual gift to move others forward in using theirs. Those gifts which emphasize verbal ministries must be attentive to be accurate to God's revelation; those gifts which emphasize service must be attentive to using God's strength (4:11). Even though God's grace is manifested in various ("manifold") ways, they all come from God (the same Giver), and glorify God (the same goal, 4:10–11). Mutual submission is shown when believers receive from and give to each other. Such intersubmission of varying precedence is egalitarian because, although the gifts are different, they are equal in worth and value. No gift is superior. Love is the great leveler. Love orders the gifts to be compassionate and in service to others.

First Corinthians 12 reiterates Ephesians 4 and 1 Peter 4 on the equality of the gifts. Paul especially writes against discouragement and entitlement. In 1 Corinthians 12:14–20, he speaks against discouragement. Even though the hand is normally situated higher and is more visible than the foot, the foot is no less important than the hand. There is no hierarchy of gifts. Also, a person with any gift should not feel more important or entitled than anyone with another (12:21). Humility sees the worth of everyone else and any other gift and oneself as only one part of a venture. In discouragement, one cannot develop; in entitlement, others cannot develop. Functional egalitarianism must be humble, according to Paul. Everyone is equal: a loss for one is a loss for all, while a win for one is a win for all (12:26). Equality is shown in each part of the body loving and using gifts for the common good (12:7). The church is one body, Christ's body, which, as a result, unites and levels all. That is why the greatest gift is love, exhibited by mutual communal service (12:31—13:13).

Paul adds a new concept here—mutual honor and the reciprocating of honor. Not all have the same initial income, but their final resources should be equal (2 Cor 8:13–15); not all have the same initial honor, but their final disbursement of honor should be equal (1 Cor 12:22–24). Those that have more worldly honor should treat with greater honor those who have less worldly honor, unlike the wealthy Corinthians who treated their poor

---

34. On team-centered organization, see also Kilinski & Wofford, *Organization*, 159–70.

believers with less honor and gave them fewer physical resources (1 Cor 11:20–22, 29–34). So "discerning the body" means sharing one's food with the more needy members of Christ's body.

Thus, "first" in 12:28 ("God has placed in the church first apostles, second prophets, third teachers, then . . .) cannot refer to hierarchy of rank or gift. That would contradict everything Paul wrote earlier. Therefore, he must be referring to the sequencing of events: the foundation of the church is built first on the testimony of the apostles to the life and resurrection of Jesus (Acts 1:21–22), then prophets proclaim God's revelation, then teachers cause disciples to learn, then the Spirit's manifestation is shown by miracles, healings, strategies of organization, and communication (1 Cor 12:28). The use of the Greek negative *mē* signifies that the answer to every question in 12:29–30 is "no": all are *not* apostles, all are *not* prophets, etc. Christ's body has variety, but everyone's contribution is crucial.

In practice, Paul's teachings are quite dramatic and revolutionary. For instance, who is most important in an educational institution? Is it the president who oversees the actualization of the school's vision and raises funds? But, how can the president raise funds without the fundraiser? Or, how can students come without people to provide financial help and receive their payments? Or, how can students stay if the buildings are falling apart and without an adequate computer network? Or, how will they stay and recommend to other students to join them if teachers do not competently teach them? We could go on. Everyone in an educational institution is equal in worth and should be equal in honor, as in Christ's body. Thus, we have seen that Christian leadership is a communal effort of love and service gifted by God to cause the body of believers to grow into Christ.[35]

Romans 12:3–8 reiterates many similar points to the earlier passages on gifts. Love is key (12:9–10). Every member of the body is equal to the other members, but different. There is no hierarchy of gifts. "Do not think of yourself more highly than you ought" (Rom 12:3 NIV) is reiterated at the end of the passage: "do not be haughty" (12:16). "The many are one body in Christ, and the one (body) is comprised of members with one another" (12:5). All of us are gathered into one body "in *Christ*" and *not* to a fan club for a particular earthly pastor. Within that one body, members are related to one another. We are each diverse and distinct but still part of Christ's larger body. We are individually interdependent. Functional egalitarianism, unlike theoretical egalitarianism, takes humility, understanding

---

35. On the theme of growth, see further Richards & Hoeldtke, *Theology of Church Leadership*, 45–55.

our real place in Christ's body, cognizant that we are each only one part of it: a necessary part, but only one part.

Paul's teachings can be compared to the analogy of construction. In 2018, we had an additional room, basement, and attic constructed (a three-level addition). The basement floor could be compared with God's mercy; the "mercies of God" undergird our presenting our bodies as a living sacrifice to God, which is our spiritual worship (Rom 12:1). The goal is genuine worship—that is the blueprint for the building. How does one get from God's mercy to the goal: worship? We individual participants work together to reach that goal. In a building, all the different tradespeople are needed to reach the goal of completion, according to the plans specified in the blueprint. Each, though, has a different function. The workers are one team, just as the components of Christ's body are one. Each worker has a different skill. The work begins with the prophets because they receive God's architectural design, the blueprints of what God wants. Faith is needed to be accurate to God's plans. The bigger the plans, the more faith is needed (12:3–6). Next come the service workers. They may bring in the supplies. All spring and summer, we had trucks coming in, bringing lumber, cement, windows, etc. No work could be done without these supplies. In the same way, in the church, those with gifts of service are the needed workers for everyday work. Then come the workers in groups of two or more. The more experienced laborers teach the less experienced workers how to do certain carpentry, roofing, or painting tasks. On our house, as on God's "house," they worked together, while teaching each other (12:7). As time went on, encouragers were needed to help discouraged workers. One task might be extremely tiring, or the sun could be very hot and an encourager would bring in a tent to help the workers cool off. When the bills mount up, the owner needs to pay the contractor. The contractor, as the leader or overseer of the project, has to remain diligent in order to keep the workers on their various jobs so that the work reaches completion according to the plans. At the same time, the contractor must show compassion with workers who may get sick or have family problems (12:8).

The workers are interdependent. After the basic walls go up, the electricians come before and after the final walls are constructed. The painters cannot come until the walls are all up and secure. The rug installer comes even later, and then the furniture is delivered, wherein all is completed. Each one has different skills and each work must be done well with good quality materials (12:9). Everyone's work must be valued and honored. If the contractor is congratulated, the honest contractor will then point out the value of everyone's work as it contributes to the whole (12:10). All the workers actualize the architectural design (12:11). The contractor should communicate with the architect to check the design and to ask for help with difficulties (12:12). And the owner should be patient if work is progressing. We had a neighbor who ridiculed the work at the beginning, when the old room had been taken apart and the dirt had been dug up to ready a space for the basement, but we treated our neighbor with respect, and encouraged him to wait for the future great work (which he did like very much, 12:14).

Romans 12:16 summarizes well the basic principle here: do not set up hierarchies of entitlement. In other words, "Live in harmony with one another; do not be haughty, but associate with the lowly; do not claim to be wiser than you are" (12:16 NRSV). The list of gifts did not begin with "leaders" (12:8). There are skills that come with each gift and with every office, even skills that come with being "governing authorities"—for example, not to be a terror to good conduct, but rather to approve of those who do good and to punish wrongdoers (13:1–4).[36] Each of us needs to submit ourselves to others as they do their work, and they submit to us as we use our spiritual gifts (13:5). Our basic leadership principle can be further summarized: Christian leadership is a communal and *interdependent* effort of love, service, and *skill* to cause the body of believers to grow into Christ and *worship God*.

How Does the Priesthood of All Believers Support Egalitarian Leadership?

In the Old Testament, active priests were Jewish men from a specific tribe (Levi) aged 30–50 who were in a state of physical purity and were called by lot to participate in the tabernacle services (Num 1:50, 4:3; Luke 1:5–9). Their service included strenuous physical activity such as carrying and repairing temple equipment, providing protection, and preparing animals for sacrifice (Num 1:50–51, 53; 3:7–9). Priestly service also consisted of keeping the fire lit in the sanctuary, burning incense, placing shrew bread on the table, lighting the lamps, and examining lepers.[37] In addition to the sacrificial system, priests pronounced the blessing, supervised tithing and the treasury, sounded the trumpet to call the assembly, acted as magistrates, and educated.[38] The sacrifice of animals was terminated by Christ's perfect sacrifice of himself.[39] But, the educational and intercessional aspects continued in the new covenant. The prophet Anna, like a

---

36. See also 1 Pet 2:11.
37. Exod 27:20–21; 30:7; Lev 1:3–9; 6:12; 13:1–44; 23:10; Heb 10:11.
38. Lev 10:10–11; Num 5:15; 6:22–26; 10:8–10; 18:1; Deut 33:10; 2 Kgs 12:10; Neh 10:38.
39. Heb 9:13–14, 25–28; 10:11–14.

priest serving at the sanctuary,[40] served at the temple in Jerusalem by praying day and night. By recognizing Jesus as the Messiah, she became one of the first evangelists (Luke 2:37–38).

God originally wanted all the Hebrew people to be a "priestly kingdom and a holy nation" (Exod 19:6 NRSV). The passage that Jesus chose as the defining one for his calling (Luke 4:17–19 citing Isa 61:1–2) includes a foreshadowing of the future: "You shall be called priests of the Lord, you shall be named ministers of our God" (Isa 61:6 NRSV). The priests were supposed to teach God's law accurately (to "guard knowledge," Mal 2:7), making distinction between the unclean and the clean, and honoring the Sabbath.[41] Because of Christ's sacrifice, now "clean" and "unclean" states are primarily expressed in good moral behavior, not obeying food laws (e.g., Acts 10:9–16, 35; 11:5–18). However, the priestly function of education and intercession continues now, fulfilling God's original intention. All believers, whether female or male of any tribe at any time are part of God's "living stones" in a "spiritual house" so as to be a "holy priesthood" now offering "spiritual sacrifices acceptable to God through Jesus Christ."[42] All believers are the "royal priesthood" who proclaim God's mighty acts (1 Pet 2:9). The priesthood and temple service are no longer limited to pure Jewish males, but are automatic for all reborn people.[43] Jesus as the perfect priest has ended the Old Testament priesthood; as a result, believers should meet together regularly to "spur" each other "toward love and good deeds" (Heb 10:10–25). Jesus also ended the temple as a physical building. The "temple" is now Christ's body, the Holy of Holies, represented by two or more believers worshiping together.[44]

Therefore, the population of God's new priestly kingdom, made of Greek and Jew, circumcised and uncircumcised, barbarian, Scythian, slave and free, all forgive one another, love one another, and teach and admonish one another, singing psalms to God (Col 3:11–16). We see the priesthood of all believers active also in James's instructions to the Twelve

---

40. The same verb *latreuō* ("render cultic service") is used of Anna and the Old Testament priestly service (Heb 8:5; 13:10). Even Old Testament precedent does not limit priestly service to all Jewish men.

41. Lev 10:10–11; Neh 8:7–9; Ezek 22:26.

42. 1 Pet 2:5. See also Rom 12:1; Heb 13:15–16; Rev 1:6; 5:10; 20:6.

43. See also Grenz, "Biblical Priesthood," 272–86.

44. *Naos* is the Holy Place and Holy of Holies of the temple (Thayer, *Lexicon*, 422). John 2:21; 1 Cor 3:17; 6:19; 2 Cor 6:16; Eph 2:21. See A. Spencer, *2 Corinthians*, 114–15. On how the Protestant Reformation supported equality, see Witte, "Human Dignity, Equality, and Liberty," 145–60, and Davies and Dodds, *Leadership*, 99–100. Davies and Dodds compare "pyramid" to "tambourine" models as symbols of leadership styles (60–63).

Tribes: confessing sins to each other, praying for each other, and seeking the wandering sinner (Jas 5:16, 19–20).[45]

How Does the New Covenant Support Christian Egalitarian Leadership?

The priesthood of all believers is one aspect of the new covenant made possible by God placing the law within people's minds and hearts. As a result, from the "least" to the "greatest" will know the Lord (Heb 8:8–11 citing Jer 31:31–34). Hierarchy of status is not a requirement for the proclamation of the gospel. Now, all believers have access to the Father by the Spirit. They are one holy temple in the Lord (Eph 2:17–22). All believers are eligible to be filled with the knowledge of God's will by the Spirit (Col 1:9).[46]

A similar message is proclaimed by the prophet Joel when God revealed that God would pour out his Spirit on all people: "I will pour out my Spirit upon all flesh, and your sons and your daughters shall prophesy, and your young men shall see visions, and your old men shall dream dreams. Even upon my slaves, both men and women, in those days, I will pour out my Spirit; and they shall prophesy" (Acts 2:17–18 citing Joel 2:28–29 NRSV). The new covenant with the permanent indwelling Spirit came upon the disciples at Pentecost in Jerusalem, making men and women, young and old, slave and free equal. "Everyone who calls on the name of the Lord will be saved" (Joel 2:32). Moreover, "everyone" includes Gentiles as well as Jews. The work of the Holy Spirit, as recorded in Acts, demonstrated equality between Jews and Gentiles when the Gentile Cornelius and his family and friends received the same gift of the Holy Spirit that the Jews had received.[47] This one incident was sufficient proof to the Jewish Christians of the Gentiles' equality with them. The familial terms of "brother" and "sister" illustrate this equality in the one united household of God.[48] Gentiles have been adopted along with Jews as heirs of God's kingdom.[49]

---

45. See A. Spencer, *James*, 281–82. Greg Ogden reminds us that Martin Luther also emphasizes that, since being made right with God is mediated directly through Jesus Christ, every Christian now should be a minister of God's word, a "priest" (Ogden, *Reformation*, 49–50).

46. See also John 7:38–39.

47. Acts 10:44–45; 11:15–18.

48. E.g., Acts 16:40; 2 Cor 8:22–23; Eph 2:19; Phlm 16–17.

49. Atkins adds that *huiothesia* ("adoption") is related to the kinship relationship, which reveals an egalitarian community. Paul uses adoption terminology without a sense of hierarchy. The members of the community have equal access to the means of achieving individual success. The gifts of the Spirit are distributed to all the siblings in

Does Egalitarian Leadership Undermine the Authority of Leaders?

Sometimes people think egalitarian leadership contradicts all godly authority of leaders. But this is not at all true. Being egalitarian contradicts bullying and unwarranted entitlement, which often usurps power over others. So understanding legitimate authority at the outset is important.

Webster's Dictionary defines "authority" as "the power to determine, adjudicate, or otherwise settle issues or disputes," "a power or right delegated or given," "right to respect or acceptance of one's word, command, thought." "Authority, control, influence denote a power or right to direct the actions or thoughts of others. Authority is a power or right, usually because of rank or office, to issue commands and to punish for violations."[50] People are given authority frequently in the Bible. The New Testament has at least eleven different word families that relate to authority.[51] Authority is needed to exercise a spiritual gift. God gives humans authority so that they can do good to others (Rom 13:1–4). However, Jesus and Paul warn against authority that tyrannizes, dominates, and is self-centered.[52] Prevention of the misuse of authority begins in the Old Testament by giving power to a plurality of leaders and by the rulers being dependent on God. Moreover, religious authority in the New Testament is not limited to Jewish wealthy free males. Since all of God's people were to be a priestly and holy dominion, at first all the people heard the voice of God on Sinai (Exod 19:8; Deut 5:22–27). Not just Moses, but the elders as well, had been sent to Pharaoh (Exod 3:18), but they shifted their responsibility onto Moses, imploring him: "Go near, you yourself, and hear all that the Lord our God will say. Then tell us everything that the Lord our God tells you" (Deut

---

Christ (xviii, 73, 169–70, 182–83, 186–90). The "Pauline church" is "a group that is a voluntary association of individuals who freely contract together. The rules for behavior in the group are individualized or personalized for the members because there are few hierarchical social controls to keep them active in the group. The participants find the group important enough to make room for it in their lives. This is visible in descriptions of the ways in which they interact and in rules associated with membership. On the other hand, there are few overt, visible social controls that determine their decisions regarding their participation. This is apparent in the lack of controls related to social hierarchy" (*Egalitarian Community*, 143–44).

50. *Random House Webster's Unabridged Dictionary*, s.v. E.g., Jesus had authority to overturn the vendors' tables in the temple because it was his Father's house (John 2:16–18). See also A. Spencer, "Biblical Equity," 112–13.

51. A. Spencer, *1 Timothy*, 64. These synonyms for "authority" are used for women, too, e.g., in Rom 16:1–2; 1 Cor 7:4; 11:10.

52. Matt 20:25–26; 2 Cor 11:20–21; 1 Tim 2:12. A. Spencer, *1 Timothy*, 63, explains the negative nature of "authority" in 1 Tim 2:12.

5:27 NRSV). When Moses is overwhelmed by leading the Hebrews (Num 11:11–15), God sends Moses seventy plus two elders to share his burden (Num 11:16–17, 26). Later, God sends Jethro, his father-in-law, to counsel him. Jethro advises Moses to divide the judging among virtuous people over groups of thousands, hundreds, fifties, and tens: "Let them sit as judges for the people at all times. . . . they will bear the burden with you" (Exod 18:21–22 NRSV).[53] In the New Testament, the Christian community as well bears each other's burdens (Gal 6:2). Moses's exclamation ("Would that all the Lord's people were prophets, that the Lord would put his Spirit on them," Num 11:29 NRSV) is fulfilled at the heavenly Pentecost (Acts 2:1–4).

God never wanted the Hebrews to have human kings; rather, God was to be their Ruler. When the judge and prophet Samuel is ready to retire, the elders demand a "king to govern us, like other nations" (1 Sam 8:5 NRSV). God responds: "They have not rejected you, but they have rejected me from being king over them" (1 Sam 8:7 NRSV). Samuel warns them how the kings will oppress them by demanding workers, land, harvests, and animals for each king's own use (1 Sam 8:9–18). In contrast, when God ruled them directly, God appointed emissaries such as Deborah, who was a moral judge and prophet who fulfilled God's commission to her by reminding the Israelites of the mighty things the Lord had done for them so they could worship and serve the Lord who brought them out of Egypt, by settling disputes, and by rescuing them from their enemies.[54]

In the New Testament, we find God gifting a plurality of leaders. For example, more than one elder represents the church and oversees it in Ephesus (Acts 20:17, 28). This group of elders lays hands on Timothy to empower him and oversee the congregation.[55] More than one elder from a church prays for the sick person (Jas 5:14). Peter speaks to a group of elders not to lord it over those in their charge, but to become humble examples.[56] A group of trustworthy people were to be trained to teach others the gospel (2 Tim 2:2). A group of overseers and ministers are present at Philippi (Phil 1:1). Jesus sent out workers two by two (Mark 6:7; Luke 10:1), and the Holy Spirit sent out both Barnabas and Saul (Paul) for a special mission (Acts 13:2). Paul continued working with male and female coworkers as his colleagues (e.g., Acts 18:2–3).[57] So human rule involves

---

53. See further Spencer and Spencer, *Joy through the Night*, 179–84.

54. Judg 2:10–11, 16–18; 3:7–9; 4:4–5. A. Spencer, "Biblical Equity," 117–18.

55. 1 Tim 3:1; 4:14; 5:17.

56. 1 Pet 5:2–3. See also Acts 14:23; Titus 1:5; Heb 13:7, 17. See also A. Spencer, *2 Timothy and Titus*, 10–20, 95.

57. See A. Spencer, *Beyond the Curse*, 117–18.

more than a single leader in complete power to provide checks and balances for that power. This is in contrast, however, to perfect divine rule. We believers have one Chief Shepherd, one High Priest, one Lord, one Mediator, one Savior, one Sovereign: Jesus Christ.[58]

With plurality of leaders comes communal decision making. For instance, the serious debate between Paul and Barnabas and the circumcision party is resolved by the church together with the group of apostles and elders in Jerusalem. Paul and Barnabas are sent by a group, the church of Antioch (Acts 15:2–6). Peter, Barnabas, and Paul inform the group of God's actions through their ministry among the Gentiles (15:7–12). James reminds the group of Old Testament prophecy that predicted such a blessing (15:13–18). Two leaders, along with Barnabas and Paul, then relay the joint decision to the Gentiles at Antioch (15:22–32). The Holy Spirit worked cooperatively with the council for the decision (15:28).[59]

A similar pattern is described by Jesus in handling disagreements between two members of a church. First, only the two people involved speak to each other; then, two or three others assist. These two or three people, and not merely one appointed "ruler" (Matt 18:15–20), represent Christ's presence. As a final step, the whole church becomes involved. Gilbert Bilezikian aptly summarizes the safety in community leadership: "Because of checks and balances, a group of leaders is less likely to become corrupted and to usurp the authority of the community than a strong individual leader who might gain ascendency over it."[60]

Nevertheless, today, some people still are asking God for the church to be like the worldly culture and give them one "king," one pastor, to govern them, missing out on the blessings from having a plurality of gifted mutually supportive leaders. The voice of that one leader standing perilously on his or her platform can overshadow the voice of God to all God's people through their variety of spiritual gifts.

---

58. Matt 2:6; Luke 2:11; John 4:42; Eph 4:5; 1 Pet 5:4; Heb 10:21; Rom 10:9; 1 Tim 2:5.

59. See also A. Spencer, "Biblical Equity," 113–14.

60. Bilezikian, *Community*, 163. "Servant leadership," he adds, "operates on the basis of group consensus or of representative consensus, not of unilateral, autocratic, top-down decision-making" (*Community*, 162). Further, see pp. 139–42, 162–63. The Trinity offers the perfect example of "collaborative leadership" in distributing spiritual gifts (165; 1 Cor 12:4–6; Rom 12:3; Eph 4:7–13). See also 2 Cor 3:3–17.

Can Someone Be a Servant or an Egalitarian Leader but not Christian?

Although a Christian value, egalitarian leadership by itself is not necessarily Christian, nor is servant leadership by itself necessarily egalitarian. For example, the couple Ananias and Sapphira were egalitarian in many ways. Together, they kept back some of the proceeds of their sale of property, but presented some money to the apostles as if it were all the proceeds. Together, they agreed to "put the Spirit of the Lord to the test" (Acts 5:1–4, 7–9). Both died and were buried together (Acts 5:5, 10). They had equality, no apparent hierarchy, shared power, and cooperated in a partnership. However, their leadership was not Christian because it was not modeled on Christ, nor did it serve Christ. Their actions aimed to deceive Christ's Spirit. Their actions were misleading, aiming to look more sacrificial and others-oriented and humble and thankful than it was in reality. Their actions were sacrificial, but not truthful.

Sometimes pastors and leaders try to be "servant leaders," for example, by serving a meal to the laypeople at a church gathering, or even doing a foot washing service, but these same leaders may run their ministries to promote themselves and do not share power in their decisions over others. They may favor those who are like themselves and are not impartial as God is. They may take credit for the work of others and not encourage their partners in ministry to use their gifts in ministry. Theoretical egalitarian leadership is not the same as *functional* active egalitarian leadership.

In summary, Christian leadership is modeled on Christ's character and actions, enabled by God-the-Trinity, and is for honoring Christ. A leader guides or shows the way in order to enable Christian maturity. Christian leadership is mutual service between partners in ministry for Christ's sake. Christian egalitarian leadership is an intrinsic aspect of servant leadership. It is characterized by a communal and interdependent effort of love, service, skill, education, intercession, confession, and forgiveness to cause the body of believers to grow into Christ and to worship God. All humans are equal in worth, rights, and status, but are not the same in gifts, skills, function, experience, sex, age, ethnic background, wealth, or education. Variety is good. Key aspects of servant and egalitarian leadership may be summarized as follows:

Servant leadership is:

1. Sacrificial service for others in Christ's behalf
2. Others-oriented power, not abusive, harmful, self-centered, or self-seeking

3. Humble, gentle, not entitled

4. Thankful

5. Loving

6. Christ honoring and promoting

The nature of *egalitarian leadership* emphasizes:

1. Equality between the genders, races, economic and social classes, differing ages, differing power, honor, and education, married and single, differently gifted

2. Outside of the hierarchy between God and humans, lacking innate or permanent hierarchy of rank, status, or authority; position is identified by gifting

3. Mutual submission, interdependence, and service out of love

4. Cooperative partnership in ministry

5. Shared power and decision-making

6. Mutual honor

References

The American Heritage Dictionary. 4th ed. New York: Dell, 2001.

Atkins, Jr., Robert A. *Egalitarian Community: Ethnography and Exegesis*. Tuscaloosa, AL: University of Alabama Press, 1991.

Barth, Marcus, and Helmut Blanke. *The Letter to Philemon: A New Translation with Notes and Commentary*. The Eerdmans Critical Commentary. Grand Rapids: Eerdmans, 2000.

Bauer, Walter, Frederick W. Danker, W. F. Arndt, and F. W. Gingrich. *A Greek-English Lexicon of the New Testament and Other Early Christian Literature*. 3d ed. Chicago: University of Chicago Press, 2000.

Bilezikian, Gilbert. *Community 101: Reclaiming the Church as a Community of Oneness*. Grand Rapids: Zondervan, 1997.

Cohick, Lynn H. "Women as Leaders." In *The IVP Women's Bible Commentary*, edited by Catherine Clark Kroeger and Mary J. Evans, 642–45. Downers Grove, IL: InterVarsity, 2002.

Davies, Mervyn, and Graham Dodds. *Leadership in the Church for a People of Hope*. New York: T & T Clark, 2011.

Everist, Norma Cook, and Craig L. Nessan. *Transforming Leadership: New Vision for a Church in Mission*. Minneapolis: Fortress, 2008.

Ford, Leighton. *Transforming Leadership: Jesus' Way of Creating Vision, Shaping Values & Empowering Change*. Downers Grove, IL: InterVarsity, 1991.

Greenleaf, Robert K. *Servant Leadership: A Journey into the Nature of Legitimate Power and Greatness*. Edited by Larry C. Spears. New York: Paulist, 2002.

Grenz, Stanley J. "Biblical Priesthood and Women in Ministry." In *Discovering Biblical Equality: Complementarity without Hierarchy*, edited by Ronald W. Pierce and Rebecca Merrill Groothuis, 272–86. 2d ed. Downers Grove, IL: InterVarsity, 2003.

Groothuis, Rebecca Merrill. *Good News for Women: A Biblical Picture of Gender Equality*. Grand Rapids: Baker, 1997.

Kilinski, Kenneth K., and Jerry C. Wofford. *Organization and Leadership in the Local Church*. Grand Rapids: Zondervan, 1973.

Northouse, Peter G. *Leadership: Theory and Practice*. 6th ed. Los Angeles: SAGE, 2013.

Ogden, Greg. *The New Reformation: Returning the Ministry to the People of God*. Grand Rapids: Zondervan, 1990.

Padgett, Alan G. *As Christ Submits to the Church: A Biblical Understanding of Leadership and Mutual Submission*. Grand Rapids: Baker, 2011.

Random House. *Random House Webster's Unabridged Dictionary*. 2d ed. New York: Random House Reference, 2001.

Richards, Lawrence O., and Clyde Hoeldtke. *A Theology of Church Leadership*. Grand Rapids: Zondervan, 1980.

Rogers, Jeffrey S. *Building a House for All God's Children: Diversity Leadership in the Church*. Nashville: Abingdon, 2008.

Schürer, Emil. *The History of the Jewish People in the Age of Jesus Christ (175 B.C.—A.D. 135)*. 2 vols. Edited by Geza Vermes and Fergus Millar. Edinburgh: T & T Clark, 1973.

Spencer, Aída Besançon. *Beyond the Curse: Women Called to Ministry*. Grand Rapids: Baker, 1985.

———. "Biblical Equity and the Meaning of Servant Leadership." In *The Quest for Gender Equity in Leadership: Biblical Teachings on Gender Equity and Illustrations of Transformation in Africa*, edited by KeumJu Jewel Hyun and Diphus C. Chemorion, 109–22. House of Prisca and Aquila Series. Eugene, OR: Wipf & Stock, 2016.

———. *2 Corinthians*. The People's Bible Commentary. Abingdon, UK: Bible Reading Fellowship, 2001.

———. "2 Corinthians: An Egalitarian Ideology for the Latinx Church." In *Latinx Perspectives in the New Testament*, edited by Osvaldo D. Vena and Leticia Guardiola-Sáenz. Lanham, MD: Lexington, 2021.

———. "'El Hogar' as Ministry Team: Stephan(s)'s Household." In *Hispanic Christian Thought at the Dawn of the 21st Century: Apuntes in Honor of Justo L. González*, edited by Alvin Padilla, Roberto Goizueta, and Eldin Villafañe, 69–77. Nashville: Abingdon, 2005.

———. *A Commentary on James*. Kregel Exegetical Library. Grand Rapids: Kregel, 2020.

———. "Jesus' Treatment of Women in the Gospels." In *Discovering Biblical Equality: Complementarity without Hierarchy*, edited by Ronald W. Pierce and Rebecca Merrill Groothuis, 126–41. 2d ed. Downers Grove, IL: InterVarsity, 2003.

———. *1 Timothy*. New Covenant Commentary Series. Eugene, OR: Cascade, 2013.

———. *2 Timothy and Titus*. New Covenant Commentary Series. Eugene, OR: Cascade, 2014.

———. "Toppling the Silent Idol: Assessing Greed as Part of an Idolatrous Meta-System and Promoting Holiness as an Antidote to Greed." *Africanus Journal* 7:2 (Nov. 2015) 29–47.
Spencer, Aída Besançon, and William David Spencer. *Joy through the Night: Biblical Resources on Suffering.* House of Prisca & Aquila Series. Eugene, OR: Wipf & Stock, 1994.
Spencer, Aída Besançon, William David Spencer, Steven R. Tracy, and Celestia G. Tracy. *Marriage at the Crossroads: Couples in Conversation about Discipleship, Gender Roles, Decision Making and Intimacy.* Downers Grove, IL: InterVarsity, 2009.
Spencer, Aída Besançon, Donna F. G. Hailson, Catherine Clark Kroeger, and William David Spencer. *The Goddess Revival: A Biblical Response to God(dess) Spirituality.* House of Prisca & Aquila Series. Eugene, OR: Wipf & Stock, 1995.
Thayer, Joseph Henry. *Thayer's Greek-English Lexicon of the New Testament.* Marshallton, DE: National Foundation for Christian Education, 1889.
Witte, John Jr. "Human Dignity, Equality, and Liberty in Classic Protestant Perspective." In *Carnival Kingdom: Biblical Justice for Global Communities,* edited by Marijke Hoek, Jonathan Ingleby, Andy Kingston-Smith, and Carol Kingston-Smith, 145–60. Gloucester, UK: Wide Margin, 2013.

2

Egalitarianism and Biblical Authority

John P. Lathrop

SOME TIME AGO, THOUGH I do not recall the source, someone made a statement that went very much like this: "Jews say 'the fathers (or rabbis) tell us,' Catholics say 'the Pope says,' and the Protestant minister says 'well, I think.'" I also do not know the exact context in which this statement was made, but it certainly lends itself nicely to the issue of authority—the authority by which religious people speak. The statement is a bit humorous once you get to the part where the Protestant minister speaks. It is also, of course, an oversimplification of the issue. However, it makes the point that people look to various sources to support what they believe, and that they, at least sometimes, cite their sources.

Some, like the Jews mentioned above, look to the trusted teachers of the past. It is true that, during the time of Jesus, a number of Jews adhered to the tradition of the elders, one of which was the washing of hands before meals which "had no direct basis in Scripture."[1] This was true of other traditions as well. Jesus described them as "merely human rules" (Mark 7:7 NIV). References to the tradition of the elders can be found in Matthew 15:1–20 and Mark 7:1–23, which are parallel passages. As these texts make clear, Jesus did not endorse the tradition of the elders. However, in a number of passages in the New Testament, we see the Jews of the first century appealing to the biblical writers of the past, referencing the writers of inspired Scripture. In Matthew 19:7, the Pharisees appealed to what Moses had written about divorce in the Old Testament (Deut 24:1–4) when

---

1. Keener, *Background*, 87.

he gave instructions about a man giving his wife a certificate of divorce and sending her away. The Sadducees also cited Moses as a source when they sought to trap Jesus in their question about the resurrection (Matt 22:24–28; Deut 25:5–6). Jesus, also on occasion, cited sources which were from the Old Testament Scriptures. In Matthew 8:4, he commanded a cleansed leper to show himself to the priest and offer a gift, as Moses had commanded (Lev 14:1–32). Early church leaders also, at times, cited sources. In his sermon on the day of Pentecost, Peter cited David (Acts 2:25–28; 2:34–35; Ps 16:8–11; 110:1). Peter also referenced Moses when he was preaching in Jerusalem and speaking to his hearers about Jesus Christ (Acts 3:22; Deut 18:15, 18). The apostle Paul also referred to the writings of Moses when he was making a case for the financial support of those in ministry (1 Cor 9:9; Deut 25:4). Citing biblical writers is a good practice. That being said, it must be acknowledged that, at times, people have misunderstood and sometimes misinterpreted what the inspired writers wrote.

In later church history, others, like the Roman Catholics mentioned above, look to the current ecclesiastical leader, the Pope, for truth; he is considered the voice of authority in matters of faith. And still others, like the Protestant minister mentioned above, frequently look to their own personal theological views (hopefully developed from Scripture). In the case of the Jews, they looked to the views of a number of respected individuals from the past: the rabbis. In the other two cases, that of the Roman Catholics and the Protestants, the view of one person determines the proper belief: the Pope for Catholics and the individual minister for the Protestants. While our denomination, education, leaders, and personal views may be helpful, and at times may even be right, they should not ultimately be what we look to in order to determine truth.

Our ultimate source should be Scripture, and our ultimate concern should be "what has God said about this?" As Craig Keener has pointed out, our concern should be "what the writers of the Bible teach."[2] God has revealed his word and will to us in the pages of Scripture, the sixty-six books of the Bible. The Lord's view is the most important one. When it comes to truth regarding matters of both temporal and eternal significance, we need a standard greater than that of mere human logic or opinion—we need God's mind, his revelation on the matter. This includes matters of our personal life and issues related to church life and practice. The Bible has much to tell us about the church. By reading the New Testament, we can learn that the church belongs to God (Matt 16:18; Acts 20:28; 1 Cor 6:19–20) and is made up of different kinds of people. The church is made up of males and females,

---

2. Keener, *Women and Wives*, 3.

from different classes in life, and from different ethnicities (Gal 3:28; Col 3:11; Rev 7:9). This is God's intention (Matt 28:19; Eph 2:14). All who are truly the church are those that the Lord has redeemed by the blood of Christ (1 Pet 1:18–19; Acts 20:28). The apostle Paul told the believers in the first century a number of times that Christ is the head of the church (Eph 1:22; 5:23; Col 1:18). Thus, as Christians, we are not our own (1 Cor 6:19–20); we are to live under the Lordship of Christ.

Because of these truths, the Lord has every right to determine how the church is set up and how it is to function. God has made his will known in the Scriptures, and it is now our responsibility to follow the instructions we have been given. In order to do this, we need to be people of the book (the Bible), who follow the practice of the Bereans who examined the Scriptures (Acts 17:11) in order to determine the truth. In addition, we need to make every effort to be those who follow Paul's instruction in 2 Timothy 2:15: we are to be those who rightly interpret the Scriptures. This holds true for every facet of church life and ministry, including the ministries of men and women in the church. Men and women have both been a part of the church since the beginning (Acts 1:12–14; 2:1–4).

Even though both genders have been part of the church from the beginning, it is no secret that there is a difference of opinion among Bible-believing Christians about the place of women in the ministry of the church. So, how should we seek to address this subject? Well, we start with the truth, the Scriptures. Christians sometimes speak of the canon of Scripture, the word appropriated to indicate a list of books.[3] However, it also means "rule or standard."[4] The Scriptures are "in a unique sense, the *rule* of belief and practice."[5] However, as scholars and seminary professors, Gordon Fee and Douglas Stuart have pointed out that does not in itself solve all of the problems. They write, "A simple look at the contemporary church, for example, makes it abundantly clear that not all 'plain meanings' are equally plain to all."[6] Nevertheless, we need to start with the Bible and work through the difficulties.

Biblical Authority

A number of years ago, a man who was attending a well-known university in the United States told me a story. He had visited a church near the dorm

---

3. Bruce, *Canon*, 18.
4. Bruce, *Canon*, 17.
5. Bruce, *Canon*, 18.
6. Fee and Stuart, *Bible*, 19.

where he was living. During the course of his sermon, the preacher said that he disagreed with the apostle Paul. Since the preacher was obviously not alive in the first century when Paul conducted his ministry, it was clear that he was taking issue with something that Paul wrote in the New Testament. This minister was disagreeing with Scripture, God's revealed truth! This is a dangerous place for anyone to be theologically. If I recall correctly, this man told me that he never went back to that church (I do not think that I would either).

Now, we may all feel uncomfortable from time to time with some of the things we read in Scripture. They make us uneasy, and that is as it should be. God wants us to be conformed to the image of Jesus (Rom 8:29). The Scriptures were not given just to make us feel good; they have multiple purposes (see 2 Tim 3:16–17), which include correcting us. For example, when Paul writes and advocates for holy behavior, that goes against our sinful nature, and we may feel uncomfortable or convicted. This is especially true if we are currently struggling with sin in one of the areas he mentions. Passages such as Romans 12:9–21, Ephesians 4:22—5:2, and Colossians 3:5–14 are examples of texts that may convict us. We may inwardly draw back from some of what Paul wrote; however, we are not free to change it or dismiss it. This is because the things that Paul and the other biblical writers wrote did not originate with them. The Bible is not ashamed to say that it is the divinely inspired record, that the Scriptures came from God (2 Tim 3:16–17; 2 Pet 1:20–21). Fee and Stuart also point out that the Bible "is the Word of God given in human words in history."[7] That is a good description of how the Scriptures came to us, highlighting the "dual nature of the Bible."[8] The Apostle Peter said that the inspired writers "spoke from God as they were carried along by the Holy Spirit" (2 Pet 1:21 NIV). The divine origin of Scripture is vital to the subject of inerrancy.

"Inerrancy" is a theological term used to describe a particular view of the Bible. People hold various views about the Bible. Christians who hold to a high view of Scripture—that is, those who believe that it is, in fact, truly the word of God—believe in inerrancy. Millard Erickson defines inerrancy this way: "The Bible, when correctly interpreted in light of the level to which culture and the means of communication had developed at the time it was written, and in view of the purposes for which it was given, is fully truthful in all that it affirms."[9] In the *International Standard Bible Encyclopedia*, under the entry "Infallibility," J. Daane wrote, "Those who

---

7. Fee and Stuart, *Bible*, 21.
8. Fee and Stuart, *Bible*, 21.
9. Erickson, *Theology*, 259.

speak of inerrancy usually mean freedom from any kind of error—scientific, historical, chronological, etc."[10] Because the Bible came from God, who is a perfect being, the Scriptures are true and accurate in what they say, they are without error. *The Holman Bible Handbook* states, "A God who is omniscient would not make a mistake, and a God who is truthful would not mislead."[11] It further goes on to say, "The doctrine of inerrancy guarantees the dependability of the Bible."[12]

The denomination that I am part of, the International Fellowship of Christian Assemblies (IFCA), has this statement in their Articles of Faith concerning the Bible:

> We believe the Holy Scriptures of the Old and New Testaments to be the verbally and plenary inspired Word of God. We accept the original autographs as God-breathed, inerrant, infallible and complete, and therefore hold the sixty-six books of the Bible as the complete and divine revelation of God to man and the final authority for faith and life. The Scriptures are to be interpreted according to their normal grammatical-historical meaning (2 Timothy 3:16–17; 2 Peter 1:20–21; Matthew 4:4).[13]

Other Bible-believing churches will have similar statements in their articles of faith. In some churches' doctrinal statements, a statement about the authority and reliability of the Bible is the first item in the list. I think this is significant. Establishing the trustworthiness of the Bible is critical because all of the other beliefs of Christian churches are to be derived from the Bible.

The concept of inerrancy is not a delusion or wishful thinking. A person does not need to disengage his or her mind in order to accept the idea of inerrancy, for the concept of inerrancy is based on certain data. The Christian Research Institute lists a number of reasons why we can trust the Bible, including manuscript evidence, archeology, biblical prophecy, and statistical probability of biblical prophecies being fulfilled.[14] New Testament scholar, F. F. Bruce, in his book *The New Testament Documents: Are They Reliable?*, also supplies information that points to the trustworthiness of the New Testament, one of which is Luke's accuracy.[15]

---

10. Daane, "Inerrancy," 821.
11. Dockery et al., *Bible Handbook*, 11.
12. Dockery et al., *Bible Handbook*, 11.
13. IFCA, "Articles of Faith," para. 1
14. CRI, "Bible Readability: M-A-P-S To Guide You Through Bible Reliability."
15. Bruce, *Documents*, 82. Luke correctly identifies individuals by their proper titles.

Believing in the inerrancy of Scripture is vital if we are going to have confidence in biblical revelation. The biblical text must be reliable if we are going to have a clear statement of the mind and will of God. If we cannot depend on the Bible, then all the other doctrines that we hold to, that are drawn from its pages, could be deemed unreliable. This would include major doctrines such as the nature of God and humanity's need for salvation. It would also include the sacrifice of Jesus Christ being the *only* basis for salvation (John 14:6; Acts 4:12; 1 Tim 2:5–6). So, a lot is at stake here.

In addition, if the Bible is inerrant, then we as Christians are not free to alter what God has said or create our own beliefs that do not agree with the biblical revelation. We cannot update, adjust, or dismiss the Bible, or parts of it, to accommodate our desires or the trends in our culture. We must take the Bible on its own terms. As my friend and former pastor John King has said, "We need to surrender to the text."

Years ago, a man I worked with told me he believed that the Bible was the word of God and that Jesus was the Son of God. But he also told me he believed that when you die you just go into the ground and that's it. I told him he did not have that option; he had to accept all that the Scriptures have to say. He could not pick and choose. Thankfully, years later this man became a believer. Sadly, there are some denominations today whose leaders are selecting what they will believe out of Scripture, and, in the process, they are setting aside some Scriptures in order to affirm what they would like to believe. Scripture tells us, "Do not go beyond what is written" (1 Cor 4:6 NIV), and yet some in our day are doing that very thing. We are also warned in Scripture, more than once, that we are not to add to or take away from the word of God (Deut 4:2; Rev 22:18–19). If we do so, we are indeed on a slippery slope. With no anchor, a church can be "blown here and there by every wind of teaching and by the cunning and craftiness of people in their deceitful scheming" (Eph 4:14 NIV). The Bible is the canon, that is, "the *rule* of belief and practice."[16] Jesus affirmed the authority of the Scriptures on a number of occasions during the course of his earthly ministry. He appealed to them three times when he was tempted in the wilderness (Matt 4:4, 7, 10). The Lord also said he came not to destroy the law and the prophets but to fulfill them (Matt 5:17). Jesus also cited the Scriptures on a number of other occasions during the course of his earthly ministry. If Jesus viewed the Old Testament as authoritative, so should we.

The New Testament also is authoritative for all these reasons, and also because of Peter's statement in 2 Peter 3:15–16:

---

16. Bruce, *Canon*, 18.

Bear in mind that our Lord's patience means salvation, just as our dear brother Paul also wrote you with the wisdom that God gave him. He writes the same way in all his letters, speaking in them of these matters. His letters contain some things that are hard to understand, which ignorant and unstable people distort, as they do the other Scriptures, to their own destruction." (NIV)

In these verses, to use the words of Douglas Moo, "Peter therefore implies that the letters of Paul have a status equivalent to that of the canon of the Old Testament itself."[17]

The Problem

Not everyone agrees on what the plain meaning of a text is.[18] From a logical point of view, we might think that, if people accept the concept of biblical inerrancy, there will not be any doctrinal disagreements. Sadly, this is not true. Both past and present church history demonstrates that this is not the case. Even in the days of the first-century church, when apostles such as Paul and John were still alive and could be consulted, there was not a uniform view among genuine believers on all matters. For example, in Romans 14, we find that there seems to have been a difference of opinion among the believers in Rome about which day should be set aside for worship and what foods one could eat. The conflict on these issues was largely between Jewish and Gentile Christians, as these were issues about which these two people groups might disagree.[19]

In more recent times, the large number of Christian denominations and independent churches that make up the church testify to the doctrinal diversity that exists within the body of Christ. There are many differing viewpoints on certain biblical teachings in the church today. Some of these differences are known as "doctrinal distinctives"—that is, key beliefs that make one group different from other Christian bodies. For example, many classical Pentecostal churches believe that speaking in tongues is the initial *physical* sign that a person has been baptized in the Holy Spirit. Also, different views exist on the doctrine of salvation (Arminian versus the Calvinistic view), eschatology (all of the rapture, tribulation, and millennium positions), worship (traditional, blended, or contemporary), church government (episcopal, presbyterian, or congregational), spiritual gifts (cessationists or continuationists), water baptism (full immersion or sprinkling, infant and adult,

---

17. Moo, *Application Commentary: 2 Peter, Jude*, 212.
18. Fee and Stuart, *Bible*, 19.
19. Osborne, *Romans*, 355.

or adult only), communion (meaning and frequency of observance), and, of course, the place of women in Christian ministry.[20] These differences of opinion do not undermine the authority of the Bible. The Bible is reliable; the problem is on our end. Jack Deere, a former professor at Dallas Theological Seminary, has written that he thinks it is "an illusion" to believe that anyone, including Christians, can arrive at "pure biblical objectivity" regarding their beliefs and practices.[21] He says that our environment, theological traditions, and teachers play a large role in forming our beliefs.[22]

These differences of opinion are based on particular understandings and interpretations of Scripture. In what follows, we will look at one issue: the ministry of women and men in the church, especially focusing on the ministry of women, as they are frequently excluded from or restricted in some aspects of ministry. This is an important subject that must be given careful and prayerful consideration while constantly referring to Scripture.

The subject of women in ministry should be given careful consideration for many reasons. First, women are human beings created in the image of God (Gen 1:26–27). Second, they make up a significant part of the church, as Carolyn Custis James's book *Half the Church* reminds us.[23] A 2014 Pew Research Center report on Religion and Public Life demonstrates that, in the United States, women, for the most part, make up more than half of the church. Their report says that 54 percent of Catholics, 55 percent of evangelical Protestants, 59 percent of historic Black Protestants, and 55 percent of mainline Protestants are women.[24] The only Christian group comprised of less than 50 percent women is the Orthodox Christian group, with 44 percent.[25] If the United States is at all representative of the rest of the world, women make up more than half of the church. Third, the mission of the church requires a great number of workers. Fourth, we should want to honor the giftings of the Holy Spirit. As one of Christians for Biblical Equality's core values states, "The unrestricted use of women's gifts is integral to the work of the Holy Spirit and essential for the advancement of the gospel in the world."[26] The Spirit decides who gets which gifts (1 Cor 12:11). If the church—the body of Christ—fails to deal adequately and biblically with each of these issues, we may indeed miss the will of God regarding this

---

20. See also Lathrop, *Answer*, 35–45.
21. Deere, *Power of the Spirit*, 46.
22. Deere, *Power of the Spirit.*, 47.
23. James, *Half the Church*, 19, 27.
24. Pew Research Center, "Gender Composition."
25. Pew Research Center, "Gender Composition."
26. Christians for Biblical Equality, "CBE's Mission and Values."

subject. In addition, this may also have an adverse effect on the difference that the church can make in this world—in other words, our impact and influence will suffer.[27]

We Are Not United

Jesus prayed for the unity of the church (John 17:20–21, 23), and Paul urged it for the congregations to whom he wrote (1 Cor 1:10; Phil 2:2).[28] As a result, the church in the first century was at times united (Acts 1:14; 2:1–4; 4:23–31).[29] Unity is the ideal, but it does not always exist. Even in the New Testament, we find churches that were founded and taught by the apostles, but were divided. They were conflicted about their teachers (1 Cor 1:12; 3:4), and, as already mentioned, about foods and special days (Rom 14), to name just a few issues.

The contemporary church is also currently divided about the place of women in ministry. Some denominations, such as the Assemblies of God, Cumberland Presbyterian and Presbyterian (USA), United Methodist, Wesleyan Methodist, and American Baptist, ordain women, while others including the Southern Baptist, Orthodox, and Presbyterian Church of America churches do not.[30] My own denomination, the International Fellowship of Christian Assemblies, wrestled with the issue of ordaining women for a number of years and finally decided in favor of ordaining them. However, we have very few women who are actually ordained.

The subject of the ministry of women in the church is a live issue and in some ways a volatile one. I once wrote, "Discussing biblical teaching about women is a lot like discussing eschatology, as there are differences of opinion and emotions can run high."[31] Scripture plays a central part in the discussion, but the discussion can become quite emotional. "Proof texts" are often cited in defense of the differing views. This does not mean, however, that all is lost. Discussion of this issue can, and should, continue.

There are two main views on the subject of women in ministry: the complementarian view and the egalitarian view. These two views are not only different from one another, but in some ways they are diametrically opposed. Generally speaking, complementarians believe that women should not teach or have authority over men. One of the chief proponents of this position

27. Keener, *Women and Wives*, 1–2.
28. See also Lathrop, *Answer*, 1–8, 55–56.
29. See also Lathrop *Answer*, 51–54.
30. See also Spencer, "Evangelicals and Gender," 113–19.
31. Lathrop, *Power and Practice*, 45.

is the Council on Biblical Manhood and Womanhood (CBMW). One section of the Danvers Statement, which the Council of Biblical Manhood and Womanhood believes demonstrates the need for the CBMW, reads: "In the church, redemption in Christ gives men and women an equal share in the blessings of salvation; nevertheless, some governing and teaching roles within the church are restricted to men (Gal 3:28; 1 Cor 11:2–16; 1 Tim 2:11–15)."[32] The last section of this statement is one of the defining marks of the complementarian position. In this view, women are excluded from the higher levels of leadership in the church, such as senior pastor. Egalitarians believe that women can serve equally with men and function in any leadership capacity that a man can, including the ministry of senior pastor. A leading voice for the egalitarian position is Christians for Biblical Equality (CBE). On their website, the purpose statement says: "CBE exists to promote biblical justice and community by educating Christians that the Bible calls women and men to share authority equally in service and leadership in the home, church, and world."[33] The scriptural support for its position is found in its document called "Statement on Men, Women, and Biblical Equality," available on its website in a number of different languages.

Much has been written concerning both views; books, blogs, position papers, editorials, and articles. Some of the books written in support of the egalitarian position have been written on a popular level and some on an academic level. An example of a book written on the popular level would be Lee Grady's book *Ten Lies the Church Tells Women*. Craig Keener's book *Paul, Women, and Wives* would be an example of an academic work on the subject. Churches and denominations need to decide what their position is, because this decision will have direct bearing on the leadership and functioning of the local church, and, in the case of denominations, the larger movement, whether national or international. However, this decision should not be based on a received tradition or preference, but must be based on the word of God. If we are going to advocate for the full and equal ministry of women in the church (and the House of Prisca and Aquila series does) we must demonstrate from Scripture that women were involved in positions of leadership in the Bible. It is perhaps especially important to show that this was the case in the New Testament, because as believers in Jesus today we are part of the church.

---

32. CBMW, "Danvers Statement," Affirmation 6, point 2.
33. CBE, "CBE's Mission and Values."

Egalitarianism

At the House of Prisca and Aquila (HPA), we publish books that hold to the egalitarian view. The mission statement for HPA reads:

> Our mission at the House of Prisca and Aquila is to produce quality books that expound accurately the word of God to empower women and men to minister together in a multicultural church. Our writers have a positive view of the Bible as God's revelation that affects both thoughts and words, so it is plenary, historically accurate, and consistent in itself; fully reliable, and authoritative as God's revelation. Because God is true, God's revelation is true, inclusive to men and women and speaking to a multicultural church, wherein all the diversity of the church is represented within the parameters of egalitarianism and inerrancy.[34]

The statement above says that our mission is to "expound accurately the word of God," and the words "inerrancy" and "egalitarianism" are included in the same sentence. Some Christians might not think that those two words belong together. They do not believe that a person can accept the Bible as accurate and without error and endorse women for some positions of leadership in the church. Linda Belleville has pointed out that traditionalists—that is, complementarians who restrict women from some leadership positions—usually focus their attention on 1 Timothy 2:11–15.[35] She further goes on to ask if 1 Timothy 2:9–15 is the only text that speaks to this issue.[36] But it, of course, is not the only Scripture regarding women in ministry, specifically women in leadership ministries in the church. Belleville knows this and so do we. The House of Prisca and Aquila maintains that there is no contradiction between inerrancy and the egalitarian viewpoint. On the contrary, we see them as totally compatible, and we are not alone in this view. A number of biblical scholars also hold this view, including Gordon Fee, Craig Keener, and others who have endorsed the ministry of Christians for Biblical Equality.[37]

Egalitarianism is not theological liberalism. We would contend that theological liberalism is inconsistent with inerrancy because liberalism typically denies, or explains away, what the Bible says. One example of such dismissal concerns the supernatural acts found in Scripture. Some liberal scholars deny the supernatural elements found in the Bible, or offer other

---

34. House of Prisca and Aquila, "About Us."
35. Gundry and Beck, *Two Views*, 70.
36. Gundry and Beck, *Two Views*, 70.
37. CBE, "Endorsement."

natural explanations for what the biblical writers wrote. One example of such thinking can be found in the work of John Dominic Crossan, who has denied the virgin birth of Christ.[38] In a statement that could be used to address the charge of theological liberalism regarding the egalitarian view, Craig Keener, who is an egalitarian, has said that no one should challenge his commitment to Scripture's authority because his views on the biblical view of women differ from that of some other evangelicals.[39] Like Keener, HPA does not hold the egalitarian view because we have caved in to the secular feminist agenda in our world.[40] We hold to the egalitarian position because we believe that it best represents the teachings of the Scriptures, which were given by the inspiration of God (2 Tim 3:16–17).

Problems arise when biblical authority is not the foundation for egalitarianism. People can join together for a good cause, such as the full equality of women in the church, but if the Bible is not the source of authority, then anyone's ethics or opinion can potentially become the governing principles of the group. This will not do. The Scriptures supply us with parameters in which to work. They are the principles of God, not the principles of human beings; the Scriptures supply us with an impartial foundation.

Dr. Aída Besançon Spencer called my attention to the women-church movement. This movement, which seeks to free women from various inequalities in church and society, has some challenges to face with regard to being truly biblical egalitarians. One article by Miriam Therese Winter, originally published in the March 1, 1989, issue of *Christian Century*, stated that the women-church movement needs to find ways to include men.[41] Other statements in the article lead me to believe that the Bible is not their primary source and that theological liberalism would be tolerated in this movement.[42]

If we, as egalitarians, were not able to demonstrate from Scripture that women were involved in ministry, including leadership ministry in the church, we would indeed be on tenuous ground. However, this is not the case. The Scriptures provide us with examples of women serving in ministry alongside of men, including the example of the husband-and-wife team of Prisca and Aquila, after which the book series is named (Acts 18:26; Rom 16:3–4; 1

---

38. Crossan, *Jesus*, 17, 18, 27–28. See also, Mohler, "Can a Christian Deny the Virgin Birth?"
39. Keener, *Women & Wives*, 12.
40. Keener, *Women & Wives*, 5–10.
41. Religion On Line, "The Woman-Church Movement."
42. Religion Online, "The Woman-Church Movement."

Cor 16:19). Below I will present a very brief overview of the equality of men and women in human history and in the church.

The Proof Is in the Texts

The tenets we believe need to be firmly founded upon biblical texts. The Bible itself tells us that we are to live by every word that comes from the mouth of God (Deut 8:3). Jesus cited and endorsed the truth of this text in the New Testament (Matt 4:4). That is to say, we must base our beliefs on *all* of what Scripture reveals and not just on a small pool of "proof texts."

Sometimes when we read Scripture regarding the ministry of men and women in the church, we look very closely at a select group of texts. We may do this consciously or unconsciously, and for any number of reasons. As important as looking at specific verses is, we also need to consider the big picture, which shows the equality of men and women throughout the Scriptures. This equality can be seen in a number of key events of human and biblical history.

CREATION

The first instance of equality is set forth in the very first book of the Bible, Genesis. Aída Besançon Spencer has pointed out that "Almost all foundational questions find their answer in the early chapters of Genesis. Male-female relations are no exception."[43] Aída's husband, William David Spencer, was my theology professor in seminary. In one class, he made a statement to the effect that, if we want to find the purest theology, we need to go back to the opening two chapters of Genesis, before the fall of humanity, for here we find God's original intention, before sin entered the world. As Gretchen Gaebelein Hull has pointed out, the biblical record shows that men and women were both created in the image and likeness of God (Gen 1:26–28).[44] Aída Besançon Spencer has also called attention to this point.[45] Adam and Eve were equal in God's creation, this was God's original intention.

---

43. Spencer, *Beyond the Curse*, 17.
44. Hull, *Gender Equality*, 4.
45. Spencer, *Beyond the Curse*, 21.

The Fall

Someone might say, "Creation was before the fall, and we are not living in that state now." That is true. However, as Gretchen Gaebelein Hull has pointed out, Scripture also sees Adam and Eve as equal in their failure and fall into sin.[46] Paul places the responsibility for the fall both at the feet of Adam (Gen 3:6; Rom 5:12; 1 Cor 15:22) and Eve (Gen 3:6; 1 Tim 2:14). Men and women are both guilty and fallen before God; this includes the entire human race (Rom 3:23).

Redemption

Even after the fall, we find that women and men are equal. Hull points out that both genders are equal in redemption.[47] She further mentions that women come to God without a male intermediary, except for Christ, who is the same basis on which men approach God (1 Tim 2:5).[48] The biblical evidence demonstrating the equality of the genders in redemption is extensive. The sacrifice of Jesus paid for the sins of the whole world (1 John 2:2) and thus avails for "whosoever will," including women (John 3:16; Acts 2:21; Rom 10:13). All of humanity is in need of a savior, and there is only one for the human race: Jesus Christ (John 14:6; Acts 4:12).

It is also clear from Scripture that both men and women were empowered by the Holy Spirit for ministry. We see this in the opening chapters of Acts. In Acts 1, women were among those present in the prayer meeting as the believers waited to be baptized with the Holy Spirit (Acts 1:12–14). They were also present when the Holy Spirit came on the day of Pentecost (Acts 2:1–4). Peter's citation of Joel 2 indicates that including both genders will be the new norm (Acts 2:16–18). All were anointed to be witnesses (Acts 1:8) and to engage in other types of ministry as well. Further evidence that women were anointed for ministry can be found in Acts 21, where we read that Philip had four virgin daughters who prophesied (Acts 21:9). The apostle Paul also acknowledged that women participated in Spirit-empowered ministry when he wrote about them prophesying (1 Cor 11:5). In addition, there are no gender restrictions on the gifts of the Spirit in 1 Corinthians 12. Aída Besançon Spencer, summarizing the ministries of women in the New Testament wrote, "Women were apostles, prophets,

---

46. Hull, *Gender Equality*, 7.
47. Hull, *Gender Equality*, 7.
48. Hull, *Gender Equality*, 7.

teachers, coworkers, ministers, and church overseers."[49] The same is true today. Women can, and do, function in many places with the ministries that women did in the first-century church.

As this brief survey shows, males and females are equal in God's eyes. This has been the case throughout biblical history. If the fall, which had such extensive and far-reaching effects, did not alter this essential truth, I can think of nothing that will.

Conclusion

One need not set aside the authority of the biblical text and the concept of inerrancy in order to hold the egalitarian view. These things do not exclude each other, but, rather, include each other; we believe that to hold one is to hold the other. A more detailed articulation of the HPA egalitarian position will be found in the pages that follow. But I hope that this brief introduction of the subject will prove to be a foundation on which the other contributors to this book can build a biblical defense of the egalitarian position of the equal leadership of women and men in the church. May the church, the whole church, capture this vision of men and women working together side by side in ministry.

References

Bromiley, Geoffrey W., et al., eds. *The International Standard Bible Encyclopedia*. Rev. ed. Vol. 2. Grand Rapids: Eerdmans, 1982.

Bruce, F. F. *The Canon of Scripture*. Downers Grove, IL: InterVarsity, 1988.

———. *The New Testament Documents: Are They Reliable?* Grand Rapids: Eerdmans/Downers Grove, IL: InterVarsity, 1988.

Christian Research Institute. "Bible Readability: M–A–P–S To Guide You Through Bible Reliability." https://www.equip.org/article/bible-reliability-m-a-p-s-to-guide-you-through-bible-reliability. Accessed Nov. 26, 2018.

Christians for Biblical Equality. www.cbeinternational.org. Accessed Nov. 26, 2018.

———. "CBE's Mission and Values." https://www.cbeinternational.org/content/cbes-mission. Accessed Nov. 19, 2018.

———. "Endorsement." https://www.cbeinternational.org/endorsements?page=1. Accessed Nov. 30, 2018.

Council for Biblical Manhood and Womanhood. "Danvers Statement." https://cbmw.org/about/danvers-statement. Accessed Nov. 19, 2018.

Crossan, John Dominic. *Jesus: A Revolutionary Biography*. New York: Harper Collins, 1994.

Deere, Jack. *Surprised by the Power of the Spirit*. Grand Rapids: Zondervan, 1993.

---

49. Spencer, *Beyond the Curse*, 135.

Dockery, David S., et al., eds. *Holman Bible Handbook*. Nashville: Holman Bible, 1992.
Erickson, Millard. *Christian Theology*. 2nd ed. Grand Rapids: Baker Academic, 1998.
Fee, Gordon D., and Douglas Stuart. *How to Read the Bible for All Its Worth*. 3rd ed. Grand Rapids: Zondervan, 2003.
Gundry, Stanley N., and James R. Beck, eds. *Two Views on Women in Ministry*. Counterpoints Series. Rev. ed. Grand Rapids: Zondervan, 2005.
House of Prisca and Aquila. "About Us." https://sites.google.com/site/houseofpriscaandaquila/about-us. Accessed Nov. 29, 2018.
Hull, Gretchen Gaebelein. *ABCs of Gender Equality*. Hightstown, NJ: CER, 1990.
International Fellowship of Christian Assemblies. "Articles of Faith." http://ifcaministry.org/about-us. Accessed Nov. 28, 2018.
James, Carolyn Custis. *Half the Church: Recapturing God's Global Vision for Women*. Grand Rapids: Zondervan, 2015.
Keener, Craig S. *Paul, Women, and Wives: Marriage and Women's Ministry in the Letters of Paul*. Peabody, MA: Hendrickson, 1992.
———. *The IVP Bible Background Commentary: New Testament*. Downers Grove, IL: InterVarsity, 1993.
Lathrop, John P. *The Power and Practice of the Church: God, Discipleship, and Ministry*. Waltham, MA: J. Timothy King, 2010.
———. *Answer the Prayer of Jesus: A Call for Biblical Unity*. Eugene, OR: Wipf & Stock, 2011.
Mohler, Albert. "Can a Christian Deny the Virgin Birth?" https://albertmohler.com/2007/12/05/can-a-christian-deny-the-virgin-birth-3/. Accessed March 3, 2020.
Moo, Douglas J. *The NIV Application Commentary: 2 Peter, Jude*. Grand Rapids: Zondervan, 1996.
Osborne, Grant R. *Romans*. The IVP New Testament Commentary Series. Downers Grove: InterVarsity, 2004.
Pew Research Center. "Gender Composition." http://www.pewforum.org/religious-landscape-study/gender-composition. Accessed March 15, 2019.
Spencer, Aída Besançon. *Beyond the Curse: Women Called to Ministry*. Grand Rapids: Baker Academic, 1985.
———. "Evangelicals and Gender." In *Evangelicals around the World: A Global Handbook for the 21st Century*, edited by Brian C. Stiller, et al. 112–19. Nashville: Thomas Nelson, 2015.
Winter, Miriam Therese. "The Woman-Church Movement." https://www.religion-online.org/article/the-women-church-movement. Accessed April 4, 2019.

3

Women Discipling Men

A Biblical Pattern of Leadership

Grace Ying May

WHILE RESPECTFUL OF CULTURE, God is not obliged to subscribe to human cultural norms. The Scriptures are replete with examples of God overturning the law of primogeniture by blessing the last over the first, beginning with the promise to Eve to give her seed or descendant the ultimate defeat over the serpent's seed, and overturning patriarchy by raising up godly women throughout history. In the long line of biblical leaders, two women are particularly deserving of our attention: Phoebe, who led Paul in the faith; and Deborah, who strengthened Barak's faith.

Phoebe in First Century Cenchreae

Everyone can benefit from the example of someone else. Even a pioneer and church planter of Paul's stature followed in someone else's footsteps. At the end of the letter to the Romans, Paul identifies his mentor, a minister of the gospel and a forerunner in the faith named Phoebe. He recognizes her as "a leader of many and also of myself" (Rom 16:2 my translation). While Phoebe did not introduce Paul to Christ, the Scriptures credit her for leading Paul in his spiritual journey. Unlike today, where some men may be embarrassed to admit that the person who discipled him was a woman, Paul made a point of announcing the fact publicly in a letter, which would have been heard by first-century Christians, but which has been muted for many in subsequent generations.

In Romans 16, Paul casts a spotlight on Phoebe by listing her name first in his long lineup of greetings. Romans 16:1–2 reads:

> I commend to you our sister Phoebe, a minister [*diakonos*] of the church at Cenchreae, so that you may receive her in the Lord as is worthy of the saints, and assist her in whatever she may need from you, for she has been a leader [*prostatis*] of many and also of myself [my translation].

The main grounds for identifying Phoebe as Paul's mentor is the way the apostle expresses his relationship to her. He calls her "a leader [*prostatis*] of many and also of myself" (Rom 16:2). Liddell and Scott's *Greek-English Lexicon* defines *prostatis* as "leader," "chief," "president," or "presiding officer."[1] Literally, *prostatis* means "one who stands before." The Contemporary English Version refers to Phoebe as "a respected leader for many others, including me" (Rom 16:2). Other forms of the word *prostatis* occur in the New Testament to describe a person exercising the gift of leadership (Rom 12:8), one in charge (1 Thess 5:12), a deacon (1 Tim 3:12), a bishop (1 Tim 3:14), or an elder (1 Tim 5:17), as all of these individuals are leading, ruling, or managing others. Curiously, despite all the New Testament instances denoting leadership, the word *prostatis* in relationship to Phoebe in Romans 16:2 has been variously translated as "helper" (NKJV, NASB, AMP), "benefactor" (NIV, NRSV), and "patron" (ESV). While Phoebe may have been a financial supporter of Paul, there is no need to assume so from the context. Why do translators eschew calling her a leader? Could it boil down to the fact that she is a woman, and, even in the twenty-first century, we are still hesitant to admit that a woman can lead or disciple a man?

In sharp contrast, Paul draws attention to the fact that Phoebe is not only *his* leader but the leader of a church. He calls her "our sister Phoebe, a minister [*diakonos*] of the church at Cenchreae" (Rom 16:1). She is a pastor.

Interpretation inevitably enters into any translation, but what is disturbing is how a particular bias has concealed Phoebe's identity as a pastor. When *diakonos* appears next to a man's name—consider the names of Timothy (1 Tim 4:6), Epaphras (Col. 1:7 NIV), and Tychicus (Col. 4:7 NRSV; Eph. 6:21 NRSV)—the translators opt for "minister"; however, when the same word describes Phoebe, the ESV, NASB, and KJV call her a "servant" while the RSV refers to her as a "deaconess." The choice of the word "deaconess," however, is a strange compromise. While it is the feminine version

---

1. LSJ, 1526.

of *diakonos*, the word used in Romans to refer to Phoebe is masculine, and the order of the deaconess did not exist until at least a hundred years after the New Testament was written.

What all of the above translations do, unfortunately, is keep English readers in the dark as to the possibility that Phoebe could be a minister. Only the Darby Translation (1890), Montgomery's *The New Testament in Modern English* (1924),[2] and the American Bible Society's Contemporary English Version (1995) actually translate the word as "minister" *in the text*. In 1989 the NRSV provided "minister" as an alternate translation in a footnote to Romans 16:1, and it was not until 2011 that the NIV translation committee chose to translate the word as "deacon." The point bears repeating that the problem is not that *diakonos* can never mean "servant," but that the translation is inconsistent. *Diakonos* can have a range of meanings, including "servant," "deacon," and "minister," but the assumption seems to be that, since women cannot be pastors, therefore, Phoebe must be a "servant" because she is a woman.

Yet the very syntax of Romans 16:1–3 bears witness to Phoebe's significance in the church. Typically New Testament churches were referred to by their location, such as the church in Corinth or the churches in Galatia. Applying the same logic to Phoebe, then, makes her the pastor of "the church in Cenchreae" (Rom 16:1). The use of the possessive genitive further underscores her close relationship to the church as between a shepherd and her flock. Serving as a pastor in the bustling seaport of Cenchreae on the eastern coast of Corinth might have had its advantages, given the exposure residents would have already had to a diversity of cultures and leaders.[3]

Holding Phoebe in high esteem, Paul wants the Christians at Rome to honor her when they meet her. He asks the church to "receive" her and to provide her with whatever she needs, not only because she is his mentor and a faithful pastor, but because she has made the arduous journey from Cenchreae to Rome, a trip that likely took two to three weeks and exposed

---

2. In 1924, Helen Barrett Montgomery (1861–1934) published her translation of the New Testament, the culmination of nine years of work, originally called *The Centenary Translation* to celebrate the 100th anniversary of the American Baptist Publication Society. Her motivation stemmed from a desire to provide a readable translation for young people, Sunday School teachers, and immigrants. The first woman President of the Northern Baptist Convention (1921–1922), she was also a civic leader and a pioneer in the women's missionary movement. See Dowd, "Helen Barrett Montgomery's Centenary."

3. It was common for churches to start in the houses of influential and wealthy women and couples: Mary (Acts 12:12), Lydia (Acts 16:14–15), Nympha (Col 4:15), Chloe (1 Cor 1:11), Prisca and Aquila (Rom 16:5), and Philemon and his sister Apphia (Philemon 2). See Giles, "House Churches."

her to the rigors of the road and sea.[4] It is reasonable, then, for Paul to expect the recipients of his letter to do whatever they can for her out of respect and gratitude for her sacrifice. According to Craig Keener, professor of New Testament at Asbury Theological Seminary, the fact that she alone is welcomed indicates that she holds the distinction of carrying the scroll with Paul's words to the church at Rome.[5] If she was the courier, she also enjoyed the privilege of reading Paul's letter out loud to the congregation.[6]

Unashamed of owning his debt to Phoebe, Paul seizes the opportunity to practice what he preaches in Romans 12. As a member of the church, he wants to function as a part of the body of Christ. By greeting members by name, Paul demonstrates his dependence on other members of the body and their outpouring of love, gifts, and service. As a leader, he is not above relying on others. It is precisely his need for Phoebe to deliver the letter to the church in Rome that brings her to the foreground. In fact, nearly half of the people that Paul greets in Romans 16 are women: Phoebe (v. 1), Prisca (v. 3), Mary (v. 4), Junia (v. 5), Tryphaena (v. 12), Tryphosa (v. 12), Persis (v. 12), Rufus' mother (v. 13), Julia (v. 15), and Nereus's sister (v. 15). Discipled by Phoebe and serving alongside women and men, he shows his trust and appreciation of other brothers and sisters.

Phoebe was by no means an isolated female minister. During the reign of Trajan (AD 98–117), Pliny recounts that "in Bithynia under Trajan there were female deacons" (*Epistuale* 10.96.8).[7] *Diakonoi*, which is masculine plural in Greek, could just as well be translated "ministers," but not "deaconesses," an office that did not exist yet and would have required the word to appear in its feminine form. In the latter half of the fourth century, the inscription on a stele reads, "*Sophia, hē diakonos, hē deutera Phoibē.*" Sophia, a woman identified as a "deacon" or "minister," is honored as "the second Phoebe." The German scholar Ute E. Eisen observes:

> In non-Christian inscriptions the description "a second Homer" or the like is applied to individuals who gave outstanding service to their city. For Sophia this could mean that her title "the

---

4. To traverse more than 600 miles from Corinth to Rome by ship and carriage or foot would require between twelve to twenty days, according to calculations by Orbis, the Stanford Geospatial Network Model of the Roman World, akin to a MapQuest for the ancient world, See http://orbis.stanford.edu.

5. Keener, *Romans*, 182.

6. BDAG, 230, offers the alternate definition of *diakonos* as "one who serves as an intermediary in a transaction." Thus, *diakonos* in the context of Romans 16:1 could be translated "courier."

7. G. H. R. Horsely, ed., *New Documents*, 239, in McCabe "A Reexamination of Phoebe."

second Phoebe" reflects aspects of Phoebe's activity beyond her work as a deacon (Rom 16:1–2), such as her title of *prostatis*.[8]

Therefore, to be called a "second Phoebe" is suggestive of the profound influence Phoebe held in her day.

Like his mentor Phoebe, Paul did not cower from danger. Paul traveled hundreds of miles to establish and strengthen the church, often hounded by his persecutors and sometimes escorted in chains. Whether by land or by sea, rarely did he travel in safety and security. Yet, before he died, he had preached to multitudes and planted churches throughout the Roman Empire. Jesus had said his disciples would do greater things than he did, given the limited years he spent in ministry and the times in which he lived. Similarly, Paul did far more than we ever hear of Phoebe's accomplishments, but he openly acknowledged his debt to her as a minister of the church in Cenchreae, courier of the epistle to the Romans, and leader of himself and many others.

In considering Phoebe's legacy, one surmises that Phoebe not only provided an excellent example for Paul, but also a positive experience working with a woman leader. Paul, in turn, made it his practice to work with women and men in his ministry and expressed high regard for his mentor, a female pastor. Starting in the first century, Phoebe and Paul establish mutual respect as the norm for church and missions.

Nancy Hudson in South Africa

Over the course of her years in missionary service, Nancy Hudson discipled men, and in 1992, she and her husband started the first church at Moshakga with the Christian Assemblies of South Africa (CASA).[9] She had worked for years in business when God called her to enter into an altogether different line of work. In 1990, while South Africa was still suffering from the scourge of apartheid, God called Nancy Hudson, a white woman, to be a missionary in Moshakga, a black village in the area of Modjadji. Then, in 1997 after her husband died and she had spent seven years loving, shepherding, counseling, and earning the respect of the people she served, the congregation turned to her and said, "You are our pastor." Like Phoebe, whom Paul recognized as his leader, Hudson was called a pastor by her followers.

---

8. Ute E. Eisen, *Women Officeholders*, 160, in McCabe, "A Reexamination of Phoebe."

9. All quotations and materials in the following three pages about Nancy Hudson are taken with her permission from an interview granted the author on August 26, 2019.

Pastor Hudson's strategy for ministry seems similar to Paul's house church model. She used home groups, generally consisting of fifteen to thirty people, to train her leaders. Members of the home group had opportunities to serve as MCs (directing the meetings), lead music, preach, and translate the message. Under Pastor Hudson's encouragement and tutelage, she could see who had which gifts and let them "practice, practice, practice" until they were ready to minister in the Sunday gatherings. The advantage of this model of discipleship is that it cultivated a *team* of leaders instead of grooming only one person to be the leader. Members also found it easier to invite neighbors to their home groups than church, and, consequently, many were saved.

What God did in the home group served as a basis for church planting. As God provided mature leaders from the base church, Pastor Hudson would assign a person with spiritual maturity and the gift of pastoring to start a church in a different area. Now, ten years later, Hudson oversees ten churches in CASA. Both her pioneering work and her oversight of multiple churches qualifies her as an "apostle" in CASA and in many charismatic circles. She shares the oversight of these churches with Apostle Jonathan Peter from Cape Town, who is the acting overseer in charge of the administration of all the churches when she is not in South Africa, and Pastor Philip Mangena, whom she has discipled and known since he became a Christian at age twelve. While initially it was challenging to release a church to the care of younger pastors, all of whom inevitably made changes to the church and some mistakes in the process, she learned "to let go and let God." In this next season of her ministry, she looks forward to going from church to church, like the apostle Paul during his missionary trips, to strengthen the churches as she preaches, teaches, and counsels. Now in her eighties, she declares with all the conviction and joy of a missionary half her age, "There's more!"

Deborah in Ancient Israel

Similar to Paul in his regard for Phoebe, Barak held Deborah in great esteem as commander in chief and ruler of Israel in the era of the judges. Like her New Testament counterpart Phoebe, Deborah raised up a male leader with enormous potential, whom she sought to release to lead in his own right. Biblical scholars Athena Gorospe and Charles Ringma elaborate:

> In Judges 4 and 5, women are celebrated for their roles in God's acts of deliverance — but never to the exclusion of men. Instead, both women and men, leaders and people, official and volunteers, prominent members of the community and low-key housewives,

outsiders and insiders—in their various capacities and roles—participate in God's work and bring about God's purposes. [10]

Deborah, who descended from the tribe of Ephraim, was the fourth judge in Israel's history. She lived in the twelfth century BC during the Iron Age when the Canaanites, led by King Jabin, sorely oppressed the Israelites. Judges (Hebrew *shophetim*) was the title given to the rulers of the twelve tribes of Israel before the days of Israel's monarchy (Judg 21:25). As a judge, Deborah held sweeping legislative, judicial, and executive powers. She "used to sit under the palm of Deborah . . . and the Israelites came up to her for judgment" (Judg 4:5), harkening back to Moses, "who sat as judge" while the people waited for their cases to be heard (Exod 18:13). God sent Deborah and Moses, respectively, in answer to the Israelites' cries to be saved from the cruel reign of King Jabin and slavery under Pharaoh. In each case, the Scriptures actually spell out the military might of the foreign countries: the Canaanite king with his 900 chariots and Pharaoh with his army of horses and riders.

The author of Judges, however, not only drew parallels between Deborah and Moses, but also between Deborah and Samuel. The location of Deborah's court between Ramah and Bethel (Judg 4:5) points forward to two prominent places associated with Samuel, the last judge of Israel. Eventually, Ramah would become famous as the hometown of Samuel, and Bethel ("the house of God" in Hebrew) would become a site in Samuel's annual circuit as judge (1 Sam 7:16). Both Deborah and Samuel held dual roles as judges and prophets. And while Deborah never held the title of priest as Samuel did, in Judges 4, Deborah serves as an intermediary between God and Barak, and in Judges 5, Deborah pronounced blessings and curses, reminiscent of Moses's actions in Deuteronomy 27:9–26 and 28:1–14.

The allusions to Moses and Samuel highlight Deborah's significance in the Scriptures. She stands as a pillar of leadership during a time of moral degradation, painful oppression, and tribal disunity. Among the major judges, she alone is portrayed without any moral blemishes. She is a woman called to proclaim God's words, and no crisis or threat of danger deters her from fulfilling her duty before God.

Biblical prophecy consists of two parts: the message, which is from the Lord, and the voice, which is distinctly the messenger's, in this case, Deborah's. The author of Judges leaves no doubt in the listeners' or readers' mind that Israel's leader is a woman by using three words in rapid succession in Judges 4:4: "Deborah," "prophetess," and "wife/woman." Deborah is a female

---

10. Gorospe and Ringma, *Judges*, 57.

name. The feminine gender is preserved in the Hebrew by calling her a prophetess.[11] Then, depending on the interpretation, she can be regarded as the wife of a man called Lappidoth, the woman from a place named Lappidoth, or the woman of "torches." According to J. Clinton McCann, professor of biblical interpretation at Eden Theological Seminary, the "torch" signifies conquering power in the prophetical books (Zech 12:6, Dan 10:6, Isa 62:1) and may be used here to allude to Deborah's military prowess.[12] All are acceptable translations of the Hebrew that attest to her female gender.

Exercising her authority as a judge and prophet, Deborah "sent and summoned Barak" (Judg 4:6 NRSV). She declared, "The Lord, the God of Israel, commands you, 'Go, take position at Mount Tabor, bringing ten thousand from the tribe of Naphtali and the tribe of Zebulun. I will draw out Sisera, the general of Jabin's army, to meet you by the Wadi Kishon with his chariots and his troops; and I will give him into your hand'" (Judg 4:6–7 NRSV). Deborah's speech in *the first person* anticipates the speech of later prophets who often began their declarations with the phrase "Thus says the Lord" and then proceeded to speak in the first person.

Barak, however, responded with a qualification. He said to Deborah, "If you go with me, I will go; but if you will not go with me, I will not go" (Judg 4:8 NRSV). Barak's words echoes Ruth's words to Naomi, "Where you go, I will go" (Ruth 1:16c NRSV). The determination and the wording are similar, but they emanate from a different source. Ruth spoke boldly in faith, whereas Barak did not have enough faith to trust in God's word alone. Like the judge Gideon, Barak wanted God's reassurance of victory. To Barak's credit, he expresses what he thinks he needs to follow through with God's command. Barak wants Deborah to accompany him because, to him, Deborah represented God's presence and power,[13] like the ark of the covenant, which Israel always took into battle.

Deborah's next words to Barak appear to bring promise and judgment. "I will surely go with you; nevertheless, the road on which you are going will not lead to your glory, for the Lord will sell Sisera into the hand of a woman" (Judg 4:9 NRSV). God grants Barak the assurance of Deborah's presence. She will go north with him to rally the troops in Zebulun and Naphtali (Judg 4:10). The tradeoff is that, by Barak's not trusting God fully to begin with, the glory of defeating the enemy would not go to Barak—unlike Ehud, the left-handed judge who killed the Moabite King Elgon (Judg 3:21–22), and

---

11. The Hebrew Bible records other "prophetesses," including Miriam (Exod 15:20), Huldah (2 Kgs 22:14), Noadiah (Neh 6:14), and an unnamed prophetess, possibly Isaiah's wife (Isa 8:3).

12. McCann, *Judges*, 52.

13. McCann, *Judges*, 52.

Shamgar, the judge who singlehandedly killed 600 Philistines with an oxgoad (Judg 3:31). While the prediction that a woman would deal the decisive blow would have been perceived as a sign of weakness on Barak's part by ancient readers in a patriarchal society, God does not hold the same bias. For God is a respecter of neither gender, having created male and female both in the divine image. Alternatively, Deborah's words may stand simply as a prediction—that is, another instance of Deborah prophesying what would take place in the future without any negative connotation, as suggested by Frederick Buechner.[14] If a rebuke is implied, it is because initially Barak did not want to obey God's words and attached conditions to his obedience. Regardless, the criticism is not directed at Barak for listening to a woman. Listening to God's word is the right response whether the mouthpiece is a man or a woman.

Deborah demonstrates her maturity as a leader in how she responds to Barak. As a prophet, she delivered God's word without compromise. At the same time, as commander in chief, she probably wished that Barak had followed through immediately with God's order. Perhaps she had worked with Barak for years, first initiating and teaching him how to follow God's ways, then sharing the responsibility of leading others, and finally, after determining Barak's readiness and receiving God's confirmation, desiring to dispense the responsibility of leading the army entirely into his hands. But he wavers. Deborah could have been filled with disappointment and abandoned him for his lack of sufficient faith. "Rather, she accompanied him and gave him strength in accomplishing God's purpose."[15] As Barak's mentor, she was willing to work with him, honor his request, and bolster his fledgling faith, emboldening him to follow through with God's commands.

Barak, on his part, seemed to have no problem with the acclaim going to someone else. What he craves is Israel's victory. Once he knows God is with him, he has the faith to enter into battle. For while 10,000 men on foot were no match for 900 iron chariots (the equivalent of tanks in the Ancient Near East), "The Lord threw Sisera and all his chariots and all his army into panic *before* [lipnê] Barak" (Judg 4:12 NRSV, italics mine). One way to understand the word *before* is temporally; that is, even before Barak arrives God "threw [*yāhām*][the army] into a panic" (Judg 4:15). The Hebrew verb *yāhām* mirrors the work of God in the Exodus (Exod 14:24).[16] The Creator of the cosmos had unleashed falling stars and torrential rains, turning a ravine into a rushing river (Judg 5:20–21). Then, like the Red Sea that came crashing down on Pharaoh and his men, the raging flood waters of the Wadi Kishon turn the earth

---

14. Buechner, "Deborah."
15. Glahn, "Java with the Judges."
16. Holbert, "Deborah and the God of Surprise."

into mud, catching the wheels of the Canaanite iron chariots and throwing commanders off their horses. By the time Barak arrives at the Wadi Kishon, all that he and his 10,000 men need to do is chase down their enemies, who are fleeing on foot, and kill them with a sword (Judg 4:16).

The slaughter is complete except for Sisera, who flees to the home of Heber the Kenite, where his wife Jael offers the weary general a covering and drink, ostensibly Ancient Near Eastern acts of hospitality (Judg 4:17–19). But once Sisera falls fast asleep, she takes a tent peg and hammers it into his head (Judg 4:22), thus, bringing full circle the story of God's deliverance.

The strategy of the narrator is to portray God's deliverance not through a single person, but through three: a judge, a general, and a homemaker.

Deborah the Judge shows Barak a patience that reflects the longsuffering that God displays time and again in the book of Judges, as God bears with the rebellion of the Israelites and even some of their judges, such as Samson, who caved in to his lusts; Gideon, who led the people into idolatry; and Samuel, who refused to discipline his sons. Deborah's decision to go with Barak appears to have been precisely the act of compassion needed to fortify his faith and galvanize him into action. After Barak arrived at Mount Tabor as God had instructed, she then uses her prophetic voice to assure Barak, "Up! For this is the day on which the Lord has given Sisera into your hand. The Lord is indeed going out before you" (Judg 4:14 NRSV). A true prophet, Deborah speaks to build up and encourage Barak (1 Cor 14:3). Then, after the defeat, Deborah magnanimously includes Barak in singing of God's triumph (Judg 5:1).[17] Instead of slighting him for his initial reluctance to do battle, she includes him with her in a joint proclamation before the assembly. What a demonstration of humble leadership and unity. Sandra Glahn, an author and Bible teacher, remarked, "We have here a great example of a man and woman partnering as they obey the commands of God."[18]

It was not, however, Barak's brinkmanship that won the battle, but the "faith" he displayed "in . . . obeying the voice of the Lord's prophetess."[19] God honored the "progress" Barak made, looking forward to Paul's exhortation of his protégé Timothy (1 Tim 4:15 NRSV). Barak's name is inscribed in the epistle to the Hebrews, because God rewards the maturing of his faith, counting him among those "who became mighty in war" and "put foreign armies to flight" (Heb 11:32, 34 NRSV).[20] Like the men with clay feet listed

---

17. The victory hymn follows the tradition of Moses's song and Miriam's song in Exodus 15 and many of David's psalms that exult in God's triumph.

18. Glahn, "Java with the Judges."

19. Anonymous, "The Faith of Barak."

20. The biblical account does not indicate that Deborah took up arms, only that she was present at the battle. If she did not fight, then this circumstance might provide the

next to his name—Gideon, Samson, Jephthah, David, and Samuel—Barak "won strength out of weakness" (Heb 11:34 NRSV). The theme of redemption runs thick through the Scriptures as time and again, God's power is made perfect in weakness (2 Cor 12:9).

Finally, Jael saves the day. Jael is not a foot soldier and may not have been an Israelite. While she is the wife of a Kenite, a descendant of Moses's father-in-law (Judg 4:11), it is unclear whether the Kenites were an ally or a foe of the Canaanites (Judg 1:16). Jael, however, is on a mission to destroy the Canaanite general. Using her well-honed skills and tools from pitching tents, which was largely women's work, a "defenseless, statusless, weaponless female becomes the victor over the erstwhile commander of 'nine hundred chariots of iron.'"[21]

A recurring theme in the book of Judges is divine prerogative. In Judges 4 and 5, God chooses the unlikely triumvirate of Deborah, Barak, and Jael to fulfill God's saving purposes. By not naming Deborah or her compatriots as the deliverer (cf. Judg 3:9, 15), the author of Judges subtly directs the reader not to a human savior, but to *none other than God*.[22] For as the opening of Judges declares, "Whenever the Lord raised up judges for them [the people], the Lord was with the judge, and he delivered them from the hand of their enemies" (Judg 2:18 NRSV). God is the true hero of the story.[23] Immediately after recounting the stories of men and women of great faith, the author of Hebrews urges, "Let us run with perseverance . . . looking to Jesus, the pioneer and perfecter of our faith" (Heb 12:1–2 NRSV). For, in the end, only God's Chosen One is wholly sufficient to be our Savior and Deliverer.

The fact that all the stories of victory in Scripture ultimately point to God as the Redeemer, however, in no way diminishes Deborah's stature. She is a distinguished and highly esteemed spiritual and political leader in an era where no other woman "arose as a mother in Israel" (Judg 5:7 NRSV). Gorospe concurs:

> Deborah's role as prophetess, judge, and co-leader in military action is surprising rather than stereotypical. This suggests that being part of the purposes of Yahweh takes precedence over cultural proprieties. This also reinforces the radical and at times

---

reason she is not included in the Hebrews account of those who showed great faith in battle.

21. Eves, "Judges," 133.

22. Yairah Amit argues that the central question in the narrative of Judges 4 is the identity of the savior and that all the central characters and structure of the chapter stress that God alone is the Savior of Israel. Amit, "Judges 4," 89–111.

23. Kenneth Way, "Handling Heroes."

subversive nature of God's work in the world. God calls whom he wills for his liberating work.[24]

The continual allusions to other respected biblical leaders show the high regard with which God views Deborah. Even the way the chapters are framed, first the prose account in Judges 4 and then the song in Judges 5, parallels the Exodus account, where the obliteration of Pharaoh's army is first narrated (Exod 14:15–31) and then sung by Moses and Miriam (Exod 15:1–18, 20–21). What is unique is that the song in Judges is told from a female perspective, as suggested by the number of lines devoted to Jael (Judg 5:24–27) and detailed ruminations of Sisera's mother (Judg 5:28–30).[25] General Sisera's mother imagines her son and his soldiers "dividing the spoil—a girl [*raham*] or two for every man" (Judg 5:30), literally in Hebrew, a *raham* is "a womb or two." The general's mother is all too familiar with the ravages of war, which included the rape of women. Deborah as a ruler and commander in chief would be aware of such casualties of war as well. How powerful to ponder that a woman, the brave and stalwart ruler Deborah, authored the Song of Deborah in Judges 5.

Naomi Dowdy in Singapore

Like Deborah, whose proclamation of God's word and commitment to those entrusted to her, Naomi Dowdy has left a remarkable legacy through her preaching and teaching and mentoring of leaders in the church and in the marketplace. More than forty years ago, after a successful business career, Dowdy responded to God's call to serve as a missionary in the Marshall Islands, then pastored Trinity Christian Centre in Singapore (which grew from forty-two to 3,000 over her thirty-year tenure), authored six books on leadership (including *Destiny Calling* and *Moving On and Moving Up*), and founded the TCA College to train pastors and leaders. Now in her mid-eighties, she continues her ministry globally through Naomi Dowdy Ministries.[26] Like Micah of old, she prophetically calls men and women to walk boldly and humbly with their God.[27]

Pastor Dowdy's greatest joy is to see people "rise to their prophetic potential." Since her earliest days of ministry, she has discipled men. She

24. Gorospe, *Judges*, 65.
25. Cundall, *Judges*, 100.
26. See the website for Naomi Dowdy Ministries: https://www.naomidowdy.com.
27. Unless otherwise indicated, all quotations and materials about Naomi Dowdy in the following pages are taken with her permission from an interview granted the author online dated November 10, 2019.

did not see any reason not to, and her investments of time and energy have borne fruit. Many years ago, Pastor Dowdy saw Dominic Yeo's potential and worked patiently and diligently with him from the time he was saved until she appointed him as her successor and the next senior pastor of Trinity Christian Centre. Now under Pastor Dominic's leadership, the church has grown to more than 8,000 members. Her goal for him, though, extended beyond the local church. She wanted to see him mature until he was ready to stand on the world stage and not be intimidated. Currently, in addition to shepherding other pastors, he also leads TCA College as the vice chancellor, serves as the secretary of the World Assemblies of God Fellowship, participates as a member of the executive committee of the Pentecostal World Fellowship, and holds the position of chairman of the Asia Pacific Assemblies of God Fellowship.

Single by choice, Pastor Dowdy has not encountered problems mentoring men because of her gender and "has never had to read the riot act" to anyone. Her premise is that one's anointing and own conduct are the most important factors in letting others know how to respond to you. In addition to the way she carries herself, she takes practical measures, such as avoiding being with members of the opposite sex in secluded places and making it a habit to keep her office door open when meeting one-on-one and having a secretary outside her door. In terms of public ministry, she explains that, when we have people come up front for prayer after a message, we do not insist on men pairing up with men and women pairing up with women, because those ministering understand that "they are not being called on to massage people, but to pray for them."

Pastor Dowdy is not naïve about verbal or sexual harassment. She has encountered her share of people who have struggled with sexual misconduct, plagiarism, and manipulation. Whatever the character issue, she states uncompromisingly the need to intervene, but, to her dismay, has found few who are willing to confront—a malaise she attributes to "weak leadership." Many pastors underestimate their spiritual authority; they are afraid of being judged, losing members, or seeing the offering decline. Often confrontation is viewed as "a fight" instead of as "a chance to resolve a problem." In contrast, Pastor Dowdy, cites Paul as a strong leader who had the integrity to confront the Corinthian church in a case of incest, even calling for the excommunication of the brother in question (1 Cor 5:1–15).

When asked about church discipline, Pastor Dowdy answered in a measured way that the discipline depends on "the person's offense and profile." For example, a pastor may be asked to step down publicly, but in a multi-staff church, where a specific pastor's influence and exposure is more limited, the whole congregation may not need to know of the censure. In either case, the purpose of the discipline is for the person's growth and restoration. The overarching principle, according to Pastor Dowdy, is that accountability grows in proportion to a person's authority and responsibility.

Pastor Dowdy points to the need for stronger leadership in the church. Starting with her own school, TCA College, a training ground for future pastors and leaders, she requires lecturers to have served in a local church prior to obtaining their advanced degrees, because she believes that they need to "be practitioners not just theorists," especially when teaching topics related to ministry. The backbone of both TCA College and Trinity Christian Centre is small groups. In TCA College, administrators, faculty, as well as students gather in small groups of their peers for spiritual growth, support, and accountability. In Trinity Christian Centre, all the pastors, staff, worship leaders and musicians, children's Sunday School teachers, and people in every level of ministry meet regularly in their own small groups. The purpose of the small groups is to allow brothers and sisters to grow, discover their spiritual gifts, and hold one another accountable under the authority of the Scriptures as they are "maturing into Kingdom leaders." The leaders and members of small groups share the responsibility of pastoring, avoiding the pitfall of becoming a church that is overly dependent on a single pastor or pastor-driven. Pastor Dowdy attributes "the metamorphosis" and exponential growth of her ministries to the system of small groups that she and her leaders have developed.

What is revealing is that both Pastor Dowdy and Pastor Hudson subscribe to a small-group model of ministry for regularly identifying and training new leaders who are given opportunities initially to exercise their gifts within their small groups and then potentially in settings of greater influence. Such a collaborative model of leadership recalls the example of Deborah, Barak, and Jael, where God appoints and orchestrates the part that each leader plays. The advantage of shared leadership is that it guards against inflated egos and self-appointed leaders while offering ample opportunity for growth and the testing of both character and skills. The value of a group or corporate identity is stressed by the New Testament and runs counter to an individualistic emphasis on the solo leader.

In Pastor Naomi's estimation, "discipleship alone is not sufficient." According to the Great Commission, discipleship must be tied in to teaching and baptism, and specifically teaching that leads to obedience to everything that Jesus commanded (Matt 28:18–20). However, "What is a disciple?" Pastor Naomi asks, "but a learner or a follower? . . . But," she stresses, "that is not all God has called us to be." Jesus "called his disciples, and chose the twelve of them, whom he also named apostles" (Luke 6:13 NRSV). Pairing Luke's teaching with Matthew's, Pastor Naomi understands that Jesus is prophetically "designating" his disciples to become "apostles"—that is, "leaders who lead other leaders."

Based on God's appointing "first apostles, second prophets, third teachers" (1 Cor 12:28), Pastor Naomi sees a design for the church that leads to growth. Adhering to the structure of the fivefold giftings established in Ephesians 4:11, the church advances as follows: Evangelists are the first tier, who go out and bring the message of salvation to individuals. Then the prophet hears from God and shares what God has revealed, followed by the teacher who searches the word of God, providing "biblical substantiation of the prophet's words." After hearing from God, "the apostle puts feet on the teaching and mobilizes people," according to Naomi. Finally, the pastor focuses on nurturing the local church under his or her care. Reflecting on Paul's practice, she sees the apostle sending out Timothy and Titus primarily as evangelists and then instructing them to appoint elders to lead and teach the respective congregations.

Returning to the biblical metaphor of the body, cell groups are not only the crucible and support net for building the character and integrity of local believers, but they are also the launching pad for leaders. For it is within the safety of the small group that individuals learn about their gifts, strengths, and weaknesses and interact regularly with fellow believers who can witness their lives and see them in action. The genius of the small group is that it encourages people to discover, develop, and deploy their gifts and creates platforms for them to exercise their gifts. Ultimately, the goal is for people to mature into leaders, not just be disciples.

Pastor Dowdy is adamant that she does not distinguish between men and women when discipling. She looks for the same qualities and seeks the same end that they will grow to be leaders of leaders, but her approach to discipling can differ. With men, she tends to be more direct and less wordy. The topics that interest women and men also seem to differ. "Although there are exceptions, women seem more drawn to topics that cover character, spiritual development, spiritual gifts being recognized . . . and discovering their spiritual identity and calling." Notwithstanding the overlaps, men focus more "on church structure, governance, spiritual gifts, the operation of the fivefold ministry . . . and church discipline issues."[28]

When asked about mentoring women and men in mixed company, Pastor Dowdy's experiences are instructive. She observed that, if all the people gathered are senior pastors, men and women speak freely and interact as equals. They regard one another as spiritual peers who have each reached

---

28. The quotations and material from the above paragraph are based on an email from Naomi Dowdy to the author dated Dec. 20, 2019.

a level of maturity and ministry, and they respond to one another "as iron sharpening iron." But when husbands and wives gather in the same room, despite the fact that the women have ministries in their own right, the wives tend to "step back" and let their husbands do the talking. In contrast, when only women are in the room, the group dynamics differ, and sisters feel free to break into a lively and meaningful exchange.

Pastor Dowdy explains, on the one hand, the deference of the wives could be an expression of honoring one another, but more often than not, she thinks it is the result of poor teaching and a kind of "domestication." Unfortunately, it is not only wives, but sisters in general who may be subject to the same lie that they cannot do this or that ministry without the covering of a man.[29] Kept under foot for years, too many sisters have grown accustomed to taking a more passive role in the presence of brothers. Pastor Dowdy declares that "bad hermeneutics" is the source of the problem. To break off the lies and intimidation of the enemy requires nothing less than the clarity of the Scriptures. "To counter the culture we may have been raised in, whether that be the family or the church, we need to ask, 'What does the Bible say?' and 'What does God say?'" For only when sisters know the truth can they be set free; only then can they know who they are in Christ and what they are truly capable of. Last but not least, sisters need to be given a platform to practice the gifts that God has given them.

Foreseeing major breakthroughs in Asia, Pastor Dowdy reports that women leaders are rising up. In 2019, "in Japan, I preached, and the Japanese Christian women leaders taught all the workshops." Next time she envisions that the women leaders will preach and teach. Her principle is that "in the first stage of leadership development, it's me, then in the second stage, it's me and them, and finally it's just them." I believe that Deborah may have followed a similar pattern in grooming Barak to lead.

Twenty years ago, heeding God's call to focus more attention on developing women leaders and pastors, Pastor Dowdy began "mentoring roundtables." Because women leaders and pastors expressed their preference to meet exclusively in groups with other women, she initially invited fifteen women to meet together. Then, in each roundtable sessions, she would encourage collaborative learning, first by sharing on a different topic, such as leadership, character, ministry, faith, etc., and then by having the women raise questions and share their insights and experiences. In Pastor Dowdy's experience, "self-discovered truth is the most impactful and transformational," and roundtables provide good soil for that process to take root. The interval

---

29. In certain Christian groups, "covering" refers to a principle of submission. For example, a woman may need to appeal to the presence of her husband or a pastor as a sign that she is ministering with the approval of a recognized spiritual leader.

between meetings started at six months and then increased to one year. Two decades later, she holds several annual roundtables with several of the founding members still participating: one in America, one in Singapore, two in Malaysia, two in Japan, and one in Asia that includes leaders from different Asian nations. The two Asian and American roundtables met jointly for the first time a couple of years ago with the combination of cultures giving rise to a very enriching experience. She prefers to keep each group between twenty to thirty people so the sharing can go deeper and everyone can have a turn to speak and to be heard. Individuals can opt out of the group if it "does not feel like a fit," and others can recommend attendees, but Pastor Dowdy reserves the right to invite people to join the roundtables.

Men and women have reaped the benefits of Pastor Naomi's corporate model of discipleship and individual mentoring. The spiritual DNA that Pastor Naomi is able to impart through small groups has allowed her to grow ministries within the local church and within the wider kingdom. She has found her current ministry particularly fulfilling as she devotes most of her time to leading a select corps of leaders or serving as a consultant to senior pastors. She compares the latter work to picking up the metaphorical "towel" or the "mop and bucket" to clean up difficult and messy situations in which leaders and churches sometimes find themselves.

Conclusion

The common thread in Phoebe, Deborah, Nancy, and Naomi's ministries is that they stayed true to God's calling and shared their gifts and years of experience by strategically investing in male leaders. In the ministries of both Pastor Hudson and Pastor Dowdy, they implemented a discipleship program that drew out the gifts of the people whom God had entrusted to them. By mentoring and training in groups, they maximized their time and energy while opening the door for others to participate in the discipleship process. God has blessed their ministries in Asia, Africa, and America, and they continue to bear fruit and spread.

References

Amit, Yairah. "Judges 4: Its Contents and Form." *Journal for the Study of the Old Testament* 12:39 (Oct. 1987) 89–111.

Anonymous. "The Faith of Barak." https://biblehub.com/sermons/pub/the_faith_of_barak.html. Accessed Nov. 25, 2019.

Bauer, Walter. *Greek-English Lexicon of the New Testament and Other Early Christian Literature*. Edited by Frederick William Danker. 3rd ed. Chicago: University of Chicago Press, 2000. (BDAG)

Buechner, Frederick. "Deborah." https://www.frederickbuechner.com/quote-of-the-day/2016/11/6/deborah. Accessed Nov. 21, 2019.

Cundall, Arthur E., and Leon Morris. *Judges and Ruth: An Introduction and Commentary*. Tyndale Old Testament Commentaries. Edited by Donald J. Wiseman. Downers Grove, IL: InterVarsity, 1968.

Dowd, Sharon. "Helen Barrett Montgomery's Centenary Translation of the New Testament Characteristics and Influences." http://godswordtowomen.org/Dowd.html. Accessed Nov. 21, 2019.

Dowdy, Naomi. "Naomi Dowdy Ministries." https://www.naomidowdy.com. Accessed Nov. 11, 2019.

Eves, Ailish Ferguson. "Judges." In *The IVP Women's Bible Commentary*, edited by Catherine Clark Kroeger and Mary J. Evans, 136–46. Downers Grove, IL: InterVarsity, 2002.

Giles, Kevin. "House Churches." *Priscilla Papers* 24:1 (Winter 2010) 6–8. http://cbeinternational.org/resources/article/priscilla-papers/house-churches. Accessed Nov. 15, 2019.

Glahn, Sandra. "Java with the Judges." https://bible.org/article/deborah-woman-god-uses. Accessed Nov. 25, 2019.

Gorospe, Athena E., and Charles Ringma. *Judges*. Asia Bible Commentary Series. Edited by Frederico Villanueva. Carlisle, UK: Langham Global Library, 2016.

Holbert, Holbert. "Deborah and the God of Surprise." https://www.patheos.com/resources/additional-resources/2011/11/deborah-and-the-god-of-surprise-john-holbert-11-07-2011. Accessed Nov. 25, 2019.

Liddell, Henry George, and Robert Scott. *A Greek-English Lexicon*. 9th edition with supplement. Oxford: Clarendon Press, 1996.

Keener, Craig S. *Romans*. New Covenant Commentary Series. Edited by Michael F. Bird and Craig S. Keener. Eugene, OR: Cascade, 2009.

McCabe, Elizabeth A. "A Reexamination of Phoebe as a '*Diakonos*' and '*Prostatis*': Exposing the Inaccuracies of English Translations." *Society of Biblical Literature* 7:5 (2009). https://sbl-site.org/publications/article.aspx?ArticleId=830. Accessed Nov. 19, 2019.

McCann, J. Clinton. *Judges*. Interpretation: A Bible Commentary for Teaching and Preaching. Edited by James Luther. Louisville: John Knox, 2002.

Montgomery, Helen Barrett, trans. *The New Testament in Modern English*. https://studybible.info/MNT/Romans%2016. Accessed Nov. 21, 2019.

Orbis, the Stanford Geospatial Network Model of the Roman World. http://orbis.stanford.edu. Accessed Nov. 9, 2019.

Way, Kenneth. "Handling Heroes." https://www.biola.edu/blogs/good-book-blog/2011/handling-heroes-in-hebrews-11. Accessed Nov. 25, 2019.

4

Equal Leadership

God's Intention at Creation

William David Spencer

IS EQUAL LEADERSHIP REALLY God's plan for humanity? Are women who are exercising leadership gifts actually rebelling against God's creation plan for a hierarchy of male leadership wherein, as our evangelical brother the Rev. Dr. Bruce Ware contends, "Male headship applies not only to marriage but equally in the church, where qualified elders, who are male, are those who rightly serve in leadership positions."[1] Worthy of note is that our brother is not just basing his view of permanent one-way female submission to male authority on his doctrine of humanity, but he is basing it on his conviction of an "*authority-submission structure* that exists eternally in the three persons in the Godhead, each of whom is equally and fully God."[2] Because of that "structure," "we are made in the image of God, and so we can live rightly and best only when we mirror in our relationships the relationships true of the eternal God himself." And, thus, "we have the opportunity to pattern what we do after God's design," since "the doctrine of the Trinity is eminently practical, and the church can ben-

---

1. Ware, *Father*, 148.
2. Ware, *Father*, 21.

efit much from understanding and modeling its own life, work, and relationships after the Trinity."[3]

But is Prof. Ware correct? Has a hierarchy within the Godhead been built into the whole intertexture of the universe that would determine that the refusal to let women lead equally is God's intention, reflected from God's nature? Or does such thinking originate elsewhere?

In theological studies, the watchword is that all good theology goes back to creation. Today, however, many scholars hesitate to make pronouncements about human actions, particularly in marriage, based on the Trinity. But, despite this caution's undeniable value, Genesis does tell us that humans are made in God's image and, thus, to test Prof. Ware's challenge to the validity of this present book's argument, we must, at the very least, explore several pertinent questions: Does the theory driving Prof. Ware's interpretation of Scripture originate with the scriptural account of God's creation that we see in Genesis 1 or does it depend on an extrabiblical philosophy that has for centuries been imposed on our readings of the Bible text? Does God's nature in the creation account in Genesis 1 reflect a cooperative or hierarchical tone in the command to rule that God gives to humanity? Is the image of God in which humans are created, therefore, intended to be, hierarchical or equal in nature? In short, is the command to rule given to men only or to both men and women together?

The intention of this chapter is to examine these questions, and, to do so, we will explore an extrabiblical source that appears to be impressing hierarchical thinking on Christian readings of the creation account. Next, we will examine God's expressed pre-fall intentions for humanity in how people should reflect God's image in ruling the earth as expressed in Genesis 1's explanation of the creation, and we will also review what happened to those intentions when disrupted by the post-fall ramifications that impacted that joint rule. Our focus in exploring this last question will be centered on God's explanation of the curse to Eve, since that is where the subject of the distribution of human rule is most affected and the future of the implications on post-fall female/male relationships are specified.

The Pagan Genesis of Hierarchical Thinking

In his classic collection of eight lectures that he "preached before the University of Oxford in the year 1886,"[4] gathered into his book *The Christian Platonists of Alexandria*, the Rev. Prof. Charles Bigg carefully traced the

---

3. Ware, *Father*, 22.
4. Bigg, *Christian Platonists*, iii.

influence of Plato on Philo, the Gnostics, Clement of Alexandria, Origen, Athenagoras, and others among the earliest church apologists and theologians. He identifies what he terms "The Reformed Paganism" that originates, as he cites the Syrian Numenius (c. AD 150), who explains he went "back to the fountain head, to Plato, Socrates and Pythagoras," to adopt his view that God, "being changeless he cannot create, hence there is derived from him a second God, the Creator." This is "the Son," who creates.[5]

Among others, Prof. Bigg highlights the impact on Origen that can be seen in such writings as the *Stromateis*, wherein: "All rational existence is figured as a vast and graduated hierarchy, like a chain of iron rings, each sustaining and sustained, each saving and saved, held together by the magnetic force of the Holy Spirit, which is Faith." Such "belief in the solidarity of all that thinks and feels, which was afterwards the master-thought of Origen," posits, "Father, Son, and Holy Spirit are succeeded by the orders of Angels, and these in their turn by men."[6]

The result is a graded hierarchy, theorized to be among human beings (thus the limitation placed by speculating men on women), and assumed, before that, to be already present in the Godhead itself, so that Christ is subordinated to the Father in such a way that, "if we look upward, the Son is 'next to the Almighty,' 'a kind of Energy of the Father.' If we look downward, He is the Great High Priest, in whom all are reconciled to God." Such a conviction that "all rational existence is figured as a vast and graduated hierarchy"[7] both in God and creation exerted such an influence on the early church theologians and apologists that it became pervasive. Some, like Clement of Alexandria, Charles Bigg sees insisting on "the essential Unity of the Father and the Son," so that Clement departs from Origen's conviction not to pray to anyone born of woman (i.e., Christ) and, therefore, "has no scruple about prayer to the latter." But, though "the idea of subordination is strictly secondary in Clement,"[8] it is still present in his theology as it is everywhere in the platonic culture of thought in which he worked.

Professor Bigg, of course, is right, because anyone can see such hierarchical thinking originating in Plato's creation account in his book, *Timaeus*, and not in the creation account in Genesis 1.

---

5. Bigg, *Christian Platonists*, 251.
6. Bigg, *Christian Platonists*, 68.
7. Bigg, *Christian Platonists*, 68–69.
8. Bigg, *Christian Platonists*, 69.

The Platonic View of God in Creation

For the ancient Greek philosopher Plato (c. 429–327 BC), hierarchy was certainly built into the whole structure of the universe. In his book of theology, his *Timaeus*, Plato claimed that the "Maker and Father of this Universe,"[9] when intending that humanity "should grow into the most god-fearing of living creatures," determined that "since human nature is two-fold, the superior sex is that which hereafter should be designated 'man.'" And, that "when, by virtue of Necessity, they should be implanted in bodies," a man's task would be to "master" his "violent affections" and control his "desire mingled with pleasure and pain" and "fear and anger and all such emotions." The indication to God that men have succeeded is: "if they shall master these they will live justly." God's resulting reward is that at death they will go to a celestial abode and "shall gain a life that is blessed and congenial." But, "whoso has failed therein" and, instead, "are mastered" by violent passions and live "unjustly," "shall be changed into woman's nature at the second birth." And, if the reincarnated man still fails to live justly in this inferior female state, "he shall be changed every time, according to the nature of his wickedness, into some bestial form after the similitude of his own nature."[10] So unjust men enter a penitential, restorative process designed to turn a bad man into a good man by making him, first, female and, should that fail, second, an animal. If he turns into a rogue tiger or junkyard dog, presumably, he may go on and on reincarnating until he is finally rescued by God, or by the lower gods, having become, at last, a good tsetse fly (if such a thing is possible) or an amiable saltwater crocodile (if that possibility is even in its routinely "short-tempered, easily provoked"[11] skill set).

To bring this system about, God "delivered over to the young gods the task of moulding mortal bodies, and of framing and controlling all the rest of the human soul which it was still necessary to add, together with all that belonged thereto, and of governing this mortal creature in the fairest and best way possible, to the utmost of their power, except insofar as it might itself become the cause of its own evils." So, having the task clear at hand, God the Father "then, having given all these commands," rested, "abiding in His own proper and wonted state." And, while the Father took a much-deserved break, "His children gave heed to their Father's command and obeyed it."[12]

---

9. Plato, *Tim.*, 51.
10. Plato, *Tim.*, 91–93.
11. Jameson, "Most Dangerous Animals in the World."
12. Plato, *Tim.*, 93.

This is Plato's view in his *Timaeus* of the way the universe works in general and male and female development works specifically.

Here we see both the subordination of the lesser gods (easily compacted and transferred onto the Son and Holy Spirit, when later transferred to Christianity) and the reduction of women to reincarnated failed men being offered a second chance to "live justly."

This immense impact of Plato's view on the early church, I note, is evident in the theology of such early church writers as Justin Martyr (c. AD 100–165), a Gentile who in his dialogue with a Jewish philosopher named Trypho explains: "God has begotten of Himself a certain rational Power as a Beginning before all other creatures. The Holy Spirit indicates this Power by various titles, sometimes the Glory of the Lord, at other times Son, or Wisdom, or Angel, or God, or Lord, or Word." The Son "performs the Father's will and that He was begotten by an act of the Father's will." Justin, then proceeds to explain the way the Son performs the Father's will by turning to Proverbs 8:22–31. According to Justin,

> The Lord begot Me in the beginning of His ways for His works. I was set up from eternity, before He made the earth, and before He made the depths, before the fountains of waters had sprung out, before the mountains had been established. Before all the hills He begets Me. God made the earth, and the desert, and the highest inhabited places under the sky. When He prepared the heavens, I was present. When he set up His throne on the winds, when He established the clouds above, and strengthened the fountains of the deep, when He balanced the foundations of the earth, I was with Him arranging all things.[13]

So, God created all things and the Son arranged them. One of the parts of creation the Son arranged appears to be humanity, similar to what we see in Plato's *Timaeus*, where the supreme God brings about the lesser gods to put the finishing touches on humanity.

Questions Concerning the Conclusions Drawn from the Platonic Element in These Early Theologians' View of Creation

Is the created and personified characteristic Wisdom really an adequate image for the person of the Trinity we know as God's Son? Is John 1:3, which says literally, "All through him became, and without him became not one

---

13. Justin, *Dial.*, 244–45.

thing,"[14] really encompassed by the attribute Wisdom "arranging" what the Father creates, as Justin reads Proverbs 8? In fact, does any New Testament writer ever refer clearly to Proverbs 8 as a prophetic declaration of what the Son of God is like and whether there are limits imposed on the Son's pre-incarnate capabilities by the Father? We note that John 1:1 states, "In the beginning was [ēn, the imperfect form of eimi, be, exist, therefore, to be understood as "was already existing"] the Word . . ." John, we note, does not write, "In the beginning God begat or gave birth to [yennaō] the Word," although John certainly could have, or should have, had that been the case. But, instead, he writes just what the Holy Spirit inspired him to write. "Becoming" language does not appear until John 1:14, when we are told, literally, "And the Word flesh became" (egeneto, the aorist, punctiliar form of ginomai, become, happen, take place, be born, signifying something that came about at one point in time). If Proverbs 8 were intended to refer to Jesus Christ, John's brilliant prologue to his gospel would have been a good place to mention it. But it is nowhere here. In fact, nowhere clearly does the Incarnated Word of the Godhead, Jesus Christ, ever connect himself with the personified feminine attribute of God, "Wisdom" in Proverbs 8, nor do any of the New Testament writers connect him with Proverbs 8 in the many Old Testament verses they identify as prophesying of Jesus.

Further, much scholarship has been expended on how much relationship can be found between the work of the brilliant, Platonism-influenced Philo (c. 20 BC– AD 45[15] or c. BC 30– AD 50[16]), and the prologue of John. But Philo's understanding of God's word is clearly set out in his *Allegorical Interpretations*, Book 3, when he writes: "And the word of God [*ho logos de tou theou*] is above [*huperanō*, as in "above the horizon,"[17]] all the world, and the oldest [*presbutatos*] and the principal[18] of those which were created."[19] I have translated this passage with the lexical meanings of the words for readers' consideration to underscore that the "word of God"

---

14. All literal Bible translations are by the present author unless otherwise noted. Please take note: the point of rendering a literal translation rather than a smoother dynamic equivalent is to produce the thoughts of Scripture as free of interpretation from reworking them as possible.

15. F. L. Cross and E. A. Livingstone, "Philo," *Oxford Dictionary of the Christian Church*, 1083, col. 2.

16. Piero Treves, "Philon (4)," *Oxford Classical Dictionary*, 822, col, 2.

17. See Liddell and Scott, *Dictionary*, s.v.

18. From *genikos*, or "typical" = type, Liddell and Scott, *Dictionary*, s.v.

19. Philo, *Allegorical Interpretations*, Book 3, para. 61:173–76. *Gegone*, "gegona" from *ginomai*, BDAG, s.v., "To come into being through process of birth . . . to come into existence, be made, be created, be manufactured," BDAG, s.v.

for Philo is clearly very different than it is for John. For Philo, the word is a creation, for John "the Word was with God ['with' from the word *prosopon*, meaning 'face,' so, 'face to face with God'] and the Word was God," hence our understanding that John here is referencing the plurality of persons in the monotheistic Godhead.

Now, as we see a distance in theology between John's elevated understanding of the Word of God as divine and Philo's view of the word of God as created, partly due to the influence of Greek philosophy on Philo's view of the Scripture,[20] so do we note, for example, another aspect of a Platonic-type of thinking transitioning into our present age in the book *Father, Son, and Holy Spirit: Relationships, Roles, and Relevance*, with which we opened this chapter. While Bruce Ware's book neither embraces Philo's view of the word of God as a creation, nor advocates for the superiority of men and the inferiority of women,[21] but affirms, "both the Father and the Son are said to create, the Father and Son are thereby identified together as the one Creator,"[22] still, it does follow Plato's view of hierarchy in its emphasis: "the Father is the Grand Architect, the Wise Designer of all that has occurred in the created order. From initial creation through ultimate consummation and everything that happens in between, it is God the Father who is the Architect, the Designer, the one who stands behind all that occurs as the one who plans and implements what he has chosen to do." [23] Thereby, the book's argument still seems to diminish the other persons of the Trinity to a lower status, somewhat reminiscent of the level of Plato's younger gods who fill in the details of creation according to the plan of the supreme God.

So, what would be reflected of God's nature in humanity would not be a mutual sharing of tasks, as Genesis 1:26–27 appears to indicate by the command to rule and steward being given to both components (male and female) that together comprise humanity, but, instead, something very different than the text states. And that difference would reflect the actual nature of the God whom humanity is imaging, as we see in Prof. Ware's theology:

> An authority-submission structure marks the very nature of the eternal Being of the one who is three. In this authority-submission structure, the three persons understand the rightful place each has. The Father possesses the place of supreme authority,

---

20. As a Jew, Philo may not have been expecting God's messiah to be revealed as the divine Word incarnated in our world, as John discovered to be the case; see John 1:11: "To (or 'in among') his own he came, and his own did not receive him."
21. Ware, *Father*, 138–39.
22. Ware, *Father*, 30–31.
23. Ware, *Father*, 51.

and the Son is the eternal Son of the eternal Father. As such, the Son submits to the Father just as the Father, as eternal Father of the eternal Son, exercises authority over the Son. And the Spirit submits to both the Father and the Son. This hierarchical structure of authority exists in the eternal Godhead even though it is also eternally true that each person is fully equal to each other in their commonly possessed essence. The implications are both manifold and wondrous as we ponder this authority-submission structure which not only is accepted but is honored, cherished, and upheld within the Godhead.[24]

As with Plato's, so with Dr. Ware's vision: divine authority-submission structuring is imaged in humanity from its beginning in a power imbalance in the relationship between man and woman as each half of the "two-fold" "human nature."[25] Dr. Ware's "manifold and wondrous" implications, as adapted through his platonic-colored lens to Christianity, are as follows:

Wives can benefit enormously from the doctrine of the Trinity in realizing that the submission required of them as wives is itself reflective of the very submission eternally given by the Son to his Father, and by the Spirit to the Father and the Son. In this sense, God calls wives to be what he *is*, just as he has also called husbands to be what he also *is*. Therefore, in obeying Scripture's command that wives submit to their husbands, it is not enough before God simply to grit your teeth, buck up, and say, "Okay, if you insist, God, even though I don't like it and I don't want to do it, I'll submit." Why is such begrudging submission insufficient? It is insufficient in part because it fails to understand the nature of submission as reflective of the Son's submission to the Father and the Spirit's submission to the Father and the Son. In the Trinity, just as the Father takes his responsibility of authority seriously and exercises it with impeccable wisdom and goodness, so the Son and Spirit render joyous and glad-hearted submission, always longing to do just what is asked or commanded of them.[26]

We should notice to his credit that Prof. Ware stops short of relating the eternally obedient Son to the attribute Wisdom in Proverbs 8 and, thereby, maintains a high ontological equality of the Son (and Spirit) to the Father,

---

24. Ware, *Father*, 21.
25. Plato, *Tim.*, 91.
26 Ware, *Father*, 145.

despite seeing "the Father as Supreme among the Persons of the Godhead,"[27] getting "top billing," and "deserving of ultimate praise."[28]

About his application of the biblical passages he references, however, readers may wonder how the relationship of a Father to a Son can apply to a husband and a wife. This gender-bending transition makes no sense, unless one is operating in Plato's framework, where women, as we have seen, are actually men who have failed in a prior life. Then the need for them to be controlled makes complete sense. The subordination in Plato, reflected in a vacuum without a change of essence by Bruce Ware, makes more sense in Plato as a second-chance opportunity that, if squandered, may end miscreants up as warthogs. And not all humans may enjoy finding themselves in such a position.

I cannot believe this pagan interpretation's connection is conscious in the view of any Christian scholar, and certainly not one as devout, distinguished, and honored within the Evangelical Theological Society as Dr. Ware. I do, however, recognize in his work what appears to be a direct link that provides a smooth philosophical transition, transforming the imagery of father-son to husband-wife, as we see in Plato's argument.[29]

In all of this light, we ask, are Plato's, Justin's, Origen's, and Bruce Ware's readings of what happens in creation commensurate with what we see in the Bible?

---

27. Ware, *Father*, 46.

28. Ware, *Father*, 51.

29. Certainly, no such connection is made in Ephesians 5:22–33. Drawing its verb from verse 21, which counsels mutual submission, even in its plainest reading, ignoring any contextual evidence that this advice is being made to a largely Gentile church, that its cult of Artemis was run by women, now presumably newly converted to Christianity and not being permitted to lead with such a toxic background that needed to be completely revamped, rather than the Ephesian church being filled with Jewish women already conversant with the Torah and the prophets, or that "head" in Gentile understanding means origin or source, so that honoring one's source is what Gentiles would understand, but just taking the passage completely out of context, still nowhere within it is a statement made specifying that, just as the Son fully submits unilaterally to the Father, should women submit unilaterally to the men. Instead, the submission the passage deals with for women concerns honoring their husbands, and husbands caretaking their wives. Wives are not being told be like the Son of God. No reference to the Trinity is being made for such an interpretation is gender-bending eisegesis.

The Biblical Picture of Cooperation within the Triune God at Work in Creation

Genesis 1:1 tells us, "In the beginning, *elohim* [the plural term for God] created the heavens and the earth." Before God [plural] speaks in Genesis 1:3, the Hebrew word (*rahap*, "brooding") depicts the Holy Spirit like a mother bird brooding over her eggs, in this case, "gestating" the primary chemicals, or "waters," that will become the building blocks of what is to be created out of earth's initial formless matter (Gen 1:2). Next, either the Father (cf. Heb 1:2, "through whom also he made all existence" [*tous aiōnas*]), or, perhaps, the entire, creating, monotheistic Godhead speaks to let creation begin, and the Apostle John is indicating that, in reality, what that "speech or speaking" signifies is the living, creating Word going forth from the Godhead to do the work of creation (John 1:1–4, esp. 1:3; cf. Gen 1:3 ff). John tells us in John 1:3–4, through (*dia*) God's living Word all creation was done, the inanimate and the animate. Paul states, in Colossians 1:16, "in him" (I might understand this as "in his power") all things were created. So, what we are seeing is a perfect triunity in cooperation, revealing the entire Godhead at work in Genesis 1:3. If the Father is speaking, all three of the persons of the Trinity are being identified, even if subtly, as being actively involved in creating humanity. The Genesis 1:2 text highlights the Spirit. John 1:1–4 identifies the speaking of *elohim* in Genesis 1:3ff as more than mere divine words, but actually indicating a creating person of the Trinity, who is being described metaphorically as God's living "Word," who would eventually "recreate" fallen humanity through providing salvation by word and deed, here initially giving all life. Such a reading certainly appears to be the Apostle John's understanding in John 1:1–14, as he presents the Word incarnating as a human.

When the creation of humanity takes place, however, the activity of each of the persons of the Godhead is not as specifically identified. Again the plural term for God, *elohim*, is used to record God saying literally in Genesis 1:26: "And God [in the plural form] said, 'Let us make the *adam* [the human] in our ṣelem ["image"] after our *demuth* ['likeness'] and let them rule."

The first thing we might wonder about is all this use of the plural form for God, so let us ask the obvious question: Does this plural suggest that a plurality of gods created humanity? No, according to Gesenius, Kautzsch, Cowley in what is considered traditionally the authoritative Hebrew grammar by scholars. They explain that the plural name *elohim* means "*Godhead, God*" and is "to be distinguished from the numerical plural gods," since "the language has entirely rejected the idea of numerical plurality."[30] A similar

---

30. Gesenius, Kautzsch, Cowley, *Gesenius' Hebrew Grammar*, §124, g-k, 398–99,

use of this plural term is matched with YHWH, the singular name for God ("the Lord"), in one of the most famous passages in the Hebrew Bible (or Old Testament), where Christians recognize the Hebrew confession of the Trinity, "Hear, Israel, the Lord [singular] your Gods [plural], the Lord [singular] is one [or united, *ehad*]" (Deut 6:4).

Israel worshiped one God, not three gods. In Genesis 1, as interpreted in John 1:1–4, we see that one monotheistic God in plurality in action.

So, such a context would lend proof to the interpretation that Genesis 1 is a primal reference to the triunity in the Godhead. In the context of the Triune God mutually cooperating to build creation, seeing the entire Triune Godhead speaking in Genesis 1:26–27 in mutual unity and delight to create humanity makes sense. Since the actual data that we have is that the Triune God is doing the creating, a full divine voice would make more sense to me than a speculation, unsupported by the plural name of God being employed in the text, that only the Father is speaking and, further, not so much inviting, but commanding the Son and Spirit to get on with the creation of humanity. (Maybe this is the first time the Son and Spirit heard about the Father's plan to create humanity? But since this is one God we are talking about, and all the persons of God are omniscient, as well as almighty,

---

see the plural use of God as "closely related to the plurals of amplification . . . which are mostly found in poetry. So especially *elohim* Godhead, God (to be distinguished from the numerical plural *gods*, Ex 1212, &c.). The supposition that *elohim* is to be regarded as merely a remnant of earlier polytheistic views (i.e. as originally only a numerical plural) is at least highly improbable, and, moreover, would not explain the analogous plurals. . . . That the language has entirely rejected the idea of numerical plurality in *elohim* (whenever it denotes *one* God), is proved especially by its being almost invariably joined with a singular attribute." This understanding can be paralleled with the use of other words for God, which, while undoubtedly plural, are regarded as singular as "*The Most Holy*" and "*The Most High*," §124h., 398–99. Contextually, "Godhead," as a translation, seems to work perfectly, the plural and yet unified singular nature of the term denoting the Trinity at work, creating a singular yet plural humanity=two parts comprising a whole identity. What this understanding contributes to our chapter has to do with the image in which God creates us. The triune Godhead makes a dual-component humanity, man and woman, to reflect God's image materially. What we are seeing here is what we might term a pedagogical (or educational) analogy, not a simple allegory. God's point is didactic; we are ourselves in our dual nature a teaching tool of God. The point is so that we can get at least a handle on how God can be one but plural, having three coeternal, coequal "faces," just as humanity has two faces to complete it. Of course, no doubt, as you have, I have heard other suggestions to explain the plural that is *elohim* as a collective singular, like "the We of Majesty," which is similar to "The Most High," "The Hosts of Heaven" (though why we would suppose God would involve angels in creation when the Godhead at work is all that is identified [or needed!] in Genesis 1 seems more a later gnostic speculation of demiurges bobbling things up because the high, holy God can't touch evil matter), and even "The Editorial We," though how the latter would relate to God, and not a scribal recorder of God's voice, is unclear to me.

and omnipresent, such a speculation would seem like nonsense, especially since the Holy Spirit searches out the depths [*bathos*] in the Godhead [1 Cor 2:10], so that would not work.) But whether the entire Godhead or the Father is speaking, we have to ask: which is the kind of attitude in our Creator we see in the intentions expressed for how we humans should be exercising our imaging of God: the hierarchical or the mutual?

As we noted, John 1:1 will revisit Genesis 1:1 and clarify the presence of the Son at the creation, literally, "In the beginning was already existing the Word, and the Word was with God (*pros* from the word for 'face,' meaning 'face to face with God') and the Word was God." In crafting the language the way he does, John could be intentionally adding the "Word was God," so that his readers do not think, as did Plato, a plurality of lesser gods were enlisted in creation. In fact, John in his gospel is reported to have been responding directly to platonically syncretized ideas promoted by the gnostic Cerinthus (c. AD 100) among others. Irenaeus, the early church theologian and overseer of the church in Lyon who had met John's disciple Polycarp, explains: "John, the Lord's disciple, proclaimed that faith. By proclaiming the gospel he wished to remove the error that was disseminated among people by Cerinthus, and long before by those who are called Nicolaitans, who are an offshoot of the falsely called 'knowledge.'"[31]

In his gospel's chapter 1 introduction or prologue, John corrects the platonic notions of Cerinthus and those he was confusing by specifying, "This one [or he] was already there in the beginning with God. All things through him became [or came into being], and without him [or this one] became not one thing" (John 1:2–3). So, in summary, in his brief commentary on Genesis 1 in the prologue to his gospel (*euaggelion*, i.e., good news)

---

31. Irenaeus, *Haer.* 3:11.1 In Book 1, chapter 26, paragraph 1 of *Against the Heresies*, Irenaeus tells us Cerinthus taught "the world was not made by the first God, but by some Power which was separated and distant from the Authority that is above all things, and which was ignorant of the God who is above all things." Cerinthus also objected to Jesus's virgin birth, contending he was "born the son of Joseph and Mary like all other men," and advocated for adoptionism, "after his baptism Christ descended on him in the shape of a dove . . . But at the end Christ again flew off from Jesus," Jesus suffering, dying, and rising again, while Christ "remained impassible, since he was spiritual." "The so-called Ebionites," Irenaeus continues in this chapter, "admit that the world was made by the true God, but in regard to the Lord they hold the same opinion as Cerinthus," while the Nicolaitans "lived unbridled lives," seeing "no difference between committing fornication and eating food sacrificed to idols" *Haer* 1:26.1–8. Irenaeus also passes on a well-publicized account reportedly from John's disciple Polycarp, "There are those who heard him say that when John the disciple of the Lord was at Ephesus and went to take a bath, on seeing Cerinthus there, he rushed out of the bathhouse without having bathed. 'Let us flee,' he explained, 'lest even the bathhouse collapse because Cerinthus the enemy of the truth is in there'" (*Haer.* 3:3.4).

about Jesus, John explains these points: that, when God began to create our world, the creating Word already existed, being "face to face" or distinct and equal with God, and yet being God (v. 1); that the Word created all that exists (v. 3) and, after our world fell, while remaining God, now became human as well, being born into our world (v. 14) on a mission from the Godhead to redeem humanity (vv. 7, 16).

So, that plurality in singularity in the Godhead is an essential aspect of understanding God's nature and thus is reflected materially in God's creation of humanity.

Further, after correcting Cerinthus, John adds a sentence that separates his gospel from Plato's view. Plato tells us that the Father "blended and mixed the Soul of the Universe" and then "mixing it in somewhat the same manner, yet no longer with a uniform and invariable purity, but second and third in degree of purity . . . He divided it into souls."[32] Again, hierarchy is built into the world Plato's Father God creates. But John tells us, literally, "In him [the Word] life was, and the life was the light of the humans. And the light in the darkness shines, and the darkness has not overtaken [or seized, or put it out]." And John caps this all in John 1:9 by telling us that the Word "was the true light, the one that lights every human" and this is the one "coming into the world" as Jesus Christ.

So, here in John 1:1, we see that the person of the Godhead who incarnated as Jesus Christ, the earthly Son of God, was thoroughly involved in the creation in Genesis 1:2, that the Holy Spirit had already begun working before we are told of the active involvement of the other persons of the Trinity.

So, in this light, we can interpret the statement in Genesis 1:26–27, attributed to the plural name of God, *elohim*, "Let us make the Adam in our image, after our likeness," as being a cooperative venture, not by necessity a one-way command by the Father to his underlings to "arrange" humanity in a similar hierarchical structure.

Quite the opposite. Genesis 1:27 tells us God created humanity male and female and commanded them both to have dominion over the land. God did not give the command solely to the man to have rule and dominion, but for women and men to share rule. So, what we are seeing is the cooperative nature of God reflected in the command to humans to rule cooperatively over the earth as God's stewards.

Where the imbalance takes place is at the fall, when God discusses the ramifications to Eve and Adam of their disobedience. Each has endangered the privileges they had before, so that Eve is told in Genesis 3:16 her *teshuqah* (desire or longing in the MT; or v. 17 in the LXX, her *apostrophē*, that is,

---

32. Plato, *Tim.*, 91.

"turning") will be for her man and he will rule over her. The term the Septuagint uses for "rule" is a pejorative one, *kurieuō*, "lord it over." It is the same word Jesus uses in Luke 22:25 to caution the disciples that "the kings of the nations (or Gentiles) lord it over them," but his followers are not to act this way with one another (Luke 22:26). So, this is not a good thing. This term describes the oppression of women and not something Eve should welcome, nor does it describe her relationship to her husband before the fall. It is a consequence of what life will be like after the fall. It does not describe God's intention for humanity and, therefore, there is no reason to believe such imbalance describes God's nature as reflected in humanity from the Trinity. It is not a pure reflection of God's image in woman and man; it is a shattered and polluted mirroring of that fallen image.

This primal truth is necessary to understand at the outset to avoid our wandering into some of the preposterous images and theories that mute the beautiful cooperation in the Godhead and substitute an oppressive structure of subjection, suppression, unilateral submission, and imbalance.

All of this informs our examination of the intentions God has for whether or not humans are to share equally in their responsibility for leading this earth. Now, we will focus more directly on God's expressed intentions and what happened to them.

What Does Genesis Tell Us God Intended for Human Leadership?

Clearly, Genesis 1:27 specifies who comprises the "*adam*" and who exactly is to rule: "And God [in the plural form] created the *adam* in his [in the singular form] image, in the image of God he created him, male and female he created them."[33] Humanity was created male and female with a joint com-

---

33. C.F. Keil and F. Delitzsch in their *Commentary on the Old Testament*, vol. 1, pp. 63-64, following Martin Luther, equate "image" and "likeness," seeing "the two words are synonymous, and are merely combined to add intensity to the thought: 'an image which is like Us.'" They also reject the various evolutionary or creationist interpretations: "Certainly not in the bodily form, the upright position, or commanding aspect of the man, since God has no bodily form, and the man's body was formed from the dust of the ground." They also reject the popular idea of "dominion of man over nature." Instead, they opt for "man is the image of God by virtue of his spiritual nature . . . the spiritual personality of man." As a "living soul" (as opposed to animals) with "free self-conscious personality," a human is "a creaturely copy of the holiness and blessedness of the divine life." They add, "This concrete essence of the divine likeness was shattered by sin; and it is only through Christ, the brightness of the glory of God and the expression of his essence (Heb. i.3), that our nature is transformed into the image of God again (Col. iii.10, Eph. iv.24)." Jamieson, Fausset, and Brown, in their *Commentary Practical*

and Explanatory on the Whole Bible, 18, col. 1, ask, "In what did this image of God consist?" and agree, "not in the erect form or features of *man*, not in his intellect," and add, "for the devil and his angels are, in this respect, far superior; not in his immortality, for he has not, like God, a past as well as a future eternity of being; but in the moral dispositions of his soul, commonly called *original righteousness* (Eccles. 7:29)." Henry in *Baker's Dictionary of Theology*, 277–78, contends, "The image of God is a recurring theme in biblical revelation. The image is man's unique endowment at creation (Gen 1:26), sullied by the Fall but not destroyed." What he means by this is that, since God "cannot be localized in space and time; the unique bearer of the divine image, in the creature world, is man himself." An image of "the Godhead, and not of the Son alone," "man" finds restoration of this image in Christ who "is the undistorted image of God in human nature." "Since Christ overcame sin in the flesh, and raised human nature to glory in his resurrection and ascension, fallen mankind again has the prospect of spiritual glory through a final and complete conformity to the image of Christ (1 John 3:2)." Along these lines, the entry on "Adam" in the *Dictionary of Biblical Imagery* (eds. Ryken, Wilhoit, Longman, 9) suggests, "Adam is first and foremost related to God. In the spare and schematized language of Genesis 1, Adam is the fleshly distillation of the creative and divine word." But, also, "Adam" is "two—male and female—... an animated, walking, talking and relating mediation of the essence, will and work of the sovereign creator God." So human male and female comprise a "living image of the living God." This privilege gives human "image bearers of the sovereign Creator ... an active rule that represents the loving dominion and care of God over the wonders of creation." Therefore, "both man and woman are commanded to 'fill the earth,' 'subdue it' and 'rule' over every living thing," under a "responsibility" to the Creator, which demands they assume a joint "creative vocation of earth-care and earth-filling (Gen, 1:28)." H. A. G. Blocher, under "Anthropology, Theological" in the *Global Dictionary of Theology*, 43–44, sees the "image" with which humanity is created as possessing "(1) limitation: created, not a god, only an image, and (2) privilege, which entails superiority over all other earthly creatures." This imaging involves: "authority and strength conferred," "domination over the animal realm," "free will" ("power of choice"), "discernment," even reflecting "God's own eternity with the calling to incorruptibility," the interpretations historically grouping under the categories "dominion" or "spirituality." The early church theologians, he notes, emphasized the spiritual aspect, after "the end of the eleventh century," moving toward "the quality of rational and moral" agency, along with a "moral-spiritual agreement" with God's attributes (e.g., "holiness, righteousness, benevolence," etc.). While the Reformers' interpretations favored the "moral-spiritual line," their critics (e.g., the anti-Trinitarian Socinians) returned to the "dominion" viewpoint, emphasizing human empowering, and, in more modern times, he notes, an interpretation by Karl Barth sees God creating the duality of female and male, suggesting "an I-Thou relationship" in humanity "that is analogous to the trinitarian I-Thou." This analogy appears only to be reflected in the human relational aspect and its binding us to Christ, as part of Christ's "bride," the church, as opposed to humans being created in the "image of God" in the unique way that only appears to be realized in Jesus Christ. B. Assohoto and S. Ngewa in their commentary on Genesis in the *Africa Bible Commentary*, 11, observe that human beings "have been made in the *image* of God.... Thus humans are different from other created beings like animals, and this fact has important consequences for how we live." This resemblance makes each human "special and important," and humans "should not worship any animal," or give "an image of an animal the place that belongs only to the Creator." "We should be able to recognize the Creator in the men and women we see around us," and "must not mistreat our own bodies or those of others." "Both men and mand to rule. This is pre-fall theology. In other words, unfallen humanity was created to share joint rule between the two sexes, as expressed in God's intention: "Let them rule" (or have dominion, *radah*, Gen 1:26).

What Happened to That Joint Rule?

After the fall, this equal rule is beset by challenges. Because of the disobedient actions of the humans against God's expressed prohibitions in Eden's garden, God explains the ramifications of what that rebellion now means for Eve's and Adam's future together. For the woman, it means that her right of joint rule will now be threatened by the man.

Since there is some confusion on this point among readers and scholars, it is worth taking a moment to examine what Genesis 3:16 in the Hebrew is actually stating. God (in the plural voice form) to the woman says, "unto your man your *teshuqah* ("desire") and he will *mashal* ("rule") over you."

How Do Prominent Bible Versions Render This Passage?

NIV: "Your desire will be for your husband, and he will rule over you."

---

women were blessed by God . . . to *rule over* creation and to *subdue* the earth." They add, "It is important to note that men and women were permitted to rule only over other living creatures, not over other human beings. Nor were men given authority to dominate women (or vice versa). Our fellow human beings bear the image of the Creator and thus are not to be dominated but to be served." Lily Yun Chu Chong in *The IVP Women's Bible Commentary*, 2-4, reminds us that ancient "kings were understood to be the image of the deity," so, "according to Genesis all human beings share the status of royalty." Summarizing Tikva Frymer-Kensky's view on monotheism replacing gendered deities, Lily Chong observes, "God is not male," being "above and beyond sexuality, it is possible for both women and men to be in the image of God." And she adds, "All humanity, women and men, are God's image." Noting the complexity surrounding many years of varying interpretations, currently involving such concepts as "being God's image is a task" as much as a status, the singularity and plurality embedded in the language, etc., she ultimately returns to her original observation to opt for "God the king creates us in his image so that we can rule in his stead." Interestingly, Bruce Ware, after noting several interpretations, reminds us that "one thing that Genesis 1:26-28 emphasizes is that the man and woman God creates in his image are commanded to 'rule over' or 'subdue' the other aspects of the created order," as representatives of God. His difference with what precedes comes with his qualification of "thoughtful, judicious authority exercised along with joyful, glad-hearted submission within the very Trinity itself" (*Father*, 132-33), but it does show some common agreement and, therefore, common currency in our interchanges on these issues, couching our differences as more familial than they might be when discussing such issues with those who do not share our agreement of the parameters of God's image within us.

NRSV: "Yet your desire shall be for your husband, and he shall rule over you."

KJV: "Thy desire shall be to thy husband, and he shall rule over thee."

NASB: "Yet your desire will be for your husband, and he will rule over you."

REB: "You will desire your husband, but he will be your master."

JB: "Yet, your yearning shall be for your husband, yet he will lord it over you."

TEV: "In spite of this, you will still have desire for your husband, yet you will be subject to him."

HCSB: "Your desire will be for your husband, yet he will rule over you."

CEV: "But, you will still desire your husband, and he will rule over you."

ESV: "Your desire shall be contrary to your husband, but he shall rule over you."

NLT: "And you will desire to control your husband, but he will rule over you."

As we review this list, we notice an interpretive difference added to the final two versions. The ESV adds the word "contrary" and the NLT adds "desire to control." Let us compare these two versions' translations to the literal Hebrew rendering for Genesis 3:16 (or 17): "And unto your man [or husband] your desire/longing (*teshuqah*) and he will rule (*mashal*) over you."

Does Any Justification Exist for These Additions to the Hebrew?

1. In New Testament times, the Jews were Hellenized (under Roman rule and schooled in Greek), so the rabbis used the Greek translation of the Hebrew Bible, called the Septuagint (LXX), as well as the original Hebrew version.

2. The translators of the ESV and NLT appear to have consulted (or at least agree with) the English translation of the Septuagint published in Great Britain by Samuel Bagster and Sons, which for many years was the version in common use. The word the Septuagint used to translate the Hebrew word for the woman's response to her husband, *teshuqah*, was *apostrophē*. This word is used elsewhere in the Septuagint.

We find it in:

- Genesis 4:7: where Cain is warned by God that sin wants to cause him to turn, but he must rule over it.
- Deuteronomy 22:1: Do not watch your neighbor's ox or sheep straying, turn (or return) them back to their owner.
- Deuteronomy 31:18: God turns God's face away from evil.
- 1 Kings 7:17 (1 Sam 7:17 MT): Samuel returns to his house.
- In the apocryphal book of Sirach (or Ecclesiasticus), Sirach 16:30: Living creatures God creates out of the earth return to it.
- Sirach 18:24: God turns away God's face.
- Sirach 41:21: To turn away your face from helping your kinsman (neglecting needy relatives)
- Micah 2:12: God's people will return to God.
- Jeremiah 5:6: Jerusalem's turning to evil.
- Jeremiah 6:19: Reaping the fruit of turning away from God's path.
- Jeremiah 8:5: Have God's people turned away?
- Jeremiah 18:11–12: God warns, let everyone turn back again from evil ways, but God's people will reply that they will keep turning to evil.
- Ezekiel 16:53: God will turn people's fortune so they can be punished.
- Ezekiel 33:11: God calls on the wicked to turn away from sin, because God does not desire the death of the people.
- The apocryphal book of 3 Maccabees 2:10 reminds God of God's promise of love, if Israel turns away from God to sin, God will listen to its prayer of repentance.

In conclusion, *apostrophē* means "turning" or "returning" everywhere else in the Septuagint, so it probably means that here in Genesis 3:17 (16 in our English Bibles) as well: "And unto your man (or husband) your turning and he will rule over you."

How Do the ESV and NLT Versions Differ from the Hebrew, Greek, and the Other Prominent English Translations?

In the Septuagint, the word *apostrophē* simply means turning or returning. Toward what one is turning identifies whether the turning is neutral, a good action, or a bad choice. An example of a neutral use is when Samuel returns to his house (1 Kgs 7:17 LXX; 1 Sam 7:17 MT). A bad turning is specified in Jeremiah 5:6, when people turn to evil. A good turning is in Micah 2:12, when people return to God. Here, in Genesis 3:16 (or 17), God explains the object to whom the woman turns is her husband. This would normally be seen as good; it is a natural part of God's plan for a female and male to be attracted to each other (Gen 2:18–24). But, now, the consequences will be bad for her, since fallen man will try to lord it over her. In other words, equality is no long assured. The introduction of sin causes imbalance and therefore oppression. The woman turns to man, but the equal companionship she seeks is no longer assured.

At this point the New Living Translation and English Standard Version choose to add an interpretation to the Genesis 3:16 explanation, suggesting the woman has a different objective in mind than simply desiring her husband: she herself will now be turning toward oppression, desiring to control him by acting contrary to the man and, as a result, he will have to rule over her to keep her in line.

We recall that both the NLT's and ESV's renderings of Genesis 1:26–28 read like all the other Bibles listed, agreeing that, before the fall, God gave joint custody and rule of the earth mutually to all of humanity: women as well as men. The lack of equity is the result of a fallen world. It is clearly not God's intention for how men and women should relate.[34] So, there is no question of whether mutual rule existed before the fall. The question is *what* the curse changed and the implications for the present day: whether

---

34. Here is the ESV's rendering of Gen 1:26–28: "Then God said, 'Let us make man in our image, after our likeness. And let them have dominion over the fish of the sea and over the birds of the heavens and over the livestock and over all the earth and over every creeping thing that creeps on the earth.' So God created man in his own image, in the image of God he created him, male and female he created them. And God blessed them. And God said to them, 'Be fruitful and multiply and fill the earth and subdue it, and have dominion.'" The NLT translates Gen 1:26–28 as follows: "Then God said, 'Let us make human beings in our image, to be like us. They will reign over the fish in the sea, the birds in the sky, the livestock, all the wild animals on the earth, and the small animals that scurry along the ground.' So God created human beings in his own image. In the image of God he created them; male and female he created them. Then God blessed them and said, 'Be fruitful and multiply. Fill the earth and govern it.'"

we Christians are supposed to live under the curse or, as being redeemed by Christ's sacrifice, to live "Beyond the Curse" as the Rev. Dr. Aída Besançon Spencer counsels in her classic book of that name.

What is clear, however, is that there is no adverb for "contrary" or infinitive for "to control" either in the Old Testament Hebrew original or in the Septuagint translation of Genesis 3:16 (17). So, no grounds exist for putting these words in. To do so is adding an object not in the text to make the woman's action bad and, therefore, an excuse for her coming oppression. And, neither of the nouns in Hebrew or in Greek for "turning" in itself contains "contrary" or "to control" to signify a rebellious aspect to the woman's yearning or desire in turning toward her husband.

This is why every other version simply translates the Hebrew noun as "yearning" or some equivalent word, like the Greek "turning," which also has no sense of control or disagreement (e.g., contrary).

How Does the Husband Rule Over the Wife in the Description of the Curse?

Both Genesis 3:16 (or 17, depending on the version being used) and Genesis 4:7, which we could view as a kind of control version, use the same term for rule: *mashal*.

When seventy or seventy-two Jewish elders translated the Torah of the Hebrew Bible, c. 250 BC, as ordered by Ptolemy II Philadelphus, they knew the description of the curse was describing an oppressive situation in Genesis 3:16 (or 17). So, while they used a positive term for rule, *arxeis*, in Genesis 4:7 to describe Cain's need to rule over sin, they used a negative term *kurieuō*, or "lording it over someone," to describe what the fallen man would do to the fallen woman now. This describes the lamented state of domestic abuse, which was a condition God never wanted for humanity.

So, a more accurately literal rendering of these two passages would be:

- Genesis 4:7 "To you its [that is, sin's] desire and you will rule it." (In other words: sin yearns to turn you, but you must rule it.)
- Genesis 3:17 (16) reads literally, "And to your man, your desire [or turning, or submission, if we adopt Bagster's Septuagint rendering], but he himself will lord it over you."

Therefore, what we can learn from these passages is, as Cain was warned in Genesis 4:7, we need to master sin. And in Genesis 3:16 (17), Eve was being warned that a war between the sexes had begun and Adam would now try to lord it over her. We need to end such strife in our lives and work for peace and equality for one hundred percent of the church.

Remember, this is a "lording over" (*kurieuō*) that Jesus warns his disciples not to do in Luke 22:25–26, when he calms their dispute about which of them is the greatest by explaining, "The kings of the nations [also 'Gentiles; pagans, heathen, unbelievers'] lord it over [*kurieuō*] them and those having authority [or power, *exousia*] over them are being called benefactors [*euergesia*], but all of you are not to be this way [or the same way, or like this]."[35]

Describing the reason for the man lording it over the woman as caused by her contrariness is not in the text. It changes the meaning and pathos of the result of the fall: oppression by the physically stronger.

In fact, if we were to see the curse as God's command that now, because of Eve's sin, Adam's duty is to "lord it over her," we would be positing a contradiction between Jesus's expressed command not to "lord it over each other," and, thereby, be putting two persons of the Trinity (Father and Son) in disagreement. Jesus, we notice, did not add, "Oh, except for women. It's okay to 'lord it over them' all you want, just don't try it with other men. The Big Guy in the Sky doesn't like that. But he's fine with whatever happens to the women—they all deserve it, because of Eve."

No. Jesus is simply applying God's pre-fall intentions to redeemed people. He is saying: Do not do what God warned would happen because of the fall, something you can see readily all around you when powerful rulers oppress their people. Do not "lord it over" others. We should be living redeemed lives, reflecting the image of mutual cooperation within the One who created us.

Conclusion

So, what can we conclude from this chapter?

God intended humans, women and men, to rule jointly, reflecting God's image in humanity, the two material and equal parts that comprise humanity, man and woman, demonstrating in our equal leadership in ruling and stewarding the earth together the perfect mutual cooperation of the three persons in the Godhead, who created us in the first place. We are ruling in a reflecting imaging of God, as an analogy, not a point by point allegory, of one aspect of the One God with Three Equal Faces who is our Creator.

This image, as in all the imagery humanity reflects from its creation by God, was shattered at the fall, effaced but not erased. Men's oppressive domineering in "lording it over" subjected women is part of that effacing,

---

35. Newman, *Dictionary of the New Testament*, 52.

not commensurate at all with what we see in Genesis 1 as God's intentions for how humans are to relate.

Therefore, a one-way, graded, hierarchical command structure among humans is not what God expressly intends and, therefore, does not reflect or image the nature of God. It reflects the plight of fallen humanity.

We are redeemed by the blood of Jesus Christ, poured out for the remission of our sins, the restoration to favor with God, and the chance to live redeemed lives of gratitude and graciousness, reflecting or imaging the God who created us. In that sense, though still fallen and doomed to die in this temporal world, we are empowered to live more and more Christlike lives that will begin for us, in prelude, the redeemed lives we will enjoy fully in heaven with our loving and redeeming God.

Therefore, we should not "lord it over each other," but live in the equal sharing of joint ruling and submission God intended for us at our creation, mutually determined in each instance by the gifts God has given us.

References

Assohoto, Barnabé, and Samuel Ngewa. "Genesis." In the *Africa Bible Commentary*, edited by Tokunboh Adeyemo. Nairobi: WordAlive/Zondervan, 2006.

Bauer, Walter, W. F. Arndt, F. W. Gingrich, and Fredrick William Danker, eds. *A Greek-English Lexicon of the New Testament and other Early Christian Literature*. 3rd ed. Chicago: University of Chicago Press, 2000. (BDAG)

Bigg, Charles. *The Christian Platonists of Alexandria*. Oxford: Oxford University Press, 1886.

Blocher, H. A. G. "Anthropology, Theological." In the *Global Dictionary of Theology*, edited by William A. Dyrness and Veli-Matti Kärkkäinen, 42–49. Downers Grove, IL: InterVarsity, 2008.

Chong, Lily Yun Chu. "Genesis." In *The IVP Women's Bible Commentary*, edited by Catherine Clark Kroeger and Mary J. Evans, 1–5. Downers Grove, IL: InterVarsity, 2002.

Cross, Frank L., and E.A. Livingstone, eds. *Oxford Dictionary of the Christian Church*. 2nd ed. Oxford: Oxford University Press, 1983.

Feyerabend, Karl. *Langenscheidt Pocket Hebrew Dictionary to the Old Testament: Hebrew to English*. Berlin: Langenscheidt, 1969.

Gesenius, William. *A Hebrew and English Lexicon of the Old Testament*, edited by Francis Brown, S. R. Driver, and Charles Briggs. Translated by Edward Robinson. Oxford: Oxford University Press, 1968.

Gesenius, William, E. Kautzsch, and A. E. Cowley. *Gesenius' Hebrew Grammar*. 2nd English ed. London: Oxford, 1976.

Hammond, N. G. L., and H. H. Scullard, eds. *Oxford Classical Dictionary*. 2nd ed. Oxford: Oxford University Press, 1970.

Henry, Carl F. H. "Image." In *Baker's Dictionary of Theology*, edited by Everett F. Harrison, Geoffrey W. Bromiley, and Carl F. H. Henry, 277–78. Grand Rapids: Baker, 1960.

St. Irenaeus of Lyons: Against the Heresies. Book 1. Ancient Christian Writers. Translated by Dominic J. Unger and John J. Dillon. Mahwah, N.J.: Paulist, 1992.

St. Irenaeus of Lyons: Against the Heresies. Book 3, edited by Matthew C. Steenberg. Translated by Dominic J. Unger. Mahwah, N.J.: Newman, 2012.

Jameson, Daniel. "The Ten Most Dangerous Animals in the World." *Condé Nast Traveler US*. https://www.cntraveler.com/stories/2016-06-21/the-10-most-dangerous-animals-in-the-world. Accessed April 2, 2020.

Jamieson, Robert, A. R. Fausset, and David Brown. *Commentary Practical and Explanatory on the Whole Bible*. Grand Rapids: Zondervan, 1961.

Saint Justin Martyr: The First Apology, The Second Apology, Dialogue with Trypho, Exhortation to the Greeks, Discourse to the Greeks, The Monarchy or The Rule of God. The Fathers of the Church. Translated and edited by Thomas B. Falls. Washington, DC: Catholic University of America Press, 1948.

Keil, C. F., and F. Delitzsch. *Commentary on the Old Testament*. Vol. 1. Grand Rapids: Eerdmans, 1973.

Liddell, Henry George, Robert Scott, Henry Stuart Jones, and Roderick McKenzie. *A Greek-English Lexicon*. Oxford: Oxford University Press, 1977.

Newman, Barclay M. *A Concise Greek-English Dictionary of the New Testament*. Rev. ed. Stuttgart: Deutsche Bibelgesellschaft/United Bible Societies, 2010.

Philo. *Allegorical Interpretations of Genesis II, III*. In *Philo*. Vol. 1. Loeb Classical Library. Translated by F. H. Colson and G. H. Whitaker. Cambridge, MA: Harvard University Press, 1929.

Plato. *Timaeus*. In *Plato in Twelve Volumes: Timaeus; Critias; Cleitophon; Menexenus; Epistles*. Vol. 9. Loeb Classical Library. Translated by R. G. Bury. Cambridge, MA: Harvard University Press, 1929, 1981.

Ryken, Leland, James C. Wilhoit, and Tremper Longman III, eds. *Dictionary of Biblical Imagery*. Downers Grove, IL: InterVarsity, 1998.

The Septuagint Version of the Old Testament and Apocrypha. London: Samuel Bagster, n.d.

Ware, Bruce. *Father, Son, and Holy Spirit: Relationships, Roles, and Relevance*. Wheaton, IL: Crossway, 2005.

5

Influence of Plato and Aristotle's Patriarchy on Christian Hierarchy Today

Jean A. Dimock

WE ARE GIVEN MANY reasons why the men in our world have traditionally been viewed as the developers of society and culture, warriors, and heads of the family. In general, men are viewed as stronger than women, not just physically, but also intellectually. Consequently, women have customarily been offered the back seat to men's tasks and careers, either by intentional or unintentional individual, institutional, or corporate discrimination. But there is a significant contribution toward the continued development of patriarchy through time that influences our thinking and beliefs today that we do not often consider: philosophy. More specifically, the thinking and the determinations of the ancient philosophers Plato and Aristotle still influence today's enlightened world as it pertains to women and their place in the family, the church, and the community.

Whom did these ancient philosophers influence? What did they ultimately shape and impact? Did any ideas of ancient philosophers, as we refer to scriptural interpretations or beliefs, carry through to the present day? If so, how did this happen? Because patriarchy today has many of its roots in the ancient philosophers, we will follow the thread that moves from Plato and Aristotle into the present day to see how, across time, they have influenced our understanding of Scripture.

To gain understanding as we read or meditate on Scripture, insight concerning the culture surrounding biblical writings helps us to discover what a particular Scripture is truly communicating to the reader. Scriptural interpretations that result from cultural biases or the injection of a philosophy, whether the biases exist today or at any point throughout the ages, do not provide a favorable outcome and can lead not only to an incorrect understanding of Scriptures, but also to faults in our daily living.

Three Ancient Philosophers

Plato (427/28–347 BC) and Aristotle (384–322 BC) are the two ancient philosophers considered here, but first we will look briefly at Socrates (469/70–399 BC), because he taught Plato, who then taught Aristotle. These and many other philosophers have made significant contributions to the way we think today, but Plato and Aristotle will be considered foremost because of their direct influence on two Christian saints.

During the time of Socrates, Plato, and Aristotle, Athens was the cultural center of the Greek world. A person's station in society became important, and so did the art of rhetoric.[1] An Athenian male believed that the best course for his life was to work toward becoming well known, to be held in a place of honor and political power.[2] To achieve this end, he needed to be able to speak well and convincingly.

Socrates (469/70–399 BC)

Socrates was born in Athens and is known mostly through the writings of Plato, one of his pupils, because Socrates did no recording of his thoughts, teachings, or philosophy. Socrates is credited with being the philosopher who moved philosophical questions from the natural sciences of the natural philosophers and settled them more within ethics and ethical conduct.[3] Another distinction given to Socrates is his view of women. Socrates spoke of "men and women, priests and priestesses," and recognized those women who were his teachers.[4] At the same time, Socrates did not always present a positive view of women.

---

1. Gaarder, *Sophie's World*, 63.
2. Nails, "Socrates," para. 4.
3. Denault, "Philosophy: The Athenian Philosophers: Socrates, Plato, and Aristotle," para. 5.
4. Nails, "Socrates," para. 5.

In the *Apology* (399 BC), Plato gives an account of the speech Socrates made at his trial, where he was found guilty of not recognizing the gods of his time and corrupting the youth of Athens. He tells the court that he will not resort to any antics or manipulations (such as presenting his three sons to the court) that would bring mercy toward him, but, rather, he will speak for himself:

> O Athenians, three in number, one of whom is growing up, and the two others are still young; and yet I will not bring any of them hither in order to petition you for an acquittal. And why not? Not from any self-will or disregard of you. Whether I am or am not afraid of death is another question, of which I will not now speak. But my reason simply is that I feel such conduct to be discreditable to myself, and you, and the whole state.... I have seen men of reputation, when they have been condemned, behaving in the strangest manner: they seemed to fancy that they were going to suffer something dreadful if they died, and that they could be immortal if you only allowed them to live; and I think that they were a dishonor to the state, and that any stranger coming in would say of them that the most imminent men of Athens, to whom the Athenians themselves give honor and command, are no better than women. And I say that these things ought not to be done by those of us who are of reputation....[5]

Here, he provides a view of women inconsistent with his view of those women who were his teachers, but consistent with the culture of Athens at that time.

In *Phaedo* (360 BC), Socrates views women as more emotional than men, with the need to be spared certain difficulties. In this instance, Xanthippe, Socrates's wife, while sitting with Socrates at the prison and learning that he will die on that very day, is described as expressing her emotions, while the men in attendance did not, but rather engaged in philosophical discourse with Socrates.

> When she saw us she uttered a cry and said, as women will: "O Socrates, this is the last time that either you will converse with your friends, or they with you." Socrates turned to Crito and said: "Crito, let someone take her home." Some of Crito's people accordingly led her away, crying out and beating herself.[6]

---

5. Plato, *Apology*, para. 62.
6. Plato, *Phaedo*, para. 26.

Xanthippe is here described as a woman who entertains a response typical of women under difficult circumstances. Upon her removal from Socrates and the men in attendance, they were able to continue with their intellectual dialogue.

Plato (427/28–347 BC)

Plato was born into a politically active and wealthy family. His mother, Perictione, followed the family line of Solon, a lawgiver, who encouraged democratic reforms. Plato grew up during the Peloponnesian War (431–404 BC), a civil war conflict that included Athens and Sparta and brought the Athenian Golden Age to an end. Philip of Macedon then took advantage of the weakness created by the war and, consequently, Athens and Sparta were emptied of the principles of democracy and their cultural wealth.[7]

The death of Socrates, Plato's teacher, as well as the executions of Plato's relatives who had introduced Plato to Socrates (Critias and Charmides), turned Plato away from politics and toward philosophy.[8] He developed a school of philosophy near Athens and called it the Academy (after the Greek hero Academus).[9] Plato's concerns were questions about what is eternal and unchanging over time in nature as well as morals and society. For him, determining what is eternal and what is unchanging are the same.

In his volume *The Republic* (380 BC), Plato described his political philosophy. *The Republic* includes his ideas about how justice is best understood. Is justice understood better as a virtue of a good city or is it better understood within good individuals? He asserts that these two concepts are inseparable, that virtue starts with the individual (who has wisdom, courage, and temperance),[10] but leads us to experience virtue in the good city if individuals have virtue. If individuals are virtuous, then the state will be virtuous as well. He also concluded that the state is supreme; thus, it is totalitarian and not democratic. Since humans are not born with equal abilities, each needs to understand his or her part in life according to each person's strengths and abilities. Some people have the skills to lead and some do not. Those who do know what is in each individual's best interest should be the rulers of the state, and those are the people who know how to use reason

---

7. Denault, "Philosophy: The Athenian Philosophers: Socrates, Plato, and Aristotle," para. 6.

8. Denault, "Philosophy: The Athenian Philosophers: Socrates, Plato, and Aristotle," para. 8.

9. Gaarder, *Sophie's World*, 83.

10. Gaarder, *Sophie's World*, 91.

(which leads to wisdom). Plato's ideas about how best to order the state can be likened to the parent-child relationship.[11]

Plato had a Theory of Forms that asserts that God created a physical world and a spiritual world. The physical world is what we experience with our senses and is constantly changing and not perfect. The spiritual realm is the realm of forms, which is perfect. The physical realm is merely a shadow of what is real—the spiritual realm. The spiritual world is more real than the shadows that exist in the physical realm. So in the physical realm we can experience a brown book, a beautiful flower, and an act of kindness, which are patterned on the forms, but the Form for each of these is brownness, beauty, and kindness.[12] Leigh Denault explains, "Plato's idea of an absolute Form of the Good was close to the Christian Monotheistic God; Neoplatonism in the Christianizing Roman Empire (100–400 CE) revived Plato as an early precursor of Christian doctrine."[13] Also in *The Republic*, Plato provides his famous "Myth of the Cave" that deals with human perceptions. In essence, "Plato likens people untutored in the Theory of Forms to prisoners chained in a cave, unable to turn their heads."[14]

In the fourth century BC, the roles played in society by men and women were determined by their physiology. Women became pregnant and gave birth to children, so their bodies could not sustain the rigors of hard work and combat. Consequently, women did not enter the public level, but stayed back in the private realm of society.[15] They needed to stay in the home and care for the children. Men were propelled into the public arena because they were stronger and did not have the same restraints or responsibilities as women.

Plato attacked the Athenian democracy of his time. He wanted to "overthrow this political system," construct a just city, and correct a system where citizenship, land ownership, and voting considered only men.[16] In the *Republic*, Plato did contend that not all individuals are born with equal abilities, but asserted that "women must be assigned social roles in the ideal state equal to (or approximate) to men."[17] He believed that women had the same ability to reason as men did if they had the same training as men had and if

---

11. Honer et al., *Invitation to* Philosophy, 217.
12. Cummings, "The Theory of Forms by Plato: Definition & Examples," para. 3.
13. Denault, "Philosophy: The Athenian Philosophers: Socrates, Plato, and Aristotle," para. 11.
14. Cohen, "The Allegory of the Cave," line 3.
15. Brisson, "Women in Plato's *Republic*," para. 5.
16. Brisson, "Women in Plato's *Republic*," para. 2.
17. Smith, "Plato and Aristotle on the Nature of Women," line 1.

they did not occupy themselves with childcare and household duties.[18] He firmly believed that women should be educated and that not to do so was cutting society short of its full capabilities.

In the *Republic*, Plato explains that humans have a body and a soul, and we are defined by our soul and the "soul's excellence," not our gender.[19] Not only does the soul take care of our "cognitive and physical movements," but it lives on after the body gives out and can be "punished or rewarded in another world."[20] This means that women should be integrated into society with the ability of becoming a part of the ruling class, becoming a warrior, or whatever their excellence indicates.[21]

Plato believed that raising children was such an important occupation that it should be left to the state.[22] He also believed in the sharing of women and children as one large community rather than as many individual families. Sex is to be viewed as the means of reproduction, and women are not to be viewed "as objects of desire or pleasure."[23]

The above description of how Plato viewed women in the *Republic* runs contrary, in many instances, to his understanding of women as described in the *Laws* (348 BC). A reading of the *Laws* reveals that Plato is sometimes more considerate of women than many others in the time of his writing, but is also more restraining of their abilities than he relays in the *Republic*. For example, in the *Laws*, women are considered citizens, can hold public office, may serve in the military, and can be included in common meals, but cannot own property. Perhaps the view of a woman's "place" in society as described in the *Republic* could be termed as Plato's ideal, and what he describes as male and female roles in the *Laws* is often more amenable to the time in which he lived. Such a difference in his view of women as expressed in the *Laws* makes one wonder if Plato was influenced by the culture of the time when he formulated his philosophy regarding government.

The *Laws* is divided into twelve books and is his last and longest writing. Subject matter ranges from political thought to "psychology, ethics, theology, epistemology, and metaphysics."[24] In Book VI, Plato states that women must be controlled by legislation, and that their nature is inferior to that of men:

---

18. Gaarder, *Sophie's World*, 92.
19. Brisson, "Women in Plato's *Republic*," para. 9.
20. Brisson, "Women in Plato's *Republic*," para. 8.
21. Brisson, "Women in Plato's *Republic*," para. 8–9.
22. Gaarder, *Sophie's World*, 92.
23. Brisson, "Women in Plato's *Republic*," para. 16.
24. Kirby, Jeremy, and Sonya Wurster, eds. "Plato: The Laws," para. 2.

> For with you, Cleinias and Megillus, the common tables of men are, as I said, a heaven-born and admirable institution, but you are mistaken in leaving the women unregulated by law. They have no similar institution of public tables in the light of day, and just that part of the human race which is by nature prone to secrecy and stealth on account of their weakness—I mean the female sex—has been left without regulation by the legislator, which is a great mistake. And, in consequence of this neglect, many things have grown lax among you, which might have been far better, if they had been only regulated by law; for the neglect of regulations about women may not only be regarded as a neglect of half the entire matter, but in proportion as women's nature is inferior to that of men in capacity for virtue, in that degree the consequence of such neglect is more than twice as important.[25]

In Book XII, Plato explains what virtue is: "courage, temperance, wisdom, justice."[26] So it is in these areas of character that Plato views women as inferior to men.

Plato further states:

> For women are accustomed to creep into dark places, and when dragged out into the light they will exert their utmost powers of resistance, and be far too much for the legislator. And therefore, as I said before, in most places they will not endure to have the truth spoken without raising a tremendous outcry, but in this state perhaps they may.[27]

In Book VII, Plato speaks about the necessity of babies nursing, moving as if they were "rocking at sea," and listening to their nurses sweetly singing to them.[28] He further tells the reader that "[T]he Bacchic women are cured of their frenzy in the same manner by the use of the dance and of music."[29] In making further reference concerning music and women, the same book says that the music women experience should be different than a man's, as women must be assigned "their proper melodies and rhythms."[30]

> Now both sexes have melodies and rhythms which of necessity belong to them; and those of women are clearly enough indicated by their natural difference. The grand, and that which tends

---

25. Plato, *Laws*, Book VI.
26. Plato, *Laws*, Book XII.
27. Plato, *Laws*, Book VI.
28. Plato, *Laws*, Book VII.
29. Plato, *Laws*, Book VII.
30. Plato, *Laws*, Book VII.

to courage, may be fairly called manly; but that which inclines to moderation and temperance, may be declared both in law and in ordinary speech to be the more womanly quality. This, then, will be the general order of them.[31]

Also, in the same book, Plato cautions the legislator to "not let the female sex live softly and waste money and have no order of life...."[32] Plato also clearly places women in a hierarchy below men:

> Now better men are the superiors of worse men, and in general elders are the superiors of the young; wherefore also parents are the superiors of their off spring, and men o [sic] women and children, and rulers of their subjects; for all men ought to reverence any one who is in any position of authority, and especially those who are in state offices.[33]

So here we can see the conflict between the *Republic* and the *Laws* as it regards Plato's views on women. In the *Republic*, he seems to want to present women as equal to men even with the understanding that, in general, women are not as strong physically. But in the *Laws*, Plato ultimately provides a hierarchical and more traditional depiction of women, with women holding a position below that of men because of their perceived inferior nature and inferior virtue.

Aristotle (384–322 BC)

Aristotle was born in northern Greece in Stagira. On the Greek island of Lesbos, he performed zoological and marine animal experiments.[34] Aristotle later traveled to Macedon and tutored the young Alexander the Great. When in Athens, he founded the Lyceum.[35]

Aristotle was considered to be the last of the three greatest Greek philosophers and concerned himself with the changes in nature far more than did Plato. Aristotle used both reason and his senses to gain knowledge. He studied nature and is considered to be the first biologist. He concluded that there was increasing sophistication from plants to animals to humans. Aristotle was the supreme organizer who initiated and classified various

---

31. Plato, *Laws*, Book VII.
32. Plato, *Laws*, Book VII.
33. Plato, *Laws*, Book XI.
34. Amadio and Kenny, "Aristotle Greek Philosopher," para. 1–2.
35. Mark, "Aristotle," para. 6.

sciences.[36] He also developed the process of scientific observation and experimentation as well as methods of scholarly research.[37] The science of logic was founded by Aristotle.[38]

For Aristotle, the "form" that exists with the things we experience with our senses is not exactly what Plato viewed as his "form." Aristotle did not believe that there were forms that existed beyond the natural world, but, rather, he believed that forms rested in those individual things we recognize with our senses and are the common characteristics that belonged to those things. For example, a fox has a particular form common to all foxes and is different than the form recognized in an elephant. Plato believed that those things we perceive with our senses exist in perfection in another realm; Aristotle believed that reality exists in what we perceive with our senses.

Aristotle also believed that people have two different purposes: natural purposes and social purposes. A person's natural purpose is *eudaimonia*, which is Greek for "happiness" or "total wellbeing."[39] He believed that all humans naturally work toward experiencing *eudaimonia*, and that a part of *eudaimonia* is not only fulfilling our social roles, but also, because we have the ability to reason, that fulfillment also becomes a part of *eudaimonia*. We are to live our lives in a disciplined way and not in extremes, but through practical wisdom that holds extremes at bay. This is moral virtue, which he explains is a "mean" (the "Golden Mean") between deficiency and excess, both of which are unacceptable. For example, eating enough to nourish the body is a moral virtue, but eating to excess or not eating enough to keep one's body nourished is neither wise nor a virtue. The other wisdom Aristotle addresses is that which comes from paying attention to the world, thinking about our surroundings and what is going on in the world, thus understanding the world. Such understanding is how one achieves total wellbeing or *eudaimonia*.[40]

Aristotle's philosophies as they relate to natural purposes contain principles that strongly influence Roman Catholic moral teaching. In essence, these philosophies are: "[E]verything in nature has a purpose . . . everything in nature has an essential nature . . . everything in nature has its proper good . . . something's natural purpose, its essential nature, and its proper good

---

36. Gaarder, *Sophie's World*, 105–06.

37. Denault, "Philosophy: The Athenian Philosophers: Socrates, Plato, and Aristotle," para. 17.

38. Gaarder, *Sophie's World*, 112.

39. Van Camp et al., *Applying Ethics*, 11.

40. Van Camp et al., *Applying Ethics*, 11.

are all intimately related."[41] In perhaps a too-simple example, the natural purpose of food is to nourish one's body; the essential nature of one's body is that it needs to be fed physically; nourishment is the proper good of food; thus, each of these three points has a relationship to the others.

Aristotle's views concerning the leadership of women were not positive. Not only did Aristotle find a kind of hierarchy or sophistication from plants to animals to humans, but he also saw a similar hierarchy among slaves, women, and men. In *Politics*, Aristotle wrote, "Again, the male is by nature superior, and the female inferior; and the one rules, and the other is ruled; this principle, of necessity, extends to all mankind."[42] He also tells us that the rule a husband has over his wife is different than constitutional or government rule in one respect:

> A husband and father, we saw, rules over wife and children, both free, but the rule differs, the rule over his children being a royal, over his wife a constitutional rule. For although there may be exceptions to the order of nature, the male is by nature fitter for command than the female, just as the elder and full-grown is superior to the younger and more immature. But in most constitutional states the citizens rule and are ruled by turns, for the idea of a constitutional state implies that the natures of the citizens are equal, and do not differ at all. Nevertheless, when one rules and the other is ruled we endeavor to create a difference of outward forms and names and titles of respect. . . . The relation of the male to the female is of this kind, but there the inequality is permanent.[43]

No turns are taken between male and female rule because men and women are not equals. Furthermore, he states, "For the actions of a ruler cannot really be honorable, unless he is as much superior to other men as a husband is to a wife, or a father to his children, or a master to his slaves."[44]

Aristotle also tells us the difference among slaves, women, and children: ". . . the slave has no deliberative faculty at all; the woman has, but it is without authority, and the child has, but it is immature . . . the courage of a man is shown in commanding, of a woman in obeying."[45] Another example of his belief in hierarchy as it pertains to men and women is provided in Book Six of *Politics*, when he provides examples of the "good order" of government:

41. Van Camp et al., *Applying Ethics*, 75.
42. Aristotle, *Politics*, Book One, Part V.
43. Aristotle, *Politics*, Book One, Part VII.
44. Aristotle, *Politics*, Book Seven, Part III.
45. Aristotle, *Politics*, Book One, Part VIII.

"Some of these are clearly not democratic offices; for example, the guardianships of women and children—the poor, not having any slaves, must employ both their women and children as servants."[46]

Aristotle believed that women should remain in their "traditional roles in the home," and also that they should remain subservient to men.[47] His beliefs carried from the household to government rule. He believed "the ideal of monarchy to be paternal rule"[48] as he explains in *Nicomachean Ethics*:

> The association of man and wife seems to be aristocratic; for the man rules in accordance with his worth, and in those matters in which a man should rule, but the matters that befit a woman he hands over to her. If the man rules in everything the relation passes over into oligarchy; for in doing so he is not acting in accordance with their respective worth, and not ruling in virtue of his superiority. Sometimes, however, women rule, because they are heiresses; so their rule is not in virtue of excellence but due to wealth and power, as in oligarchies.[49]

Aristotle believed that the character and nature of men and women are different and explains in *Politics* what he means:

> For a man would be thought a coward if he had no more courage than a courageous woman, and a woman would be thought loquacious if she imposed no more restraint on her conversation than the good man; and indeed their part in the management of the household is different, for the duty of the one is to acquire, and of the other to preserve.[50]

There are traits he believes are good for one to have, but not necessarily the other, for example: "Silence is a woman's glory, but that is not equally the glory of man."[51] Aristotle's delineation of male and female roles runs contrary to the activities of a capable woman as described in Proverbs 31, where we are told that she engages in business (acquiring fields and selling her goods), helps the poor, provides wisdom, teaches, and her presence and good work are recognized not only by her family, but, also throughout her community. Aristotle also states:

---

46. Aristotle, *Politics*, Book Six, Part VIII.
47. Smith, "Plato and Aristotle on the Nature of Women," line 2.
48. Aristotle, *Nicomachean Ethics*, Book VIII, Chapter 10.
49. Aristotle, *Nicomachean Ethics*, Book VIII, Chapter 10.
50. Aristotle, *Politics*, Book Three, Part IV.
51. Aristotle, *Politics*, Book One, Part VIII.

> [P]eople of a manly nature guard against making their friends grieve with them, and, unless he be exceptionally insensible to pain, such a man cannot stand the pain that ensues for his friends, and in general does not admit fellow-mourners because he is not himself given to mourning; but women and womanly men enjoy sympathisers in their grief, and love them as friends and companions in sorrow. But in all things one obviously ought to imitate the better type of person.[52]

In reading Aristotle's *The History of Animals*, even more differences between men and women surface:

> The fact is, the nature of man is the most rounded off and complete, and consequently in man the qualities or capacities above referred to are found in their perfection. Hence woman is more compassionate than man, more easily moved to tears, at the same time is more jealous, more querulous, more apt to scold and to strike. She is, furthermore, more prone to despondency and less hopeful than the man, more void of shame or self-respect, more false of speech, more deceptive, and of more retentive memory. She is also more wakeful, more shrinking, more difficult to rouse to action, and requires a smaller quantity of nutriment.[53]

> As was previously stated, the male is more courageous than the female, and more sympathetic in the say of standing by to help. Even in the case of molluscs, when the cuttle-fish is struck with the trident the male stands by to help the female; but when the male is struck the female runs away.[54]

Within Aristotle's philosophical reality, women have a "natural deficiency" and are inferior:

> For females are weaker and colder in nature, and we must look upon the female character as being a sort of natural deficiency. Accordingly while it is within the mother it develops slowly because of its coldness (for development is concoction, and it is heat that concocts, and what is hotter is easily concocted); but after birth it quickly arrives at maturity and old age on account of its weakness, for all inferior things come sooner to their perfection or end, and as this is true of works of art so it is of what is formed by Nature.[55]

---

52. Aristotle, *Nicomachean Ethics*, Book IX, Chapter 11.
53. Aristotle, *The History of Animals*, Book IX, Part 1.
54. Aristotle, *The History of Animals*, Book IX, Part 1.
55. Aristotle, *On the Generation of Animals*, Book IV, Part 6.

Aristotle believed that male semen provided all the characteristics of a resulting child, while the woman's role was providing the environment in which this new life could develop: "For . . . the male and female principles may be put down first and foremost as origins of generation, the former as containing the efficient cause of generation, the latter the material of it."[56] Furthermore,

> Now since this is what corresponds in the female to the semen in the male, and since it is not possible that two such discharges should be found together, it is plain that the female does not contribute semen to the generation of the offspring. For if she had semen she would not have the catamenia [menses]; but, as it is, because she has the latter she has not the former.[57]

One could say he viewed women as incomplete or unfinished men with the natural purpose of reproduction.

> For there must needs be that which generates and that from which it generates; even if these be one, still they must be distinct in form and their essence must be different; and in those animals that have these powers separate in two sexes the body and nature of the active and the passive sex must also differ. If, then, the male stands for the effective and active, and the female, considered as female, for the passive, it follows that what the female would contribute to the semen of the male would not be semen but material for the semen to work upon. This is just what we find to be the case, for the catamenia have in their nature an affinity to the primitive matter.[58]

Gaarder summarizes Aristotle's philosophy of human generation this way:

> In reproduction, woman is passive and receptive whilst man is active and productive; for the child inherits only the male characteristics. . . . He believed that all the child's characteristics lay complete in the male sperm. The woman was the soil, receiving and bringing forth the seed, whilst the man was the "sower."[59]

But Aristotle digs even deeper by saying that the material that becomes male is superior in divinity than that which becomes female:

---

56. Aristotle, *On the Generation of Animals*, Book I, Part 2.
57. Aristotle, *On the Generation of Animals*, Book I, Part 19.
58. Aristotle, *On the Generation of Animals*, Book I, Part 20.
59. Gaarder, *Sophie's World*, 115.

> For the first principle of the movement, or efficient cause, whereby that which comes into being is male, is better and more divine than the material whereby it is female. The male, however, comes together and mingles with the female for the work of generation, because this is common to both.[60]

He views the semen as containing that which is necessary for the soul: "For the female is, as it were, a mutilated male, and the catamenia are semen, only not pure; for there is only one thing they have not in them, the principle of the soul."[61] For "[I]t is the soul that is from the male, for the soul is the reality of a particular body."[62]

Aristotle puts the diminishing importance of a woman's contribution yet another way:

> Now a boy is like a woman in form, and the woman is as it were an impotent male, for it is through a certain incapacity that the female is female, being incapable of concocting the nutriment in its last stage into semen (and this is either blood or that which is analogous to it in animals which are bloodless owing to the coldness of their nature).[63]

> To recapitulate, we say that the semen, which is the foundation of the embryo, is the ultimate secretion of the nutriment. By ultimate I mean that which is carried to every part of the body, and this is also the reason why the offspring is like the parent. For it makes no difference whether we say that the semen comes from all the parts or goes to all of them, but the latter is the better. But the semen of the male differs from the corresponding secretion of the female in that it contains a principle within itself of such a kind as to set up movements also in the embryo and to concoct thoroughly the ultimate nourishment, whereas the secretion of the female contains material alone.[64]

And it is this material that the female contributes and that the semen works upon.

---

60. Aristotle, *On the Generation of Animals*, Book II, Part 1.
61. Aristotle, *On the Generation of Animals*, Book II, Part 3.
62. Aristotle, *On the Generation of Animals*, Book II, Part 4.
63. Aristotle, *On the Generation of Animals*, Book I, Part 20.
64. Aristotle, *On the Generation of Animals*, Book IV, Part 1.

Impact of the Ancient through the Middle Ages

The ancient philosophers still had influence through the Middle Ages, even within Christianity. In examining modern-day patriarchy, we begin to understand the intellectual pathway the ancient philosophers' ideas took through time.

Although Athens lost its control after Aristotle died (322 BC), Alexander the Great (356–323 BC), through his many conquests, managed to connect civilizations that ran from Egypt to Asia and India to Greek civilization.[65] During this time period, Greek culture played a leading role. The thread of Greek philosophy followed into the Middle Ages.

Rome's military and political dominance was the reason for the inception of the Roman period, and this dominance took over Hellenistic culture.[66] Latin was mainly spoken from Spain into Asia.[67] Nonetheless, there is a good reason why the influence of Greek culture and philosophy still persisted. Just as we experience globalism today, so did those in this area of the world during this early time. Borders between countries and cultures lifted, leaving a meshing of religious, philosophical, and scientific beliefs, when, before the amalgamation of cultures, each area had its own religion and philosophical ideas. Now, a single, unique culture evolved and long-held beliefs were questioned. Also, during this time of melding cultures, people searched for the meaning of life and the best way to live.

The Middle Ages existed between the fifth to fifteenth centuries AD, from the fall of the Roman Empire to the Renaissance (roughly 1350–1550). The Medieval Era is sometimes called the Dark Ages because of the "political, economic and social set back" of the time and also a lack of information compared with other time periods.[68] Providing education and all that belongs to a life of faith became the responsibility of monasteries. There were convent schools, cathedral schools, and, around 1200, the first universities were founded. At the same time, not all the Greek philosophers were forgotten.

The "old" Roman Empire became three different, distinct cultures: In the West, a Christian culture with its capital in Rome; in the East, Greek Christian culture had Constantinople as the capital; and an Arabic-speaking

---

65. Gaarder, *Sophie's World*, 126.
66. Simonin, "Hellenistic Period," para. 1, 3.
67. Gaarder, *Sophie's World*, 126.
68. Newman, "The Dark Ages," para. 1.

Muslim culture developed in North Africa and the Middle East, and later, Spain was joined to them.[69]

During the Middle Ages, the Roman Church had great power and dominated people's lives through its own laws, lands, and taxes.[70] At the same time, the Arabs carried Aristotelian philosophy through the Middle Ages while the church tried to maintain strict adherence to what it believed the Bible taught, well seasoned with Neoplatonism. Toward the end of the 1100s, Arab scholars landed in northern Italy.[71] Aristotle's writings were translated into Latin and passed along to the people of this region, bringing increased interest in the sciences. In the midst of this consideration, questions arose concerning the relationship, if any, of Christianity to Greek philosophy. Aristotle had proven himself brilliant as matters pertained to the natural sciences, but was this also true of his philosophical thought?

The Ancients' Influence on Early Christian Philosophers

St. Augustine (AD 354–430)

St. Augustine, born in North Africa, lived in the early Middle Ages, in Tagaste (now in Algeria). He studied in Carthage and traveled to Rome and Milan, spending the last years of his life in Hippo, west of Carthage.[72] He was not a Christian all his life, but, in formulating his beliefs, he examined different religions as well as philosophies before becoming a Christian, and eventually became influenced by Manicheanism, a sect with a doctrine that included both religion and philosophy.[73] Manicheanism became more appealing to Augustine because it rejects the Old Testament, which Augustine did also.[74]

Augustine found himself unimpressed with the sect's leaders and their inability to think, so he left.[75] He concerned himself with the "problem of evil" and questioned the Manichaean ideas of dualism, or "good and evil, light and darkness, spirit and matter."[76] Augustine then became acquainted with the Bible and the Christian faith and developed a new understanding.

---

69. Gaarder, *Sophie's World*, 170.
70. Alchin, "Middle Ages Religion," para. 3, 5.
71. Gaarder, *Sophie's World*, 177.
72. Kiefer, "Augustine of Hippo, Bishop and Theologian," para. 1, 2, 5, 24.
73. Kiefer, "Augustine of Hippo, Bishop and Theologian," para. 4.
74. Brown, "The 'Woman' of Augustine of Hippo," para. 9.
75. Kiefer, "Augustine of Hippo, Bishop and Theologian," para. 4.
76. Gaarder, *Sophie's World*, 172.

Influence of Plato and Aristotle's Patriarchy   99

During the time of Augustine, culture accepted men having concubines. Augustine had one at the age of seventeen, and had a child as well.[77] The church also found having a concubine acceptable as long as a man was faithful to her, until he sent the concubine away when he became engaged to be married, because he had to remain monogamous.[78]

Augustine then leaned toward Neoplatonism and the idea that only God is fully real and everything outside of God is degraded.[79] Neoplatonism is a present-day term used to describe the dominant philosophical school of thought from the middle of the third century to the middle of the seventh century in the Greco-Roman world. It provided an understanding of the universe and the human's place in it, based on Plato's views.[80] St. Augustine infused Christian doctrine with Neoplatonism. Consequently, there was no clean break from Greek philosophy as society entered the Christian Middle Ages.

Augustine's overall view of women meshed with his support of Plato's Theory of Forms. Drawing more on Plato's *Laws*, than on his *Republic*, Augustine, in his effort to Christianize Plato, viewed the City of God as "the eternal order which transcends and yet pervades the City of Man [i.e., humanity], the temporal order of human society and government."[81] To substantiate his views about women, he used Ephesians 5:22–23, "Wives, be subject to your husbands as you are to the Lord. For the husband is the head of the wife just as Christ is the head of the church, the body of which he is the Savior." Augustine compared man to the City of God, but the status of woman he lowered to the City of Man.[82] The City of God he viewed as higher, more transcendent, and more spiritual, as well as eternal. David Withun views Augustine's ideas on women as a mix of "Platonism, Ancient Jewish thought, early Christian belief, and his own ideas."[83]

How can Christianity and Plato's philosophies meet in unity? Many scholars believe that St. Augustine saw no difference between Plato's philosophy and Christianity. For example, St. Augustine saw Plato's concept of eternal ideas as how God viewed his creation: the perfection that exists in the Theory of Forms (or Realm of Ideas/Ideals) is more real than what we

---

77. Brown, "The 'Woman' of Augustine of Hippo," para. 6.
78. Brown, "The 'Woman' of Augustine of Hippo," para. 6. As found in Chadwick, "The Early Church," 216.
79. Kiefer, "Augustine of Hippo, Bishop and Theologian," para. 9.
80. Wildberg, "Neoplatonism." para 1.
81. Withun, "Christianity, Ethics, and Ecology," para. 1.
82. Withun, "Christianity, Ethics, and Ecology," para. 2.
83. Withun, "Christianity, Ethics, and Ecology," para. 2.

are able to sense in the physical world, and Augustine added that God is the source of these forms.[84] The physical world is incomplete or imperfect. The spiritual world, or Realm of Ideas, is perfect. Individuals, he believed, are spiritual beings with a material or physical body that deteriorates.

Augustine recognized that there is a division between God and the world. He also agreed with Plato when considering good and evil: that evil is the absence of God. St. Augustine believed that good comes from doing God's work and evil occurs when we remove ourselves from God's work or when we are rebellious.[85] Humanity was lost after the fall, so no person deserves redemption, but God has made a way of salvation. St. Augustine believed that God preordains who will be saved and who will not.[86] This is all explained in St. Augustine's *City of God*, where he describes the struggle for supremacy between God and the world.

For women, only in the union with her husband does she bear the image of God.[87] Therefore, women are not intended or equipped by God to lead.

St. Thomas of Aquinas (AD 1224/5–1274)

St. Thomas of Aquinas was from Roccasecca, Italy, taught at the University of Paris,[88] and was also a theologian and a philosopher. Aristotle greatly influenced his theology. St. Thomas is responsible for incorporating many of Aristotle's ideas into church doctrine; thus, many of Aristotle's philosophies were injected into Christian theology. Many view this process as St. Thomas christianizing Aristotle as St. Augustine christianized Plato, and believe this was done to make these philosophers no longer a threat to Christian teachings.[89]

St. Thomas believed that reason shows us what Christianity teaches. Reason and Christian teachings are compatible. He believed that there is no conflict between reason or the senses and Christianity or faith. Consequently, God can be revealed in both reason and the Bible, providing us with a "theology of faith" and a "natural theology."[90] St. Thomas believed that there is really only one truth, "so when Aristotle shows us something our reason tells us is

---

84. Robinson, "Platonic Influence on St. Augustine's Philosophy," para. 2.
85. Koukl, "Augustine on Evil," para. 16.
86. Samples, "Augustine's View of Predestination: St. Augustine, Part 9," para. 3.
87. Withun, "Christianity, Ethics, and Ecology," para. 3.
88. Brown, "Thomas Aquinas (1224/6–1274)," para. 4, 8–11.
89. Gaarder, *Sophie's World*, 177.
90. Gaarder, *Sophie's World*, 179.

true, it is not in conflict with Christian teaching."[91] Furthermore, he believed that Aristotle's philosophies proved the existence of God.[92]

Aristotle viewed the progression of living things as hierarchical. While God holds the highest position in this progression, plants hold the least of all stations. After plants were animals; after animals, humans. St. Thomas built upon this hierarchical idea, adding that angels come after humans, and, finally, God appears at the very top. While humans have intelligence and the power of reason that place them above animals, angels, who are also God's creation, have no need to think or reason toward conclusions and also have no body, so they cannot die.[93]

St. Thomas used "natural law," a concept provided by Aristotle, as the basis for ethical reasoning, still used today by people of faith and many others.[94] Natural law, or Aristotle's belief that everything in nature has a purpose, has influenced the Roman Catholic Church. For example, with regard to sex, because human reproduction is the natural purpose of sex, any artificial means to prevent pregnancy (e.g., condoms, birth control pills) is seen as immoral, since it is unnatural. The essential nature of humans is to experience the love that comes from being a parent. The Catholic Church encourages the use of a natural method of preventing or planning a pregnancy: the rhythm method, in which the menstrual cycle is tracked over a period of time to determine when ovulation occurs.

Aristotle also influenced St. Thomas's view about women. Thomas said that woman is "an 'imperfect man' and an 'incidental' being."[95] At the same time, he believed that a woman's soul carried as much value as a man's, and that there are no physical gender differences in heaven,[96] revealing St. Thomas did not subscribe to every idea Aristotle had about women.

Thomas's views on women are included in his *Summa Theologiae*, and much can be credited to Aristotle. In this work, Thomas considers whether the woman should have been part of the original creation, since, after all, she is a clear imperfection.[97] St. Thomas believed that, because women are necessary for the continuation of humanity, and this is a woman's inherent value, she should have been created, but, at the same time, he agrees with Aristotle

---

91. Gaarder, *Sophie's World*, 179.
92. Gaarder, *Sophie's World*, 179.
93. Gaarder, *Sophie's World*, 181.
94. Van Camp et al., *Applying Ethics*, 84.
95. Honer et al., *Invitation to Philosophy*, 107.
96. Gaarder, *Sophie's World*, 182.
97. James, "Thomas Aquinas on Women," para. 2.

that a "woman is naturally subject to man."[98] As a result, Thomas believed that women are to be subject to men, as this "subjection existed even before sin."[99] He asserted that this submission is not the result of sin, but, rather, the result of the order of creation. Women's subordination is for their own good, as it is necessary for proper family order.[100] After all, men are wiser than women, being made superior in "intellect and reason," and the ones who are wise must govern those who are not.[101] In God's creation of women, God did not make a mistake, as God does not make mistakes, but his creation of the woman was necessary to enable humanity to reproduce.[102]

St. Thomas reasons that "there is no justice or injustice absolutely speaking toward a slave or a son," as the slave belongs to the man and a child contains a part of the father.[103] The relationship between a woman and her husband, however, is more equitable, because her husband does not own her and she is not a part of her husband. In his *Supplement* to the *Summa Theologiae*, Thomas writes that the subservience of the woman is not that of a servant, even though she is in subjection to her husband. The marriage relationship is a permanent one between equals with the consent of both required for the marriage to occur, so marriage does not exist as the result of a man's procurement. In *Summa Contra Gentiles*, St. Thomas teaches that neither husband nor wife can break the bond of marriage. Each owes fidelity to the other because they are equal,[104] since woman came from man's side, but this does not change the necessity of women being subservient to men.[105]

So St. Thomas held these two ideas in tension: that women are equal to men, but also that women are inferior to men. He believed that women and men are both made in the image of God, but with a qualification:

> The image of God, in its principal signification, namely the intellectual nature, is found both in man and in women. Hence after the words, To the image of God He created him, it is added, Male and female He created them.... Moreover it is said "them," in the plural, as Augustine ... remarks, lest it should be thought that both sexes were united in one individual. But in a secondary sense the image of God is found in man, and not in woman,

---

98. James, "Thomas Aquinas on Women," para. 3.
99. James, "Thomas Aquinas on Women," para. 6.
100. James, "Thomas Aquinas on Women," para. 6.
101. James, "Thomas Aquinas on Women," para. 7.
102. James, "Thomas Aquinas on Women," para. 3.
103. Popik. "The Philosophy of Woman of St. Thomas Aquinas," Part Two, 5.
104. Popik. "The Philosophy of Woman of St. Thomas Aquinas," Part Two, 5, 6.
105. Magee, "Thomistic Philosophy," para. 9.

for man is the beginning and end of woman, just as God is the beginning and end of every creature. So when the Apostle had said that man is the image and glory of God but woman is the glory of man, he adds his reason for saying this: For man is not of woman, but woman of man; and man [is] not created for woman, but woman for man.[106]

St. Thomas recognized that men and women are both members of the same species, and they both have the ability to arrive at the same supernatural end, as both are "saved by the grace of Christ, before which there is no distinction between male and female."[107] Yet, he believed women to be inferior, as man came first and woman came from man; men have a God-given higher reasoning and, therefore, are more attuned to eternal things, making them wiser. Women pay attention more to temporal matters. (Mary, mother of Jesus, is one of some exceptions.) Nature tends to produce males, making women a God-planned mistake of nature.

St. Thomas tells us in *Summa Theologica*:

> Vis-à-vis [being caused by] the *natura particularis* [i.e., the action of the male semen], a female is deficient and unintentionally caused. For the active power of the semen always seeks to produce a thing completely like itself, something male. So if a female is produced, this must be because the semen is weak or because the material [provided by the female parent] is unsuitable, or because of the action of some external factor such as the winds from the south which make the atmosphere humid.[108]

St. Thomas continues, clarifying:

> But vis-à-vis [being caused by] *natura universalis* [general Nature] the female is not accidentally caused but is intended by Nature for the work of generation. Now the intentions of Nature come from God, who is its author. This is why, when he created Nature, he made not only the male but also the female.[109]

Christ was male, so femininity is inferior and passive, while males are superior and active. Women cannot generate the necessary seed for procreation, making males the primary contributor to generation. Women are

---

106. St. Thomas, *Summa Theologica*, Volume I.

107. Popik, "The Philosophy of Woman of St. Thomas Aquinas," part one, 3.

108. St. Thomas of Aquinas. *Summa Theologica (On how a woman is born to be a woman)*, para. 2–4.

109. St. Thomas of Aquinas. *Summa Theologica (On how a woman is born to be a woman)*, para. 2–4.

weaker physically (and therefore their souls are weaker) and in "temperament and constitution."[110]

So, once again, St. Thomas holds two contradictory concepts in tension. First, he believes that imperfect sperm will create a woman, but at the same time, he believes that God intended for women to be formed, even though the material a woman provides is not perfect, because they are needed for procreation.

St. Thomas believed that, as with society, the family needs a ruler. Just as living in societies helps provide the necessities of life, family life also provides the basics of life: food, a place to live, basic education, etc. Men rule the society and the family because they are naturally superior to women in "wisdom, virtue, reason, strength, and nobility" and, therefore, are natural leaders.[111] Men direct household tasks and women must submit to them. Thomas believed that St. Paul's direction to Timothy, that women must be subject and silent (1 Tim 2:12), was given because Eve was the one originally seduced and caused Adam's downfall.[112]

St. Thomas also refers to Ephesians 5:22, where Paul writes that women are to be subject to their husbands as to the Lord. Thus, Thomas viewed women as morally inferior and easily swayed toward "deception and temptation."[113] Consequently, a woman's safest course of action is to obey her husband even against her own will, as this benefits her in her weakness. St. Thomas does recognize that, in the midst of all men's superiority in the home, they are to "love their wives as they love their own bodies, and as Christ loves the Church" (Eph 5:10). Loving one's wife should be a natural attachment, since woman was made from man.[114]

The husband is to provide order, correction, wisdom, instruction, and physical necessities for the home, wife, and children, so he is the one who engages in business outside the home to make those provisions. The wife takes care of the needs as directed by the husband, so wives are necessary to preserve the household environment.[115]

If her husband approves, a wife may earn money and own and dispose of her own property, and spend or give common household money on her own without "impoverishing her husband."[116] A wife can also

---

110. Popik. "The Philosophy of Woman of St. Thomas Aquinas," part one, 3.
111. Popik, "The Philosophy of Woman of St. Thomas Aquinas," part one, 3.
112. Popik, "The Philosophy of Woman of St. Thomas Aquinas," part two, 3.
113. Popik, "The Philosophy of Woman of St. Thomas Aquinas," part two, 3.
114. Popik, "The Philosophy of Woman of St. Thomas Aquinas," part two, 3, 6, 7.
115. Popik, "The Philosophy of Woman of St. Thomas Aquinas," part two, 7.
116. Popik, "The Philosophy of Woman of St. Thomas Aquinas," part two, 8.

proclaim a certain faith, convert, and be baptized, which runs contrary to Proverbs 31.[117]

Aristotle believed that men are better at leading, which meant that women were not to participate in certain areas of life, such as politics.[118] St. Thomas agreed. Women have no public role and must refrain from "civic activities, from warfare, and even from being lawyers . . ." as both disputing and teaching in public are considered "shameful."[119] Women are not able to reason sufficiently; Aristotle believed that reason is necessary to engage in public life and women are unable to do so adequately. Understanding Aristotle in this regard, St. Thomas viewed a woman as a citizen, but not one who can rule—one who must simply follow the law.[120]

Women are allowed to teach in the home, but not publicly, including preaching and teaching in the church. While women may receive prophecy and other gifts as well as men, they may never receive Holy Orders, because they are inferior and need to be ruled over. In general, one must not risk women assuming power. One exception is in the monastery where women may have power to teach or correct women under them, as having men in a female monastery could be compromising.[121] Today, in some Protestant churches, as well as the Roman Catholic Church, women still are not allowed to be pastors or priests.

St. Thomas permitted women to be full members of the church and to receive all the sacraments (except for Holy Orders). They could baptize in an emergency, meaning that there is no man present who can perform the baptism. A female must always be subject to someone (unless she is a harlot) because men are superior; she must be subject either to her father or her husband, not men in general.[122]

We can see that Aristotle influenced St. Thomas's ideas about women. St. Thomas was not only a "product of his times," but also "a casualty of his devotion to the pagan Aristotle."[123] Pagan philosophy, not Scripture, determined a woman's value and place in the medieval era. The overarching view Thomas took of women is not biblical, and many scholars believe that the scriptural passages he used to describe a woman's weakness or inferiority are employed to back up his already-formed opinions that are based on

---

117. Popik, "The Philosophy of Woman of St. Thomas Aquinas," part two, 8.
118. Clayton, "Aristotle: Politics," para. 52–53.
119. Popik, "The Philosophy of Woman of St. Thomas Aquinas," part two, 10.
120. Popik, "The Philosophy of Woman of St. Thomas Aquinas," part two, 10.
121. Popik, "The Philosophy of Woman of St. Thomas Aquinas," part two, 7, 10, 11.
122. Popik, "The Philosophy of Woman of St. Thomas Aquinas," part two, 11.
123. James, "Thomas Aquinas on Women," para. 8.

Aristotle's ideas, and not the result of properly understanding, or rightly dividing, God's word.[124]

St. Thomas provided an essential influence that helped transport Aristotle through the Middle Ages and onward:

> [Aristotle] was the author of a philosophical and scientific system that became the framework and vehicle for both Christian Scholasticism and medieval Islamic philosophy. Even after the intellectual revolutions of the Renaissance, the Reformation, and the Enlightenment, Aristotelian concepts remained embedded in Western thinking.[125]

Conclusion

The ideas about women that came from ancient philosophers and the early church still exist today. We viewed philosophy and the resulting theology as they moved through time and geography to see how two ancient philosophers significantly contributed to a view of women that propelled itself through the Middle Ages to today. These ideas have not only affected the secular view of women, but also the view the church too often believes and teaches about women.

In the *Republic*, Plato had generous views of women for his time, but then his assertions in the *Laws* ran contrary to his more positive view in the *Republic*. The *Laws* contained unfavorable views of women, a view that fit more with the culture he lived in at the time. Aristotle's view of women as defective,[126] incomplete, and as unfinished men, along with the many other deprecating assertions regarding women, carried through alongside Plato's ideas to the present day, affecting philosophy, theology, culture, and, consequently, family life.

St. Augustine was strongly influenced by Plato, and St. Thomas used Aristotle's philosophies as the framework for his own theological beliefs. Plato's and Aristotle's ideas about women have been filtered through the thought of St. Augustine and St. Thomas, with both early church theologians subscribing to many of the philosophers' ideas about women. Therefore, St. Augustine's christianization of Plato along with St. Thomas's christianization of Aristotle carried through the Middle Ages to the present day with the resulting erroneous theology of women. Injecting the ancient philosophers into the understanding of Scripture helped keep

---

124. Popik, "The Philosophy of Woman of St. Thomas Aquinas," part two, 12.
125. Amadio and Kenny, "Aristotle: Greek Philosopher," para. 1.
126. Honer et al., *Invitation to Philosophy*, 107.

Christianity alive during the Middle Ages when the philosophies of Plato and Aristotle were very influential.

While St. Augustine and St. Thomas are deemed as experts by some, and may be theologically correct in many of their assertions, believing they are correct in *all* of their theological assessments is problematic, especially where these assessments pertain to women. All humans are fallible, so the scriptural understandings of scholars of theology, well-known Christian leaders, and saints of old are always subject to careful review. A responsible scholar welcomes such an examination.

Sadly, Platonic and Aristotelian pagan influences upon the interpretation of Hebrew and Christian Scripture continue to color the way Bible texts are interpreted. Some contemporary Christian teachers and writers adhere to these ideas and their resulting interpretations of Scripture that agree with many of Plato and Aristotle's ideas about women, continuing to pass these views along.

The Danvers Statement on Biblical Manhood and Womanhood supports such a view of Scripture. It was formulated by the Council on Biblical Manhood and Womanhood (CBMW) in Danvers, Massachusetts, in 1987 and published in Wheaton, Illinois, in 1988.[127] The statement was written by some evangelical leaders to present their core beliefs relating to the biblical responsibilities of men and women in the church, including the limitations of women. The document encapsulates the overarching beliefs of those who follow Plato's and Aristotle's patriarchal views as they have influenced the interpretation of Scripture and remain in the church today.

The Danvers Statement is divided into two parts: rationale and affirmation. The rationale section makes many points resonate with Plato and Aristotle and oppose sound theology. The third point, a reason for drafting the document, cites "The increasing promotion given to feminist egalitarianism with accompanying distortions or neglect of the glad harmony portrayed in Scripture between the loving, humble leadership of redeemed husbands and the intelligent, willing support of that leadership by redeemed wives."[128] The assertion that a husband is his wife's leader and the separation of responsibilities echoes the statement in Plato's *Laws* that women must be controlled by legislation because their nature is inferior to that of men. We are reminded that Plato places women in a hierarchy below men. Likewise, Aristotle states that a husband must rule over the wife because the man is superior to the woman. Furthermore, he tells us in *Politics* that, through subservience, a woman's courage is revealed through obeying her husband. He also views a

---

127. CBMW, "Danvers Statement," 1.
128. CBMW, "Danvers Statement," 1.

woman's courage as lacking compared to a man's. Aristotle's *On the Generation of Animals* tells us that women are by nature substandard.

Point 4 in the Danvers rationale provides another reason for the document: "The widespread ambivalence regarding the values of motherhood, vocational homemaking, and the many ministries historically performed by women."[129] The word "historically" tells us that the framers of this statement refer to those roles that are a matter of tradition rather than an understanding of exercising God-given gifts formed by good theology. Philosophies from Plato and Aristotle, passed through St. Augustine and St. Thomas, provide an errant pagan tradition that influences our theology today. Aristotle also referred to the importance of letting tradition inform male and female duties.

Point 8 shows CBMW's concern for "hermeneutical oddities devised to reinterpret apparently plain meanings of Biblical texts."[130] The questions here are: Are so-called "plain meanings" filtered through pagan philosophers rather than responsible scholarship? In viewing the Scriptures in Hebrew and Greek, is the English translation being automatically influenced by the patriarchal interpretation, such as in Ephesians 5? Is objectivity and good scholarship being nudged aside to make room for the patriarchal slant?

Point 10 expresses concern for the "accommodation of some within the church to the spirit of the age at the expense of winsome, radical Biblical authenticity which in the power of the Holy Spirit may reform rather than reflect our ailing culture."[131] In this techno-culture, "the spirit of the age" is an Aristotelian spirit that remains to influence how we view theology and life in general. If there exists, in this age, an objection to the patriarchy that the Danvers Statement promotes, it is one in which women (and also men) are rebelling against the Platonic and Aristotelian pagan philosophies.

The Danvers Statement's second section, Affirmations, contains more examples of Platonic and Aristotelian influence on their theology. Point 2 of the affirmations states: "Distinctions in masculine and feminine roles are ordained by God as part of the created order, and should find an echo in every human heart."[132] Why should pagan philosophy "echo in every human heart"? This view comes from St. Thomas as he was influenced by Aristotle.

The third point tells us: "Adam's headship in marriage was established by God before the Fall, and was not a result of sin."[133] We might

---

129. CBMW, "Danvers Statement," 1.
130. CBMW, "Danvers Statement," 1.
131. CBMW, "Danvers Statement," 1.
132. CBMW, "Danvers Statement," 2.
133. CBMW, "Danvers Statement," 2.

remember that God gave both the man and the woman dominion over creation. The Scriptures cited to bolster the affirmations do not prove that Adam's headship was given to him before the fall (Gen 2:16–18, 21–24; 3:1–13; 1 Cor 11:7–9).

In point 4, the wife is exhorted to submit to her husband while the husband engages in "headship" over her. We too often forget that Ephesians 5 describes the Christian household as one where we must "be subject to one another out of reverence for Christ" (Eph 5:21 NRSV). Also, within the same Danvers Statement, women are told to adhere to "the use of their gifts in appropriate ministries." Here again, the word "appropriate" tells us that women have limitations as previously placed on them by Plato and Aristotle.

Point 4 also speaks of the necessity of a husband using "humble headship." In Gen 3:16, we are told that, as the result of the fall, the man will lord over the woman. As the result of the fall, or sin, we have male headship. But the redemption we receive in Christ takes us beyond the curse. Point 6 tells us that "redemption in Christ aims at removing the distortions introduced by the curse."[134] Wives are to engage in "joyful submission to their husbands' leadership."[135] This presentation is contradictory. Removing distortions resulting from the fall and curse means women should experience mutual submission with their husbands; husbands are no longer to lord over their wives. This is true also of the statement's assertion that there are ministerial restrictions for women in the church. We again see Platonic and Aristotelian imbalance. Contemporary Christian consciousness needs to be injected with the reality that there is equality in Christ.

In point 9, we read, "no man or woman who feels a passion from God to make His grace known in word and deed need ever live without a fulfilling ministry for the glory of Christ and the good of this fallen world." Again, this is a good statement, but, of course, it comes with limitations on women and their ability to serve in a calling given by God. The question here is: Who approves of the ministry? Does God, through his word, or does complementarian theology, which is influenced by Platonic and Aristotelian philosophy, inform this question?

Overall, the influence of Plato and Aristotle, through the advancement of St. Augustine and St. Thomas, has influenced some of our theology and is strikingly present in the Danvers Statement. God has given each of us gifts that need to be nurtured and used in his service for his glory. Complementarianism stifles and negates a woman's God-given gifts, which hinders the advancement of the church.

---

134. CBMW, "Danvers Statement," 2.
135. CBMW, "Danvers Statement," 2.

The Danvers document cautions against a man's "harsh or selfish leadership," and women are cautioned against resisting their husbands' authority and not submitting to spousal leadership.[136] Plato, in Book VI of the *Laws*, tells us that women need to be regulated by legislation because of their inferior nature. CBMW agrees that both men and women are equally able to share in the blessings of salvation, but warns that "denial or neglect" of the principles in the document will "lead to increasingly destructive consequences in our families, our churches, and the culture at large."[137] However, even though the Danvers rationale is not in agreement with "the upsurge of physical and emotional abuse in the family,"[138] it is the complementarian understanding of Scriptures that exacerbates domestic violence in Christian homes where that propensity exists. The following information is from a paper written for a New South Wales Presbyterian Church training day that was a response to domestic violence (DV):

> The connection between complementarianism and DV has received plenty of attention over the last few years. It is important that complementarian churches recognize the risk that the position can be misused, and do all they can to guard against that. The biblical teaching on submission does not give a husband any right to abuse his family members.[139]

Since one of the concerns of the CBMW is the increase of abuse in the home, let us take a look at what the church does to encourage and perpetuate domestic violence. Within the complementarian view, a woman cannot assume a leadership role and must submit to her husband (she is "lesser than"). A woman is also told that she is the reason for the downfall of humankind (which is shaming), and is told that she must keep silent and not teach men (making her ideas, understanding, and/or intelligence insignificant). All of this sounds startlingly like the writings of Plato and Aristotle. These are the very ideas abusive men convey to the women and children they abuse: they are unworthy and less important; shameful; insignificant; and even stupid. The more these ideas take root in the women and children in domestic violence families, the more control a man has over them. The patriarchal understanding of Scripture is erroneous but also dangerous, as women are viewed as inferior and therefore must be ruled over. Attempting

---

136. CBMW, "Danvers Statement," 2.
137. CBMW, "Danvers Statement," 2.
138. CBMW, "Danvers Statement," 1.
139. McClean, "Domestic and Family Violence – Biblical and Theological Resources," para. 18.

to control his victim is the foundational reason a man engages in domestic violence. Complementarianism controls rather than sets free.

How much headship is enough headship? For example, is a woman allowed to teach in seminary where there are men? Host a neighborhood Bible study? Engage in employment where she supervises men? One must ask the person who has headship. He will make those determinations. Will one man's answer remain consistent among all men who are "heads" of women?

Domestic violence specialists witness many different responses from church leadership when they are confronted with a DV situation. Pastors too often put the pressure on women (not men) to put a stop to the abuse they are experiencing; consequently, women (and children) continue to experience the abuse. Pastors will often put the blame on women, saying they need to be more submissive, affirming that doing so will help encourage their husband toward less abusive behavior. In truth, acquiescing often serves to increase abusive behaviors. When a woman's ability to submit becomes a measure for her relationship with Christ, she becomes a failure and takes the responsibility for the abuse. Consider the following from an article written for *Priscilla Papers* by Steven Tracy, whose experience includes professorial duties in theology and ethics, as well as serving on Arizona's Governor's Commission for the Prevention of Violence against Women:

> Some pastors simply emphasize that abused wives should stay and trust God.... Other clergy imply or assert that the submission mandate essentially strips wives, apparently even abused wives, of their personal rights, but not of their responsibility to submit.... [I]t is common for pastors to tell abused wives that they must be more submissive.... Sadly, submission does not stop abuse.... In fact, it often serves to intensify the abuse....[140]

When women who have children do not leave their domestic violence situations, children are put at very high risk. Considerably more than half of the men who abuse their wives will hurt their children. Understand that children are abused when they experience the abuse of their mother. Children who witness domestic violence have higher rates of suicide and drug and alcohol usage as well as other mental illness challenges, and contribute to higher crime rates.[141]

Many pastors, as well as some prominent Christian writers who are not qualified to give counsel or write about domestic violence issues, diminish

---

140. Tracy, "Clergy Responses to Domestic Violence," 9–10.
141. Edwards, "Alarming Effects to Children's Exposure to Domestic Violence," para. 1–6.

the seriousness of the problem and provide treacherous advice. Consider that neither women nor men get help if men who abuse are not exposed.

Not only is the Danvers Statement a conduit for continued Platonic and Aristotelian philosophy as it is injected into Christian theology, but its complementarian theology hinders the ministerial gifts God has given women, and the harmony spoken about in the statement is challenged. Complementarianism runs contrary to the statement that there is neither male nor female, Jew nor Greek, slave or free, when in Christ, our Redeemer (Gal 3:28). The Danvers Statement aligns more with Plato and Aristotle than with Scripture.

If Augustine, St. Thomas, and complementarians were theologically correct in their assessment of women and what they should and should not do, was our Lord in error when he anointed women for very responsible and recognizable positions in ancient Israel, the early church, and in society outside their families? Among numerous examples, consider Deborah: a judge of Israel who is referred to as the mother of Israel, a ruler, a prophet who gave Israel new energy, a successful warrior, and a poet (Judg 4–5). Paul commended Junia as being "prominent amongst the apostles" (Rom 16:7). Huldah was a prophet (2 Kgs 22:14–20; 2 Chr 34:22–33). Then there is Priscilla, Esther, the Proverbs 31 woman, and too many others to list here.

Allowing a culture other than the biblical culture in which or for which the Scriptures were written to influence our interpretation or understanding of Scripture leads to the danger of misinterpreting and misunderstanding biblical passages. Rather than allow philosophers of any time period to inform the Bible, we should allow the Bible to inform the veracity of any philosopher's ideas, including those who are also theologians. As we rightly divide and explain God's word (2 Tim 2:15), we are also providing a light or lamp, not a burden, unto the feet of those who hear.

References

Alchin, Linda. "Middle Ages Religion." LordsandLadies.org. (2017). http://www.lordsandladies.org/middle-ages-religion.htm.

Amadio, Anselm H., and Anthony J. P. Kenny. "Aristotle Greek Philosopher." (Alternative title "Aristoteles"). *Encyclopedia Britannica* (Jan. 11, 2019). https://www.britannica.com/biography/Aristotle.

Aristotle. *Nicomachean Ethics*. Translated by W. D. Ross. (1994–2009). http://classics.mit.edu/Aristotle/nicomachaen.html.

———. *On the Generation of Animals*. Translated by Arthur Platt. (March 8, 2020). https://en.wikisource.org/wiki/On_the_Generation_of_Animals.

———. *Politics*. Translated by Benjamin Jowett. (1994–2009). http://classics.mit.edu/Aristotle/politics.html.

———. *The History of Animals*. Translated by D'Arcy Wentworth Thompson. (1994–2009). http://classics.mit.edu/Aristotle/history_anim.html.

Baima, Nicholas R. "Plato: The Laws." *Internet Encyclopedia of Philosophy*. (no date) https://www.iep.utm.edu/pla-laws.

Brisson, Luc. "Women in Plato's *Republic.*" *Etudes Platoniciennes* (2012). https://journals.openedition.org/etudesplatoniciennes/277.

Brown, Christopher M. "Thomas Aquinas (1224/6–1274)." *Internet Encyclopedia of Philosophy*. (no date). https://www.iep.utm.edu/aquinas.

Brown, Matthew V. "The 'Woman' of Augustine of Hippo." *Priscilla Papers* 4:4 (Fall 1990). https://www.cbeinternational.org/resources/article/priscilla-papers/woman-augustine-hippo.

Chadwick, Henry. *The Early Church*. The Pelican History of the Church. Vol. 1. New York: Penguin, 1967.

Clayton, Edward. "Aristotle: Politics." *Internet Encyclopedia of Philosophy*. (no date). https://www.iep.utm.edu/aris-pol/#SH7e.

Cohen, S. Marc. "The Allegory of the Cave." (2006, updated on July 24, 2015). https://faculty.washington.edu/smcohen/320/cave.htm.

Council on Biblical Manhood and Womanhood. "The Danvers Statement on Biblical Manhood and Womanhood." (Nov. 1988). http://www.grbc.net/wp-content/uploads/2015/09/The-Danvers-Statement-on-Biblical-Manhood-and-Womanhood.pdf.

Cummings, Erica. "The Theory of Forms by Plato: Definition & Examples." Study.com. (No date). https://study.com/academy/lesson/the-theory-of-forms-by-plato-definition-lesson-quiz.html.

Denault, Leigh. "Aristotle." Hellenic Foundation for Culture. (2015). http://hfc-worldwide.org/blog/2015/01/30/aristotle.

———. "Philosophy: The Athenian Philosophers: Socrates, Plato, and Aristotle." The Glory that was Greece: History and Culture in Ancient Athens. (2003). http://www.watson.org/~leigh/philo.html.

Edwards, Blake Edwin. "Alarming Effects of Children's Exposure to Domestic Violence." *Psychology Today* (Feb. 26, 2019). https://www.psychologytoday.com/us/blog/progress-notes/201902/alarming-effects-childrens-exposure-domestic-violence.

Gaarder, Jostein. *Sophie's World: A Novel about the History of Philosophy*. New York: Farrar, Straus and Giroux, 2007.

Honer, Stanley M., Thomas C. Hunt, Dennis L. Okholm, and John L. Safford, eds. *Invitation to Philosophy*. Belmont, CA: Wadsworth Cengage Learning, 2006.

James, Frank A. "Thomas Aquinas on Women." (Aug. 6, 2013). https://carolyncustisjames.com/2013/08/06/thomas-aquinas-on-women.

Kiefer, James E. "Augustine of Hippo, Bishop and Theologian." In *Biographical Sketches of Memorable Christians of the Past* (Aug. 29, 1999). http://justus.anglican.org/resources/bio/50.html.

Koukl, Gregory. "Augustine on Evil" from radio show transcript: Stand to Reason. (2002). https://www.str.org/articles/augustine-on-evil-1.

Magee, Joseph M. "Women." *Thomistic Philosophy* (March 21, 2015). http://www.aquinasonline.com/Questions/women.html.

McClean, John. "Domestic and Family Violence – Biblical and Theological Resources." *The Gospel Coalition* (Oct. 7, 2019). https://au.thegospelcoalition.org/article/domestic-family-violence-biblical-theological-resources.

Mark, Joshua J. "Aristotle." In *Ancient History Encyclopedia* (Sept. 2, 2009). https://www.ancient.eu/aristotle.

Nails, Debra. "Socrates." *The Stanford Encyclopedia of Philosophy* (Spring 2018). Edited by Edward N. Zalta. https://plato.stanford.edu/archives/spr2018/entries/socrates.

Newman, Simon. "The Dark Ages." In *The Finer Times: Excellence in Content*. (No date.) http://www.thefinertimes.com/Middle-Ages/the-dark-ages.html.

Plato. *Apology*. The Internet Classics Archive. Translated by Benjamin Jowett. (1994–2009). http://classics.mit.edu/Plato/apology.html.

———. *Laws*. The Internet Classics Archive. Translated by Benjamin Jowett. (1994–2009). http://classics.mit.edu/Plato/laws.7.vii.html.

———. *Phaedo*. The Internet Classics Archive. Translated by Benjamin Jowett. (1994–2009). http://classics.mit.edu/Plato/phaedo.html.

Popik, Kristin M. "The Philosophy of Women of St. Thomas Aquinas. Part One: The Nature of Woman." In *Faith & Reason: The Journal of Christendom College* 4:4 (Winter 1978). https://media.christendom.edu/wp-content/uploads/2016/07/Kristin-M.-Popik-The-Philosophy-of-Women-of-St.-Thomas-Aquinas.pdf.

———. "The Philosophy of Women of St. Thomas Aquinas. Part Two: The Role of Women." In *Faith & Reason: The Journal of Christendom College* 5:1 (Spring 1979). https://media.christendom.edu/wp-content/uploads/2017/05/Kristin-M-Popik-The-Philosophy-of-Woman-of-St-Thomas-Aquinas.pdf.

Robinson, Nick. "Platonic Influence on St. Augustine's Philosophy." Hearst Seattle Media, LLC. (2019). https://education.seattlepi.com/platonic-influence-st-augustines-philosophy-5566.html.

Samples, Kenneth. "Augustine's View of Predestination: St. Augustine, Part 9." *Reflections* (Aug. 28, 2012). https://reflectionsbyken.wordpress.com/2012/08/28/top-ten-things-augustine-contributed-to-philosophy-part-ii-2.

Simonin, Antoine. "Hellenistic Period." *Ancient History Encyclopedia* (April 28, 2011). https://www.ancient.eu/Hellenistic_Period.

Smith, Nicholas D. "Plato and Aristotle on the Nature of Women." *Journal of the History of Philosophy*. John Hopkins University Press. 21:4 (Oct. 1983). https://muse.jhu.edu/article/226997.

Thomas of Aquinas. *Summa Theologica (On How a Woman is Born to be a Woman)*. "Wijngaards Institute for Catholic Research." Translation by the Fathers of the English Dominican Province (1947). http://www.womenpriests.org/theology/aqui_wom.asp.

———. *Summa Theologica (Whether the Image of God Is Found in Every Man?)*. Translation by the Fathers of the English Dominican Province and Revised by Daniel J. Sullivan. *Encyclopedia Britannica*. Chicago: William Benton, 1923. https://archive.org/stream/in.ernet.dli.2015.126741/2015.126741.The-Summa-Theologica-Vol1_djvu.txt.

Tracy, Steven R. "Clergy Responses to Domestic Violence." *Priscilla Papers* 21:2 (Spring 2007): 9–16. https://www.cbeinternational.org/sites/default/files/pp212_3crtdv.pdf.

Van Camp, Julie C., Jeffrey Olen, and Vincent Barry, eds. *Applying Ethics*. Stamford, CT: Cengage Learning, 2015.

Wildberg, Christian. "Neoplatonism." *The Stanford Encyclopedia of Philosophy* (Summer 2019), edited by Edward N. Zalta. https://plato.stanford.edu/archives/sum2019/entries/neoplatonism.

Withun, David. "Christianity, Ethics, and Ecology." Wordpress.com. (2013). https://davidwithun.com/category/neoplatonism.

PART 2

Practice

6

The Multicultural Aspect of Egalitarian Leadership

Jeanne DeFazio

THE MISSION AT THE House of Prisca and Aquila (HPA) is to produce quality books that expound accurately the word of God to empower women and men to minister together in a multicultural church. Through HPA, I have had the opportunity to edit *Creative Ways to Build Christian Community*, *Redeeming the Screens*, and *Berkeley Street Theatre*. These books describe my ministry experience working with dynamic Spirit-filled Christian men and women ministering in the multicultural church. My latest HPA publication, *Empowering English Language Learners: Successful Strategies of Christian Educators,* is authored by racially diverse educators (men and women) who teach English language learners (ELL). These books explore the advantage gained as men and women minister and share God's word side by side. These books model HPA's egalitarian view that women and men are equally made in the image of God, with the implication that they are equally gifted for ministering the word of God. I am contributing to this dialogue by referring to Psalm 133:1 as a guideline of practical theology: "How very good and pleasant it is when kindred live together in unity!"[1]

---

1. Orthodox Jewish Bible.

The Multicultural Church

HPA's egalitarian mandate is timely and critical to the millennial multicultural church. Paul warned against a factious spirit in the early Corinthian church that would block the flow of God's Holy Spirit and generate a church of insiders and outsiders: "For when one says, 'I follow Paul,' and another, 'I follow Apollos,' are you not mere human beings?" (1 Cor 3:4).[2] Two thousand years after Paul reprimanded the Corinthian church, Martin Luther King Jr. observed that Sunday morning remains the most segregated hour in America. Two in three (66 percent) Americans have never regularly attended a place of worship where there was an ethnic minority, according to a polling analysis released by LifeWay Research.[3] When they do, however, the experience is eye-opening and uplifting. African American church leader Yvonnette O'Neal, founder of My Child Ministry, attended the memorial celebration of the fiftieth anniversary of Dr. King's March on the Washington D.C. Mall and commented on the strong feeling of goodwill that prevailed among brothers and sisters of every color who attended. Ms. O'Neal explained that Dr. King was a pastor who understood that each Christian serves God by bringing souls to Jesus, and that his civil rights activism sprang from his devotion to prayer and his obedience to God's word.[4]

Yvonnette's ministry is chronicled in *Creative Ways to Build Christian Community* in the HPA Series. As an African American child at the height of the civil rights movement in Mississippi, she was integrated into all-white schools. This experience taught her to relate to the individual, independent of race, color, or creed. In Southeast Washington, DC, as a young adult on staff at the Frederick Douglass Center and the Fishing School, her ethnic background gave her the education and social skills necessary to teach the predominately African American inner city students how to develop in order to succeed in a multicultural society.[5] Through overcoming the challenges of her background, Yvonnette has developed the ability to reach out in a multicultural church. She has ministered to mayors and members of Congress and city councils. Yvonnette expounds God's word by organizing all-night Gospel praise-a-thons at the Lincoln Memorial, prayer events of Christian leaders from across the nation at historic churches in the DC metro area, and Wailing Women International intercessory prayer events in key locations in the nation's capital. Her civil rights background has influenced

---

2. All Bible quotations are from NIV 2011 unless otherwise indicated.

3. Grossman, "US Churchgoers still sit in segregated pews and most are okay with that," line 4–6.

4. DeFazio, "We Shall Overcome."

5. DeFazio and Lathrop, *Creative Ways*, 24.

her latest initiative to institute Bible clubs as electives in U.S. public school systems. Yvonnette aligns her ministry with HPA's objective to expound accurately the word of God to empower spiritually multicultural inner-city public school students.

In *Redeeming the Screens*, Mel Novak, founder of Heavenly Manna, Inc., chronicles his ministry to a multicultural prison community: "I had the opportunity to minister at Pelican Bay Penitentiary, Washington State County Rehabilitative Facilities, and many others. Many inmates I counsel are the highest levels of security. In the prisons, they call me 'machine gun' because I back up everything that I say with Scriptures."[6]

Mel models and repeats Scripture sharing the understanding that the word of God is a manifestation of heavenly manna to the incarcerated. As Mel infuses Scripture into the inmates' lives, he reports that revival has been occurring in the prisons. Since January of 2013, 97 percent of those who attend Mel's services have accepted Jesus as Lord and Savior. In his monthly newsletters, Mel explains that he distributes Bibles and his *Arsenal Prayer* so the word of God impacts the diverse prison populations for Jesus. Mel claims that God's word and his testimony have brought more than 100,000 incarcerated people to Jesus. He receives numerous letters from inmates whose lives have been changed as he teaches God's word. For example, one wrote:

> I landed in a cell with a friend of mine. He was my yard dog when we were in Corcoran together back in 2011. We both got out and came back, but to my surprise, he is walking with the Lord these days. And to his surprise, I am also walking with the Lord. In the morning we start out our day by reading the *Daily Bread*, then reading the Scripture aloud with a small prayer. I gave him the *Arsenal Prayer* as well. I still have the Bible you gave me and wrote on the inside.[7]

Chaplain Jozy Pollock[8] invited Mel to minister with her in the Los Angeles County Jail:

> Although I felt quite comfortable walking the high-power rows alone, God gave me the desire to minister on the mental rows. I

---

6. DeFazio and Spencer, *Redeeming the Screens*, 77–78. "In 2014, African Americans constituted 2.3 million, or 34 percent, of the total 6.8 million correctional population. African Americans are incarcerated at more than 5 times the rate of whites. Though African Americans and Hispanics make up approximately 32 percent of the US population, they comprised 56 percent of all incarcerated people in 2015." NAACP "Criminal Fact Sheet," lines 7–10, 18–23.

7. DeFazio and Spencer, *Redeeming the Screens*, 77–79.

8. Jozy Pollock, email interview with the author, March 15, 2019.

called Mel Novak, an actor who was a minister in prisons and on skid row. We had met on prison tour with Calvary Chapel. I told him I could get him a chaplain badge if he would accompany me.[9]

Jozy recently reflected on the multicultural community she developed as a chaplain ministering alongside Mel at the Los Angeles County Jail. She commented that, while watching a recent Christian television program, she was shocked to hear a white pastor say that if a Latino or African American attends his church he redirects them to a church of their ethnicity where they would be more comfortable. In her own words: "He wasn't even wearing a hood." Jozy's main ministry as chaplain focused on the incarcerated in the Los Angeles County Jail, which is multicultural, but has fewer whites. Racism was rampant in the jail. God moved her to write a sermon on racism, which she preached to the inmates. She was surprised when God told her to take the same sermon to the church. She was on pastoral staff at a church called The Hiding Place (a multicultural church filled with "the beautiful people" in the entertainment industry), and she preached her sermon when the pastor was away. Out of obedience, after Jozy preached the sermon, she shocked herself by inviting people who were racist to come forward for prayer. People did come forward and received prayer.

During Jozy's decades ministering at the jail, she explains that she got along with all the gangs except the white supremacists, who one day explained to her that heaven was "all white." She replied: "No, it isn't." One white supremacist exclaimed: "Well, if it's not, I don't want to go there." Jozy's responded: "Don't worry. You won't be going there." Currently, she happily attends a multicultural church with a tattooed ex-gang-banger pastor who, prior to conversion, was shot five times and stabbed three times. This pastor was converted in a facility where Jozy preached the word.

Jozy and Mel and Gemma Wenger ministered side by side in the Los Angeles County Jail. Gemma Wenger is a woman in leadership in another multicultural church. In *Redeeming the Screens,* she details joining forces with Mel Novak to minister the word of God on skid row and in jail.[10] Gemma explains how the Holy Spirit aligned her in ministry with Mel to preach the word of God and how, as a result of joining forces with spiritual powerhouses like Mel and Jozy, she grew spiritually and continued to minister God's word in editorials in *The Hollywood Times* (edited by her mother, Bee Beyer) and in her international television program, *Beauty for Ashes*:

---

9. DeFazio and Spencer, *Redeeming the Screens*, 69.
10 DeFazio and Spencer, *Redeeming the Screens*, 69.

> At seventeen, I was asked to sing at the Los Angeles Mission on Skid Row by Mel Novak, a prison minister whom I met at the Southern California Motion Picture Council (SCMPC), an organization that awards morally uplifting movies and television shows.... At twenty-one, I began ministering to the youths in juvenile hall. From the prisons and skid row, God increased my ministry to churches, radio, books, newspapers (*The Hollywood Times*), evangelical outreaches, and television ministry.[11]

Through the united ministry of Mel, Jozy, and Gemma, the Word became flesh and made his dwelling in the hearts of inmates and skid row homeless people (John 1:14). These three saints of the church manifested the Holy Spirit by speaking God's word into the lives of those who have nothing and with whom nobody wants anything to do.[12]

One of the most powerful witnesses to the move of the Holy Spirit recorded in *Redeeming the Screens* is the testimony of Susan Stafford, world famous former *Wheel of Fortune* hostess. Susan had achieved major success and fame in Hollywood. After a divorce and her disenchantment with *Wheel of Fortune* after her cohost Chuck Woolery left the program, Susan experienced a great void in her life. She describes visiting India with Father Herbert DeSouza and ministering with Mother Teresa among the lepers and the dying as an experience that revived her spiritually and renewed her sense of purpose. Susan left *Wheel of Fortune* on October 22, 1982. Her popularity had engaged Susan in a life relating to fans, many of whom wrote her about their battles with cancer. She began ministering to cancer patients at the Dr. John Stehlin Cancer Center in Houston's St. Joseph Hospital in 1982. Subsequently, Susan cared for Rock Hudson during his much-publicized death from AIDS in the mid-1980s. Joining spiritual forces with Pat and Shirley Boone, Gavin and Patti MacLeod, and Father Terry Sweeney, Susan brought the word of God to Rock Hudson in a critical moment of his life:

> The fear of contagion at Rock Hudson's deathbed was great. Shirley and Pat Boone, Gavin and Patti MacLeod, and I were the only outsiders who came in to minister at Rock's deathbed. We called in Father Terry Sweeney S.J. because Rock was a Roman Catholic. The loss of Rock as a friend was heartbreaking. I am

---

11. DeFazio and Spencer, *Redeeming the Screens*, 118.

12. "Every time you sacrifice something at great cost, every time you renounce something that appeals to you for the sake of the poor, you are feeding a hungry Christ. You are clothing His nakedness. You are offering shelter to a homeless Christ. Every time we are concerned about the poor, whether they are near or far away we do it all for Him." Saint Teresa of Calcutta, "Mother Teresa Quotations," lines 46–47.

grateful that Rock came to Jesus on his deathbed, and I have the promise of seeing this beloved friend again in heaven.[13]

Susan's ministry flourished, and she prays and ministers with prominent Christian men and women in the entertainment world: Pat and his belated wife Shirley Boone, Marilyn McCoo and Billy Davis, Bob Rieth, and Bob Yerkes. She continues reaching out to the sick and dying in the gay community, teaching the word of God and through the power of the Holy Spirit.

When men and women align to teach accurately the word of God around the world, the Holy Spirit infuses the attributes of Jesus so that Scripture is interpreted by actions more than words. For example, I organized homeless outreaches for MP Grace II in the early 1990s. Located on the third floor of McDonald's on 58th Street in New York City, these meetings were open to anyone who needed prayer or just a comfortable place to receive encouragement and a meal. The events were culturally and economically diverse, drawing everyone from executives of the business world to the homeless. In *Redeeming the Screens*, author and ambassador of prayer April Shenandoah describes a powerful move of the Holy Spirit through the teaching of the word in one of those meetings:

> During one evening at a McDonald's meeting, a small elderly man stood up to share. I do not know if he was homeless or just down on his luck, but I do know that I will never forget him. As he reached into his pocket and pulled out a small Bible, he spoke words filled with faith and such conviction that my spirit leaped for joy. His soft-spoken passion raised my faith when he told us not to look to people for anything, but to trust God for every need. This man was rich in my eyes. That is what these meetings were all about: being inspired and led by the Holy Spirit.[14]

Charlene Eber, founder and board member of World Alliance for Peace, sponsored these outreaches. In *Redeeming the Screens*, Charlene details a powerful experience while ministering in China with spiritual powerhouses Joanne Petronella and Michelle Corral of Breath of the Spirit Ministries. It is a beautiful description of egalitarian ministry recounting how the Holy Spirit used Joanne and Michelle, founders of a major Christian ministry; and Charlene, a highly successful Hollywood producer; to bring the word of God to Chinese peasants in an open field:

> I traveled with Breath of the Spirit Ministries and smuggled five hundred Bibles into Communist China. The penalty for

---

13. DeFazio and Spencer, *Redeeming the Screens*, 50.
14. DeFazio and Spencer, *Redeeming the Screens*, 101–02.

this crime at that time was very harsh. Joanne Petronella and Michelle Corral met with the customs officials who inspected their bags, which contained Bibles. They explained later that the man was "blinded in the Holy Spirit" and never saw the Bibles. I did not understand what "blinded in the Holy Spirit" meant at the time. We distributed Bibles to strangers on the street in Canton. Then, on a train ride headed to the next ministry point, Joanne said we had to get rid of the remaining Bibles because there would be an inspection at the next stop. I opened the door and started to throw Bibles off the train. There were people in the rice paddies running toward the train to receive the Bibles. There are no words to describe the experience of seeing these people in the water of the rice paddies coming to receive what they did not know was the word of God. . . . This experience was one of the most awesome in my life. At the next train stop, there were indeed many soldiers inspecting the train.[15]

The Multicultural Church Has Artists

The artistic world becomes a type of multicultural ministry when men and women speak God's word through the performing arts. For example, to reach the idealists of the 1970s counterculture, Berkeley Street Theatre presented the gospel in a pre-Christian message to engage audiences on Sproul Plaza. In a retrospective chapter, I chronicle a meeting with Berkeley Street Theatre members. In a coffeehouse more than three decades later, this group of talented men and women paused to reflect on Berkeley Street Theatre, how they worked together in mutual accord, and the lasting impact of the Jesus Movement. Asian tourists at an adjacent table took our photos. I described Berkeley Street Theatre to them as a talented and prayerful team that successfully brought youth to Jesus. How? they wondered. I quoted Revelation 12:11 to explain: "We were victorious by the blood of the Lamb and the word of his testimony."[16] The directors and artists of Berkeley Street Theatre were men and women who aligned their performances with the mission goals of HPA. As a cultural melting pot, these team players put aside their differences to study and teach the word of God through performance. The members were Puerto Rican, Asian, Creole, Southern folk, New Yorkers, and California-born men and women, but all cultural differences were set aside as they prayed and studied God's word so that dramatic outpourings of the Holy Spirit reached the counterculture for Jesus.

15. DeFazio and Spencer, *Redeeming the Screens*, 132.
16. Aramaic Bible in Plain English. DeFazio, *Berkeley Street Theatre*, 6.

Olga Soler in *Berkeley Street Theatre* describes a miraculous move of the Holy Spirit as the word of God is spoken through multicultural performing artists working together:

> Then I was led to Texas where music and puppetry, comedy and drama turned into "Midnight Oil"—my first theater company. That ministry was beset with one miracle after another as we prayed for people who were cured of drug addiction, temptation to suicide, and cancer. I first started to see the healing power of sacred art at that time. God was punctuating his work in us as artists with an infusion of grace into human pain to heal and help. We took this as confirmation that we were doing His will and it made the opposition from many quarters bearable. We were doing what we were meant to do.[17]

The Multicultural Church Has Jews and Gentiles

Paul, in Romans 2:10, explains that "glory, honor and peace [are available] for everyone who does good: first for the Jew, then for the Gentile." Academy Award–winning producer Aaron Mann (aka Ezra Mann) was reared in an Orthodox Jewish tradition. His parents were Holocaust survivors. He is acknowledged in *Berkeley Street Theatre* for making a courageous paradigm cultural shift in the Hollywood community by accepting Jesus as Messiah Lord and Savior. His powerful play *Otto and the White Dove* is an autobiographical account of his conversion. In it, the White Dove (a manifestation of the Holy Spirit) expounds the word of God and brings Otto, a Holocaust survivor, to Jesus.

Aaron identifies his life-changing experience as he broke orthodox Hebrew tradition through the power of the Holy Spirit to encounter the risen Jesus in Hollywood's evangelistic Christian communities. Along with Susan Stafford, Patti Zuckor, Gavin and Patti MacLeod, LeaAnn Pendergrass, and Linda Chapman, Aaron prays for and ministers God's word to Jewish and Gentile members of the entertainment industry.

---

17. DeFazio, *Berkeley Street Theatre*, 85.

MULTICULTURAL MINISTRY INCLUDES TEACHING ENGLISH LANGUAGE LEARNERS

Mutual leadership should be taught early, as the Bible explains the importance of educating youth in positive ways: "Train up a child in the way he should go, and even when he is old he will not depart from it" (Prov 22:6 ESV).

Julia Davis, in an insightful chapter in the book *Empowering English Language Learners*, aligns herself with HPA's mission objective when she explains that children need the wisdom of God's word interpreted by actions more than words. She identifies the way that the Holy Spirit infused the word of God into her public school classroom, resolving discipline problems in a completely politically correct fashion by drawing on the children to step up and take leadership in devising rules for class behavioral protocol:[18]

> Scripturally based Classroom Rules are a way to bring the practice of Christian principle into the public school classroom without being "politically incorrect." My students begin each class by devising classroom principles. When students have written the Classroom Rules, they are more apt to abide by them. For example, "I am ready to be respectful and responsible and a good classroom citizen" reflects the values of Psalm 19:14,[19] Proverbs 18:24[20] and Mark 12:31.[21] "Listening without interrupting" describes the wisdom of Proverbs 18:2.[22] "Speaking without accusing" is a mandate of James 1:19.[23] "Answering without

---

18. "Discipline problems in schools continue to be one of the greatest causes of concern for educators in schools today. The Bible, in Proverbs 22:6, commands, 'train up a child in the way he should go, and even when he is old he will not depart from it.' This verse is a clear promise and direction from God. As such, it is not a coincidence that as prayer and the Bible are removed from schools, children are able to test the boundaries of their teachers and parents, which in turn leads to disciplinary challenges. As training opportunities are removed, discipline problems are increased. Many public opinion polls have cited discipline as a major problem in the schools." DeFazio and Spencer, *Empowering English Language Learners*, 40.

19. Ps 19:14: "May these words of my mouth and this meditation of my heart be pleasing in your sight, Lord, my Rock and my Redeemer."

20. Prov 18:24: "A person who has friends may be harmed by them, but there is a friend who sticks closer than a brother."

21. Mark 12:31: "The second is this: 'Love your neighbor as yourself.' There is no commandment greater than these."

22. Prov 18:2: "Fools find no pleasure in understanding, but delight in airing their own opinions."

23. Jas 1:19: "My dear brothers and sisters, take note of this: Everyone should be quick to listen, slow to speak and slow to become angry."

arguing" is an instruction of Proverbs 17:1.[24] Ephesians 4:15 outlines the importance of "sharing."[25] "Forgiveness without retribution" is a mandate of Colossians 3:13.[26]

This shared creating of classroom rules not only encourages ownership of the educational experience, but also helps students begin to exercise leadership skills.

I contributed a chapter to *Empowering English Language Learners* entitled "Teaching Migrant Children Prepared Me to Teach Theology to At Risk English Language Learners." In the close of that chapter, I outline how I integrate Scripture to teach English language learners effectively as an Athanasian Scholar at Gordon-Conwell's Center for Urban Ministerial Education.

The New International Version of the Bible translates Deuteronomy 32:2 as follows: "Let my teaching fall like rain and my words descend like dew, like showers on new grass, like abundant rain on tender plants." As an Athanasian Scholar, I pray this Song of Moses in Ellicott's commentary: "Everything that comes down from the 'Father of lights' is handed on by one heavenly messenger to another, until it falls upon the hearts of men [and women from every race and cultural background] in just that form in which he can best receive it."[27]

> At the end of each course, I am grateful for these strategies that helped my [multicultural] students learn, but my heart gives thanks to God who faithfully answers my prayer for supernatural aptitude for learning for each student. The look of understanding in the students' eyes, the pride in their accomplishments as a result of the extent of their efforts, and the joy they experience in the process of acquiring understanding is the greatest reward to me for teaching theology to English learners.[28]

24. Prov 17:1: "It is better to eat a dry crust of bread in peace and quiet than to eat a big dinner in a house that is full of fighting" (NIRV).

25. Acts 2:42–47: "And they devoted themselves to the apostles' teaching and the fellowship, to the breaking of bread and the prayers. And awe came upon every soul, and many wonders and signs were being done through the apostles. And all who believed were together and had all things in common. And they were selling their possessions and belongings and distributing the proceeds to all, as any had need. And day by day, attending the temple together and breaking bread in their homes, they received their food with glad and generous hearts, praising God and having favor with all the people. And the Lord added to their number day by day those who were being saved" (ESV).

26. Col 3:13: "Bear with each other and forgive one another if any of you has a grievance against someone. Forgive as the Lord forgave you." DeFazio and Spencer, *Empowering English Language Learners*, 41.

27. Waller, "Deuteronomy," para. 2.

28. DeFazio and Spencer, *Empowering English Language Learners*, 92.

Prayer and the correct application of God's word are key spiritual strategies for teaching English language learners and for modeling a form of education they can themselves adapt. As a teacher of ELLs at Gordon-Conwell's Boston urban campus, I learn from the cultural exchange so that the teacher-student relationship accomplishes the HPA goal of being multicultural and egalitarian!

Conclusion

The House of Prisca and Aquila's mission clearly aligns with Paul's commendation of the Bereans in Acts 17:11,[29] who diligently studied and searched the Scriptures to expound accurately the word of God: "The word of God is what we are expounding, thereby empowering women and men" to join one another to minister "in all levels of the church and home."

In this chapter, I contributed to the dialogue on the HPA's goal to encourage mutual, multicultural leadership by referencing four of my HPA books to identify ways the Holy Spirit unites the multicultural church as Christian men and women minister the word of God. I cited references in each book identifying men and women in ministry leadership and service, as well as students and teachers, performers and audiences, chaplains and inmates, who through God's grace and the power of the Holy Spirit experienced how good and how pleasant it is for kindred to dwell together in unity (Ps 133:1).

In John 17:20– 23, Jesus firmly identified unity in the body of Christ as a reflection of God's presence and love:

> My prayer is not for them alone. I pray also for those who will believe in me through their message that all of them may be one, Father, just as you are in me and I am in you. May they also be in us so that the world may believe that you have sent me. I have given them the glory that you gave me, that they may be one as we are one—I in them and you in me—so that they may be brought to complete unity. Then the world will know that you sent me and have loved them even as you have loved me (NLT).

The House of Prisca and Aquila's mission statement is aligned with John the Apostle's. The unity of the church is the work of the Spirit *with and through* the written word of God. In the preface of *Creative Ways to Build Christian Community*, HPA cofounder William David Spencer explains why unity of the multicultural millennial church is critical:

---

29. Acts 17:11: "Now the Berean Jews were of more noble character than those in Thessalonica, for they received the message with great eagerness and examined the Scriptures every day to see if what Paul said was true."

As the future continues to isolate us into solitary individuals, the Church of Jesus Christ may very well be the chief architect of face-to-face community. Because of our beliefs in a God who met us face to face and walked among us and calls us to be the body of the Christ, God's anointed one on earth, we may be the only network left standing, able completely to assure humanity that, despite the strides of artificial intelligence, the valuable work of hands, humans alone are made in the image of God and therefore never obsolete, that we are worth more than a handful of bolts. This book will continually help remind us of that truth, as it helps us ensure a Christian communal future for humanity as well as a recognizable body of believers for our Lord when he finally comes back to gather us up to himself in God's everlasting arms of love.[30]

References

DeFazio, Jeanne, ed. *Berkeley Street Theatre: How Improvisation and Street Theater Emerged as a Christian Outreach to the Culture of the Time.* Eugene, OR: Wipf and Stock, 2017.

———. "We Shall Overcome." http://blogs.christianpost.com/scriptural-truths/we-shall- overcome- 177918/14. Sept. 2013.

DeFazio, Jeanne, and John P. Lathrop, eds. *Creative Ways to Build Christian Community.* Eugene, OR: Wipf and Stock, 2013.

DeFazio, Jeanne, and William David Spencer, eds. *Empowering English Language Learners: Successful Strategies of Christian Educators.* Eugene, OR: Wipf and Stock, 2018.

———. *Redeeming the Screens: Living Stories of Media "Ministers" Bringing the Message of Jesus Christ to the Entertainment Industry.* Eugene: OR: Wipf and Stock, 2016.

Grossman, Cathy Lynn. "US Churchgoers still sit in segregated pews and most are okay with that." https://www.christiancentury.org/article/2015-01/us-churchgoers-still-sit-segregated-pews-and-most-are-ok. Accessed April 12, 2019.

NAACP. "Criminal Fact Sheet." http://www.naacp.org/criminal-justice-fact-sheet. Accessed April 12, 2019.

Pollock, Jozy. Email interview with the author. March 15, 2019.

Teresa of Calcutta. "Mother Teresa Quotations." http://www.iskandar.com/waleed911/motherteresa.html. Accessed April 12, 2019.

Waller, C. H. "Deuteronomy." In *A Bible Commentary for English Readers*, edited by Charles John Ellicott. London: Cassell, 1905. https://biblehub.com/commentaries/ellicott/deuteronomy/32.htm/. Accessed May 20, 2020.

---

30. DeFazio and Lathrop, *Creative Ways*, xv.

7

Egalitarian Multiethnic Leadership in the United States

Francois W. Augustin

MY ATTEMPT IN THIS chapter is to propose how the Christian church in America can demonstrate egalitarian multiethnic leadership. I propose a change in attitude, in belief, and in practice, reaching to the very depth of the culture's character. However, what I hope to convey finds its source in none other than the Bible. In the first half of this chapter, I make the case for egalitarian multiethnic leadership by leveraging biblical passages, as I seek to establish the ethical norms upon which I will build my arguments. The second half is the problem, as I understand it to be, in the American context. The final segment highlights a proposed solution to promote egalitarian multiethnic leadership. It has been more than a half century since the late Baptist preacher Dr. Martin Luther King Jr. exhorted us in his book *Where Do We Go from Here: Chaos or Community?* stating, "Let us be dissatisfied until America will no longer have a high blood pressure of creeds and an anemia of deeds."[1] My hope is for the chapter to help the Christian church in the United States demonstrate its creed of egalitarian multiethnic leadership by moving from awareness of multiethnic leaders to a full embrace of the latter's leadership through the practice of physi-

---

1. King, *Where Do We Go From Here?*, para. 53.

cal proximity that leads to deliberate integration and by rethinking the culture's highest ideal.

The Biblical Foundation

In the New Testament, the nations (or the non-Jews) were often referred to as *ethnos* or Gentiles. Jewish religious leadership despised the *ethnos*[2] and saw them as an unclean and inferior class of people. In Acts 21, for example, Paul was arrested by the Jewish leaders based on their accusation of Paul having brought an Ephesian man, a Gentile named Trophimus, into the temple (Acts 21:28–29). Despite the negative sentiment the Jewish leaders harbored toward the *ethnos*, one thing that remains clear is the gospel's dignified and positive view of them. Throughout Jesus's ministry, we see extensive outreach to the *ethnos* and Jesus advocating on their behalf. For example, Jesus cleared out the temple with a whip by chasing away, with heightened zeal, those who made the temple off limits to the *ethnos*. Jesus exclaimed, "My house shall be called a house of prayer for all the nations (*ethnos*)" (Mark 11:17 NRSV). Later, in Mark 13:10, he underscores the fact that the good news must be preached to all *ethnos*. We see a similar emphasis in Matthew 28:19–20 when Jesus commanded his apostles to go into all the *ethnos* to make disciples.

The gospels feature multiple stories in which Jesus ministered quite extensively in Gentile (*ethnos*) territory. For example, Jesus ministered to the centurion, who was a Gentile, an officer of the Roman army in Capernaum (Matt 8:5–13; Luke 7:1–10; John 4:46–54). He delivered the demon-possessed man in Gadara (Matt 8:28–34; Mark 5:1–20; Luke 8:26–39). He ministered to a Samaritan woman at a well (John 4), along with many other things. In these three cases, we see these *ethnos* becoming agents of proclamation of the gospel of Jesus, a task designated to the early apostles and leaders (see Matt 28:16–20). After healing the servant of the centurion, Jesus used that centurion's faith to teach the Jews how to respond to God in faith. He said, "Truly I tell you, I have not found anyone in Israel with such great faith" (Matt 8:10, 26, NIV). After Jesus healed the demon-possessed man, Mark and Luke record how that man became a traveling evangelist in the region and made quite an impact: "And he went away and began to

---

2. I believe the message of the Bible views the word *ethnos* positively, although, in the New Testament, Jews considered the *ethnos* to be culturally and religiously inferior. Many Bible translations translate the word *ethnos* as Gentiles or nations, but in so doing they dilute the cultural connotations Jews attributed to the *ethnos* during New Testament times.

proclaim in the Decapolis how much Jesus had done for him; and everyone was amazed" (Mark 5:20; Luke 8:39). In the story of the Samaritan woman at the well, the gospel of John records how that woman became the leading evangelist in her town, and that many came to faith in Jesus Christ through her ministry (John 4:39). But Jesus's outreach to the *ethnos* was not merely to transform them into passive recipients of his good news. We see in Jesus's ministry deliberate embrace of the *ethnos* as leaders as well.

Jesus's intentions with leadership started out with the recruitment of a diverse group of Jewish disciples, which spread into a multiethnic community of leaders. Jesus's choice of his first disciples, along with the spread of the gospel message in the Greco-Roman world, clearly demonstrates that egalitarian multi-*ethnos* leadership was both Jesus's and the early church's deliberate approach to leadership. Perhaps most striking is Christ's approach to the *ethnos* in the Gospel of John. Twice we see Jesus mentioning that his hour had not yet come (John 2:4 and John 7:6). In John 2:4, Jesus tells Mary, his mother, while they are at a Judean wedding, that the hour for him to reveal himself to the world as Messiah has not yet come. Later, in John 7:6, in the context of a Judean festival, Jesus tells his family members that his hour has not come. However, in John 12, we see Jesus finally mentioning that his hour has come. The context in John 12 is telling, for the people involved are the *ethnos*, whose diversity demonstrates Christ's global perspective of inclusion and equal footing of all groups when it comes to salvation. John 12 shows that a group of Greeks, which were part of the *ethnos*, wanted to talk to Jesus. Since they could not get to him, they found Philip. But why Philip? This, I believe, was not accidental, because Philip's name was Greek. This implies that Philip, very likely, was of Hellenistic Jewish background. But what Philip does next is also very telling. The text says that Philip found Andrew: the same Andrew who also found Peter and brought the latter to Jesus to tell him that they had found the Messiah. Why was Andrew and not Peter often viewed as the leader of the group? It appears that those who wanted to get to Jesus needed to go through Andrew. But Andrew, by his name, was also of Hellenistic background. Among the Twelve, he and Philip were the only two with Greek names. Andrew was clearly biethnic or bicultural, to say the least. Andrew, who could bring the very Jewish Peter to Jesus (John 1:41), was the same Andrew who could bring the Greeks, the members of the *ethnos*, to Jesus. Philip, who knew to find Andrew so the Greeks could meet Jesus (John 12:22), was also the one to connect the very Jewish Nathanael to Jesus (John 1:46). And when Andrew brought the Greeks to Jesus, Jesus exclaimed that his hour had finally come (John 12:23). All subsequent mentions of Jesus's hour beyond John 12 are references to the fulfillment of Jesus's hour of glory. Jesus's hour did not come until the *ethnos* were included in the plan of salvation, and members of the *ethnos* served as bridge builders for those who needed to be added to God's fold.

All the apostles were on equal footing before Christ, and these apostles were not a monolithic group.[3] They were a group with Jewish heritage but with ethnic characteristics that bridged the gap between them and those who were considered part of the *ethnos*. If Jesus wanted a purely Jewish leadership cadre, he would have chosen everybody out of the same group, particularly out of the priestly class, to ensure that everyone was ethnically pure. But we see leaders like Andrew and Philip, who were hybrids: bridge builders to non-Jewish groups.

Moreover, as the gospel message spread throughout the Greco-Roman world, we also see a new cadre of non-Jewish or hybrid Jewish leaders coming from among the *ethnos*. For example, Timothy, who was the leader of the church at Ephesus, was the child of an *ethnos* father (Acts 16:1). Titus, another leader of the early church, whose name was of Latin origin, was also of the *ethnos* (Gal 2:3). Titus was Paul's "partner and fellow worker in service" (2 Cor 8:23) who shared in Paul's burdens toward the Corinthians and was dispatched to restore peace in Corinth (2 Cor 7:6–7, 13). Titus was also exhorted by Paul to teach the faithful all things excellent and profitable (Titus 3:8).

We encounter in the New Testament communities that are culturally and ethnically diverse with leadership models reflecting that same degree of diversity. But, more so, we see the expansion of the kingdom of God, the spread of the gospel message, being directly tied to multiethnic leadership structures, and, more precisely, an egalitarian form of multiethnic leadership. Besides Jesus choosing two early apostles with Hellenistic Jewish backgrounds (Philip and Andrew), we also see Jesus choosing Paul, who, although being a Hebrew of Hebrews (Phil 3:4–8), had Roman citizenship, was from Tarsus, was profiled as an Egyptian, spoke fluent Greek (Acts 21:37–38; 22:28), and possibly spoke comfortably in Latin.[4] Later, we encounter the ministry of Apollos, clearly Greek, or a Hellenized Jew by name, who was from Alexandria in Egypt and who "was a great help to those who by grace had believed. For he vigorously refuted his Jewish opponents in public debate, proving from the Scriptures that Jesus was the Messiah" (Acts

---

3. Acts 6 highlights the fact that the Jews were not monolithic. There were Greek-speaking Jews and Aramaic/Hebrew-speaking Jews. This is akin to saying there are Haitians with American heritage and Haitians from the native land. One has the added dimension of English being a dominant part of his/her culture, while the other maintains a more indigenous form of the identity by having Haitian Creole and French as the dominant languages.

4. Porter, "Did Paul Speak Latin?," 290.

18:24, 27–28 NIV). Later, in the first epistle to the Corinthians, Apollos was put on the same leadership footing as Paul, Peter, or even Christ, when Paul addressed a schism in the Corinthian church (1 Cor 3:1–9). Notice, however, how the schism involving Apollos was just as much along ethnic lines as it was along theological lines. The name used for Peter is not *Petros*, as he is often referred to in the epistles, but, rather, *Cephas*, his Aramaic name, thus highlighting his Hebrew ethnic heritage. So it appears that Corinth, being the port city at the edge of the Roman empire, was a confluence of cultures and ethnic groups[5] and the Christian church that Paul planted there reflected that diversity. That diverse group of Christians had among them some who wanted to act more tribally than the gospel would warrant. Those with affinities for Greek and Alexandrian culture or heritage probably wanted to follow Apollos, and those with Jewish heritage probably wanted to follow Cephas, while those with Roman affinities probably wanted to associate with Paul.[6] Paul's answer, however, brings everyone back to the ethos of egalitarian leadership when he states:

> What then is Apollos? What is Paul? Servants through whom you came to believe, as the Lord assigned to each. I planted, Apollos watered, but God gave the growth. So neither the one who plants nor the one who waters is anything, but only God who gives the growth. The one who plants and the one who waters have a common purpose, and each will receive wages according to the labor of each. For we are God's servants, working together; you are God's field, God's building (1 Cor 3:5–9 NRSV).

What we see here is egalitarian multiethnic leadership at its best. This, along with the other examples listed above, underscore the fact that both Jesus's choice of leaders and the early church's leadership structure consisted of a cadre of multiethnic leaders who were all on equal footing before Christ. Jesus had a ministry to the Jews, but not a ministry exclusively to Jews. He promoted Jewish-based leaders, but did not see leadership pertaining to the advancement of his message and kingdom as being exclusively Jewish. Non-Jews were not merely recipients of salvation, but were active participants in leading the advancement of the salvation message to the ends of the earth. In Jesus's eyes, the non-Jews served as leaders and were on equal leadership footing with the Jews.

---

5. Myers, *The Eerdmans Bible Dictionary*, 234–35.
6. Richards and O'Brien, *Misreading Scripture with Western Eyes*, 66.

The Problem

Some have argued that the Bible's notion of ethnicity does not perfectly correlate to our modern understanding of the concept.[7] However, we can extrapolate the ethical norms found in Christianity with respect to the dignity and worth that the Bible accorded to all ethnic groups, especially as it applies to leadership. In this chapter, ethnicity is viewed from the perspective of differences in history, nationhood, language, ancestry, and even biology. Hence, we see ethnic diversity as cultural varieties that emanate from and are informed by the characteristics listed above in order to produce behaviors and to establish norms that can support the advancement of the gospel message to the ends of the earth.

Jesus's commission in Matthew 28 is not to the early apostles alone. One can safely conclude that discipling the nations and spreading the gospel message require the involvement of all *ethnos*. The American Christian church will not be able to live up to Jesus's expectations of gospel expansion and kingdom advancement apart from an egalitarian multiethnic leadership model. Martin Luther King Jr.'s lament of the segregated posture of American Christianity[8] continues to haunt this nation and stir the conscience of those who are passionate about getting the gospel through the *ethnos* and to the *ethnos*. America is among a handful of nations in the world that have a unique position and ability to fulfill this mission. The gospel message spread rapidly through the multiethnic communities in Roman cities, which were connected by Roman roads and other components of the Roman infrastructure.[9] The *ethnos* came to Roman cities because that was where they stood a better chance at life. No wonder Paul's missionary journeys spanned multiple cities and his many letters were addressed to Christian communities in those cities. The Roman Empire had a unique position in the world that made the *ethnos* gravitate to Roman cities. At the same time, the Roman Empire's infrastructure and confluence of cultures significantly facilitated the spread of the gospel message in the early days of Christianity.[10]

Today, America is the new Roman Empire. It is one of the few places in the world toward which the *ethnos* gravitate because America offers opportunities that are not easily found elsewhere. Immigration data from

---

7. See Berzon, "Ethnicity and Early Christianity," 191–227.

8. King, "Interview on Meet the Press." During an interview on NBC's Meet the Press with Ned Brooks on April 17, 1960, Martin Luther King Jr. pointed out that the most tragic example of segregation in America was eleven o'clock on Sunday morning. See interview transcripts from The Martin Luther King, Jr. Papers Project.

9. Latourette, *A History of Christianity* vol. 1, 74–75.

10. Kaatz, *The Rise of Early Christianity*, 3.

the United States government shows that, between 2015 and 2017 alone, more than three million immigrants from countries spanning Asia, North America, Africa, Oceania, Europe, and South America were granted permanent legal status in America.[11] Often overlooked is the fact that a great number of those who migrate to America are Christians from other shores who, at some point, had received the gospel from Americans and other missionaries. Now, many of those same immigrants who find themselves on American soil have become the new evangelists, bringing the gospel back to America. And because of the transnational nature of those immigrants, they are not only evangelizing America through the churches they plant and integrate as they maintain ties to their countries of origin, but they have also become gospel agents to and from America. This new multiethnic, Christian, immigrant leadership cadre on American soil now comprises the missionaries to America from America.

But the task of these multiethnic leaders cannot be accomplished without the recognition, support, and empowerment from all Christian leaders in America, particularly those of America's dominant cultural class, namely white evangelical Christians. Sadly, America's white dominant culture does not always have a positive relationship with other members of the *ethnos*. The white American church, for example, sometimes tends to have a relationship fraught with unjust attitudes and actions toward nonwhites, particularly toward its black, Latino, and Asian counterparts.[12] Further, a similar antagonism to that which existed between the Jews and Gentiles in the New Testament exists in contemporary American society between whites and nonwhites, especially with the former treating the latter as inferior groups of people. This sentiment, as it relates to the American Christian experience, is what many Christian writers are now calling "white evangelicalism"[13] or white cultural hegemony clothed with religious beliefs and practices. We cannot get to the development of an egalitarian multiethnic Christian leadership model in America that will help advance the gospel message through the nations until the American Christian church does away with such "white evangelicalism."

---

11. U.S. Department of Homeland Security, Annual Flow Report: Lawful Permanent Residents: August 2018.

12. Emerson and Smith. *Divided by Faith*, 1–2.

13. Soong Chan Rah, in his two books, *The Next Evangelicalism* and *Many Colors*, explains what is meant by white evangelicalism. Bryan Loritts, in his book *Inside Outsider*, echoes Rah and elaborates on the impact of white evangelicalism on the church and the wider culture.

The Solution

I propose three strategies to help normalize multiethnic leadership while addressing the hurdles that the American Christian church needs to overcome as we strive toward this new leadership model. The American Christian church can never live up to its calling of getting the gospel through the nations and to the nations if it does not first move from awareness and recognition to full embrace of nonwhite Christian leadership; second, practice proximity and deliberate integration; and, third, redefine the pursuit of happiness.

Move from Awareness and Recognition to Full Embrace of Nonwhite Christian Leadership

The first strategy toward the normalization of multiethnic leadership in American Christianity is moving from awareness and recognition to full embrace of nonwhite Christian leadership. Plenty of reasons exist to believe that this approach is doable among Christians. For example, American evangelicals prize high-quality preaching and usually promote it as a sign of effective and strong leadership. With such a belief, one would expect that, if a preacher is recognized as one of the most effective preachers in America, that same preacher would have a multiethnic following. This has not necessarily proved to be the case.

In May 2018, Truett Seminary conducted a second round of its twelve most effective preachers survey[14] with the purpose of identifying the most effective preachers in the English language since its last ranking in 1996. The survey was conducted among scholars and practitioners of preaching who belong to the Evangelical Homiletics Society and the Academy of Homiletics. The preachers were evaluated and chosen according to the following seven criteria: biblical/exegetical, that is, the careful study of the selected text, taking into account grammar, syntax, history, culture, etc.; relevance, reinforcing a text's meaning to today's hearers; person of the preacher, or the preacher's degree of authenticity, integrity, and commitment to the Christian faith; theological/orthodox, that is, the degree to which the preacher's sermons line up with the historic faith; sermon form, the degree to which the preacher's sermon is engaging and understandable; effective communication, or the effectiveness of the preacher's use of language, images, and illustrations; and, lastly, delivery, the degree to which the preacher skillfully shares his or her message with authenticity that maximized the hearers' reception and understanding of that message.

---

14. See "Baylor University's Truett Seminary."

Not only do America's evangelicals prize preaching, but these seven criteria also provide the measuring sticks for evaluating what American evangelicals call a "good" sermon. These are also the guidelines taught in preaching classes at evangelical seminaries.

Three of the twelve preachers identified are Drs. Anthony Evans, Ralph Douglas West, and Otis Moss III. All three are African Americans who pastor large churches. Two of them, Evans and West, are products of prestigious evangelical seminaries. And one, in particular, Dr. Evans, is a household name among white evangelicals. However, the recognition these three preachers received did not result in a multiethnic church audience with a significant number of white evangelical Christians in attendance. Dr. Tony Evans's church is in the Dallas area. According to the Pew Research Center, white evangelical Protestants represent nearly one-quarter of the population in the Dallas/Fort Worth area,[15] a region of nearly 2 million people. If one includes the larger metro area, the population swells to more than 6 million residents.[16] This would translate as half a million white evangelicals based on the 2 million population estimate and 1.5 million white evangelicals if we include the larger metro area. Given this data, one would expect that Oak Cliff Bible Fellowship of Dallas, Texas, where Evans pastors, would be well attended by white evangelicals, especially given Dr. Evans's preaching ability.

I contacted the church to see if it recorded statistics of the ethnic percentages of its weekly attendance. The Oak Cliff Bible Fellowship staff chose not to share this information. However, they do provide video broadcasts of the Sunday services. Camera sweeps of the congregation reveal, in my own estimation, that fewer than five percent of attendees appear to be white.[17] It defies logic that a preacher such as Evans, who meets every criterion that white evangelicals deem high on their list, from theology and character, to preaching and community leadership, would lead a church that is barely attended by white evangelicals, especially given the fact that white evangelicals alone make up 38 percent of the total population of Dallas/Fort Worth. One could argue that perhaps white evangelicals are not attending Evans's church because they do not know about him. But such an argument would not make any sense. Dr. Evans has been pastoring in Dallas since 1976 and is a household name in white evangelical circles. He served for decades as

15. See "Evangelical Protestants Who Are." Thirty eight percent of the total population is evangelical with 64 percent of that number being white evangelicals, alone.

16. See "Fort Worth Population, 2020."

17. There are many examples of online sermons delivered by Dr. Evans at Oak Cliff Bible Fellowship. One such example that shows camera sweeps of the church can be seen on YouTube. See "God Can Turn Things Completely Around for You."

chaplain of the Dallas Mavericks and Dallas Cowboys professional sports teams. He is a prolific writer who taught for many years and sits on the board of the most respected evangelical seminary in Dallas, and he hosts a nationally syndicated radio program.[18] Being a popular figure is an understatement when thinking of Pastor Evans. So why are there so few white evangelicals attending his church?

The issue lies with the fact that white evangelicals need to move from awareness and recognition of nonwhite leadership to a full embrace of nonwhite leadership. It is very clear that white evangelicals have acknowledged Evans's gift of preaching, following Evans's selection as one of the twelve most effective preachers in the United States. However, that acknowledgement needs to be translated into the embrace that clearly demonstrates that Evans's gift is good for all Christians—white evangelicals as well as their nonwhite siblings. A full embrace of Evans's leadership should equate to a larger share of the white evangelicals in the Dallas area attending his church. Acknowledgement without embrace perpetuates the power distance that racial segregation has established. The greatest weapon against the dividing wall of racial hostility in America would be white evangelicals' full embrace of nonwhite leadership from nonwhite leaders such as Evans.

In my home state of Massachusetts, a well-known and mostly white evangelical church with a total attendance of three thousand members has a membership makeup that is 70 percent white; 20 percent Asian and Pacific Islanders; 4 percent African Americans, Africans, and Caribbeans; 4 percent Hispanic/Latino; and 2 percent multiethnic/other.[19] Pleasantly surprising is the fact that the percentage of the nonwhite population[20] in the metro area of that church correlates with the church's membership data, and, at times, the church's data even surpasses that of the metro area. Asians, for example, make up only 12 percent of the population of the metro area, but represent 20 percent of that church's membership. Hispanics and Latinos make up 8 percent of the metro area, but represent 4 percent of the church's membership. Blacks and African Americans represent 5 percent of the metro area and represent 4 percent of the church. There is no doubt that the gospel will continue to advance through that church, especially given a membership that is on par with the general population.

It is more likely to see a diverse membership in an American church when its pastor is white. However, the book of Acts, in chapters 4, 9, and 13, teaches us that empowering a diverse leadership cadre breeds a multiethnic

---

18. See "About" section of Dr. Tony Evans's website.
19. Deymaz and Li, *Ethnic Blends*, 155.
20. See "Middlesex County, Massachusetts."

congregation. In the American church, it appears that nonwhites have no problem joining a church that is predominantly white and that is led by a white pastor, as is the case of the church highlighted above. It is when the roles are reversed that American Christianity has not been supportive of multiethnic Christian leadership.

Many nonwhite Christians deliberately embrace the leadership of a good preacher in their metropolitan area and willfully overlook the fact that the preacher is white. I wonder what message the American church would communicate to the wider society should white evangelicals deliberately begin to integrate churches like Evans's. This act would be a direct blow to the ethnocentric practice that too many white Christians have embraced in America. It would reinforce the message of Christ that everyone, irrespective of ethnicity, is on an equal footing before Christ, a perspective the American society desperately needs. It would also promote egalitarian multiethnic leadership, and, above all, demonstrate the oneness that Jesus prayed for in the garden of Gethsemane, and thus tell the world that Jesus is the Messiah who unifies all people (John 17:20–23). The church in America will never get to that oneness if our white brothers and sisters in Christ, particularly our white evangelical brothers and sisters, continue to be race-centered in their choices of leaders and overlook nonwhite leadership. In the long run, this undermines multiethnic leadership and thus undermines gospel expansion.

Acknowledging, affirming, and embracing nonwhite Christian leadership is not the task of the average white congregant alone. It is also the duty of white Christian leaders in predominantly white Christian institutions. I once attended a local conference headlined A Life Fashioned after the Gospel of Jesus Christ.[21] At that conference, all the plenary speakers were white. Three of them were national figures and two were locals. Even though this might not have been intentional, such planning on the part of the organizers indicated that white evangelical speakers were the only ones considered competent enough to educate the audience on how to fashion one's life after the gospel. But most shocking was the absence of that city's well-known cadre of highly respected and qualified multiethnic Christian leaders. For a conference that had a local and regional focus, overlooking the contribution of nonwhite leadership as it relates to the theme of that conference was nothing short of scandalous.

I happen to know of many nonwhite pastors in that city who would have very well fit that bill. One, in particular, has an impeccable academic

---

21. I am using a modified version of the conference's name here to protect the identity of its leaders.

pedigree from Ivy League schools and more than twenty years of pastoral experience leading the city's largest Hispanic church. He had abandoned a career in academia twenty years prior to become the full-time pastor of a church of just a few immigrants. Was not his faithfulness to the cause of Christ enough of an example to teach the attendees of that local conference about a life fashioned after the gospel of Christ? Maybe one could excuse the organizers' mistake due to their lack of connections with well established, experienced, respected, and godly nonwhite leaders in that city. But that was not the case at all. First, that city is small, and its Christian population is even smaller. Shockingly, two of the lead organizers were on the faculty of the only evangelical seminary in that city. That same seminary, to this day, has on its board the former pastor of the second oldest African American church in that city. He pastored for more than fifty years and was still serving on the board at the time of that conference. If he was not available, could not the organizers have reached out to the sitting pastor of the oldest African American church in that city, who, at some point, was on the faculty of that same seminary with which the organizers were associated? How about the senior pastor of the largest evangelical church, who, at the time of the conference, was a doctoral student at that same local seminary and had more than forty years of pastoral ministry experience in that city? There were many others with ties to the seminary whom these organizers could have recruited as plenary speakers. In fact, two other pastors who lead large and well-known churches had cofounded an organization to help stem the tide of gun violence in that city. One, in particular, used his body to shield a young man who was the target of a violent attack. This incident was captured in the news and is well known. If this pastor's well publicized heroism is not evidence of a life fashioned after the gospel, I do not know what is! Sadly, such news did not reach the ears or capture the sights of the organizers.

It is impossible to believe that all these nonwhite leaders were unwilling, unavailable, or worse, incapable of teaching about what it means to fashion one's life after the gospel. The truth[22] is they were not contacted. These exemplars are just a few among many other local leaders who were more than qualified to teach on the subject. But they were overlooked. The core issue is that their leadership is not fully embraced by their white evangelical counterparts. These nonwhite leaders are just the ones I know about, but, together, they had more than a century's worth of experience in gospel-centered ministry in the community. These multiethnic leaders

---

22. During a personal conversation, one of the staff members of the organizing committee admitted to not having reached out to the nonwhite leaders of that city.

had plenty to teach an audience that was eager to learn how to fashion one's life after the Gospel.

The problem with "white evangelicalism," as Bryan Lorrits and Soong Chan Rah define it, is its belief that white Christianity is the only form of Christianity that has a right to lead everyone, and, therefore, the best one qualified to teach Christianity to others. And when one ethnic group thinks that it is the only one fit to teach about God, and that no one else is as qualified to teach about God, it automatically disqualifies those it deems inappropriate, not according to God's standards, but its own.

If we want to move past this oppressive model of the nonwhite person perceived as lesser than his or her white counterpart, then, for the sake of the gospel message and the advancement of Christ's kingdom, white evangelicalism must not simply be reformed, but it must be transformed multiculturally to reflect God's full ethnically global body of Christ.

Practice Proximity and Deliberate Integration

Full proximity to nonwhite Christian leadership should flow into the practice of the kind of embrace that leads to deliberate integration of white Christians into nonwhite-dominant churches. Ethicist and theologian Dietrich Bonhoeffer has a lot to teach today's church concerning the practice of proximity and the power of deliberate integration as a platform for gospel expansion. During his experience in America in the 1920s, Bonhoeffer became a member at the Abyssinian Baptist Church in New York's Harlem neighborhood, an African American church in an African American neighborhood at a time when racial segregation was enshrined in American law and practiced vigorously. Bonhoeffer, a white German man, befriended an African American classmate from Union Theological Seminary in New York by the name of Albert Franklin Fisher, who took him to Abyssinian, since Franklin was a member there. Bonhoeffer's soul at the time thirsted for sound doctrine and sound preaching. He lamented to a friend that he could not find Christ-centered preaching at the white churches he had attended in New York. In a letter to that friend, he wrote, "I have only heard one sermon in which you could hear something like a genuine proclamation, and that was delivered by a Negro (indeed, in general I'm increasingly discovering greater religious power and originality in Negroes)."[23]

When Bonhoeffer deliberately attended Abyssinian, and even served as a Sunday School teacher there, his life was radically transformed by the overall experience. The message delivered by Pastor Adam Clayton Powell

23. Metaxas, *Bonhoeffer*, 106.

to his African American congregants—that Christ identifies with and delivers the oppressed—inspired Bonhoeffer to see Christ as the liberator of German Jews who were soon being oppressed under Hitler. In addition, Bonhoeffer's soul was revived through the gift of African American music and hymns. Later, he took many records with him to Germany and taught his students the lyrics of African American hymns to provide them with inspiration and encouragement. Bonhoeffer's positive life transformation at Abyssinian was not possible at the white churches of his day, as these white churches did not see Christ as being the liberator of the oppressed. But, because Bonhoeffer deliberately integrated a nonwhite church, he was able to benefit from leadership that taught him about Christ in a manner no one else did for him, which, in turn, transformed him into a change agent in his own right. Reggie L. Williams, in his book *Bonhoeffer's Black Jesus*, underscores this point when he states,

> In Harlem Bonhoeffer learned of a black tradition of Jesus that connected faithfulness to God, the recognition of suffering, and the presence of Christ as cosufferer. The ministries that Bonhoeffer participated in at Abyssinian Baptist Church, coupled with the intellectual interrogation of Jesus within the Harlem Renaissance, provided Bonhoeffer with new resources to filter the nationalism from his Christianity and helped to develop him into an advocate of ecumenism, of peacemaking, and of social justice. As a consequence of that black experience with Jesus, his theology became more than conceptual, his Christology became more prominent, and Bonhoeffer became more serious about his faith."[24]

Now, this is not to say that the only place a white Christian can hear the gospel preached with integrity is in a nonwhite church. What Bonhoeffer's experience tells us is that there is as much, and, sometimes, even more to gain when one decides deliberately to integrate a community of Christian believers from a different ethnic group. That community can lead and teach one in ways that cannot be found elsewhere, even in one's own ethnic community. And, just like Bonhoeffer, a white Christian who deliberately joined the membership of a nonwhite church, one does not need to remain a passive congregant. A white evangelical Christian can also be an active congregant and serve, as Bonhoeffer did when he taught Sunday school classes to boys at Abyssinian Baptist Church.

Dietrich Bonhoeffer's action should teach all of us, particularly those who are beholden to white evangelicalism, that a call to Christianity is not an

---

24. Metaxas, *Bonhoeffer*, 107.

invitation to consume a product, but a radical mandate to advance discipleship for the kingdom of God. Bonhoeffer reminds the church of what that kind of discipleship looks like when he writes, "The church is her true self only when she exists for humanity . . . not lording it over men but helping and serving them. She must tell men, whatever their calling, what it means to live in Christ, to exist for others."[25] The disciple of Christ chooses to belong to a church community in order to live out a mission for God and to fulfill a calling. Too many Christians forgo the opportunity to become servant leaders when they bypass the opportunity to integrate the membership of a church whose congregants have ethnicities that are different from their own. As seen in the case of the predominantly white evangelical megachurch in my home state noted above, deliberate church membership integration is an act of service that more nonwhite Christians are willing to make, but too few white evangelicals are practicing. This act of service is leadership at its best and must be pursued by all, thus fulfilling a mission of interdependence, integration, healing, and reconciliation in the body of Christ.

Lack of proximity to nonwhite Christians is at the heart of the separation between white and nonwhite Christians in America, and also an impediment to the flourishing of egalitarian multiethnic leadership. Survey specialist George Gallup exposed the degree to which white evangelicals want physical separation from nonwhites. In their 1989 book *The People's Religion*, George Gallup Jr. and James Castelli showed that white evangelicals, more than any other group in America, are in favor of objecting to a black person moving into their neighborhoods at a rate considerably higher than that of all other groups.[26] Such attitudes persist into more recent times. According to another Gallup poll from August 2004, white evangelicals among all ethnic groups are least likely to worship in congregations where the racial makeup is predominantly different from themselves.[27] Lack of proximity leads to apathy and indifference on the part of white evangelicals toward those who should be considered brothers and sisters in Christ. The more separated we are from each other, the less likely we will benefit each other through our gifts and services. Since leadership is first and foremost a matter of service, lack of proximity leads to absence of cross-cultural service, and thus cross-cultural leadership.

The story of the Good Samaritan in the Bible has a lot to teach us concerning the power of proximity. Without proximity, no one is aware of another's need. And that lack of awareness impoverishes both groups. The

---

25. Bonhoeffer, *Letters from Prison*, ch. 3.
26. Gallup and Castelli, *The People's Religion*, 188.
27. Winseman, "Race and Religion: Divisions Steeped in History," line 9.

person in need loses the opportunity to receive treatment and care, and the person in a position to meet that need loses an opportunity to please God. White evangelicals practicing proximity and deliberate integration can get their needs met and please God while at the same time helping others, and, in that way, advancing the cause of the gospel.

With proximity and deliberate integration, multilateral exchanges take place and cross-pollination of service and leadership among all ethnic groups can become a recipe for revival. The Azusa Street Revival of 1906–1909 and its aftermath provide clear examples of the power of egalitarian multiethnic leadership undergirded by the practice of proximity and deliberate integration. The revival was led by an African American by the name of William Seymour. The team Seymour led was made up of blacks and whites alike, with the whites embracing and promoting Seymour's leadership.[28] Those whites were countercultural, as they put aside their ethnic pride and false sense of superiority to pursue God's objective of making Christ known to the world. In his landmark book on the history of the Azusa Street Revival, historian Cecil M. Robeck writes,

> Pastor Seymour surrounded himself with [a] very capable, interracial staff of women and men. Together they provided the planning and forethought required by the revival. It was they who commissioned a significant number of missionaries and evangelists, and supported a rescue mission in Los Angeles. They coordinated workers who traveled on the streetcar system to predetermined sites. They communicated with these workers, keeping tabs on the progress of their work and encouraging them to think of the Azusa Street Mission as their connective center. They accepted invitations to speak and hold meetings in other cities in congregations that wanted to identify with the revival. In a sense, they laid out the plans that might have developed into a new Pentecostal denomination with Azusa Street Mission at its core. Pastor Seymour clearly helped to define this interracial mission and its message, but he did not do it alone.[29]

---

28. Historian Cecil M. Robeck shows that such behavior was not always the case when Seymour first started. One of his key leaders, Glenn A. Cook, actually attended one of Seymour's first revival meetings with the intention to shame and rebuke Seymour publicly. He stood up and began deriding Seymour in the general assembly. In the middle of his speech, he became convinced that he was wrong, and that Seymour was right. Cook openly repented and signed up for the movement to assist Seymour. Robeck, *The Azusa Street Mission and Revival*, 101.

29. Robeck, *The Azusa Street Mission and Revival*, 100–01.

The impact of Azusa was so significant in promoting multiethnic leadership and the embrace of nonwhite leadership that, despite many Pentecostal denominations making distinctions along the color line, many white Pentecostals exchanged bigotry for deliberate integration. In *Ecclesiology and Exclusion*, David D. Daniels III, professor of world Christianity at McCormick Theological Seminary, shares how powerful Christian witness becomes when proximity is the product of deliberate integration. He gives examples from Pentecostal churches in Azusa's wake. In a chapter entitled "Transcending the Exclusionary Ecclesial Practices of Racial Hierarchies of Authority: An Early Pentecostal Trajectory," he states,

> Resisting the dominant pattern of race dictating the criteria for membership in a congregation, some white Christians joined black congregations when the vast majority of whites distanced themselves from African Americans and supported enshrining their exclusionary practices into both denominational polity and the U.S. legal system. Challenging the dominant pattern of race being a criterion for congregations connecting or being assigned to particular denominational associations or judicatories, some white congregations joined black denominations when the vast majority of white congregations belonged to all white denominations or denominations led by white Christians, both native-born and immigrant. Countering the dominant pattern of race being the criterion for membership within the denominational leadership, some white Christians submitted to the authority of their African American leadership when the vast majority of white Christians refused to recognize any authority exercised by African Americans. . . . Vital to resisting racial hierarchies of authority is the construction of an alternative system of authority. Inclusionary practices of ecclesial governance rooted in the races being "equal in power and authority" served as this alternative. The degrees of participation by African Americans and whites needed to go beyond mere association as an inclusionary accommodation to shared authority. . . . [T]hese Pentecostal resisters of the status quo rejected hierarchies of authority that promoted hypertrophy, where one race, in practice, assumes all the authority and power and does "everything in the church," coupled with atrophy, where one race is functionally denied authority and power and rendered passive. Deeming race as an invalid basis of allocating authority, these Pentecostals imagined ecclesial authority shared by both, if not all, races.[30]

---

30. See Daniels, *Ecclesiology and Exclusion*, 142–43.

The greatest antidote to self-centeredness is proximity, especially the kind that goes beyond the "separate but equal" paradigm. This kind of proximity promotes a comingling of beings over the mere coexistence of beings. This kind of proximity also enables learning to take place where the one being taught or led can also be from the dominant culture.

Proximity should not merely mean the sharing of space or belonging to the same organization, but entails active, selfless mutual submission. Otherwise, proximity without humility is the same as distance with arrogance. Practicing proximity without a learning posture will always embolden those who are beholden to white cultural hegemony to overlook and disqualify nonwhite leaders. However, the kind of proximity that leads to deliberate integration is always accompanied with a letting go of privileges that stand in the way of gospel expansion. David Daniels adds,

> These white Pentecostal individuals put on hold the privileges granted to them by the exclusionary practices of racial segregation when they joined majority African American congregations and denominations. White Pentecostal congregations put on hold the privileges granted to them by the exclusionary practices of racial segregation when they joined predominantly black Pentecostal denominations headed by African Americans and placed on hold the power distributed to them by their race. These white Pentecostal individuals and congregations placed on hold or even rejected the prejudices about black people that the American society inscribed into federal law and state laws and that American Christianity structured into their church order."[31]

American Christianity is not without adequate examples of deliberate integration. An example such as the Azusa Street Mission and Revival ought to be replicated today in a world that desperately needs to know Christ. Proximity that leads to deliberate integration forms the bedrock of Christian oneness. Oneness is possible when we empty ourselves of toxic ethnic pride to make room for the embrace of the brother and sister from another ethnic group. It is that oneness that becomes countercultural and that promotes Gospel advancement.

---

31. See Daniels, *Ecclesiology and Exclusion*, 143–46.

Rethinking the Culture's Highest Ideal: The Pursuit of Happiness

What could serve as impediments to deliberate integration? One is ideological and the other practical. Perhaps, ideologically, the most subtle form of resistance the Christian church in America will encounter while pursuing deliberate integration across ethnic lines is a racist interpretation of the American ideal, namely, the pursuit of happiness.[32] What form has the pursuit of happiness taken for white evangelicals? It has led to the development of segregated communities and churches. For example, as white North America pursued happiness through white flight to the suburbs and redlining in the cities, white evangelicals bought into the wider culture's offer of happiness by creating enclaves for themselves and building institutions such as schools and churches in order to provide themselves with what amounts to a false sense of peace and safety. Sadly, this kind of behavior, fueled by a segregationist ethos, ended up preserving an ungodly status quo, all in the pursuit of happiness. Such a segregationist ethos also hindered gospel expansion and the growth of healthy United States churches.

Paul Louis Metzger is keen in his insight when he states in *Consuming Jesus*, "Many evangelical church leaders believe that the best way to multiply churches quickly is to make the members feel comfortable rather than comfort them with the cross that breaks down the divisions between God, us, and others."[33] Comfort, which is another expression for "the pursuit of happiness," is the enemy of mission, and comfort almost always undermines gospel movements. Many white evangelical brothers and sisters are not incentivized to leave their comfort zones to practice deliberate integration because such practice would threaten their right to be happy. Such practice would also be too costly because it assumes a "greater potential for internal conflict."[34] In the final analysis, the right to be happy wins—not the need to be godly.

Today, the concept of church in the North American context, for the most part, is one that reinforces our sense of rights, not one that encourages the giving up of rights for the sake of the gospel. Today, many churches exist to make people happy, as so many of us think. And when our sense of happiness is threatened, we swiftly make our way to the nearest church that would give us the happiness we seek. The pursuit of happiness is the guide by which we evaluate every aspect of our lives, from the church we attend, to the neighborhood we live in, to the careers we choose, even

---

32. *The Declaration of Independence*.
33. Metzger, *Consuming Jesus*, 9–10.
34. Emerson and Smith, *Divided by Faith*, 145.

down to the cars we drive. Happiness has become our national idol, and the pursuit of happiness is nothing short of addictive. The words of Alexis De Toqueville in 1833 describe the continuing futility in our culture's pursuit of happiness: "At every moment [those who pursue happiness] think they are about to grasp it; it escapes at every moment from their hold. They are near enough to see its charms, but too far off to enjoy them; and before they have fully tasted its delights, they die."[35]

Sadly, our culture's pursuit of happiness makes empty promises and yields empty results. It is also void of a sense of the ultimate, as it is its own end. Instead, we should see God as the ultimate aim of all humans, and thus the only one who can bring ultimate happiness. As Thomas Aquinas wrote, "Happiness is the same as God."[36] Since happiness is always a fleeting experience, Aquinas reminds us of the fact that God is reliable and everlasting. Therefore, true happiness is when we actively pursue a relationship with God, as all other forms of happiness in this life are temporary. In pursuing true happiness through our everlasting creator God, we receive all the satisfactions that our pursuit of happiness in the context of the American dream had promised, but could not deliver. Just as the pursuit of happiness is being instructed by the overarching culture, seeking God's true happiness can also be taught with the same fervor. In practicality, Thomas Aquinas's form of happiness echoed what Jesus himself taught his disciples when he stated, "Happy are those whose greatest desire is to do what God requires; God will satisfy them fully!" (Matt. 5:5, GNT). Therefore, we Christians can learn to pursue true happiness, the desire to do what God requires, by promoting a vision of egalitarian multiethnic leadership.

Practically speaking, the challenge that deliberate integration poses must not be overlooked, as the instability that defines the communities to be integrated presents challenges that require systemic solutions. When white Christians deliberately integrate nonwhite churches, it is likely that they will be in community with people who have been marginalized economically. A call to deliberate integration is a call to experience the financial and other structural limitations that currently exist in the environments to be integrated. This means, if there is poverty, one will experience poverty. If there is economic insecurity and other forms of scarcity, one will live and exist in the confines of such insecurity and scarcity. I personally know of a few brave souls, who, in their young years, decided to follow John Perkins's model of relocation. Some moved to urban centers and ended up as members of nonwhite dominant churches. These were post-college idealists. However,

---

35. De Toqueville, *Democracy in America*, 494.
36. Aquinas, *Summa Theologica: What Is Happiness*, Objection 3.

when they started to form families and rear children, they found it nearly impossible to rear children in an urban context where they were the minority, and in one that lacks resources. Such white Christian risk takers needed the support of a wider network that would enable them to remain in place while committing to the ideal of integration.

The kinds of structural support that would be needed to keep white integrators stable in the communities they integrate require logistical support for childcare, school, and other tools for healthy socialization and human development. Networks of churches both local and beyond, denominations, and other parachurch organizations would need to consider providing the requisite tools that can ensure long-term success, from mentoring to social and spiritual covering. In addition, our white integrators should never venture on their own. Groups are better than individuals, and families of integrators should be friends with local church families, with the latter reaching out to the former. Lastly, white Christian integrators bring in a wealth of human resources that can and must be leveraged in the local churches and communities. Their membership in churches should be an impetus that keeps them engaged, nurtured, and challenged. They need to be invited to serve according to their gifts and callings while remaining open to mentorship from local multiethnic leaders. In the end, they will be one with the community, just like everyone else, except, to the outsider, they display a counterchultural attitude that calls attention to a God of love. As our white brothers and sisters deliberately integrate communities that are predominantly nonwhite, not to dominate, but to serve and embrace nonwhite multiethnic leadership while living as equals before Christ, they will practice an egalitarian leadership model that sets a high bar for discipleship for the entire body of Christ.

References

Baylor University website. "Baylor University's Truett Seminary Announces 12 Most Effective Preachers in English-Speaking World." https://www.baylor.edu/mediacommunications/news.php?action=story&story=198528. Accessed April 1, 2019.

Berzon, Todd. "Ethnicity and Early Christianity." *Currents in Biblical Research* 16:2 (2018): 191–227.

Bonhoeffer, Dietrich. *Prisoner for God: Letters and Papers from Prison*. Edited by Eberhard Bethge. Translated by Fuller H. Regina. https://www.academia.edu/38108724/Letters_and_papers_from_prison_-Dietrich_Bonhoeffer.

Daniels, David D. III. "Transcending the Exclusionary Ecclesial Practices of Racial Hierarchies and Authority: An Early Pentecostal Trajectory." In *Ecclesiology and Exclusion: Boundaries of Being and Belonging in Postmodern Times,* edited by

Dennis M. Doyle, Timothy J. Furry, and Pascal D. Bazzell, 137–151. Maryknoll, NY: Orbis, 2012.

Data USA website. "Middlesex County, Massachusetts." https://datausa.io/profile/geo/middlesex-county-ma/#demographics. Accessed April 17, 2019.

De Toqueville, Alexis. *Democracy in America*. Edited by Bruce Frohnen. Translated by Henry Reeve. Washington, DC: Regnery, 2002.

Deymaz, Mark, and Harry Li. *Ethnic Blends: Mixing Diversity into Your Local Church*. Grand Rapids: Zondervan, 2010.

Emerson, Michael O., and Christian Smith. *Divided by Faith: Evangelical Religion and the Problem of Race in America*. New York: Oxford University Press, 2000.

Evans, Tony. "God Can Turn Things Completely Around for You." Online video clip. Tony Evans Ministries, March 10, 2020. https://www.youtube.com/watch?v=9W_EY7mkzT4.

Gallup, George Jr., and James Castille. *The People's Religion: American Faith in the 90s*. New York: Macmillan, 1989.

Kaatz, Kevin W. *The Rise of Early Christianity: History, Documents, and Key Questions*. Santa Barbara, CA: ABC–CLIO, 2016.

King, Martin. L. "Where Do We Go from Here?" Address Delivered at the Eleventh Annual SLCL Convention. http://www.stanford.edu/group/King/publications/speeches/Where_do_we_go_from_here.html. Accessed May 1, 2019.

———. NBC's Meet the Press with Ned Brooks, April 17, 1960. http://okra.stanford.edu/transcription/document_images/Vol05Scans/17Apr1960_InterviewonMeetthePress.pdf. Accessed April 22, 2019.

Latourette, Kenneth S. *A History of Christianity, Volume 1, Beginnings to 1500*. Revised Edition. New York: HarperCollins, 1975.

Loritts, Bryan. *Inside Outsider: My Journey as a Stranger in White Evangelicalism and My Hope for Us All*. Grand Rapids: Zondervan, 2018.

Metaxas, Eric. *Bonhoeffer: Pastor, Martyr, Prophet, Spy: A Righteous Gentile vs. The Third Reich*. Nashville: Thomas Nelson, 2010.

Metzger, Paul Louis. *Consuming Jesus: Beyond Race and Class Divisions in a Consumer Church*. Grand Rapids: Eerdmans, 2007.

Myers, Allen. C. *The Eerdmans Bible Dictionary*. Grand Rapids: Eerdmans, 1993.

Pew Research Center, Religion and Public Life. "Evangelical Protestants Who Are in the Dallas/Fort Worth Area." https://www.pewforum.org/religious-landscape-study/metro-area/dallasfort-worth-metro-area/religious-tradition/evangelical-protestant. Accessed May 23, 2020.

Porter, Stanley. E. "Did Paul Speak Latin?" In *Paul, Jew, Greek, and Roman. Pauline Studies*. Vol. 5. Brill. Online Publication (Jan 31, 2009). https://brill.com/view/book/edcoll/9789047424918/Bej.9789004171596.i-370_014.xml. Accessed May 25, 2020.

Rah, Soong C. *The Next Evangelicalism: Freeing the Church from Western Cultural Captivity*. Downers Grove, IL: InterVarsity, 2009.

———. *Many Colors: Cultural Intelligence for a Changing Church*. Chicago: Moody, 2010.

Richards, E. Randolph, and Brandon J. O'Brien. *Misreading Scripture with Western Eyes: Removing Cultural Blinders to Better Understand the Bible*. Downers Grove, IL: InterVarsity, 2012.

Robeck, Cecil M. Jr. *The Azusa Street Mission and Revival: The Birth of the Global Pentecostal Movement*. Nashville: Thomas Nelson, 2006.
Thomas, Aquinas. *Summa Theologica: What Is Happiness*. https://www.sacred-texts.com/chr/aquinas/summa/sum136.htm. Accessed April 1, 2019.
Tony Evans: The Urban Alternative website. https://tonyevans.org/about/tony-evans.
United States Declaration of Independence. National Archives. https://www.archives.gov/founding-docs/declaration-transcript. Accessed April 22, 2019.
United States Department of Homeland Security. *Annual Flow Report: Lawful Permanent Residents: August 2018*. https://www.dhs.gov/sites/default/files/publications/Lawful-Permanent-Residents-2017.pdf. Accessed April 1, 2019.
Williams, Reggie L. *Bonhoeffer's Black Jesus: Harlem Renaissance Theology and an Ethic of Resistance*. Waco, TX: Baylor University Press, 2014.
Winseman, Albert L. "Race and Religion: Divisions Steeped in History," 2004. https://news.gallup.com/poll/12664/race-religion-divisions-steeped-history.aspx. Accessed May 23, 2020.
World Population Review website. "Fort Worth Population, 2020." http://worldpopulationreview.com/us-cities/fort-worth-population/. Accessed April 5, 2019.

8

Egalitarian Faith Nurturing in the African Context

Julius K. Kithinji

WHEN PAUL IN 2 Timothy 1:5 invokes Timothy's childhood Christian experiences, not only does he encourage him to remain in the faith, but also to be a champion of the faith. In Paul's understanding, these beautiful childhood faith experiences for Timothy were rooted in a sequentially passed-on faith stemming from his grandmother Lois, flowing through his mother Eunice, and residing in him. Now, Paul argues for that faith to be spread out to others under Timothy's spiritual patronage, thus forming an extended spiritual family tree and an endless faith lineage, or what I term a *faith genealogy*. By mentioning Timothy's grandmother and mother in matters of his faith, Paul delineates Timothy's faith genealogy. And in doing so, Paul necessarily excludes fathers and grandfathers in this lineage. Mostly, this is because Timothy's father was not a believer (Acts 16:1), thus, unable to guide his son to Christian maturity or to exonerate male characters from essential religious upbringing of children, but also to notify readers of paternal deficiency or negligence in matters of faith upbringing. But, since later Paul presents himself as Timothy's paternal faith figure, Paul's adopted faith genealogy thus indicates an essential aspect of Christian upbringing that needs to be encouraged and brought into perspective within a framework of Christian egalitarian leadership and mutuality in matters of faith nurturing.

In this chapter, I bring out issues not only in Timothy's life, but also in the Greco-Roman context that could have made Paul bring to our attention Timothy's faith life in such a manner. The purpose of such an undertaking is not only to point out the necessity of male figures in generational faith, but also to critique and appraise dimensions of African life that promote or hinder an envisaged gender-complete promotion of faith. Such a discourse comes at a time when many African contexts are experiencing a resurgence of cultural values steeped in patriarchy. These values are bound to undermine gains from gender movements, church campaigns, and government policies in the war against negative patriarchal cultures.

Previous chapters of this book have already said much about Christian egalitarian leadership and servant leadership. Many models have already been proposed pointing to the church and how it can be empowered through this concept. This chapter considers Christian egalitarian leadership and servant leadership as a product of upbringing; this is upbringing based on faith from an African perspective as anchored in biblical teaching. It is a recognition that, more often than not, upbringing brings us to the points where we find ourselves in life. Therefore, the early years of a child, running all through teenage and young adults, determines if we shall have an egalitarian society or not. They dictate if we shall have the requisite heritage for maintaining a legacy of Christian egalitarian leadership or not.

For many years African Christian leaders have battled the effects of patriarchy. The infiltration of the effects of a harmful heritage of patriarchy even in the church was not an accidental rearrangement. It owes much of its existence to layers and layers of generations who through upbringing were socialized and oriented to this demeaning heritage. Although proponents of patriarchy in Africa have perceptions of its relative and arguable advantages, Christian egalitarian leadership does not share that perspective.[1] Therefore, there must be deliberate efforts to develop, raise, and nurture a generation that owes itself to Christian egalitarian leadership, as a product of upbringing. And, although the Bible has much to say concerning this topic, I purposely and mainly anchor my thoughts and reflections on Paul's description of Timothy in 2 Timothy 1:5. Suffice it to say that it is through the lens of 2 Timothy that I view the examples of African upbringing of children and attune them to the biblical model. This is done as a way of critiquing contemporary African models that are quickly forgetting or abandoning their root and rich African and Christian heritage, much to their detriment. Toward the end of this chapter, I shall propose models for faith nurturing in Africa

---

1. Those who practiced patriarchy were socialized to think that it was practiced in the best interests of the society.

that assure deliberate steps are taken to nurture a heritage of Christian egalitarian faith leadership in Africa.

Timothy's Responsibilities and Faith Upbringing

In 2 Timothy 1:5, Paul draws attention to Timothy's faith and ascribes to it a genealogical dimension because it had been passed on through two, and perhaps several, successive generations. It is not possible with certitude to know how far back it goes, but Paul acknowledges Timothy's faith was first resident in his grandmother Lois and then in his mother, Eunice. This faith was passed on through upbringing. To understand the depth and breadth of Paul's statement, consider the full sweep of Timothy's context.

Timothy[2] is first mentioned in the book of Acts, and little information is given about him there. He was a product of a mixed marriage between a Jewish woman and an unnamed Gentile father. His mother was devout in Jewish and Christian beliefs (Acts 16:1; 2 Tim 1:5), and, with her mother Lois, had a great influence on Timothy's faith, raising him to learn the Torah and, perhaps, the "memoirs" of Jesus's disciples, as the gospels were called, within a Gentile environment with an absentee father.[3] As has been mentioned, the most important detail on this is found in 2 Timothy 1:5 where Timothy's egalitarian faith leadership qualities are attributed to the imbibed example of his mother, Eunice, and grandmother Lois.

It can also be deduced that, from them, Timothy learned the Scriptures from a very tender age: infancy (2 Tim 3:15). From Acts and the Epistles, we learn that Timothy grew up to become an influential church leader responsible for the faith of a complex community comprised of the young, widows, slaves, and elders alike (1 Tim 5). Timothy was responsible for sound doctrine and theology (1 Tim 1:3–7). On this point, and that of his character, Timothy's leadership can be termed Christian egalitarian because sound doctrine involves sound egalitarian belief flowing through sound character. He was responsible for maintaining a sound church which

---

2. His name was common among the Greeks (Keener, *Acts*, vol. 3, 2335). *Timau* and *theos* could mean "one who honors God." Other references in the New Testament include 1 Tim 1:2; 4:14; 2 Tim 1:5; 3:11; 4:13; Acts 16:1–3; 19:22; 20:4; 17:14–15; 1 Thess 1:1; 3:2; 2 Thess 1:1; Phil 1:1; Heb 13:23.

3. About his father's absence and his mother's and grandmother's influence, most scholars conjecture that his father must have already been dead (this is also the opinion of Keener, *Acts*, vol. 3, 2317) by the time of his interaction with Paul. Since the phrase "he was" in Acts 16:3 uses the past tense, many scholars agree it can be used to justify the absence of any reference to him as well as by the strong influence assigned in reliable tradition to his mother.

valued healthy relationships through prayer and teaching (1 Tim 2:1– 4). He was responsible for maintaining healthy relationships with both genders (1 Tim 2:9–15), so his leadership had to cut across gender lines, making him a perfect example of reliable Christian egalitarian leadership.

Though not expressly alone, Timothy was in charge of discerning and qualifying those who claimed to have a calling for ecclesiastical offices, including deacons and overseers. For this reason, Paul gives him criteria to which he could refer in such circumstances (1 Tim 3). Though a young minister, Timothy was in charge of general church morality; moreover, he was in charge of himself: both his spiritual and physical health. And, in all this, Paul noted that his source of authority and model for leadership was his faith, which was a continuation of that of his Jewish mother, Eunice, and his grandmother, Lois. Paul also noted that part of Timothy's faith heritage could be attributed to him, because he had modeled faith as a father figure to Timothy (1 Tim 1:2). The richness of Timothy's egalitarian leadership could have continued until his death as a martyr. Christian tradition states that Timothy died in Ephesus when he was more than 80 years old.[4]

Mothers and Grandmothers and Faith Upbringing in the Greco-Roman World

The grandmother hypothesis[5] or matrilineal principle[6] for matters of faith in the Greco-Roman setting states that "rather than continuing to have their own children, older women, especially maternal grandmothers, would contribute more to the survival and transfer of their line (and thus of their genes) by taking care of their younger female relatives and their children." Studies have shown that, just as marriageable mothers were relatively young, so were grandmothers.[7] There were situations that found grandmothers

4. According to the first chapter of *Foxe's Book of Martyrs*, he died in CE 97 upholding the truth of the Bible. Foxe's states he was the bishop of Ephesus, and was murdered when he told a crowd of pagans that their idolatrous celebrations were ridiculous. Owing to this, some traditions have equated and regarded him as the angel of the church at Ephesus (Rev 2:1–7). See Catholic Online, "Epistles to Timothy and Titus."

5. Vuolanto, "Grandmothers in Roman Egypt," 372–402.

6. Cohen, "Timothy" (Acts 16:1–3), 265.

7. Vuolanto points out that women, who married earlier, could have become grandparents quite young. The youngest grandmother who appears in census documents is only 42 years old, and the youngest grandfather 54, while the oldest grandparents of both sexes were 75 years old. The average age was 60 for grandmothers and 63 for grandfathers—not any great difference here. Becoming a grandparent did not necessarily mean growing old in years, but rather marked a growing maturity within the family. "Grandmothers in Roman Egypt," 377.

cohabiting with their grandchildren, mostly because the mothers of these children—their daughters—were not in full control of their marriages, or the grandmothers were widowed. According to Ville Vuolanto, women had limited capacity for legal guardianship under Roman law; however, this did not curtail them from providing the necessary guidance for their children. Grandmothers had considerable authority over their daughters and their children, particularly in matters of culture and faith. Because maternal grandparents were active on the maternal side of the marriage,[8] it is possible that Timothy was reared in such a situation.

Although there is no express data to support this assertion, even in Africa, most children who grew up in the care of their grandparents exhibited more maturity than those who grew up only under the care of their parents. In Africa, the agency of paternal (mostly) grandmothers toward their younger relatives is limited to situations in which the mother and/or the father of the child was dead. The role of grandmothers, even in the presence of fathers, uncles, and stepfathers, is pronounced in the lives of many children. They act as backups in case parents die or are for some other reason absent or temporarily unable to bring up their children. In the Greco-Roman culture, grandchildren meant the survival of the family and its traditions, security in old age, and the maintenance and continuity of the names and memories of older generations.[9] Since maternal grandparents, especially grandmothers, appear in cases involving infants, it meant that pregnant women, and those with a newborn child, would have been in frequent interaction with their own parents and would have sought support and comfort, especially from their mothers. In African situations, mothers sought help more from their mothers because they were the primary nurses for their children.

Although involvement of maternal or paternal grandmothers was the norm in the Greco-Roman world, the case of Timothy, however, could have been different. It is possible that Timothy found himself in a maternal space because mixed marriages for Jews in Greco-Roman culture presented complications for children. According to Shaye Cohen, their citizenship status may have been a difficult issue, because children in a legal marriage follow the status of the father; however, children from a marriage between a citizen and a non-citizen follow the status of the mother, meaning, the offspring of intermarriage are judged matrilineally: a Jewish woman bears a Jewish child, and a Gentile woman bears a Gentile child.[10]

---

8. Vuolanto, "Grandmothers in Roman Egypt," 387.
9. Nuorluoto, "Emphasizing matrilineal ancestry in a patrilineal system," 257.
10. See Cohen "Was Timothy a Jew?" 265. See also Neuffer, "First-Century Cultural

Ordinarily, Timothy would have been educated by his father, for boys' education was a father's responsibility. However, from Paul we know that most of Timothy's influential education came from his mother and grandmother. Although education for most ordinary Greco-Roman women included little more than the domestic arts taught by mothers, there was elementary religious instruction enough to pass on to children. In spite of the girls' lack of opportunity for an education, there were women who somehow acquired considerable knowledge of the Torah and even of other subjects. This could have been the case for Timothy. There are records of some rabbis whose wives were learned in the law. It is not strange to argue, therefore, that Timothy's mother and grandmother had enough knowledge to give him a solid grounding in the Scriptures.[11]

Finally, the maternal side of Timothy's family struggled to give him the best upbringing in their power. Based on patriarchal understandings, Timothy was a proper Gentile. However, based on the matrilineal principle of the first century, most likely he was reared as a Jew even though he was not circumcised. His circumcision later in life and his influence in the mission of the church all bear witness to his Jewishness.[12] Therefore, as is already emerging, Timothy's mother, grandmother, and Paul laid the foundation for Timothy becoming a great Christian egalitarian leader.

Biblical Principle on Egalitarian Faith and Upbringing

Whereas Timothy's faith leadership is a product of mothers and grandmothers, there is biblical evidence that his leadership was supported and supplemented by male figures, including Paul and others in the Christian community. Failure to acknowledge male influence in his life would imply that the faith of mothers and grandmothers is all sufficient. Psychological studies have consistently shown the importance of both parents in upbringing.[13] The biblical point is also clear that "it is not good for man to be alone" (Gen 2:18–25), and this applies to parenting as well. The Bible reveals that fathers and mothers, grandfathers and grandmothers, should all be visible in the nurturing of generational faith.[14] There are many instances where the Bible encourages egalitarian faith upbringing in families and community.

Backgrounds in the Greco-Roman Empire."
    11. See Cohen, "Was Timothy a Jew?" 243.
    12. Gen 17:10; Lev 12:3; Acts 16.
    13. Tong, Baghurst, Vimpani, and McMichael. "Socioeconomic Position," 286.
    14. See especially Exod 13:8, 14; Deut 4:9–10, 6; 11:19–23; Prov 1–9.

Though with their unique problems, the families of Abraham, Isaac and Rebecca, and David serve as such. The book of Proverbs also contains many exhortations on how children should be brought up by both parents. In Proverbs, parenting is viewed as a God-given mandate, and parents are viewed as representatives of God in this matter. Biblical evidence also points to the fact that Jesus was brought up by both parents.[15] His teachings in many places also assume that both parents are in control of upbringing in a Christian setting. Paul's household codes likewise expect that both parents will be responsible for raising up a generation of faith.[16] Faith is a tradition to be passed on, making it a genealogical matter. Therefore, Christian faith is a genealogical issue if the family is Christian.

African Faith Children Upbringing

The African context is experiencing many challenges insofar as faith upbringing of children is concerned. There are far too many absentee fathers, irresponsible mothers, a proliferation of single parenthood, and deliberate single mothers—things that were unheard of in the past.[17] The emergence of daunting behavioral changes arouses a desire to look back to once-held beliefs and practices of any given community. Africa is known for its communal or *Ubuntu*[18] philosophical heritage. African society still embraces the values that ensure solid founding of *Ubuntu* philosophy, and parenting is not an exception.

Parenting, in spite of its many manifestations,[19] was well institutionalized in African societies. An African child went through two main processes: first, a transitional process that began just before birth and continued to adulthood, embracing cultural values that were important in particular contexts, and, second, parenting adopted a contextual dimension in terms of environment, culture, and heritage. African strategies for parenting were distinctively embraced by the African people, who treasured a communal ordering within their societies. Parenting systems were geared toward protecting and enhancing the values that upheld oneness. Thus, African

---

15. Matthew's and Luke's infancy narratives reveal that Jesus was parented by both parents. See, for example, Matt 2:14, 23, 39 and Luke 2:39–52.

16. Eph 6:1–4.

17. Abuya, Mutisya, and Onsumu, "Family Structure," shows that 19.5 percent of African children currently live in single-parent or -guardian families.

18. Ubuntu philosophy summarized by John Mbiti states that "You are; therefore, I am." In other words, one exists because the other is. *African Religion and Philosophy*, 106.

19. Amos, "Parenting and Culture Evidence," 23.

parenting drew from indispensable importance of oneness, where the values of common good, peace, cohesion, and hard work were expected to be passed down through generations.[20]

In Africa, it was the prerogative of every elder, male and female, to ensure that values that enhance social cohesion and development were embraced by the younger generations. The importance of this demand rested on the value placed on children, who were a man's source of pride, power, social status, and wealth, and a woman's assurance of standing in society. Values were handed down in a gendered structure. Boys were nurtured by their male figures, including grandfathers and fathers, while girls spent most of the time with grandmothers, mothers, and other women.

Since African parenting was communal in nature, upbringing and socialization of children was not the purview of the parents only. Africans believed that a child belongs to community, and this gave every elder a duty of rearing up a child into a responsible man or woman. Although individual homes had distinct strategies of parenting, all pointed toward maintenance of high levels of integrity, hard work, and respect, though along gender lines. Although not common, some children were reared by their mothers. This occurred only when the mother was accorded the status of an outcast. Children brought up by only mothers exhibited certain social deficiencies, for example, lack of esteem, meanness, and problems with social integration.[21] Although these could be attributed to one-sided upbringing, they could also be on account of the social prejudice against them.

The value placed on a child in Africa is traceable from the respect accorded an expectant woman. Parenting begins even before the child is born. Expected mothers are accorded special treatment in preparation for the incoming addition to the family. C. N. Nwadiokwu asserts:

> in many African societies a pregnant woman is supposed to observe certain taboos and regulations so as to protect herself and the unborn child. "Some of these taboos include wearing protective amulets which have the virtue of preventing evil spirits such as witches and also helping in delivery. She avoids doubtful foods for fear that these foods would interfere with the health and safety of the mother or child or could cause misfortune for either of them after birth."[22]

Protection of mothers and infants was not the role of expectant mothers only, but also of her clan. African society loves to have children. In

---

20. Idang, "African Culture and Values," 101.
21. Amos, "Parenting and Culture Evidence," 68.
22. Nwadiokwu, "Rites of Passage," 42.

ancient and not so ancient times, a woman derived her social status and her indispensable value from her role as child bearer.[23]

Even with the value of a child, preference was, and is still, largely accorded to male children. Upon birth, the gender of the child determines upbringing strategies and guidelines. Additionally, firstborn boys were parented differently from other boys. They were trained to take up the responsibilities of protection and provision that were a reserve for fathers and grandfathers. They were also the spokespersons of their clans and family. The same case applied to firstborn girls who took up the maternal roles of nurturing their young siblings as well as helping manage their homes.[24]

According to Robert Serpell, parenting in Africa adopted a "socially distributed model for socialization,"[25] which placed children in a kin group. While in the kin group, the child learned within a larger kin system about gender differences, norms, and value boundaries for behavior. In the extended family setting, grandparents, uncles, aunties, other blood relatives, and neighbors were naturally included in the duty of parenting. This explains the African adage, "It takes a village to raise a child."[26] Every person in the community had a right to discipline and guide a child. Communal and kinship parenting and upbringing styles provided children with a continuum of character endowments for leadership, and, although within a patriarchal mold, they included intellectual and psychological benefits as well as a lifelong sense of belonging. Since there was no dichotomy between the sacred and the secular dimensions of reality, these values were intertwined with the respect for the supreme being. People who were brought up within such a system to a large extent were responsible, reliable to the community, and faithful to values of their communal religion.

With the advent of Christianity, many of these values were integrated within the faith and philosophy of the Christian religion. Many means to the achieving of these values which were not in tandem with Christianity were challenged and even abandoned. This blend is what is today celebrated as African Christianity. However, the African Christian posture is also bombarded and challenged in many quarters insofar as fostering and sustaining egalitarian faith and servant leadership is concerned.

---

23 Nwadiokwu, "Rites of Passage," 43.

24. Rossi and Rouanet, "Gender Preferences in Africa," 326–45.

25. Serpell "Interface between sociocultural and psychological aspects of cognition," 357–68.

26. Serpell "Interface between sociocultural and psychological aspects of cognition," 362.

Upbringing in Africa Today

The African society described above has tremendously changed. *Ubuntu* philosophy is nowadays more ontological than functional. In a globalized society, many of the values that used to be African have slowly vanished or mutated as Africa locates herself in new world realities. Instead of a communal dimension to issues, there are more privatized approaches to life that have their own limited advantages and numerous disadvantages. The African church is still at the crossroads[27] insofar as raising future generations is concerned. Fathers are increasingly absent and removed from the roles of bringing up children. Mothers, too, increasingly delegate this role to home nurses, grandmothers, or caretakers. In the church, it is not different. In the early years of Christianity, Sunday school teaching was normally voluntary in churches as more fathers and mothers volunteered to teach children. Today, however, there are fewer volunteers, especially in city churches, so this role has been left to hired people who are equipped with more theoretical curriculums than real-life experiences and whose contact with the church ends when Sunday church sessions end. Many formal learning institutions are also experiencing less gender balance among teachers. The early years of learning by many contemporary African children have fewer male figures present, which leads to confused faith genealogies. It is all too possible to use 2 Timothy 1:5 to argue that the role of faith upbringing is a matter for mothers and grandmothers and not fathers and grandfathers. Within such an atmosphere, it is a daunting task to rear children in an egalitarian manner.

Christian Models for Nurturing Egalitarian Leadership

Whereas it may seem like an impossible task given the current difficult realities, the Bible retains cues, potentialities, and mysteries without which raising an egalitarian faith generation will not be possible. Whereas African values have been seriously eroded and their transformational potential curtailed in modern times, Christianity retains the potential for reviving these values in Africa. Reading 2 Timothy 1:5 on African soil, therefore, brings out some of these potentialities, and it is to them that I now turn.

First, the communal model presented in African tradition is useful for developing egalitarian Christian leadership. Apart from its patriarchal mold, a communal model ensures that leadership is negotiated for the benefit of leaders and community. A communal model not only benefits

---

27. Nthamburi, *African Church at the Crossroads*, 145.

individuals, but the entire community as well. Vices such as patriarchy are renegotiated and, with the community's participation, shunned or abandoned. The community sphere provides the necessary arena for playing out agreed-upon virtues. Here, checks and balances may be provided, and the potentialities of Christianity can be enhanced by the voice of the whole community. The communal model advocates for an "all of us, or none of us" philosophy, which can be useful when dealing with socialized vices that are deeply entrenched in the fabric of communal life. A communal model would also guarantee the participation of fathers and mothers. In an Africa that is increasingly witnessing absentee parents, and especially absentee fathers, a communal model would ensure that children grow up in an atmosphere that understands that the whole community is our parent. In ancient Africa, bringing up children was everyone's business. All parents would nurture and discipline all children, providing checks and balances at various levels, from the nuclear family to larger groups. Raising a community was everyone's business. It is in a communal model, that aspects of the fatherhood of Paul, the motherhood of Eunice, and the grandparenthood of Lois can be assured in the rearing of a sound Christian generation. In Africa, a communal approach to egalitarian faith leadership would be the best approach for rearing a generation of servant leaders who are accountable to the community and to Christianity. Coupled with Africa's respect for mothers, from whom children get their social standing, the communal model would promote a world that enjoys the fruit of egalitarian leadership modeled from infancy.

Second, the African church must deliberately have the foresight to rear a generation that preserves and practices Christian egalitarian leadership. More than any other institution, the African church still retains the requisite authority, influence, and space to ensure that a promising legacy of faith genealogy for leadership is preserved for Christ. Since Christianity is pictured as ocean-wide in Africa (though an inch deep),[28] African Christianity still holds the key to Christian social transformation. The ocean-wide space that Christianity enjoys holds great potential that should be translated into depth through egalitarian faith leadership. The potential of African life and its worldview can be tapped toward this end.

In Africa, faith was a communal matter and not a private affair. As in the cases of Lois and Eunice, the faith of the community was what they were passing on to Timothy. They were passing on a priceless heritage that may not necessarily have been found on Timothy's father's side, since he may have been a pagan. When faith is molded within a Christian community, it

---

28. Bediako, *Christianity in Africa*, 62.

becomes a way of life, a worldview, rather than an individual's view. Such a community of the faithful living every day for Christ holds the key to Africa's transformation.

Conclusion

Paul completes the full picture of Timothy's upbringing by taking upon himself a fatherly role. When Christian men do not follow his example, egalitarian faith leadership can be complicated in societies where deliberate Christian parenting is not taken up by both fathers and mothers—and, in the case of Africa, community-oriented men and women. For Timothy, though he had an absent and non-Christian father, the community provided him such guidance. Ultimately, the voice of God in Scripture, which was part of his infancy, completed the whole picture. It is possible to empower the whole African church for Christian egalitarian leadership and servant leadership through providing full parenting. Where parental abilities are curtailed, like those of Timothy's father, the whole community of grandmothers and grandfathers, other mothers, other fathers, and siblings, all of whom are found in the Christian church community, should be availed.

References

Abuya, Benta A., Maurice Mutisya, and Elijah O. Onsumu. "Family Structure and Child Educational Attainment in the Slums of Nairobi, Kenya." *Sage Open* (April–June, 2019): 1–11. https://journals.sagepub.com/doi/full/10.1177/2158244019855849. Accessed May 26, 2020.

Amos, Patricia Mawusi. "Parenting and Culture—Evidence from Some African Communities." In *Parenting in South American and African Contexts*, edited by Maria Lucia Seidl-de-Moura. *IntechOpen*, Dec. 18, 2013. https://www.intechopen.com/books/parenting-in-south-american-and-african-contexts/parenting-and-culture-evidence-from-some-african-communities. Accessed May 27, 2020.

Bediako, Kwame. *Christianity in Africa: Renewal of a Non-Western Religion*. Maryknoll, NY: Orbis, 1996.

Catholic Online Encyclopedia, "Epistles to Timothy and Titus." Vol. E, updated 2020. https://www.catholic.org/encyclopedia/view.php?id=11593. Accessed May 27, 2020.

Cohen, Shaye J. D. "Was Timothy a Jew (Acts 16:1 –3)? Patristic Exegesis, Rabbinic Law, and Matrilineal Descent." *Journal of Biblical Literature* 105:2 (1996): 251–68.

Foxe, John. *Foxe's Book of Martyrs*. Greenville: Ambassador, 2005. https://books.google.co.ke/books?id=HAE3DwAAQBAJ&printsec=frontcover&dq=foxe%27s+book+of+martyrs&hl=en&sa=X&ved=0ahUKEwjboPiZ2tXoAhWRiVwKHTm vCqUQ6AEILjAB#v=onepage&q=foxe's%20book%20of%20martyrs&f=false. Accessed May 27, 2020.

Hemelrijk, Emily A. "Fictive Motherhood and Female Authority in Roman Cities." *Hermes* 138:4 (2010): 455–69.

Hezser, Catherine. "The Graeco-Roman Context of Jewish Daily Life in Roman Palestine." In *The Oxford Handbook of Jewish Daily Life in Roman Palestine*, edited by Catherine Hezser. New York: Oxford University Press, 2010. https://www.oxfordhandbooks.com/view/10.1093/oxfordhb/9780199216437.001.0001/oxfordhb-9780199216437?rskey=DW3ODl&result=1. Accessed May 27, 2020.

Idang, Gabriel E. "African Culture and Values." *Phronimon* 16:2 (2015): 97–111.

Keener, Craig S. *Acts: An Exegetical Commentary: Vol. 3*. Grand Rapids: Baker Academic, 2013.

———. *The IVP Bible Background Commentary: New Testament*. 2nd ed. Downers Grove, IL: IVP Academic, 2014.

Keller, Heidi. "Dual and Communal Parenting: Implications in Young Adulthood." In *The Oxford Handbook of Human Development and Culture: An Interdisciplinary Perspective*, edited by Lene Arnett Jensen, 586–601. Oxford: Oxford University Press, 2015.

Laes, Christian. "Grandmothers in Roman Antiquity: A Note on Avia Nutrix, in Melita Classica." *Journal of the Malta Classics Association* 2:2 (2015): 99–113.

Madhavan, Sangeetha, and Mark Gross. "Kin in Daily Routines: Time Use and Childrearing in Rural South Africa." *Journal of Comparative Family Studies* 44:2 (2013): 175–91.

Mbiti, John S. *African Religion and Philosophy*. Oxford: Heinemann Educational, 1989.

Mbugua, Stella W., ed. *Reflections on Africa's Indigenous Knowledge on Parenting*. Mombasa: Parenting in Africa Network, 2014.

Mutai, James. "New Testament Women: Acts and Romans." *Semeia* 5:24 (2019): 23–67.

Nthamburi, Zablon. *The African Church at the Crossroads: Strategies for Indigenization*. Nairobi: Uzima, 1991.

Neuffer, Julia. "First Century Cultural Backgrounds in the Greco-Roman Empire." In *Symposium on the Role of Women in the Church*, edited by Gordon M. Hyde, 50–62. General Conference of Seventh Day Adventists, 1984. https://www.adventistarchives.org/first-century-cultural-backgrounds-in-the-greco-roman-empire.pdf.

Nuorluoto, Tuomo. "Emphasizing Matrilineal Ancestry in a Patrilineal System: Maternal Name Preference in the Roman World." In *Tell Me Who You Are: Labelling Status in the Greco-Roman World*, edited by Maria Nowak et al., 257–89. Truekaw, Poland: Sub Lupa Academic, 2017.

Nwadiokwu, Charles, E. S. Nwadiokwu, E. N. Favour, and M. E. Okwuazun. "Rites of Passage in African Traditional Religion." *International Journal of Education and Research* 4:9 (2016): 41–50.

Oduyoye, Mercy Amba. *Daughters of Anowa: African Women and Patriarchy*. Maryknoll, NY: Orbis, 1995.

Richardson, Cyril. *Early Christian Fathers*. New York: Collier, Macmillan, 1970.

Rossi, Pauline, and Lea Rouanet. "Gender Preferences in Africa: A Comparative Analysis of Fertility Choices." *World Development* 4:72 (2015): 326–45.

Serpell, Robert. "Interface between Sociocultural and Psychological Aspects of Cognition." In *Contexts for Learning: Sociocultural Dynamics in Children's Development*, edited by. E. Forman, N. Minick and A. Stone, 357–68. New York: Oxford University Press, 1993.

Tong, Shilu, Peter Baghurst, Graham Vimpani, and Anthony McMichael. "Socioeconomic Position, Maternal IQ, Home Environment, and Cognitive Development." *The Journal of Pediatrics* 151:3 (2007): 284–88.

Van Leeuwen, Mary Stewart. *After Eden: Facing the Challenge of Gender Reconciliation.* Grand Rapids: Eerdmans, 1993.

Vuolanto, Ville. "Grandmothers in Roman Egypt." *Greek, Roman and Byzantine Studies* 57 (2017): 372–402.

9

Our Egalitarian Marriage

Diverse yet United and Completing and Complementing Each Other

Benjamin Fung and Scarlet Tsao Fung

IN THIS SINFUL, BROKEN, and postmodern world, we see lots of broken marriages and divorces not just in the media, but perhaps even among people we know. We see in history a gradual disintegration of the institution of marriage since God established it (see Gen 2:24). Growing up in Hong Kong, we still recall when we were small in the 1970s, movies and soap operas on television celebrated traditional family values and marriage, but TV series started to portray cohabitation in the early '90s. Now, cohabitation and divorces are commonplace. People do not seem to know what marriage is about or why people should bother getting married at all. Recently, one episode of a popular United States television series even openly celebrated "open marriage," showing at the end of that episode a couple agreeing that once in a month, they could go out to engage in adultery, and everyone was portrayed as then living happily ever after.

Yet, from our experience of God's faithfulness in putting us together as husband and wife and walking with us throughout our past twenty years of marriage, we hope to testify to the fact that a happy, fulfilling, and egalitarian marriage is absolutely possible even in this broken and postmodern world. It is a relationship for life between two people who go through ups and downs together with the grace and leading of God. It can be beautiful and happy beyond description. It is also a partnership to work on projects big and small, in our daily lives and ministries together every day, which can be fulfilling and fun.

God's Intended Purpose of Marriage

In order to aspire toward and live out a fulfilling marriage relationship, which is "good" in God's eyes, one must first look to Scripture to ascertain God's intention as to the purpose of marriage. The answer to this can, indeed, be found in God's creation account in Genesis 1–2, where two paradoxes seem to have arisen from the text. Both paradoxes appear in chapter 2 with the first in Genesis 2:18: everything, including the man and the environment God has created for him, is good in God's sight.[1] Yet, God finds something which is "not good" when he puts them together, namely, the loneliness of man. This contradicts general belief that putting two good things together will only generate better things. This is followed by a second paradox in Genesis 2:21–22. Common sense might dictate that, in order to resolve the "not good" problem in Genesis 2:18, God could just make either the man, or the environment, or both, better. However, God took out one of the ribs from Adam, to make him even "less" (not more or better) than what God has originally designed. God made Adam less than "good" and used that bone to create a woman (Gen 2:22). Like Adam, Eve was also an entity who was less than what God had originally designed for human beings to be, for originally she was just one of Adam's ribs. In other words, she was also less than "good." Hence, only when a man and woman cleave together (i.e., figuratively putting the bone back to the man's body) can they have a taste of what God originally designed human beings to be, and what God deems to be "good." Man and woman are therefore equal, in the sense that both of them are lacking something that God has originally designed for human beings, and, without each other, neither will fully understand what is "good" according to what God intended humans to be like.

These two paradoxes have taught us that, by analogy, the marriage of two seemingly "good" persons does not necessarily guarantee a "happily ever after" ending. Adam and the garden of Eden were both good in the sight of God, but putting them together generated a less-than-ideal result. Issues and problems may occur in a marriage (in Adam's case, it is

---

1. The word "good" (*kalon* or *kala*) appears in the description of most of the first six days of God's creation account (Gen 1:4, 10, 12, 18, 21, 25) in the Septuagint, and Gen 1:31 says on the sixth day God sees all the things he has created as "very good" (*kala lian*).

the loneliness of man), and sometimes God's ways to resolve problems may be very different from what the world expects a couple should do to resolve these issues—just as we never would have thought God would take out a bone from Adam to create Eve to resolve the problem of loneliness. By God's grace we have to humble ourselves, follow his will, and work hard toward a happy marriage. The second paradox also shows us that God's original intention is for a man and a woman through marriage to complete each other, becoming "good," as we will always be incomplete without our union and help from each other. Marriage opens a door for us even further to understand God's perfect design for our lives.[2] God has helped us come to realize and experience these two truths from our twenty years of union with him leading us in each of our steps.

Diversity yet Unity and Completing Each Other

The importance of working hard on our relationship has certainly been something we have learned since the first day of our marriage, as we have in fact completely different characters and gifts. Ben was reared in a traditional Chinese family that emphasized the significance of having a son, because the son will carry forward the family name and tradition. So Ben was the center of his family, and his parents gave him their best attention in rearing him. Yet, although Ben was reared in a very loving and caring environment, he could become insensitive to others' feelings, self-centered, and easily agitated at times. On the other hand, Scarlet was reared in a very different family from Ben's. As Scarlet's parents separated when she was very young, Scarlet was reared by her grandmother, who was a very godly and loving woman. Her grandmother gave her lots of freedom to explore the world, and this has led to Scarlet's adventurous and independent character. Scarlet had also become very resourceful and good at resolving her own problems. Whereas Ben is not a very social person who would prefer to be a caveman, Scarlet can be a social butterfly. Scarlet is also by nature a perfectionist with an A-type personality who strives to achieve high standards in whatever she does; Ben is generally very relaxed on whatever he does except on certain matters. In terms of gifts, Ben has a mathematical mind, so he used to be an accountant. Scarlet is terrible at math, but good at language, so she is a lawyer and professor. Scarlet is good at planning, organization, and leadership, but Ben is weak in administration. Ben is called and gifted to be a preacher

---

2. For those who keep celibacy for life, we believe that celibacy is a gift from God (see Matt 19:11–12 and 1 Cor 7:7), and God will have special grace and mercy for them to make them complete.

and teacher of God's word while Scarlet is a worship leader and is gifted and called to network, pioneer, and organize ministries to serve youths and underprivileged children.

Our very different characters, gifts, and callings have certainly been a source of conflicts in our marriage, especially at the beginning. Yet, such conflicts were overcome as we realized marriage is a lifelong commitment. Ben remembers that we quarreled over a small issue when we were driving in a car in our first year of marriage. Then Scarlet, in her wisdom, said to Ben, "We should not argue with each other, because, as believers, we are going to spend eternity together!" Her insight immediately calmed Ben down: That's true! Why do we have to insist on something so insignificant in view of eternity? As we are going to be together forever, what was the point of arguing instead of trying to work things out? Such a realization has helped us strive to work on unconditional acceptance as well as better conflict resolution and compromise skills (e.g., trying not to insist on resolving matters right away until both parties cool down, which is difficult) for the rest of our marriage.

However, most importantly, since God is the foundation of our family and it has been our common goal to seek and serve God as a family, we can unite in Christ despite our differences. Looking back, we see how miraculously God has clearly ordained us, two very different people, to be together. In doing so, God has made us complete each other as he had originally intended all married couples to do, enabling us to answer God's calling and arrive at the positions in which God has ordained for us to serve him.

God's Putting Two Very Different People Together: Our Courtship and Marriage

Scarlet was Ben's first girlfriend, and vice versa, for we both felt that we only wanted to start a relationship with a person whom God had clearly ordained for us. After Ben became a Christian and dedicated his life to Christ, he frequently prayed that God would provide him with a lifelong partner whom he would love and treasure deeply, and the two would pursue God's way together. God did answer his prayer in a very special way. One day, when he was doing devotions, he sensed the prompting from the Holy Spirit that God would specifically choose a wife for him, and he had to trust God on this matter. This prompting from the Spirit reminded Ben to seek God first and his kingdom, trusting that God would, in return, in his time, provide him with the things that Ben needed (Matt 6:33), in this case, the love of his life. Throughout his twenties and early thirties, Ben had quite a number of opportunities to develop serious relationships with women; but, strangely, every time when he tried to develop further in a relationship, there was a "voice" inside him telling him that that each one was not the right one. This restrained him from developing further with her, no matter how attractive she was. Consequently, he did not have a specific girlfriend in that ten-year period. It was not until he was in his early thirties that he met Scarlet. We attended the same church in Hong Kong, and were introduced to each other by Ben's Sunday school students. At first, Ben would not imagine starting a relationship with Scarlet, because she was just a freshman in college and ten years younger than him. On the other hand, Ben had been working for a number of years and was about the age to settle into a serious relationship for marriage. So he could not conceive of waiting an additional three to four years for a university student to graduate and become ready for marriage.

God changed Ben's mind though. The church we attended at that time encouraged individual congregants to pray in silence in the sanctuary after each Sunday service. Most congregants would leave immediately and some would have a short prayer and leave afterward. As Ben liked to take the opportunity to spend some time with God after the service, he was usually among the very last congregants to leave. Once or twice after he finished his prayer and was about to leave, he saw Scarlet, in a far corner praying alone, earnestly, with her two hands put together. This image of her in fervent prayer gave Ben a profound impression which drove him to want to know more about Scarlet. Around that time, on another occasion after a Sunday service, when Ben saw Scarlet coming out from the church in the crowd at the entrance, he had a clear impression from the Holy Spirit that this was the woman God had prepared for him. However, for a young man who never dated any woman before, Ben did not know how to begin a relationship with the opposite sex. Worse still, because of their age difference they did not have any common circle of friends either inside or outside the church. But God already had a perfect plan for us. Because both of us were keen to learn more about evangelism, we had separately enrolled in an evangelistic training program organized by the church, and, through that opportunity, Ben finally had the chance to talk to Scarlet during an outreach activity to the poor.

As for Scarlet, in fact, she always had an impression that she should find a spouse ten years older than she was, and that was one of the reasons that made her recognize that Ben was the one! But, more importantly, God had put an inexplicable and unceasing love in Scarlet for Ben and a conviction to support Ben to go into full-time ministry to serve God since the beginning of our relationship. Therefore, although the beginning few years of our courtship were rough and we had lots of arguments, mostly because of Ben's insensibility and character flaws, Scarlet stayed by Ben's side, encouraging him not to ignore God's calling and gifts bestowed on him to preach and teach God's word. In fact, Scarlet recalls one day God asked her whether she was willing to support and encourage him to go into full-time ministry. She said yes, although it seemed really hard at that time as Ben, like the rich young man in the Bible, was quite unwilling to give up affluence and position to tread an unknown path of full-time ministry and financial insecurity in his family's eyes. Yet, God was so faithful that he even sent a godly counselor who not only helped with our relationship, but also our personal growth. So eventually, we married after seven years of courtship.

United Under One Vision and Unconditional Love— Answering God's Calling and Leaving Earthly Matters Behind

When Scarlet and Ben got married, Ben was already a certified public accountant climbing his career ladder. Although he had a clear calling from God, he was quite reluctant to give up his career prospects to serve God. We had discussed this from time to time, but we did not come to a decision in the first two years of our marriage. Then, Scarlet had an opportunity to pursue a Master of Law degree at Yale University in the United States in 2002, so Ben accompanied Scarlet to Yale and helped her settle there. Scarlet, knowing Ben's indecisiveness about full-time ministry, arranged for us to meet with the associate dean of Yale's Divinity School to inquire about seminary education. Ben asked that associate dean how long it would take to become a Bible scholar and he answered, "About ten years!" As Ben had always envisaged himself to become a Bible scholar, he was alarmed at the fact that he would be close to fifty even if he entered into a seminary for training at that very moment and might not have much time left to serve God! This encounter with the associate dean had given him a sense of urgency to give up his career for seminary training.

At that time, Ben had two apartments in Hong Kong,[3] and they were mortgaged, so he had to pay monthly payments for them. Originally, Ben thought that the most logical way should be for him to work for a few more years until he paid off the mortgage loan of one of the apartments. In this case, he could rent out both apartments while he studied at the seminary. He could use the monthly rental income of the paid-up apartment to meet the monthly mortgage payments of the other apartment and support the tuition

---

3. As the property price in Hong Kong soared to an unbelievable and unaffordable level in the recent decades, owning apartment(s) in Hong Kong, in addition to meeting up with the housing needs, becomes a sign of achievement for many people there.

and living expenses of his seminary study. Yet, on two separate occasions, God clearly told Ben, through the Scripture the account of the rich young man in Matthew 19:16–22 that he should sell his "houses" to follow God now. At first, Ben was reluctant to do so and asked God that, if God really wanted him to sell the apartments, he would move Scarlet's heart to accept the sale. So Ben called Scarlet at Yale and, to Ben's surprise, Scarlet encouraged Ben to do what God had commanded him, contrary to his belief that she would hesitate and show concern on the sale because of its probable disruption to their financial plan for the future.

Subsequently, we had determined to sell all our apartments to go to study in a seminary in the United States, but the years 2002–2003 were not a good time to sell them, as the market experienced a slump in property prices due to a highly contagious disease called SARS (severe acute respiratory syndrome). Yet, we experienced God's miracle once again. When we offered the apartments for sale, we managed to sell them right before we had to leave Hong Kong for seminary study in the U.S. The apartments sold within a short period of time, both above the market price, despite the fact that the property market was quite soft. As both of our apartments had negative equity[4] when we sold them, Ben had to sell everything he had to settle the mortgage loans: stocks, foreign currencies, and even the furniture in the apartments. Ben incurred a huge loss and lost almost all the money he had earned in the past. But strangely, after we had settled all the bills, the money we had left was just enough for our settlement as well as the tuition and living expenses for Ben's first year of our seminary study in the U.S. After having graduated from the master of laws program at Yale, Scarlet also enrolled in the master of arts in religion program at Gordon-Conwell Theological Seminary the following year, as she hoped to learn more about God's word and ministries so she could better serve God with Ben as a team.

When we first started our study at Gordon-Conwell, we did not plan to stay for long. Ben intended to finish his master of divinity in three to four years' time, and then we would return to Hong Kong to serve the Lord. We had never imagined that, in the years to come, Ben would finish not only a master of divinity, but a master of theology, and more. He could never imagine that God would lead him into pursuing a Ph.D. degree. Consequently, Ben also had the opportunity to teach a course at Gordon-Conwell Theological Seminary as an adjunct professor and serve as the sole pastor for a Chinese Alliance church in the Greater Boston Area for two years. It turned out that we stayed for a total of nine years until we returned to Hong Kong in 2012,

---

4. The selling price of the property cannot fully cover the outstanding mortgage loan, so one has to pay extra to settle the loan.

after receiving a very clear calling from God to do so. With the money that was only enough for our first year of seminary study, God had miraculously and abundantly provided for us for eight more years. We never lacked anything in those nine years. Every need of our family was well taken care of.

God's abundant provision became even more apparent after we discovered in 2009 that our daughter Theodora is on the autistic disorder spectrum and had lots of other medical issues (which we will discuss more below). As a result, we needed lots of money for her therapies and medical treatments, not to mention the cost of the expensive special diet that she has to follow strictly even now. Yet, God abundantly provided for all the medical and therapy expenses for our daughter even to date. Today, God has also opened the door for Ben to continue to teach at the Hong Kong Baptist Theological Seminary as a visiting assistant professor[5] and to preach at different churches, and for Scarlet to serve young people as an adjunct professor at a university as well as serving underprivileged children in Hong Kong.

The experience from all these years has shown us how faithful, powerful, and loving God has been to us and our family, and for all these blessings we are eternally grateful. We have experienced how God put us together and united us under one vision to serve him with unconditional love for each other so that we could complete and support each other to take a leap of faith onto the path of serving him, thus experiencing the surpassing joy of serving him and, most importantly, experiencing his guidance and many miracles in every turn of our lives. In particular, Ben believes he would not have taken that leap of faith had it not been for the support and encouragement of Scarlet by his side.

Egalitarian Marriage: Complementing and Supporting Each Other in All Matters

Our vision with God as our family's foundation has helped us walk together, going through ups and downs in life, despite our many differences. In fact, it is beautiful to see how God in marriage unites two people of very different character and gifts to work together for his glory in ministry and the family. As it turned out, our different character and gifts totally complemented each other, so we have been able to work very effectively both in the day-to-day management and operation of our household and in our different ministries.

---

5. Ben cannot serve full time because of the intensive care he has to provide for Theodora.

Practical Day-to-Day Household Operations

We share our thoughts on every subject and work on almost everything as a team, making all important decisions together. We also share our possessions with each other (e.g., we have joint bank accounts). Our very different gifts have helped us work together effectively. As Ben is an accountant, he is the chief financial officer of the family while Scarlet, with her strength in planning, leadership, and management, is the chief executive officer. As time goes by, in the past eleven years, we have become used to working on all of our household matters together, especially having gone through, working hand in hand, the ordeal of helping our older daughter, Theodora, who has special needs.

Our Daughter Theodora

Theodora was born in 2007 when Ben was studying in the master of theology program at Gordon-Conwell. Theodora is a Greek name which means "the gift of God." And, indeed, she is a very special gift to us from God! Although our precious daughter is on the autistic disorder spectrum (and not on the light side) and has many medical issues, through her we have learned much more about our limitations, our weaknesses, and our faithlessness; and, in contrast, God's all-powerfulness, faithfulness, and unconditional love. God has used these understandings to sustain us in difficult times, teach us how to endure, and wait for him in life.

In the first year after Theodora was born, we did not even know that our daughter had problems—we had no experience in rearing a child. As our parents were in Hong Kong, they were unable to observe our child and give us advice. Almost right from the time when Theodora was born, we noticed that she had great difficulty latching for breastfeeding, but because this could easily be resolved by giving her the bottle, we did not pay much attention to this issue, as long as she was gaining weight. The real problem came after Theodora turned one. We soon noticed that she had difficulty consuming solid food, and the only food she preferred was milk or fluids. As a result, her body weight kept dropping. When we forced her to take solid food, she would throw up. We knew that, after a baby turns one, milk or fluid alone could not sustain her growth, and Theodora needed to eat nutritious solid food. So we took Theodora to see doctors. After a few medical consultations, we discovered that she had acid reflux in her stomach. That explained why she usually threw up after she ate, so we put her on medication to control the acid reflux. However, the situation did not improve afterward, and Theodora still was not willing to eat. Then we discovered that Theodora very likely had a number of food allergies and had to be on a restrictive special diet. Scarlet spent a lot of time designing and preparing the new diet for Theodora, but we noticed that, even when she wanted to eat, she ate very slowly. A few more medical consultations revealed that the muscles in her mouth had not been fully developed, and this was the reason why she could not bite and swallow. What she did was to pocket the food in her mouth and wait until the food was soft enough to swallow. Consequently, we had to arrange for a nurse to come almost every day to use a device to stimulate the muscles in her mouth to help her eat. It finally took us almost nine months to figure out how we could help Theodora eat better. We were both exhausted at the end, but the bigger issue was yet to come.

When Theodora was about one and a half years old, we brought her back to Hong Kong to visit our parents. We discussed with friends and relatives about Theodora's eating problem and one suggested we take her to see a famous pediatrician in Hong Kong. After we went into the pediatrician's office, he observed Theodora for about ten to fifteen minutes while listening to our description of her eating problems, then he turned around and spoke to us in a serious manner, "Her eating problem is a relatively minor issue, I believe that she is autistic." Then he explained to us that autism is not curable and is a lifelong condition and we need to prepare ourselves to face it. We never expected such a comment from the pediatrician when we went into his office—we only wanted to know how to deal with Theodora's eating problems! That was a great shock for us. That meeting with the doctor ended quite abruptly. The doctor did not have much to say, and neither did we. We decided to get a second medical opinion for Theodora after we returned to the States, and we (especially Ben) both underwent a short period of denial. It was not until May 2009 when Theodora was one year and nine months old, that we (especially Ben) had come to accept that Theodora is autistic.

In the following year, we were under tremendous stress, trying to ascertain all possible ways to help our daughter, not only with her autism and global development delay (i.e., she is delayed in her motor, speech, cognitive, and social/emotional development), but also various medical problems. Yet our unconditional love for our daughter enabled us to work together using our respective gifts to try to obtain the best treatments for her. When we accepted Theodora's diagnosis, we flew to another state to attend a conference and, subsequently, met with so many experts and parents with children on the autism spectrum. We learned an enormous amount about different treatments and therapies for autistic children. Eventually, also with God's miraculous assistance, we were able to source and obtain all kinds of treatments and therapies for our daughter—floor time, ABA, occupational therapy, physiotherapy, music therapy, and aqua therapy—from three child psychologists and our gastroenterologist at Massachusetts General Hospital, one of the finest hospitals in the world. We also drove our daughter to New York, which was five hours away from our home, to visit an integrative medical doctor regularly. In fact, as Theodora was on a restrictive gluten-free, casein-free, and soy-free diet, one time when she was sick and needed antibiotics, Ben had to drive in the middle of the night five hours straight from our home in Massachusetts to New York to a special pharmacy in order to obtain a specially made allergen-free medicine we needed for Theodora, and then drive five hours back. We even tried a doctor in Mexico and took our daughter to do examinations and consultations with the doctor's team in both Hong Kong and Singapore. We also worked together to obtain resources from the insurance company, school district, and other sources to finance all the therapies and treatments for our daughter. More importantly, we bore the yoke and shared responsibilities together so that we could both have the rest we badly needed from time to time, allowing each of us to have some prayer and retreat time to restore our individual strength. Those were really dark hours in our life, which we certainly could not go through without each other and God's numerous divine interventions, comfort, and support.

Theodora's entire story is too long to be covered in this chapter. In fact, it would take a whole book to describe how God has miraculously led us, step by step, into different therapies,[6] met with different people and doctors, and eventually led us back to Hong Kong for Theodora's settlement in a school specifically designed for autistic students—not to mention God's amazing provision for the enormous sum of money Theodora needed for her diet, therapies, and schooling—which was many times more than the financial loss Ben had incurred from the sale of his two apartments before we went to study at the seminary in the United States. When we took a leap of faith to follow God, God kept his promise and has been taking care of all our needs since then. We never lack anything. As Deuteronomy 33:25 says, "And as your days, so shall your strength be."[7] We had been experiencing God's presence and power since we took the path to walk with God. He has made us much stronger spiritually through our beloved daughter Theodora's ordeals.

---

6. A helpful book was Wiseman, *The First Year*.
7. All the Scriptures quoted in this chapter are from the ESV.

Ministry

Our very different gifts and callings have certainly enabled us to serve God together in ministries at church and other contexts. Those were beautiful moments when Ben would preach and teach God's word at church while Scarlet was the worship team leader. Yet, it did not mean that we were instantly supportive of each other's ministry and could collaborate effectively on projects from day one. Mutual collaboration has involved lots of learning and constant reflection on our part to make us an effective team in ministry.

Ben still recalls in the first year when we were studying at Gordon-Conwell. Ben had a wrong belief that only he was called by God to be God's servant so, therefore, Scarlet should put aside all other things and focus on supporting him—ignoring the fact that God had also called Scarlet into ministry and had made her a born leader with many gifts. Yet, God knew that such a belief could be damaging to our marriage and took an opportunity to teach Ben a lesson.

One day in the first semester after we first arrived at Gordon-Conwell, Scarlet told Ben she had decided to join a worship team to practice for a worship event to be held at the seminary chapel. As Ben was busy adapting to the new environment and course schedule at Gordon-Conwell at that time, he strongly objected to her idea. This was particularly the case as Ben thought it would take up a lot of Scarlet's time and he would have to do the housework instead, thus adding a burden to his already very busy schedule. But, although Ben kept discouraging Scarlet throughout the next few weeks of her practice, she persisted. To protest against her decision, Ben did not show up at her performance, and pulled a long face to give her a hard time after she came home from the worship service. That night both of us were not happy: Scarlet was sad at Ben's rejection, and Ben was angry with her disregarding his objection to her participation in the worship service.

We went to bed without saying much to each other. Ben usually slept through the night, but, in the middle of that night, God woke Ben up and he could not sleep again. So Ben went to the living room, sat on the sofa, opened the Bible and began to flip through the pages. Then the first part of John 1:14 came into his sight and caught his attention. It says "and the Word became flesh and dwelt among us." Ben felt that God was asking him a question: "Do you know what it means for the word (i.e., God) to become flesh?" While Ben was meditating over this question, a concept he already knew resurfaced in his mind: it means that God has chosen to confine himself. God is spirit (John 4:24). He can go anywhere in the universe at anytime he likes, but having confined himself to a physical body, his movements have been restricted by the limitations of that body. God confined to a body is comparable to a person confined to a prison. Another question then came to Ben: "Do you know why I have to put myself into a prison?" An inspiration from God came to Ben: "Because I love you—I chose to confine and sacrifice myself because of you." Deeply touched, Ben's mind turned to Romans 5:8: "but God shows his love for us in that, while we were still sinners, Christ died for us." Then an understanding came into his mind: I sacrificed myself for you even though you are a sinner.

The many wrongdoings Ben had done to Scarlet in the past few weeks flashed back into his mind. Ben knew he was wrong, and he regretted his actions and cried in shame. This encounter with God had lasted for hours. When it was about to come to the end, it was already dawn. Scarlet awoke, came out from the room, and walked toward Ben, opening her arms to hug him, notwithstanding all the hurt he had caused her in the past weeks. Momentarily, there seemed to be a voice speaking to Ben in his heart: "Look at Scarlet! This is the unconditional love I am talking about, and this love you do not have!" Ben broke down into tears. He held Scarlet tightly into his arms and cried aloud. Ben sincerely apologized to Scarlet. This lesson, together with the many similar ones to come, bit by bit, reshaped Ben's understanding of how we should minister together—Scarlet is not a subsidiary product God had produced to support him. She is a unique individual and should be respected as his equal, both in life and in ministry. Scarlet, meanwhile, was happy because God had vindicated her desire to serve God.

With that change in attitude, we had now come to a point when we could ascertain and respect that a certain project was assigned to each of us respectively from time to time, and we would be supportive of each other in doing the ministry. For example, in 2006, God had inspired Scarlet to help some Christian organizations from Hong Kong to organize a trip to visit a number of pro-family organizations in the United States. Ben, therefore, accompanied Scarlet to travel to different states and cities in the U.S., including Massachusetts, Washington, Florida, and Colorado, to meet with those in charge of the organizations to arrange for the trip. Subsequently, Ben also accompanied Scarlet and the delegates from Hong Kong on the trip to visit these organizations, although, honestly, this was not a project God had directly put in Ben's heart.

Yet, there were also times when we would also work together on the same project. While we were in the United States, we spearheaded a ministry doing outreach to underprivileged children living in three relatively poor neighborhoods in Massachusetts. We paid frequent visits to families in these poor neighborhoods to mentor the children and youths living there. (They were usually from broken families.) Using her organization and leadership gifts, Scarlet organized educational and fun group activities for these children and youths to attend three times a month on Sundays (e.g., visits to zoos, museums, boat trips, and pottery workshops). She also recruited and coordinated among church volunteers to chaperone and mentor them with the hope to bring them to Christ. Subsequently, when Ben became the sole pastor of the Greater Boston Chinese Alliance Church, he did a lot of preaching and teaching work, while Scarlet ministered to some women at the church. We also cowrote this article, which required our collaboration amid our busy daily schedule. While Ben wrote the first draft, Scarlet added and rewrote some of the parts and proofread the whole chapter.

Conclusion

Looking back, in fact, it has taken us twenty-seven years (through courtship and marriage) to get us to this stage: simultaneously loving, sharing, ministering, helping, and supporting each other as equals. We both understand that we are not walking on an easy road, but we are confident that, with the grace of God, we can see an even brighter tomorrow. God is a never-changing God. As he has been faithful, providing and leading us in our every step in the past, he will certainly continue to do so for us and our family.

References

Wiseman, Nancy, with Robert L. Rich. *The First Year: Autism Spectrum Disorders: An Essential Guide for the Newly Diagnosed Child*. Cambridge, MA: Da Capo Life Long, 2009.

10

Rearing Egalitarian Children

Karen Sue Smith

IT WAS EARLY MORNING and we should have been sleeping. Instead, our eyes rested on our newborn daughter as she lay in her crib fast asleep. Our first child was stillborn, so this moment was all the more precious as we thanked God for this new life entrusted into our care. Fast forward twenty years. Our daughter, Sara, is now joined by her sister, Hannah, in college, and her brother, Jonathan, in high school. Now we watch as she writes her lab report that is due on Monday for her microbiology class. With joy, we observe her heart and life as she grows in her relationship with God!

Sara, Hannah, and Jonathan all opened their hearts to God before the age of six. Sara writes, "I sat on the couch listening as my mom read a story to me about how a little girl's journey ended in her receiving the gift of salvation. I told my mom I wanted to receive this gift too! She prayed with me, and from that moment on I began the adventure of knowing God!" That week we invited Sara to take communion during our Sunday service. As we left our seats, Hannah proclaimed in her sweet four-year-old voice, "I believe too!" That was the beginning of Hannah's personal relationship with God. She writes, "As long as I can remember, my parents took me to church, but there have been several moments where I expressed my personal desire to follow God with all my heart." When Jonathan was four, he would often play church with his cars. He would line the cars in straight rows to hear the sermon, and then form them in long lines to receive communion. One day Sara was playing with him. They were having the cars leave the church to tell other cars about Jesus. It was in this context that Jonathan asked Sara if he had received the gift of salvation. She sent him to me, and it was on that day that Jonathan asked Jesus into his heart! We treasured each one of these moments, and with each passing year we noted how God was at work in the lives of our children. We worked to weave in their lives and daily routines special times with God. Our desire was to help them grow in favor with God and in their relationships both at home and in their larger communities.

The loss of our firstborn brought intentionality to our parenting and helped us to treasure each moment, even ones filled with struggle. We searched for answers of how to steward the time that we have with our children, especially during their formative years. How do parents equip the hearts of their children to love God, especially in our increasingly technology-dependent culture? How do we help them to grow to be servant egalitarian leaders in their generations? These are questions that we have asked as we have parented our three children. What follows is a window into our journey of being parents, and what we have discovered along the way.

General Principles Learned on Rearing Servant Egalitarian Disciples

First, we have learned to ask God constantly for wisdom, since there is no one formula for rearing children that works every time. Each of our three children needed different care to help each flourish. James 1:5 tells us that if we lack wisdom then we should ask God, and he will give us what we need. This is so important, because each of our children is a unique creation of God and needs different keys to help mine all of her or his God-given gifts and talents.

Second, we learned to keep our focus on God as the source of all growth. We needed to be intentional about nurturing our children, but God would bring the harvest (1 Cor 3:6–7). Maintaining a constant connection with God and continuing to examine our hearts and grow in our relationships with God was essential to rearing our children.

Finally, we learned that we could not pass on to our children what we did not possess in our own lives. What is in our hearts and minds will be reproduced in our children. I remember questioning why Sara kept saying a particular phrase until I heard myself saying the same thing. Our lives are powerful teachers, so we need to make certain we possess what we want reproduced in our children. We need to examine our own lives to make sure we are living the life that we desire for our children. What does our relationship with God look like? Are the words that we speak in line with God's truth? Are our relationships characterized by mutual submission, honoring others, and operating out of our giftedness rather than roles?

How we think and how we train our children to think is so important. For example, if you know something is valuable, you will sacrifice time and energy to obtain what you are looking for. You only have one opportunity to shape the lives of your children. What you think, say, and demonstrate is creating a framework that will not only affect your attitude, motivation, and daily choices, but also those of your children.

Our lives are made up of moments, and how we spend those moments will determine the pattern of the fabric of each of our lives. It is challenging to make the right choice, even if that means taking the road less traveled. You may stand out from the crowd because you are not making the popular choice or be in sync with what everyone else is doing. But, if you persevere, in time you will see those moments add up to make a beautiful masterpiece.

In this chapter, we will explore together three truths that have guided our thinking as parents that we have gleaned from God's word and have woven into the fabric of our life as a family. We have noted that we need to join with the heart of God for our children, journey with our children as equals, and, finally, joyfully accept our parental role in the lives of our children.

Join with the Heart of God for Children

First, we need to join with God's heart for our children. There is a passage that gives us a glimpse into the heart of God for children. This moment in Jesus's ministry occurs in all three Synoptic Gospels, but we will focus our attention on the account in Mark 10:13–16:

> People were bringing little children to Jesus for him to place his hands on them, but the disciples rebuked them. When Jesus saw this, he was indignant. He said to them, "Let the little children come to me, and do not hinder them, for the kingdom of God belongs to such as these. Truly I tell you, anyone who will not receive the kingdom of God like a little child will never enter it." And he took the children in his arms, placed his hands on them and blessed them.[1]

In these verses, we see a contrast of attitudes. As the parents brought their children to Jesus, they were met with resistance. The disciples rebuked them for bringing the children. However, Jesus's attitude was different. He

---

1. All Bible quotations, unless otherwise indicated, are from the NIV, or are translations by the author.

was angry at the words of the disciples. In the face of opposition, he sided with the parents, telling them to bring their children to him. And what was the result? Jesus blessed the children. Jesus did not just look at the children. He took them in his arms, he placed his hands on them, and he blessed them. Jesus made room for the children to come.

In another passage Jesus speaks of the gravity of causing a child to stumble. Better someone be drowned than cause a child to go the wrong direction (Matt 18:6).

What you do during the early years of your children's development is of great importance. The typical way of thinking may be that, during the early years, your children are too little, so what you expose them to will go over their heads or not harm them. However, we found that, the smaller our children were, the more access we had to their hearts, so we were even more vigilant to nurture their spiritual lives when they were small. We needed to join with God in blessing our children. We needed to bring them to God. What we did mattered.

We learned this when we purchased our first home. Sara was six months old when we moved. We loved everything about our new house. However, since we were only a few minutes from the local hospital, each day we heard siren after siren. I noticed that this sound distressed Sara, so I decided we should use the sound of the siren as a call to pray for the people who were in trouble. Several months went by, and I prayed as the ambulances rushed by our home. One day I was busy and forgot to pray, and Sara, less than a year old, looked at me with an anxious face and lifted up her hands. She wanted to pray! This encouraged me to continue with consistency the routines of praying, reading Bible stories, and playing music full of Scripture to her.

As Hannah was born and both girls grew, we expanded the concept of something we saw prompting us to pray. We picked other things that we saw repeatedly and used those as clues to either pray for someone or something, or to stop and give thanks for something in our lives. We called each signal to pray a prayer marker. This was a great way to weave prayer into and throughout our days.

Know, however, as you bring your little ones to God, you can expect to find resistance. Be willing to persist, and you will not be disappointed, as God will bless your efforts. This resistance may not be as clear as the sound of the disciples' voices trying to turn you away, but obstacles will come. We are living in an increasingly technological society. There are more options than ever of how to spend our time. Many of these options are fun and engaging, and often good ways to spend time. However, we have learned that it is often the good things that keep us from the best choices. So identify the voices calling to you to stop your efforts to bring your children to Jesus. Are they the voices of family, friends, unfinished work, or activities that are calling for your time? Then you can agree with the heart of God that he wants you to come.

Keep bringing your children to Jesus until eventually they will come to Jesus on their own. Help them to learn that, no matter what age they are, God welcomes them. This is an important truth for us as parents to realize as well. No matter what we have done, there is always forgiveness. Demonstrating what to do when we make a mistake is so powerful. Let your children see you coming to Jesus. Demonstrate for them that God's arms of love are always open and ready to receive us when we come to him. James tells us that, when we draw near to God, he draws near to us (James 4:8). What a beautiful promise to teach our children! *We need to let our children know that they matter to God and are always invited into his arms, where he will bless them.*

Journey with Our Children as Equals

There are many places in the Bible where we see God speaking to and working through the lives of children. Here are just a few: God spoke to the boy Samuel as he lay on his bed (1 Sam 3). Naaman's servant girl urged him to seek God for his physical healing (2 Kgs 5:2–3). The boy Josiah became king at the age of eight and would later go on to make repairs to the temple (2 Kgs 22:1–2). We see John the Baptist in the womb worshiping Jesus as Lord (Luke 1:41). Many of Jesus's healing miracles involved children as he delivered them from demons (Matt 15:28) and raised them from the dead (Mark 5:38–42). It was a little boy's lunch that Jesus used to feed the five thousand (Matt 14:13–21). Timothy was trained in the Scriptures from infancy (2 Tim 3:15).

Children are important to God and have the same access to God that we as adults enjoy. Therefore, it is essential that we listen to what they have to say and pay attention to what God is doing in their lives. We also need to ask how God may be speaking to us through our children. When we were moving across the country, some of my deepest encouragements came through the songs and words of my children. God has ordained praise to come from the mouths of babes (Ps 8:2), so, value what God is doing in your children's lives.

Also, ask God to show you the unique gifts and talents that he has given your children. We kept a written record of what we were observing in our children, and what verses God was highlighting to us to pray for them. We also noted the observations of family and friends that gave us insight into the lives of our children. We also paid particular attention to activities that each of our children enjoyed and tried to expose them to as much variety as possible, especially when they were young. Sometimes even they were surprised at what they enjoyed. One fall we enrolled Jonathan in several new classes. The one he enjoyed most was archery, which was a last-minute addition to our schedule.

When we observed what God was doing, we nurtured that growth. For example, when Sara was four, we received a recording of her cousin participating in a dance worship service. As we played this video, we noticed Sara had an amazing ability and desire to learn the dance moves, and wanted to play the tape again and again and participate in the dancing. Even though we had no dance background, we recognized this gift in her. When we moved to the Midwest, God connected us with an amazing Christian dance studio. We not only enrolled Sara, but also Hannah in dance classes. This began a fifteen-year journey of dance instruction. Today, both Sara and Hannah are teaching dance and helping young girls to use their gifts of movement to praise God.

It is essential to listen to our children and pay attention to how God is speaking to them and you through their voices and lives. As you honor their desires and find the gifts that God has given them, this will aide them in learning to honor the gifts in others. Show them by your words and actions that you are listening to what they are saying and that you value their input. Help them to notice what God is doing in their own lives.

As you seek to raise up servant egalitarian children, along with your attention to their lives, you must also examine your relationships. Are you modeling equality in your relationships with your spouse, your friends, in your business and ministry? Are these relationships characterized by mutual submission, placing value on the hearts and words of those with whom you are in relationship? Do you seek to serve those around you? Do you honor the spiritual gifts and talents that God has placed in their lives and give opportunity for those you love to flourish? This is so important, because our lives are an open book that our children will read daily and from which they will learn both good and bad attitudes and balances.

Finally, live with a thankful heart for your children's presence in your life and treasure the lessons they can teach you. Children are a gift from God to us, as they can call us to live with heart postures that are pleasing to God. We see this illustrated as Jesus addresses the dispute among his disciples. In Matthew 18, the disciples began asking, "Who is the greatest in the kingdom of heaven?" Often, when Jesus was asked a question, he responded with another question or a story. But, in this passage, he uses a child to communicate his heart and help his listeners understand his answer to their question. Jesus calls them to become like the child that he brings into their midst.

Jesus is not talking about childish living. We are instructed in 1 Corinthians 13:11 to put away childish things, but, in this passage, Jesus is highlighting the humility and dependence of a child. Let your children help you cultivate and maintain the heart characteristics that are important to God. Our children have helped us to keep joy, wonder, and the beauty of the present moment in the forefront of our hearts. They have also helped us to remember that God is our provider and our source of life and provision.

Joyfully Accept Our Role as Parent

Although your children are equal in dignity and in the Holy Spirit, you are called to a unique relationship with your children. Joyfully accept your role as a parent in the life of your children. In Ephesians 6, we find a call to children and a call to parents. Children are to obey and honor their parents. This command comes with a promise. Parents[2] are not to exasperate their children, but to train them up in the fear of the Lord. These commands are temporary, as the children will grow up and one day become parents themselves. This unique relationship is designed so that parents can train their children how to walk with God and to know what things are right and what things to avoid.

We have noted from 2 Timothy 3:15 that, from childhood, Timothy was taught the Scriptures, which were able to make him wise unto salvation. How blessed Timothy was to have God's word in his life from the time he was a young child. The verse that follows shows these same writings also equip us to live a life pleasing to God. "Everything in the Scriptures is God's Word. All of it is useful for teaching and helping people and for correcting them and showing them how to live" (CEV).

As parents, we are to train our children. For the rest of this chapter, I want to continue to give you a glimpse into our family, what worked for us as we nurtured the spiritual life of our children, and how we practically worked out the command to rear our children, teaching them and instructing them about the Lord (Eph 6:4). Some of the ideas that follow might be a perfect fit for your family to implement right now. Other ideas may act as springboards to help you find what works for you and your

---

2. Liddell and Scott, *Lexicon*, 786, notes that the plural of *patēr* signifies "forefathers" or "parents." This is reflected correctly in the CEV translation of this verse, "Parents, don't be hard on your children. Raise them properly. Teach them and instruct them about the Lord."

children. I recommend reading this section with a pen in hand, an open mind, and an open heart.

Teach Your Children to Treasure God's Word

Make sure that your children know God's story. How was the world created? Why is the world so broken? How will everything end? Tell them the stories of great men and women of the Bible. Let them see their faith, their mistakes, and, most of all, God's great love and faithfulness in each of their lives. Our hearts are made for stories. I was always surprised how much my children liked to hear the same stories over and over. As they grow older, help them to develop a biblical timeline and also expose them to historical facts, to show that these stories happened in a certain time period at a specific location. Have fun acting out stories and singing music that contains God's stories.

We had each of our children make their own book of questions and answers about God and spiritual things. By writing these questions in their own handwriting and personalizing each page, the book became not only a reference, but also something they enjoy looking at. We memorized Bible verses as a family. We put our verse for the week in a central location and reviewed the verses often. We found the first moments when we entered the car before we turned on the radio or began engaging in separate activities were great times to review our memory verses. At first, starting a new pattern may meet resistance, but you will be glad that you created this habit once it becomes natural. I love the verses from Deuteronomy 6 that call us to keep God in all parts of our life, together with our children:

> These commandments that I give you today are to be on your hearts. Impress them on your children. Talk about them when you sit at home and when you walk along the road, when you lie down and when you get up. Tie them as symbols on your hands and bind them on your foreheads. Write them on the doorframes of your houses and on your gates." (Deut 6:6–9).

Teach Your Children to Trust God and Know His Ways

When you know God, it will impact the way you live (Dan 11:32). Teach your children the character of God. Start with creation and let them see

God's handiwork all around them. Then tell them the names of God, and how each reveals his nature and heart.

Tell your children what God has done in your life, and then help them to record their own history with God. We did this by creating a prayer wall. When we moved into our house in Wheaton, Illinois, my eyes were drawn to the beautiful built-in bookshelves. During our move, when I was crying out to God in prayer for help, a woman I was praying with told me, "God has done so much in your life, and he wants you to remember all the times that he has answered your prayers. Your past deliverances are to be for you a source of hope and thanksgiving." These words are what gave me the idea to place in the bookshelves only things that reminded us of answers to prayer. Among the many items on our shelves are the FedEx package that delivered the job offer for Dwight, and the tea set I acquired in China when God provided the last $300 I needed for the mission trip the night before I boarded the plane. We particularly enjoy watching Sara, Hannah, and Jonathan add their own objects to the wall as God answers their prayers.

Talk: Communication Is Key

Keep tabs on what is happening in the lives of each of your children. What is connecting with their hearts? What is God doing in their lives? Staying connected with your children's hearts is one of the most valuable things that you can do. In Proverbs 4:23, we are exhorted to guard our heart, for from it flows the wellsprings of life. It is worth the effort to keep this heart connection strong. You can do an activity, but your heart may not be involved. Sometimes, we had our children do something that we knew was good for them, but their hearts were not in it. To engage their hearts, we offered them a reward that we knew would connect with their hearts. The byproduct of this approach was that, often, when the activity was completed, they ended up enjoying what at first they were reluctant to do. For example, we attended a Christian conference together, and then went out to eat at one of their favorite restaurants on the way home.

Another way we stayed connected to their hearts was using a notebook as part of our homeschool. The idea was that I would write a question each day in the notebook, and then they would have to answer the question in a complete sentence. As they grew older, they also had to write a question for me to respond to. At first, most of the questions were about trivial things. As they grew, we were able to ask questions that, if asked in another way, would not have received a response, or may have been heard with the wrong tone. For example, on Monday I could ask, "What stood out to you yesterday when we attended church?" Instead of feeling like I was asking a question to see if they were listening, they now had the context in which to respond with an answer from their heart.

Seek to awaken desire in your children. How do you know if you like something if you never have taken the first bite? Expose them to the beautiful things that God has created. Give them opportunities to try new activities. When they do, ask questions and listen to their answers. What did you like best about that class? Did you learn anything new? If you would do that activity again, would you change anything about it?

Employ Two Important Tools: Stories and Songs

Another way to connect with the heart of your child is through stories. All of our hearts were made for stories, and that is why they are so important in training the heart of your child. Reading good books out loud creates spaces for wonderful conversations to take place. Make the stories of the Bible your main focus, especially when your children are young. Help them see how the Bible fits together and always leads us to hope.

If you are struggling with a specific problem, look for a story or biography of someone who had this same problem and found success in this area. Read stories that help you see life through the eyes of someone who lives in a different country or time period. Read a story that illustrates a truth about which you are learning. When you read, ask questions and pay attention to how your children answer. What part of the story did they like most and why? Have they ever felt that way or had that question? How would they have reacted in this situation?

Singing is also a valuable tool. Not only is singing a great way to memorize verses from the Bible, it is also a way to express our praise and thanksgiving to God. Songs can also help you create traditions that will shape the hearts of your children. Each year when we took our family vacation, I picked a worship song that we would play every morning of our trip. When we returned home, we would use this song to create a slideshow of our travels. Songs helped us create traditions and connections.

Take Care with Your Words

Proverbs 18:21 tells us that the power of life and death is in our tongues. When our children speak, we are given the opportunity to see into their hearts, so pay attention to them when they are speaking. Help them to see the importance of their words and of speaking in a way that aligns with God's word.

We take care of our children's physical needs by providing food and clothes for them. We care for their hearts and minds by the words that we speak. So, what and how we speak to our children is so important. Use your words to speak the truth about how God sees them. They are loved (John 3:16), chosen (Eph 1:4), and a child of God (1 John 3:1–2). God will never leave them (Heb 13:5) or give up on them (Phil 1:6). Bless them with your words (Num 6:24–26).

Travel

Invest in experiences. We made family vacations a priority for our family. As we started the planning process, we would always seek God for the location and details of the trip. We attached truths to experiences though travel. For example, after reading all the "Little House on the Prairie" books, we traveled to Missouri and explored the original house that Almanzo Wilder built for Laura. We visited caves, climbed mountains, walked through the desert, and played in the ocean waters. All these experiences not only are beautiful memories we now cherish, but added a depth to our reading. When we read *The Silver Chair* by C.S. Lewis, the story came alive as we could remember our own underground experiences. Traveling also gave us many opportunities to stand in awe of God's creation.

Beware of Temptations

One thing that you can be certain of is that you and your children will face temptation. We are in a battle, but God has given us the armor we need to walk in victory. We read about this gift at the end of Ephesians 6, which began with the command for children to obey their parents. We must be vigilant in this battle. We need to live disciplined lives and help our children to do the same. We have found that we always gravitate toward the choice that takes the least amount of energy and appears to be the most favorable. Often, we are far too easily satisfied.[3] That is why helping our children make the right choices versus the wrong ones, and best versus other good choices, will bring great blessing to their lives.

---

3. "We are half-hearted creatures, fooling about with drink and sex and ambition when infinite joy is offered us, like an ignorant child who wants to go on making mud pies in a slum because he cannot imagine what is meant by the offer of a holiday at the sea. We are far too easily pleased." Lewis, *The Weight of Glory*, 1–2.

Help Them Know God So that They Can Develop a Discerning Heart

Think of helping them to create a framework in which to put information. When they find a truth that fits, then there is a place for them to integrate it into their lives. The framework allows them to judge new information by saying, "Yes, this fits," or "This is something I need to disregard."

Help Them Develop Habits that Create Hunger

We have found that spiritual disciplines often do not look appealing to us or to our children. But, when we take the time to incorporate a new way to connect with God, the result will be a desire for more. The goal is that they will transfer their obedience from you to God. They never stop obeying! It is wonderful when you help them cultivate the discipline of obeying.

TAKE TIME TO MAKE MINISTRY TO OTHERS A PRIORITY

Make time for ministry together at every stage of their childhood. We taught our children they did not have to grow up before they could have a ministry. When they were small, we made cards for people who needed encouragement. We cooked a meal together to take to a new mother, or someone who was battling an illness. We prayed for people, danced God's truth, or shared a story of how God had answered prayer in our lives. These were all things in which everyone could participate and see God's love extended to others through our actions.

GIVE THEM OPPORTUNITIES TO DEVELOP A SERVANT'S HEART

Placing your children in contexts where they have something that depends on them will be the perfect context for a servant's heart to be cultivated. On Hannah's birthday, we surprised her with a baby bunny. She loves animals, so she embraced this gift with enthusiasm. We have now had her bunny Lilly for more than five years. Our hearts have been so encouraged to watch Hannah's servant heart grow as she has taken excellent care of her rabbit, even though the care became costly when Lilly developed several infections. Another idea that could produce the same result would be to involve your children in planting and caring for a garden. Giving them something that is directly dependent on their actions is a great way to help them learn to serve. Show them how they can enter in caring for their environment. Giving them responsibilities and showing them that their efforts are making a real difference in the life of your family will make an impact on their hearts.

Model Growth for Them

God created us to be lifelong learners. As you model growing to your children, they will follow your example. Seek to grow in your relationship with God. Look for ways that God wants you to serve those around you. Seek out mentors and learn from them. Whenever I met another mom, I consistently asked what resources made a difference in her family. Here are a few gems that I have found along the way. I love Susan Schaeffer Macaulay's book *For the Children's Sake: Foundations of Education for Home and School* and Monte Swan's and David Biebel's book *Romancing Your Child's Heart*.

Be Tenacious

These ways of thinking are not something that you obtain or a goal you reach. They are attitudes that must be maintained. You will often find that the path that brings growth will be the one that takes the most energy to walk. Being a parent is all about sacrifice and love, but each time you make the decision to love and to do what is best for your children, you will be rewarded.

I asked each of my children what we did as parents that helped them grow in their relationship with God. Sara wrote, "It is hard to know what one thing that my family did to help me grow spiritually. I think it is just an accumulation of all the daily choices that my parents made as I saw their love for God and His Word." When we asked Hannah this same question she said, "Having a place to ask all my questions was a big help to me. Also developing my own consistent Bible reading and study has helped me grow in my relationship with God." Jonathan replied, "Our daily prayer times are what has made a big difference in my relationship with God."

Final Thoughts

We need to look at our children through the lenses that we have examined in this chapter. I emphasize again that these will not flow naturally, but will need to be chosen and executed with sacrifice and love. We need to remember it is in those small decisions made in our daily rhythms that our children's hearts are fashioned. Always look for opportunities to bring your children to God. Listen to your children and learn from them. Finally, be intentional about teaching them to love God. Together, may we seek to know God and make him known.

References

Lewis, C.S. *The Weight of Glory and Other Addresses.* Grand Rapids: Eerdmans, 1965.
———. *The Silver Chair.* New York: Collier, 1971.
Liddell, Henry George, Robert Scott, and Henry Stuart Jones. *A Greek–English Lexicon.* 9th ed. Oxford: Clarendon, 1996.
Macaulay, Susan Schaeffer. *For the Children's Sake: Foundations of Education for Home and School.* Westchester, IL: Crossway, 1984.
Swan, Monte, and David Biebel. *Romancing Your Child's Heart.* 2d ed. Bristol, VA: Healthy Life, 2015.

11

Equipping Young People to Build Healthy Relationships

Consider It, Take Counsel, and Speak Up

Sandra Gatlin Whitley

> Let the little children come to me, and do not hinder them, for the kingdom of heaven belongs to such as these. (Matt 19:14 NIV)

ACCORDING TO THE 2017 United States Census, about 42 million young people between the ages of 10 and 19 comprise 13 percent of the United States population[1]—but they are 100 percent of our future in society and the church. As this population of 51 percent girls and 49 percent boys grows up and develops into women and men, they must be equipped now to build healthy relationships of gender equality. Why? If the Swahili proverb "A son will be what he was taught," still means young people learn from examples set by those around them,[2] then we are at a critical time in the history of humankind to "flip the script" back to what God, our Creator, originally intended in gender relationships.

In the beginning, God said,

---

1. According to U.S. Census Bureau estimates, there were about 42 million youth ages 10–19 in the United States. Racial/ethnic diversity is greater in the child population than in the adult U.S. population, and diversity among adolescents is increasing. The census bureau projects that, as soon as 2020, children and youth from ethnic/racial minorities will together comprise half of the population under age 18. See U.S. Department of Health and Human Services, "The Changing Face of America's Adolescents."

2. See UNICEF, *Adolescence*.

> Let us make humankind in our image, in our likeness, so that they may rule over the fish in the sea and the birds in the sky, over the livestock and all the wild animals, and over all the creatures that move along the ground. So God created humankind in his own image, in the image of God he created them; male and female he created them (Gen 1:26–27 NRSV).

When God said, "Let us make humans in our image and likeness," in his own image he created them, which means both male and female were created equally as *breathing, living, and reasoning* beings reflecting God's communicable characteristics and attributes.[3] When someone does harm to another human being, especially to another person physically, emotionally, mentally, or spiritually, he or she hurts God—the part of God that is reflected in that individual, the person God created in his image and likeness. God cast the human relationship between himself and his created beings as reflecting equally his own personal relationship with himself.

This chapter highlights why adolescent girls and boys should be taught, nurtured, and empowered to grow up knowing and living out their identity in Christ Jesus based on Ephesians 5:21: "Submit to one another out of reverence for Christ."

Jesus's Mandate to His Disciples and Leaders

Children have to be taught how to be in relationship with others. The first relationship must be with God, who is revealed to them through reading the Bible. Therefore, "Let the little children come to me, and do not hinder them, for the kingdom of heaven belongs to such as these" (Matt 19:14 NIV). Parents and church leaders must rear children by teaching the Bible to them. Children must not be hindered from coming to God's Son, Jesus, and receiving his love. Jesus loves them and knows children have a guileless trust in God, our heavenly Father. They have the potential for a simple faith needed to believe.

> Therefore, whoever takes the lowly position of this child is the greatest in the kingdom of heaven. And whoever welcomes one such child in my name welcomes me. If anyone causes one of these little ones—those who believe in me—to stumble, it would be better for them to have a large millstone hung around their neck and to be drowned in the depths of the sea. (Matt 18:4–6 NIV).

---

3. Erickson, *Christian Theology*, 293.

The lowly position Jesus is teaching his disciples in this text is the Greek *tapeinoō*, which figuratively means to humiliate (in condition or heart) or abase, bring low, humble (the self).[4] Jesus's divine purpose in an earthly kingdom is for all to be welcomed, including little children. Because children—non-gender specific, girls and boys—are trusting by nature, they are equally welcomed as if either boy or girl were Jesus himself. Since boys and girls are born innocent and reared to trust adults, they can also be easily led to faith in Jesus.

But anyone who causes a boy or girl to stumble (the Greek *skandalizō*), to trip up, or entice to sin, or make to offend, it would be better for that person to have a millstone hung around their neck and drowned. God holds parents and other adults accountable for how they influence children or harm them. And the disciples and church leaders reading the Bible to the children are warned that, if anyone turns girls or boys away from faith in Jesus, they will receive severe punishment. The two ways to cause children to sin or stumble are by tempting them and by neglecting or demeaning them (Matt 18:7–14). Adults, leaders, and parents are to help young people avoid anything that would cause them to stumble in their faith or lead them to sin against God. Parents and leaders of young people should never take lightly the spiritual education and protection of those young in age or young in their faith (Matt 18:4–6). We adults must be careful about judging others and must ourselves come to Jesus as little children, male and female, boys and girls equally.

So, it is time to reevaluate the stumbling blocks of patriarchy and hierarchy that are hindering boys and girls from growing in the saving knowledge of Jesus Christ and causing them to sin against God. The rising inequality in male-female relationships, shown in verbal and emotional abuse, encourages intimate partner abuse, domestic violence, and sexual assault against women. These sins are running rampant in our society.[5] A protest is needed today, just as the outcry among the Israelites burst forth when the common-law wife of a Levite was not treated as an equal in marriage with

---

4. *Strong's Greek Dictionary of the New Testament*, s.v.

5. On average, 24 people per minute are victims of rape, physical violence, or stalking by an intimate partner in the United States — more than 12 million women and men over the course of a year. From 1994 to 2010, about four in five victims of intimate partner violence were female. Most female victims of intimate partner violence were previously victimized by the same offender, including 77% of females ages 18 to 24, 76% of females ages 25 to 34, and 81% of females ages 35 to 49. A child witnessed violence in 22% (nearly one in four) of intimate partner violence cases filed in state courts. There is a link between domestic violence and child abuse. Among victims of child abuse, 40 percent report domestic violence in the home. See National Domestic Violence Hotline, "Get the Facts & Figures."

her husband nor by the male head of the household they were visiting. She had become a voiceless victim of sexual violation. Both men—the head of the household who offered his daughter and the visiting Levite's husband—acted in a patriarchal manner by giving the woman over to demanding men instead of protecting her as if she were part of her husband's body (see 1 Cor 7:4). As a result, she was violently raped throughout the night by the other men in the city until she died (Judg 19–20). Neither her husband nor the male head of household did what Christ would suggest in Ephesians 5, for a man to love his wife as Christ loves the church and give up his own body (flesh) for her (Eph 5:25–28). However, in the book of Judges, the woman was brutally violated by men in the city, resulting in God's chosen people seeking God about what to do. God decreed punishment. With the outcry of young people in America and around the world,[6] leaders of the church and society need to stand up for righteousness: "And all who saw it said . . . 'consider it, take counsel, and speak up'" (Judg 19:30 ESV).

Today, believers should follow Jesus's words and those of the Apostle Paul in 1 Corinthians, "so that there should be no division in the body, but that the members may have the same care for one another. If one member suffers, all suffer together" (1 Cor 12:25–26 ESV). Our children are suffering, including those who are the offspring of believers in Christ: the same children who are reared in the church. Remember, in our relationships with one another, there is no such thing as private or individualistic Christianity, but humble, mutually supportive Christian community.[7] We need to become involved in the lives of others to dispel the practices of patriarchy and hierarchy in systems of government, education, churches, and families.

Consider It: Patriarchy, Hierarchy, and Equality Defined

Both boys and girls must understand the differences among hierarchical, patriarchal, and egalitarian leadership in order to become effective Christlike servant leaders. From the many generations past up to now, gender stereotypes have become incorporated into systems in our homes, society, and churches. According to psychologists, the family is the first relationship where children become aware of their identity.[8] Children look to their

---

6. In one study, one-third of adolescent girls report that their first sexual experience was forced. When it is not fatal, youth violence has a serious, often lifelong, impact on a person's physical, psychological and social functioning. See Krug, "World Report," 149.

7. *Life Application Bible*, footnotes for Matt 18:4–6.

8. Aldridge, *Self Esteem*, 27.

parents and siblings to discover if they are loveable and capable, which determines whether they will have positive or negative self-esteem.[9] As they observe family members, they begin to practice how to behave the same way. Similarly noted by Nelson Mandela in the World Health Summary report, the pain of children being abused by people who should be protecting them is reproducing a legacy of itself.[10] As new generations learn from the violence of generations past, as victims learn from victimizers, and as the social conditions that nurture violence are allowed to continue, then no country, no city, no community is immune.[11] Our children deserve, and we owe them, a life free from violence and fear.

Subconsciously, as well as consciously, parents and society have fallen prey to the practice of assigning gender-specific roles to boys and girls based upon a patriarchal mindset. These practices are embedded in ways we as a society think, behave, and teach within our households. A girl is taught that womanhood means being married, being submissive, and being obedient to her husband rather than decisive and active. Boys are taught that manhood is exercising authority and control over girls and women, which is often the onset of verbal and emotional abuse and subsequently violent behavior toward them as men strive to keep control.[12] For this reason and others, it is paramount that the cycle of patriarchy and hierarchy be broken.

Since gender inequality harms everyone, a mindset shift, or even a generational shift, is required.[13] Once parents and grandparents recognize the harm of hierarchy or patriarchal lifestyles, the hope is they will be less likely to repeat the same pattern.

"Patriarchy" is "the rule of the father," and historically means men ruling their families as the male head of a household or male domination. To "rule" means to have control of and dominion over an area or people, according to the *Oxford Dictionary*.[14] Not only does patriarchy refer to male domination or autocratic rule primarily in a home (with husband, wife, and children), but since the late twentieth century, patriarchy also refers to men controlling social systems, including nuclear family units, communities, cities, nations, college campuses, corporations, and industries in which power is primarily held by adult men.[15]

9. Clark. *Self Esteem*, 4.
10. Krug, "World Report," ix.
11. Krug, "World Report," ix.
12. UNICEF, *Adolescence*, 5.
13. Chiu, "Gender Inequality Harms."
14. *New Oxford American Dictionary*, s.v.
15. *New Oxford American Dictionary*, s.v.

"Hierarchy" means the "rule of a high priest," or "president of sacred rites."[16] Hierarchy is an arrangement of items, such as objects, names, values, categories, and so forth. The arrangement of the items is represented as being "above," "below," or "at the same level as" another.[17] Simply stated, hierarchy is a group of people or things arranged in order of rank. Examples of hierarchy can be seen in the business world, where a person is ranked on the corporate ladder, and the religious community in the Catholic or highly liturgical Protestant churches, where various levels of leadership are ranked, such as priests, bishops, and deacons.[18]

"Equality" is the state of being equal, especially in status, rights, and opportunities, or relating to or believing in the principle that all people are created equal and deserve equal rights and opportunities. *Merriam-Webster* defines "egalitarianism" as the belief in human equality, especially with respect to social, political, and economic affairs, or a social philosophy advocating the removal of inequalities among people.[19] Egalitarian servant leadership is the philosophy in which there is equality of all people, and an egalitarian society gives everyone equal rights. Egalitarianism is a belief that everyone should be treated the same or equally and all should have the same rights. In the same way as the persons of the Trinity are equal to one another, human beings are to be equal to one another. Scriptural examples of Jesus and equality include:

> This was why the Jews were seeking all the more to kill [Jesus], because not only was he breaking the Sabbath, but he was even calling God his own Father, making himself equal with God. (John 5:18 ESV)

16. *New Oxford American Dictionary*, s.v.
17. *New Oxford American Dictionary*, s.v.
18. *New Oxford American Dictionary*, s.v. Similarly, military ranks are a system of hierarchical relationships, meaning the police, intelligence agencies, and other institutions have key leaders serving in top positions of authority with subordinates specializing in interdependent jobs to accomplish their joint mission together. Military members serving under a hierarchical structure gain a better understanding of authority, discipline, and teamwork while also enhancing their own personal, social, and relational skills. Historically, military members, male and female, were equally able to achieve higher ranks with equal status across every specialty. However, with one exception, women were not being promoted to the highest rank of general officer. Why? They had not served in a combat zone, so were not getting a specified number of combat hours. After learning of the barrier, they challenged the rationale to allow women to go into combat and the barriers were slowly removed. As a result, the ranks of female general officers have increased. Women are now serving in all specialties, including combat, and are achieving all the top hierarchal ranks of general officer. So, even in a hierarchical structure, gender equality of opportunity can be introduced.
19. *Merriam-Webster Dictionary*, s.v.

> In your relationships with one another, have the same mindset as Christ Jesus: Who, being in very nature God, did not consider equality with God something to be used to his own advantage; rather, he made himself nothing by taking the very nature of a servant, being made in human likeness. (Phil 2:5–6 NIV)
>
> Submit to one another out of reverence for Christ. (Eph 5:21 NIV)

Consider It: Effects of Hierarchy and Patriarchy on Adolescent Development

Adolescent boys and girls experience significant changes in their bodies as well as the ways they begin to see the world. They grow up and develop in three stages of early, middle, and late adolescence to adulthood, while the body is also developing in five areas:

1. *Physical,* including hormonal changes and development, physical appearance and body image, puberty and sexual development, physical activity and weight.

2. *Cognitive/intellectual* changes in the way the brain functions, which affects learning, including learning disabilities, academic achievements, grades, choice of music and movies, response to television programs, and response to sexist advertising/marketing.

3. *Emotional,* including how adolescents process emotions and stress, sense of identity, and relationship skills.

4. *Social* changes in familial, social, and romantic relationships, peer relationships, familial and parent relationships, school, work, community, faith institutions, media, popularity, discrimination, racism, and sexism.

5. *Behavioral or morals and values,* encompassing how adolescents' self-identity is defined, how adolescents regard their place in the world, which affects risk-taking behavior, temptation of alcohol and drug abuse, unwanted pregnancy and sexually transmitted diseases (STDs), school failure and dropping out, delinquency, crime, and violence.[20]

Of these five areas of development, some may overlap and possibly produce negative outcomes in the way both genders interact with each other.

A *Psychology Today* article entitled "Are You Dating an Abuser?" notes that the negative outcomes of emotional abuse, verbal abuse, and domestic

---

20. Gentry and Campbell, *Developing Adolescents,* 29.

violence are on the rise, particularly among young people.[21] Emotional abuse is any nonphysical behavior or attitude designed to control, subdue, punish, or isolate another person through the use of humiliation or fear.[22] It can also include verbal assault, dominance, control, isolation, ridicule, or the use of intimate knowledge for degradation. Emotional abuse is known for targeting the emotional and psychological wellbeing of the victim, primarily girls and women. Oftentimes, in more cases than not, it is also a precursor to physical abuse.[23] Therefore, the risk is great for young people falling into abusive relationships.[24]

Dating abuse statistics research reveals that nearly 1.5 million high school students nationwide experience physical abuse from a dating partner in a single year.[25] Specifically, one in three adolescents in the United States is a victim of physical, sexual, emotional, or verbal abuse from a dating partner. This figure far exceeds the rates of other types of youth violence. One in ten high school students has been purposefully hit, slapped, or physically hurt by a boyfriend or girlfriend.[26]

Take Counsel: Teens' Lack of Understanding about Their Identity and Equality

Why should we focus on teaching, nurturing, and empowering young people, boys and girls? We should because:

- Girls and young women between the ages of 16 and 24 experience the highest rate of intimate partner violence—almost triple the national average.

- Among female victims of intimate partner violence, 94 percent of those aged 16–19 and 70 percent of those aged 20–24 were victimized by a current or former boyfriend or girlfriend.

- Violent behavior typically begins between the adolescent ages of 12 and 18.

---

21. Stosny, "Are You Dating an Abuser?"
22. Karakurt and Silver, "Emotional Abuse," 2.
23. Karakurt and Silver, "Emotional Abuse," 2.
24. Stosny, "Are You Dating an Abuser?"
25. "Dating Abuse Statistics."
26. "Dating Abuse Statistics." See Grunbaum et al., "Youth Risk Behavior Surveillance."

- The severity of intimate partner violence is often greater in cases where the pattern of abuse was established in adolescence.[27]

- Violence against children is a growing, and underreported, phenomenon among the undocumented. Some forms of violence against children are socially accepted, implicitly condoned, or not perceived as being abusive. Many victims are too young or too vulnerable to disclose their experience or to protect themselves.[28]

- Around the world, one in ten girls (120 million) under the age of 20 have been subjected to forced sexual intercourse or other forced sexual acts at some point in their lives.[29]

- Close to half of all girls aged 15–19 worldwide think a husband is sometimes justified in hitting or beating his wife.[30]

This is a major problem globally. Our youth across this nation[31] and around the world are growing up in family environments where physical violence and strong patriarchal relationships exist. This significantly increases the likelihood of men and boys exhibiting violent behavior.[32] At the heart of sexual violence against women is gender inequality.[33] Gender inequality ignites unnecessary spiritual battles among young people and those they emulate. Interestingly, when children attend church and grow up hearing the teachings of Jesus Christ, they are not focused on gender as much as on the Spirit of God within them speaking to their childlike faith. When barriers such as restricting the role of women in the church or levying prohibitions on ordaining women become topics of division among church leadership, then girls and boys become the victims of an identity crisis and lose sight of their purpose in the body of Christ. In short, the body of Christ is attacking itself, male and female, because God created it to be one with specific gifts fitted together in the body (1 Cor 12:4–27).

27. "Dating Abuse Statistics." See Feld and Strauss, "Escalation."
28. UNICEF, *Hidden in Plain Sight*, 7.
29. UNICEF, *Hidden in Plain Sight*, 7.
30. UNICEF, *Hidden in Plain Sight*, 7.
31. "Dating Abuse Statistics."
32. The World Health Organization reports most of the violence is intimate-partner related. Globally, almost one third (30%) of all women have experienced either physical and/or sexual violence by their intimate partner; in some regions, intimate partner violence affected about 38% of women. The numbers of children who suffer sexual abuse or violence is unknown. However, researchers suggest about 20% of women and 5–10% men suffered abuse as children, with the highest rate occurring during puberty and adolescence. See "World Report on Violence and Health," 159, 174.

Therefore, each of our bodies is sacred to God, who does not want them abused by us or anyone else. Each one of us will give an account of ourselves to God (Rom 14:12). Paul writes:

> The body is not meant for sexual immorality, but for the Lord, and the Lord for the body. By his power God raised the Lord from the dead, and he will raise us also. Do you not know that your bodies are members of Christ himself? Shall I then take the members of Christ and unite them with a prostitute? Never! Do you not know that he who unites himself with a prostitute is one with her in body? For it is said, "The two will become one flesh." But he who unites himself with the Lord is one with him in spirit. Flee from sexual immorality. All other sins a person commits are outside the body, but whoever sins sexually, sins against their own body. Do you not know that your bodies are temples of the Holy Spirit, who is in you, whom you have received from God? You are not your own; you were bought at a price. Therefore, honor God with your bodies. (1 Cor 6:13–20 NIV)

This lack of understanding of mutual interdependence is escalating beyond measure and stifling our young people's growth and development in conforming to the image of Christ (Rom 8:29).

When children grow up in church receiving biblical teachings of Christ, there is no gender-specific way of hearing and responding to God's message of love other than in a childlike way of innocence. Children grow up to become adults, and some are drawn to wanting to know more about God. Could this have been the reason for the 1980s influx of Protestant and Roman Catholic women entering seminaries after barriers were removed from within the established systems of male-dominated leadership roles? These same barriers that permeated homes, churches, workplaces, and society have prevailed for generations.[34]

God's empowering is always perfect. So over the decades, God kept revealing in individuals and social systems various facets of patriarchal and hierarchal causes for childhood trauma, as it is written: "For there is nothing hidden that will not be disclosed, and nothing concealed that will not be known or brought out into the open" (Luke 8:17 NIV). How many of the women who entered seminary, after the falling away of barriers, were adolescent victims who grew up attending church? And, if so, were they able to receive spiritual guidance and direction from their fathers, male pastors, or male church leaders? Are these women on a journey to God's healing and calling into ordained ministry for such a time as this?

---

34. Hyer, "Surge in Seminary," lines 13–15.

Girls undoubtedly grow up believing they should be treated by men in the way their mothers were treated by their fathers. Girls and boys are learning in the home how to treat the opposite gender. Statistically, 66 percent of the boys who grow up in violent homes, where there is chronic arguing, yelling, controlling behaviors, intimidation, threats, and serious injuries,[35] go on to treat their wives or girlfriends and dating partners the same abusive way. About 50 percent of the abusive boys come out of the Christian church.[36] According to a report from the Center for Disease Control and Prevention, almost 60 percent of American adults have been exposed to at least one adverse childhood experience, such as verbal, physical, or sexual abuse as well as family dysfunction (e.g., an incarcerated, mentally ill, or substance-abusing family member; domestic violence; or absence of parents because of divorce or separation).[37]

The impact of these adverse childhood experiences on into adulthood is expressed in Ally Kern's profound pronouncement, "that one of the most prolific forms of injustice within the U.S. and the Christian church is domestic violence."[38]

> Domestic violence (also called intimate partner violence, or relationship abuse) is a pattern of behaviors used by one partner to maintain power and control over another partner in an intimate relationship. Domestic violence includes behaviors that physically harm, cause fear, prevent a partner from doing what they wish, or force them to behave in ways they do not want.[39]

Kern further states that domestic violence affects at least one in three women during her lifetime. It can happen to anyone at any point in a relationship.

> Relationship violence is a deeply embedded, often hidden, and yet a profoundly traumatic communal reality. Considering that the Christian church remains the largest institution in the U.S.—and represents the increasing socio-economic and ethnic diversity of the nation—it is imperative to address the role of the local church in survivor support, counsel, and healing.

---

35. Edwards, "Alarming Effects," line 5.

36. See Centers for Disease Control and Prevention, "Adverse Childhood Experiences," and Fletcher, "God, Faith, and Healing."

37. See Centers for Disease Control and Prevention, "Adverse Childhood Experiences," and Fletcher, "God, Faith, and Healing."

38. Kern, "The Role of Pastors."

39. National Domestic Violence Hotline, "The What, Why, and How of DVAM," lines 1–5.

Christian survivors most often reveal their experience of abuse first—and often only—to their pastor. This puts pastors in the place of a first responder. . . . Pastoral caregiving involves resisting forces that contribute to oppressing women and confronting the patriarchal theology and practices of the church.[40]

For instance, up until the age of fifteen, "Maryanne" dreamed of one day marrying, and having and rearing children just like her parents did. Then her parents separated and divorced. Back in the south, every week, her mother dropped her and the siblings off at Sunday school and came back to join them for the church service. One Sunday, Maryanne discovered an all-loving God while reading Matthew 6:6: "But thou, when thou prayest, enter into thy closet, and when thou hast shut thy door, pray to thy Father which is in secret; and thy Father which seeth in secret shall reward thee openly" (KJV). She took the words literally and faithfully went into her clothes closet to pray, asking God to bring her parents back together. Sometime later, on another Sunday morning during worship service, while listening attentively to her pastor preach his regular sermon proclaiming how Christians should live, Maryanne decided this time to pray silently right there on the pew with her eyes closed: "Lord, I want to know You like the pastor seems to know You." After that prayer, she tried to live and put into practice the principles the preacher taught her. She did not think anything of what seemed to be the norm for church leaders: the pastor, deacon, trustee board, and Sunday School superintendent were always male. Yet, the Sunday school teachers, secretary, ushers, nurse's guild, and auxiliaries were usually all female, including a congregation comprised of about 90 percent women and children. Living without her father as "head of household" and her mother becoming single head of household, Maryanne found solace in reading the Bible and praying.[41] She was really concerned about obeying God's commands as the preacher preached and teachers taught in Sunday school.

When teenager Maryanne started dating, while also going to the church where she was taught to read and live obeying the Bible, how was she to handle the human situations and temptations she faced that felt contrary to what she was being taught? Her father was not physically in her life any longer to protect her. She soon had a boyfriend. But the arguing, fighting, and hitting finally gave her the nerve to hit back after it became too much for her to bear. She could not tell her mother for fear of what her mother

---

40. Kern, "The Role of Pastors," lines 2–9, 64.

41. Scriptures important to her were: "'Love the Lord your God with all your heart and with all your soul and with all your mind.' This is the first and greatest commandment" (Matt 22:37–38 NIV) and "One does not live on bread alone, but by every word that comes from the mouth of God" (Matt 4:4 NRSV).

would do to him and what the ramifications of that might be once the truth of the abusive relationship was known. She might then not have a mother either. She ran to her closet to pray to God in private because of what she was taught from the Bible.

In the midst of human suffering, people go to church to be closer to God, to build a moral foundation and to find comfort in times of crisis. The dichotomy in the understanding of gender roles is influenced by societal systems, family structure, and, most recently, the media and the environment in which people live.[42] How are boys and girls to understand adolescence and the transition going on in their bodies, minds, and hearts? How are boys and girls to be in a right relationship with one another? Boys and girls, in addition to the obvious physiological differences, should also be aware of personality differences in each other's character and nature, the way God intended each individual to be.

The family structure of households with two married parents is on the decline as divorce, remarriage, and cohabitation are on the rise.[43] From the height of the post–World War II baby boom in the 1960s, children living with both of their married parents went from 73 percent to 61 percent in the 1980s and 46 percent in 2015.[44] Consequently, trying to figure out and understand the dynamics of relationships between male and female has become very complicated. Males and females must first understand that, although men and women as humans are more alike than different, both biologically and psychologically,[45] they also have differences. Yet, God said his creation is good (Gen 1:27, 31 NIV).

Speak Up: What Egalitarian Relationships and Servant Leadership Looks Like in Teenagers

Generally speaking, girls and boys are clearly and uniquely designed by God to be complete humanity together. Any differences are intended to balance their similarities. By beginning to understand the fact that differences are good, leaders are in a position to equip girls and boys for leadership roles of equality. General physical differences do not affect one's intellectual capacity or ability to lead. This knowledge also helps build positive self-esteem in each one as individuals. But, first, if a person has experienced any childhood trauma or was exposed to it, they will need some tender loving care from

---

42. Wikipedia contributors, "Gender Roles in Childhood."
43. Pew Research Center, "Parenting in America."
44. Pew Research Center, "Parenting in America."
45. Van Leeuwen, *Gender and Grace*, 76.

pastoral first-responders who have also received the healing love of Christ. In order for young people to accept their own unique differences, appreciate the differences in the opposite gender, and not sabotage their relationships with each other, God is raising up servant leaders to draw his children back to him. Adults must bring youth back to God in order for them to be healed of their trauma and to help them discover their identity and be set free.

After an adult's traumatic experience and healing, their new sense of clarity, purpose, and direction will help the next generation of boys and girls break through the barriers of patriarchy or male domination and control. All we are really sure of is that women can bear children and men can achieve greater physical strength. The impact of these physical properties is often different in individuals because of hereditary family traits or environmental experiences, all conditioned by varying societal rules. Because of so much patriarchy and sexual exploitation aimed at women, we hardly know what an untraumatized woman can do.

In becoming a servant leader, the best example to follow is that of Jesus Christ. John Maxwell defines a leader as "one who knows the way, goes the way, and shows the way."[46] Jesus Christ is both God and human, who lived out his earthly identity by affirming he is the way to the Father, teaching the truth about how to go to the Father, and showing the way to live a life in submission to Father God in heaven and to one another.

In Jesus's human nature, he was an egalitarian with other humans on earth (Rom 8:17). In his divine nature, Jesus was also equal with God, but had a temporary hierarchical relationship with God, the Father in heaven, to show his fellow humans how we should follow God's commands on earth. As the mediator between God and humans (1 Tim 2:5), Jesus communed with Father God in heaven and communed with human beings on earth, conveying messages from the Father. While Jesus was human on earth, he directly connected with God the Father in heaven for wisdom, direction, and purpose.

Jesus's egalitarian mutual submission is also commanded of believers in Ephesians 5:21: "submit to one another out of reverence for Christ." Submitting or subjecting oneself to another is not about gender-based headship, being unilaterally authoritative, or having an entitlement to rule over another person. Both male and female submit to each other equally, reflecting the individual relationship they each have with Jesus Christ. Throughout Ephesians, Paul exhorts Christian believers, who are male and female, to live a holy and blameless life. By the time we arrive at chapter 5, Paul further builds on this truth. It is through Jesus Christ that

---

46. Maxwell, *AZ Quotes*.

God chose boys and girls before the creation of the world to be holy and blameless before him (Eph 1:4). God reconciled humanity to himself by making us alive together in Christ, despite our sinful nature in which we have been saved by grace through faith.

Paul uses the word "submit" or "subject" (*hupotassō*) as an instruction to be under obedience, put under, subdue, submit oneself unto, and be imitators of God (1:22; 5:21). Paul could have used *archē* (ruler) for men, but since man and woman's relationship is closer because of how God created them, flesh from one creating the other, he used "head" (*kephalē*). Man is not the ruler over woman. In God's image he made them "male and female" (Gen 1:27). God graciously loves us, and it is not by power or might, but by his Spirit that we can surrender to God's will. If we understand that submission to Christ is not bondage, but a choice, then submitting to one another is also a choice made because of our adoration and love for the Father, who gave authority to his Son while on earth. Humans were given dominion together over things and creatures, but not each other. Alice Mathews comments that God placed man and woman without hierarchy. They are a team working together as parents and as caretakers of God's new world.[47] To have the attitude of mutual submission means both men and women should place themselves under each other's authority.

To be imitators means being in obedience to "Emmanuel," God with us (Matt 1:23), in the same way God surrendered his will out of love for humankind and came to earth as a baby born of a virgin, assumed the responsibility of the name "Jesus" ("he will save his people from their sins," Matt 1:21), and submitted to earthly authority. Therefore, imitating God means submitting or subjecting our will to one another in fear and reverence of God, who is Father in heaven and also on earth. Believers of Christ should be imitators of this heavenly God-among-us who submitted or subjected himself to earthly authority, not out of selfish ambition, but solely out of unconditional love, making the sacrifice for us, first to the Father, and second before humans on earth.

Boys and girls are earthly human beings who should submit to each other out of reverence for Christ (Eph 5:21). Male and female submission is egalitarian throughout the entire letter of Ephesians. It is evident that Christians must voluntarily yield to one another in love due to their respect and reverence for Christ and what he did out of reverence for the Father. Out of obedience, husbands and wives submit one to another and to their Savior. Male and female should humbly submit to one another just as they would to Christ. Christians are to submit to one another out of respect and devotion for Christ. Subjecting or submitting is the voluntary

---

47. Mathews, *Gender Roles and the People of God*, 37.

"yielding in love" to one another" (1 Cor 16:16; Eph 5:21; 1 Pet 5:5b).[48] Paul is conveying to believers that, just as they surrender their will by consciously making the choice to receive Christ as their Savior, they should also follow and obey Christ's commands. Christ gives individuals the choice to accept him as their Savior; he is not an oppressor or controller. Both boys and girls should willfully choose as Christians to yield lovingly to each other out of reverence and respect for Jesus Christ, exhibiting the same type of *agapē* love Paul mentions in 1 Corinthians 13.

When believers submit one to another out of fear and reverence of Christ, they are recognizing God's divine purpose. In order to receive spiritual blessings in heavenly places, one must live a holy and blameless life, being filled with the Holy Spirit and being subject to other believers as to the Lord. When one is filled with the Spirit, one speaks to others in psalms, spiritual songs, and hymns, while singing praises in one's heart to the Lord and giving thanks to God the Father for all things in Christ. Believers surrender their wills to those of other believers to show respect to Christ, the Son of God. Gilbert Bilezikian concludes that "consequently, there is no mandate and no allowance in the New Testament for one adult believer to hold authority over another adult believer. Instead, the overall rule calls for mutual submission among all believers out of reverence for Christ" (Eph 5:21).[49] The same mutual submission is applicable to teenage girls and boys and should be taught, modeled, and nurtured in the church. Unless the church makes a mindset shift, young people will continue to perpetuate patriarchal lifestyles.

Jesus led by example in mutual submission when he prayed to his Father in heaven about his disciples: "I have revealed you to those whom you gave me out of the world. They were yours; you gave them to me and they have obeyed your word" (John 17:6 NIV). Jesus continued praying to the Father, "I brought you glory on earth by finishing the work you gave me to do" (John 17:4). Jesus, in humble submission, as a model of servant leadership, asked the heavenly Father to glorify him in God's presence with the glory he had with Father God before the world began. Jesus further prays that he had revealed the Father God to those whom he was given out of the world. They were God's chosen who were given to Jesus and they, male and female, obeyed God's word. Jesus prayed without discriminating between genders. He prayed:

"Holy Father, protect them [male and female] by the power of your name, the name you gave me, so that they may be one as we are one. While I was with them [male and female], I protected them and kept them safe"

---

48. BDAG, s.v.
49. Bilezikian, *Beyond Sex Roles*, 176.

by my earthly name, Jesus Christ, and none but one was lost. Take them not out of the world but "protect them from the evil one . . . Sanctify them [males and females] by the truth; your word is truth" (John 17:11–12, 15, 17 NIV). As God sent Jesus into the world, Jesus sent males and females into the world to follow his example, for Jesus sanctified himself for males and females so that males and females may be "truly sanctified" (John 17:19). His prayer included all who would believe through that message (John 17:20).

So how does all of this apply? Let us return to our illustration: God loves his sons and daughters and knows each one by name. When Maryanne experienced the trauma of her parents' divorce, she ended up in an abusive dating relationship while also going through the middle adolescent stages of development. She did not consult with a pastor, but prayed to God, her heavenly Father. God gave her instructions on what to do about the arguing and fighting. She had been praying regularly in her own literal prayer closet. The Spirit of God gave her the impetus to seek a mature woman for guidance. Maryanne told her that her boyfriend was hitting her. The woman simply stated, "You do not deserve to be treated that way." That simple statement was liberating and empowered her no longer to accept the physical abuse.

As time went by, she was advancing in her career and meeting men. After having a number of failed relationships, she realized she needed to pray to God about sending the right husband he had for her. Years later, God answered her prayer and sent her a Christian husband, "John." They were both equal in position in their careers. God and John built her self-esteem and she naturally did likewise because she felt loved and accepted. John was a gentleman who respected and treated her as an equal. When they started talking about the possibility of marriage, they sought premarital counseling by attending an engaged couples retreat, group premarital sessions, and couples counseling with an associate minister of their local church. John asked her in what duties as a couple she would like to engage, and he shared his ideas. When they married, it seemed insignificant to him who did the typical home duties because his mother had taught him to cook, iron, and clean house. Apparently, he was not expecting his wife to do what he could do for himself, unless she wanted to.

Once in seminary, Maryanne's goal was to search the Scriptures for God to reveal the real truth about women in ministry and ordination. As she was approaching graduation, she searched for ministry-related jobs, but not pastoring. Maryanne did not realize that all her life she had been the victim of degrees of abuse: repression by a series of churches and oppression by a series of boyfriends. Eventually, her boyfriend from her youth regretted his actions. Because of her experiences of serving in churches where leadership was male, it still took Maryanne several years to accept God's gifting of her as a pastor.

Kern sounds the alarm that the crisis of domestic violence, primarily men toward women, is the most prolific form of injustice within the United States and the Christian church. Domestic violence is the reason for the need of local churches to provide survivor support, counsel, and healing to girls and women in crisis and boys as needed, too. God is calling girls and boys, men and women, to him to be in a relationship with him in order to receive his love and discover their identity in him. God's children, created in his image and likeness, are masterpieces who possess his character and values, and therefore should circumvent abusive behavior in relationships. (Ps 139; Gen 1:27; Eph 2:10). Girls and boys should be taught more about who they are in Christ and how to be in a relationship with him and others, and less about the dos and don'ts of Christianity. This resource Maryanne had been missing.

Eventually, men and women should be equipped as first responders to serve together in egalitarian leadership, using their giftedness and oneness to accomplish God's eternal will on earth in the body of Jesus Christ. Ephesians 4:15–16 shows us the relationship of the head to the body. The whole body is being fitted and held together by every joint according to the proper working of each individual part and the growth of the body for the building up of itself in love. *Haphē* means "ligaments," which fasten together. The pituitary gland from the head regulates the growth of all connective tissues of the body, which is symbolically the church. The husband is not the head of a wife as a dictator, controller, or ruler being a supreme being over her, but the source from which God created the woman as Christ is the source of the church. The male is to emulate Christ giving himself as a living sacrifice, willfully surrendering his life for his bride, as Christ did for the church.[50]

---

50. In Eph 5:21–31, the male is the "head" of the same body from which God the Father took the rib and made female to be the helper whom the male is to care and nourish as a part of his body (*sōma*). When God said in Gen 2:18, "I will make a fitting helper for him," the literal Hebrew translation is "a helper who is equal." Dennis Prager points out in the *Rational Bible* this description of a woman's relationship to her man: she is both his helper and his equal. The Hebrew is clear, Prager says, since *k'negdo*—even in modern Hebrew—means "equal to him." And the word "helper," *ezer*, does not imply an inferior role. God himself is called an "*ezer*" in the Hebrew Bible. From a part of man's body the female was made. Paul uses body (*sōma*) in Ephesians to represent the true bodily union of the community of Christ and emphasizes the unity that manifests itself in the body of believers of Jesus Christ. Each record of *sōma* in this epistle refers to the total being of a person in mind, soul, and spirit. *Sōma* is a term for humankind in totality, which is different from what Paul writes, "for no one ever hated his own flesh (*sarx*) but nourishes and cherishes it" (5:29). In verses 29 and 31, Paul refers to the husband not hating his own flesh and both husband and wife becoming

Maryanne graduated from seminary with a better understanding that God calls us not by gender to be servant leaders, but by the giftedness he has given each one by the Holy Spirit. Maryanne was appointed senior pastor in a local church. God revealed her gifts are faith, teaching, pastoring/shepherding, exhortation, and knowledge. Her husband John's gifts are discernment, service, faith, miracles, and intercession. He joined her in serving in the ministry of the local church, both of them using their God-given gifts fitted together in oneness. Aída Besançon Spencer makes an interesting point of how God created man and woman to share in ministry and marriage, to share tasks, and share authority. Both male and female are needed to reflect God's image.[51] Obviously, God knew what Maryanne did not when he called her to be a pastor/teacher. In their mothers' wombs, God already knew the plans for Maryanne's and John's lives individually and collectively. Their cooperative ministry is a model of mutual submission (Eph 5:21).

Practical Application: Girls and Boys Growing Up in Healthy and Nonabusive Relationships

Since God made us relational beings, we must take concerted action to teach, nurture, and empower young people (boys and girls) to seek a relationship with God and discover gender equality is uniquely given to them by him. In finding solutions for eliminating the severity of intimate partner violence,[52] the research-based Strengthening Families Program by Dr. Karol Kumpfer is one resource that has proven skills to promote happy families, healthy brains, and alcohol- and drug-free kids. Adults can equip young people to build healthy relationships in the church and live them out at home, in the school, and in society by creating or implementing ministries and programs with the following foci:[53]

1. Develop Christian self-awareness youth programs with a focus on their identity in Christ, such as who you are, who loves you, who values you, and how to build healthy relationships.[54]

---

one flesh. The body *(sarx)* functions with man and wife comprising a living entity being one body or flesh. The body of believers represents the church. Christ is head of that body *(sōma)* and the husband and wife are one, the husband being the "head" *(kephalē)*, the source of her body *(sarx)*, one flesh without separation.

51. Spencer, *Beyond the Curse*, 39.
52. "Dating Abuse Statistics."
53. https://strengtheningfamiliesprogram.org.
54. See book written by author, *Daughters, You Are Special*.

2. Teach how to read, study, and apply the Bible to everyday life and the discipline of prayer.

3. Teach self-awareness on the topics of self-esteem, gender equality, and how to resolve relationship conflict. We are children of God and his heirs and coheirs with Christ. For example, from my observation, girls tend to verbalize and feel suppressed when they cannot express themselves. Knowing this might help boys who are quiet.

4. Seek guidance on topics about godly character, identity, self-esteem, value, love, respect, worth, how to value and interact with one another, etc.

5. Encourage more participation of both genders in activities and ministries of the church in collaboration with community-based programs.

6. Encourage seeking and consulting with mature Christian women and men.

7. Create gender-specific ministries for boys and girls to be taught, nurtured, and empowered to avoid sinning or being tempted, and to avoid neglecting or demeaning each other (Matt 18:7–14).

8. Conduct mission trips with the purpose of empowering young people to appreciate and celebrate their native ethnic heritage.

9. Develop and make a victim's resource list of support agencies with hopes it will encourage victims and offenders to seek counsel from their pastor.[55]

10. Train men and women to get past their fears by completing a questionnaire addressing key concerns about their childhood, adult relationships, and parenting.[56]

11. Empower both girls and boys to serve in mutual submission leadership roles in the church (Eph 4:21–24; John 17)

Since God made us relational beings to live in relationships of love and mutual respect for one another, we have to find solutions for eliminating the severity of intimate partner violence.[57] Gender equality is important in building healthy relationships among boys and girls, their families, and communities. By equipping the population's 51 percent girls and 49 percent boys to understand and appreciate each other's differences and uniqueness, they will have greater benefits in adulthood, such as positive self-esteem and stronger

---

55. Van Leeuwen, *Gender and Grace*, 76.
56. Ashcroft, *Balancing Act*, 86–87.
57. "Dating Abuse Statistics."

relationships with parents, teachers, pastors, and peers.[58] They will be less likely to drop out of school, experience mental illness, use substances such as drugs and alcohol, practice intimate partner violence or male domination, or enact ethnic prejudice toward those who are different than they are. By being willing to "submit to one another out of reverence for Christ," young people will be disciples of Jesus Christ living out equality for people by following his example to love everyone equally as they love themselves.

References

Aldridge, Jerry. *Self-Esteem: Loving Yourself at Every Age*. Birmingham, AL: Doxa, 1993.

Ashcroft, Mary Ellen. *Balancing Act: How Women Can Lose Their Roles and Find Their Callings*. Downers Grove, IL: InterVarsity, 1996.

Bauer, Walter, Frederick W. Danker, W. F. Arndt, and F. W. Gingrich. *A Greek–English Lexicon of the New Testament and Other Early Christian Literature*. 3rd ed. Chicago: University of Chicago Press, 2000. (BDAG)

Bilezikian, Gilbert. *Beyond Sex Roles: What the Bible Says about a Woman's Place in Church and Family*. 3rd ed. Grand Rapids: Baker, 2006.

Centers for Disease Control and Prevention. "Adverse Childhood Experiences Reported by Adults." *Morbidity and Mortality Weekly Report* 59:49 (Dec. 17, 2010): 1609–13. https://www.cdc.gov/mmwr/preview/mmwrhtml/mm5949a1.htm?s_cid=mm5949a1_w. Accessed May 28, 2020.

———. "Physical Dating Violence among High School Students—United States, 2003." *Morbidity and Mortality Weekly Report* 55:19 (May 19, 2006): 532–35. https://www.cdc.gov/mmwr/preview/mmwrhtml/mm5519a3.htm. Accessed May 28, 2020.

Chiu, Bonnie. "Gender Inequality Harms Not Only Women and Girls, but Also Men and Boys." *Forbes* (May 28, 2019). https://www.forbes.com/sites/bonniechiu/2019/05/28/gender-inequality-harms-not-only-women-and-girls-but-also-men-and-boys/#4b7131184d9f. Accessed May 28, 2020.

Clark, Jean Illsley. *Self-Esteem: A Family Affair*. Minneapolis: Winston, 1978.

Edwards, Blake G. "Alarming Effects of Children's Exposure to Domestic Violence." *Psychology Today* (Feb. 26, 2019). https://www.psychologytoday.com/us/blog/progress-notes/201902/alarming-effects-childrens-exposure-domestic-violence. Accessed May 28, 2020.

Erickson, Millard. *Christian Theology*. 2nd edition. Grand Rapids: Baker, 1999.

Feld, S., and M. A. Strauss. "Escalation and Desistance of Wife Assault in Marriage." *Criminology* 27 (1989): 141–61.

Fletcher, Dale. "Adverse Child Experiences Affect Health—God, Faith, and Healing." *Faith and Health Connection* website (Dec. 17, 2010). https://www.faithandhealthconnection.org/adverse-childhood-experiences-faith-and-health-link. Accessed May 29, 2020.

Gentry, Jacqueline H., and Mary Campbell. *Developing Adolescents: A Reference for Professionals*. Washington, D.C.: American Psychological Association, 2002.

---

58. See book written by author, *Daughters, You Are Special*.

Grunbaum, Jo Anne, Laura Kann, Steve Kinchen, James Ross, Joseph Hawkins, Richard Lowry, William A. Harris, Tim McManus, David Chyen, and Janet Collins. "Youth Risk Behavior Surveillance—United States." *Morbidity and Mortality Weekly Report* 53:2 (2003) 1–96. http://www.cdc.gov/mmwr/preview/mmwrhtml/ss5302a1.htm.
Hyer, Marjorie. "Surge in Seminary Enrollments Paced by an Influx of Women." *Washington Post* (Nov. 21, 1981). https://www.washingtonpost.com/archive/local/1981/11/21/surge-in-seminary-enrollments-paced-by-an-influx-of-women/7f9342fe-e799-444a-82aa-2b4a77efff9e. Accessed May 28, 2020.
Karakurt, Günnur, and Kristin Silver. "Emotional Abuse in Intimate Relationships: The Role of Gender and Age." *Violence and Victims* 28:5 (2013): 804–21. https://www.ncbi.nlm.nih.gov/pmc/articles/PMC3876290. Accessed May 29, 2020.
Kern, Ally. "The Role of Pastors: The Vital Link in Stopping Domestic Violence." *Yale University Reflections: A Magazine of Theological and Ethical Inquiry from Yale Divinity School* (2018). https://reflections.yale.edu/article/sex-gender-power-reckoning/role-pastors-vital-link-stopping-domestic-violence-ally-kern. Accessed May 29, 2020.
Krug, Etienne G., Linda L. Dahlberg, James A. Mercy, Anthony B. Zwi, and Rafael Lozano, eds. *World Report on Violence and Health*. Geneva: World Health Organization, 2002.
Life Application Bible: New International Version. Wheaton, IL: Tyndale, 1991.
Love Is Respect website. "Dating Abuse Statistics." https://www.loveisrespect.org/resources/dating-violence-statistics. Accessed May 28, 2020.
Mathews, Alice. *Gender Roles and the People of God: Rethinking What We Were Taught about Men and Women in the Church*. Grand Rapids: Zondervan, 2017.
Maxwell, John C. Quoted in *AZ Quotes* website. https://www.azquotes.com/quote/190563. Accessed May 29, 2020.
Merriam-Webster.com Dictionary. https://www.merriam-webster.com/dictionary/. Accessed May 29, 2020.
National Domestic Violence Hotline website. "Get the Facts & Figures." https://www.thehotline.org/resources/statistics. Accessed May 28, 2020.
———. "The What, Why, and How of DVAM." Sept. 26, 2019. https://www.thehotline.org/2019/09/26/whatisdvam. Accessed May 28, 2020.
Pew Research Center. "Parenting in America." Dec. 17, 2015. https://www.pewsocialtrends.org/2015/12/17/parenting-in-america. Accessed May 29, 2020.
Prager, Dennis. *The Rational Bible: Genesis, God, Creation, and Destruction*. New York: Regnery, 2019.
Spencer, Aída Besançon. *Beyond the Curse: Women Called to Ministry*. Grand Rapids: Baker, 1985.
Stevenson, Angus, and Christine A. Lindberg, eds. *New Oxford American Dictionary*. Electronic ed. New York: Oxford University Press, 2017.
Stosny, Steven. "Are You Dating an Abuser? 9 Early Signs of Emotional and Verbal Abuse." *Psychology Today* (Dec. 17, 2008). https://www.psychologytoday.com/us/blog/anger-in-the-age-entitlement/200812/are-you-dating-abuser. Accessed May 28, 2020.
Strengthening Families Program website. https://strengtheningfamiliesprogram.org. Accessed May 29, 2020.
Strong's Greek Dictionary of the New Testament (Greek Strong's). Accordance ed. 12.3.6. Oaktree Software.

Van Leeuwen, Mary S. *Gender and Grace*. Downers Grove, IL: InterVarsity, 1990.

UNICEF. *Adolescence: A Time that Matters*. New York: United Nations, 2002.

———. *Hidden in Plain Sight: A Statistical Analysis of Violence against Children*. New York, UNICEF, 2014. https://www.unicef.org/publications/index_74865.html. Accessed May 28, 2020.

United States Department of Health and Human Services website. "The Changing Face of America's Adolescents." https://www.hhs.gov/ash/oah/facts-and-stats/changing-face-of-americas-adolescents/index.html. Accessed May 28, 2020.

Whitley, Sandra Gatlin. *Daughters, You Are Special: To Love and Be Loved by Your Heavenly Father*. Bloomington, IN: Westbow, 2020.

Wikipedia contributors. "Gender roles in childhood." *Wikipedia, The Free Encyclopedia*. https://en.wikipedia.org/w/index.php?title=Gender_roles_in_childhood&oldid=959233389. Accessed May 29, 2020.

———. "Hierarchy." *Wikipedia, The Free Encyclopedia*. https://en.wikipedia.org/wiki/Hierarchy. Accessed May 29, 2020.

———. "Patriarchy." *Wikipedia, The Free Encyclopedia*. https://en.wikipedia.org/wiki/Patriarchy. Accessed March 29, 2020.

12

God's People for All Seasons

Sharing Ministry with Laypeople

Lydia M. Sarandan

IT HAS BEEN A privilege for me for almost fifty years to interface with the adults in the church and do my small part to help "to prepare God's people for works of service, so that the body of Christ may be built up until we all reach unity in the faith and in the knowledge of the Son of God and become mature, attaining to the whole measure of the fullness of Christ" (Eph 4:12–13 NIV). This has been and continues to be an awesome and humbling gift from God.

The men and women in this chapter represent scores of committed Christians who have served in the church. They continue to flourish as they use their gifts, skills, and open hearts to serve Christ and his church. These faithful saints often go unnoticed and at times are undervalued. However, as they continue to bear fruit attached to the Vine, Jesus Christ, they leave their imprint on many whose lives are enriched and changed by their witness.

While denominations and churches continue to debate the role of women in ministry, I continue to celebrate men and women together in ministry. This has been a part of my early history in the Baptist church (the Conservative Baptist Church then headquartered in Denver, Colorado). It all began in a church that had as its focus to help young people grow up in the faith. No distinctions were made between girls and boys, and *leadership development* was the goal of our pastors, youth sponsors, and Sunday school teachers. Equipping adults for ministry ideally begins early on.

The church (and family) that values training children, youth, young adults, and mature adults for ministry and authentic Christian living best fulfills the mandate of the Scriptures. Let me illustrate.

Back in the 1950s, our youth groups had lay "sponsors." They were parent couples who cared about kids and dedicated themselves to being with them. They were usually selected by the oversight pastor who gave them simple instruction on what was required of them as sponsors. The sponsors opened their homes, fed us, and took us on camping trips and adventure day outings. We had monthly Saturday night mission trips to Skid Row in downtown Detroit and conducted teen services for the homeless. At times, this seemed scary to us, but the sponsors were our "backup"!

Our sponsors listened to us and gave us advice with our dating struggles, home issues, and school setbacks. Their presence was steady and caring. They led us in Bible study and made sure we each had our own Bible. We sang choruses, and had a good time singing—at times with a beginning piano player. When one of our group members became an awarded musician in high school, we all started to sound better.

Our sponsors were always on the lookout for those who were extroverted, could read Scripture well, give a devotional, and play an instrument. When we were absent, they called us on the telephone, wrote us notes, and urged us to be back with the group. They made it a point to know our parents. I can tell you that, if they were not happy about whom I was dating in high school, my parents knew about it. Our sponsors were not formally theologically trained, but they had good standing in the church as faithful, loyal, caring, and trustworthy couples. They had families and they enjoyed us as kids.

An opportunity opened up for our church to have a Saturday morning radio show called the *Good News* children's program. It was emceed by the children and youth pastors. On the program, we sang, read Scripture, competed in Bible quizzes, and shared Bible stories to our listening audience. I have no idea of our "ratings," but it was all a part of developing us as Christian youth and preparing us for our future work in the church. It was a unique experience!

Why do I write this? Because the church was part of my spiritual formation, my rootedness in faith, along with my immigrant parents who came to faith in Eastern Europe in the early 1920s. God uses his people in amazing ways that are never forgotten. This is the church!

I happened to be one of the early trainees called to ministry. (We affirmed that *all* Christians are called to ministry in their chosen vocations. Mine happened to be in the church.) Back then, Baptists did not affirm women as pastors. God took care of that through a Presbyterian pastor,

Bartlett Hess, who became my mentor for many years. Dr. Hess shared his wisdom through consistent wise counsel as he guided me through my seminary years in preparation for ordination in the Presbyterian church. My work began in youth ministry, and eventually I began working with adults in two large churches. (I realize that not all churches are able to hire an adult education pastor.)

Over the years, the mandate affirming and confirming the call of both men and women in ministry has always been clear to me. I am grateful for this confirmation. It is through the continued study of the Scriptures, the early church scholarship of recent years, dedicated mentors, and the evidence of the maturing church in action that I turn my attention to share a few examples of God at work through the combined ministry of gifted, called, and flourishing women and men.

As I reflect on the past and the present, I have learned the importance of the following:

1. *Selecting* men and women of strong faith, commitment, and passion for service
2. A confident *concurrence* that the person is suited or teachable for the particular ministry
3. *Identifying and appropriating the gifts* for ministry
4. A *humble willingness* of the women and men to serve and be equipped for ministry
5. *Pastoral oversight and availability*, especially when there are questions, insecurities, and issues to be ironed out or redirected in the ministry
6. *Reasonable accountability* to ensure the ministries are moving forward and comply with the mission, goals, and values of the church
7. *Continued skill building and spiritual formation* opportunities in order for the church to be "built up into maturity"
8. A safe place for *conflict resolution with confidentiality*

In a crisis, community wisdom, discernment, intervention, and resolution are critical.

Growing up in faith is hard work; it is labor intensive; it takes time and is painful. This is true personally and corporately in the life of the church. We only have to turn to the leaders of the early church to know the struggles of the Christians growing into the likeness of Christ.

Let me begin with stories that have encouraged me and continue to give me joy. These are stories of ordinary men and women whose hearts, minds, and abilities were offered up to God to be used for God's glory. Some have moved on to their "new address," and many are serving today. Their lives reflect the power of God's Spirit at work growing the mind, heart, and will into conformity with the living Christ.

Growing the Young

Jeris and Joyce Eikenberry made music that ignited youth and brought joy to the church. Using the ageless template of parents as youth sponsors, Jeris and Joyce were the ideal young parents where I first served in the church. Just as I had experienced as a teen, they loved their family and kids. They were solid Midwest stock living in a vibrant college town. Both had creative, joyful musical talent that continues to follow them to this day. They are now in their 80s, singing and entertaining the Purdue University staff and students as well as the church and college community at large.

As youth sponsors, Joyce and Jeris's hearts ran deep with desire to grow in their faith, study the Scriptures, read spiritual writings, and immerse themselves in writings by professors such as Elton Trueblood, C. S. Lewis, Henri Nouwen, and others.[1] Their spiritual depth spilled over to the youth. There was music in the air, and *spiritual music* resounding in the souls of the teens who were blessed by their love and nonjudgmental nurture.

Devoted to the high school youth group, they were front and center in the revolutionary Jesus Movement of the 1970s. We know that something happened in the '70s that can only be attributed to the Holy Spirit's revival movement. It was "hip" to be a part of the Jesus Movement. Youth groups flourished, schools opened their doors to their Christian clubs, and youth pastors were busy and popular.

The Eikenberrys were creative and innovative. Because they were musically gifted, they gave hours of their time choreographing and coaching the youth as they performed popular Christian musicals. (The support of parents, the church family, and the teens themselves ignited other churches to follow suit and challenge their ministries to risk new adventures with teens.)

The *Tuesday Morning Breakfast Club* was the innovative idea of the youth during the Jesus Movement. More than 100 gathered weekly in the spacious basements of teen homes. Donuts, hot chocolate, and cider were served and funded by parents. There was vibrant singing to guitar music coming of age in the church along with a biblical devotional by the youth pastor, in this case, me. This set the stage for the 6:45 a.m. weekly event to

---

1. Some resources used were by E. M. Bounds; Fleming, *Ignatian Spirituality*; Lewis, *Mere Christianity*; *The Great Divorce*; Nouwen, *Out of Solitude*; *Reaching Out*.

be the talk of the college town. Parents were pleased and competed to offer their large home basements. However, all was not as easily received by the neighbors who complained about car doors slamming at the early hour along the streets. Who were these teens creating a disturbance in the neighborhood? (To say nothing of their energetic, boisterous voices greeting one other.) The issues were resolved when the neighbors realized that the youth club attached to the vibrant neighborhood church was a good thing.

Prayer: The Foundation for Leadership

I continue with *Audrey*—an anchor with our new member team in the church. Her gift was prayer, and she was sincere in her prayer discipline, enrolling in the church's prayer classes as she kept growing in her prayer life.

The new member team was assigned ministry responsibilities that best fit their interests as well as their skills. One of the men on the team was skilled in art, and we never forgot how the room was decorated and ready to welcome the new members. It was like a classy Disney adventure. At that time, we had large new member classes. The numbers did not matter; it was the attention to each member that was emphasized. What Audrey did as a part of the team was significant.

Audrey's task was to call each of the candidates and establish a friendly relationship with all of them as they anticipated the membership classes. As the classes progressed, questions emerged, and the members called Audrey. She loved the challenge! (I think they may have been too embarrassed to ask the pastors their questions for fear of looking inadequate.) When Audrey did not have the answer, she would call me as the oversight pastor and take notes on my responses. Most of the time, the questions centered around Reformed baptism, the statements of faith required for membership, and how to share their stories with the elders prior to being voted on by the session. These were hard questions! Audrey was ready with her answers. During her conversations, she made it a point to pray with each candidate. By the time they all officially joined the church, Audrey had had five conversations with each person. It was fixed in their minds that our church was anchored in prayer and assumed that members used their gifts in the congregation. Without question, Audrey did pastoral work.

To this day, tears well up in me when I think of her loyalty, faithfulness, maturity, and grace in ministry. She will be one of the first that I will want to meet in heaven.

A Sacred Ministry to the "Least"

Larry is a church statesman: a man of intellect, compassion, skill, and humility. It was years until I finally discovered that he was a biochemist geneticist. Larry owned his company, which invented and manufactured calibrators for medical instruments for blood tests that could detect proteins which could assist with difficult diagnoses in various organ functioning issues—including those of the heart and brain. Recently, Larry sold his successful company, giving him time, financial resources, and visionary space to think about future kingdom possibilities.

Over the years, Larry never called attention to himself or his accomplishments. Whenever I asked about his work, he managed to skirt the answer. As an elder on the governing body of our church, when he spoke, everyone listened. He had wisdom, discernment, maturity, and respect.

Larry's passion was the mentally challenged men and women at St. Andrew's Church. He knew they were often shunned and not understood or affirmed. Their presence for some became troublesome in the church's singles ministry. After a series of sobering discussions at our session meetings, Larry was determined that the emotionally and mentally challenged would not be discouraged from becoming enfolded in the community of the church. The consensus was: "We're not equipped to handle the mentally challenged. They need to go elsewhere." The message was direct and stern.

Larry invited Mike, who had severe emotional issues and was the center of the elder discussion, to meet with him over breakfast in 1992. It was a most revealing, challenging, and moving encounter for Larry as he and Mike sat for hours in conversation. That meeting changed Larry's life. Within six weeks, five members came together and a group was formed initiated by Larry. They began to meet each Wednesday night from 7:00–8:15 p.m. as a "covenant group." Eventually, it was included as part of the adult education small group ministry of the church.

In this newly formed group, some were more severely challenged and could not drive. Larry would pick them up and bring them to the group. Many lived in less than lovely surroundings and needed a warm and homey environment. My office looked like a living room and became their "home," where they relaxed, had their snacks, and laughed heartily. They always left my office looking even better than when they entered.

Being a geneticist, Larry was interested in their histories and understood their challenges. A gifted listener, he provided space for them to share their stories, hurts, and challenges. They studied the Bible and prayed together. The group became the safe space to share and feel each other's pain. They understood isolation, being marginalized in society, lacking self-worth, experiencing loss, and rejection by family. And, yes, some felt rejection by God. The weekly community brought them joy, and over time they began to reach out to communicate and help one another during the week. One group member had been kicked out of nineteen churches. Now, he had a "home" and felt safe.

When the weekly group time concluded, Larry took them out for pie and coffee. By the time the last member was driven home, it was close to midnight. This ministry not only continued to fuel Larry's life and spiritual growth, it changed and saved the lives of the group members. His generosity stretched beyond the Wednesday gathering. Larry often paid their rent and utility bills as well as provided their needed meals. The group continues to meet and is now in its twenty-eighth year. By the way, the pie and coffee has been upgraded to dinner, with a $300 tab that Larry picks up each week!

Larry has shared that Mike, the initial member of the group and still an active participant after twenty-eight years, will eat part of his dinner, take the rest home (including the bread remaining on the table), and ration it out over two to three evenings for his dinner.

To date, the group includes ten to twelve members including men and women and one married couple who are numbered among Larry's closest friends. Over the years, Larry has ministered to dozens in the group, facilitated at four memorials, officiated one wedding, and *declares this group to be the greatest highlight of his spiritual journey.* When tempted to be discouraged, he credits his mother's admonition over the years, "Larry, don't leave the group!"

Larry's wife, *Sue Ann,* was his partner in ministry. She, too, was in the medical field. They joined one another to pick up the physically challenged for the church's Saturday night worship service. Week after week, they faithfully brought them to hear the message, join in the praise singing, and to be nourished and accepted in worship with God's people.

For twenty years now, Sue Ann has prepared meals for the physically challenged who attend the Saturday worship service and feeds them after the service. Several of the Wednesday evening group members arrive one hour early to meet the taxicab and van. They greet Annie (now 60+ years old) and Kathy, who are both in wheelchairs, and help Sue Ann feed them dinner.

Larry and Sue Ann are stellar witnesses to the beauty of God's gifts faithfully shared as a team—reaching out to those neglected and on the margins of society. There's more.

Larry's ministry is diverse, exciting, and continues to flourish. Today, he partners with a team that directs a unique mission in Africa, reaching out to educate young children in the village of Agongo, in the Midori County of Kenya. In the surrounding counties, 27 percent of the people had AIDS, which left hundreds of children orphaned. Pastor Joel Amonde, the local pastor in the county, adopted seven children. Now, through compassionate hearts, 450 have been adopted. Knowing that the children needed to be educated, Pastor Joel sent an email to a church in Santa Ana, California, pleading for resources to help build a school to educate the orphaned children.

To shorten the story, after ninety days, a 501(c)(3) nonprofit certification was secured and the Seeds of Joy Foundation was established. The generous capital funds were on their way—with $200,000 of the $400,000 needed donated from Larry. Within three years and ten trips back and forth by Larry and his team, a K-8 school was erected. In February 2020, a new dispensary clinic was added to the compound and dedicated in honor of the deceased St. Andrew's children's pastor, Candy Baylis, who served our congregation for over forty years. The children are financed one by one as "adopted," and the ministry is flourishing.

Larry's spiritual depth, business acumen, and financial generosity are not easily overlooked. One of Larry's friends shares that, when a videographer was hired to document the story of the new school, he refused. He wanted first to know the story of Larry, the man behind the school, who had captivated his attention. Naturally, Larry was reluctant, but finally gave in.[2]

Tom Brock, a retired blue-ribbon school principal in California and a member of our church, is Larry's "balcony person"—his cheerleader friend. Tom is a man of unique wit, sensibility, educational experience, and patience. Tom relates that his job is to come alongside Larry, keep him excited, be an encourager, and keep the mission team transparent. There is a dignified African word that the team uses often to communicate when transparency is being thwarted. With a smile on their faces they call out, "Remember, no *matope*!" The word basically implies communicating love with no *waste* (dung!) or hindrance on the path of getting the job done.

When asked to reflect on the best part of the past years in ministry, Larry comments with humility, "For me, it has been the Wednesday night group."

I asked Larry: "Larry, what do you do to stay centered, relaxed from your long trips and full schedule, and keep going at 83?" Larry climbed into his new red shiny truck and said, "I bought this truck so I could take my telescopes out to the desert and look up into the heavens."

As I drove away, I thought about the words of the psalmist, "I lift my eyes to the hills [stars!]—where does my help come from? My help comes from the Lord, the maker of heaven and earth" (121:1-2 NIV).

---

2. See *The Seed Academy*.

And one more thing: Larry has suffered most of his adult life from debilitating spinal issues due to injury and is in constant pain.

Larry is a man of hope. When he is weary, his strength is renewed, and he continues to soar on wings like eagles, just as Isaiah wrote (40:31).

The Church, Equipped to Care

Tom T. is a man of courage, care, and commitment. It all began when Tom was diagnosed with liver disease that eventually required a liver transplant. Tom had served as a military officer in the Vietnam War, and experience with crisis was no stranger to him. His Christian faith was strong, and he was anchored.

His business career flourished, and he was a happy husband, father of two children, grandfather, and friend to many. He was comfortable with people of all ages and stages in life.

As a Christian, Tom handled his onset illness with grace. The genetic enzyme deficiencies in his liver that caused the failure, along with the transplant process, made a difficult journey. There were times when his prognosis did not look hopeful, but God had a plan, and it matured in God's timing.

With only a few unexpected days' notice, the Mayo Clinic was standing by 2,500 miles away to give Tom a new liver. His limp, gray, and weak body barely made it on the flight to the hospital. But God was there waiting to guide the hands in the surgeons' gloves and the surgery was performed successfully. Tom lived ten years with his new liver, and, thanks to his faithful and devoted wife Nancy, they were able to travel and enjoy their families and friends. Tom had a second chance with continued ministry waiting ahead.

Tom was drawn to the Stephen Ministry at the church because he was a caring person. He understood people's suffering and hardship. He was interviewed for the ministry and accepted for the fifty hours of required training. The one-on-one ministry focused on a caregiver and care-receiver bonding together in a weekly meeting. The ministry is designed to help men and women in the congregation who are going through tough times and would benefit from an empathetic, caring, and sensitive friend.

Thousands of churches are enrolled in this ministry that has expanded to train adults in the church to care with basic skills that translate into all avenues of relationships with family, friends, neighbors, work colleagues, as well as local and global mission endeavors. The Stephen Minister (SM) is trained to listen well, give support, offer encouragement, exercise assertiveness when needed, validate feelings, and refrain from giving advice and pronouncing a "cure." In essence, the SM is a caregiver, not a cure-giver.

In this confidential ministry, men are assigned to men and women to women. Regular supervision meetings are required with assured accountability. Tom appreciated the format and discipline of the ministry as the women and men gathered to share their caregiving highlights and encourage one another, especially when they felt "stuck" in the relationship with their care-receiver. The team sharing gave perspective to the ministry as the caregivers became bonded with one another. Supervision meetings became a time for sharing their stories and issues, receiving and giving spiritual support, and praying for one another.

Tom's care-receivers were a gift to him—giving him an opportunity to share his faith experiences, gifts, and skills where they were needed most. Tom blessed the men and related authentically as a trusted friend who cared deeply, with empathy, sensitivity, and depth.

As a result of Tom's successful transplant, word of his survival spread through the hospital networks. He received calls from patients around the country who were waiting for new livers and those who were struggling with organ rejection. Tom's SM training equipped him to stretch and apply what he had learned and experienced. His caring and compassionate heart, along with his sharpened skills, extended his witness beyond the church into the world of many who needed hope, comfort, and encouragement to get through their dark, difficult days.

After living with the new liver for ten years and continuing to serve others, Tom died, leaving a beautiful legacy that, when we let God use our gifts and experiences to bring healing and help to others, it blesses beyond any earthly measure and for all eternity.

Ordained to Serve

The Scriptures outline the office of the deacon as one of sympathy, witness, and service after the example of Jesus Christ. The Scriptures explain that those called to this office are to be men and women of spiritual character and compassion, living exemplary lives fit for the office (1 Tim 3:8–13). The duties of the deacons are to minister to those in need: the sick, the friendless, any in distress both within and beyond the community of faith.

Our deacon ministry was ready to be reorganized. As the congregation grew, so did the growing needs of the congregation. For many years, the culture of the church was to choose men as elders (adding a few token women) and women as deacons. As a result of repeated conversations—at times strong—we were successful in presenting men as candidates for deacons and began by identifying couples for this ministry of service. This opened the door for successive inclusivity. Women elders increased in number over the years. Today, the ratio is three to one, with men in the majority. Over the years, as women were invited to serve, some declined because they felt their husbands were more qualified. One elder in particular was gifted in relating to the staff and used her gifts to listen, care, and inform the pastor (when appropriate) of important staff issues. Some staff issues were personal; other issues were professional. Another woman elder was a national officer in Presbyterian Women, PCUSA, and was helpful in developing the ministry to a greater potential in our presbytery.

The adult education ministry was a natural training ground for developing the skills for both men and women to serve as deacons. Men were enrolled in the prayer classes, were commissioned as Stephen Ministers, served on the telephone helpline, attended our ongoing adult education classes, facilitated small groups, and demonstrated deep care and sensitivity in the life of the church. We also made it a practice to invite elders who had served their term to consider serving as deacons. By the time their governance term was concluded, many were attracted to the hands-on caregiving opportunities of service as a deacon. It was a change from the administrative governance of the past.

Thurmond was an adult education "regular." He attended the biblical classes, enrolled in our ongoing prayer and healing courses, and served as a deacon. He was a businessman who made worship and continued education a priority—often attending alone.

As a deacon, he was prompt to visit the sick, pray with them, and follow through with any requests and needs. One significant experience that has never left my mind was his work as a deacon with a member of the congregation who was very ill.

Don was in Thurmond's deacon area and had severe heart issues. One day, Thurmond was summoned to visit Don, who had suffered a severe heart setback. Conscientious and available, Thurmond was at his bedside visiting Don day after day giving comfort, reading Scripture, and serving as the presence of Jesus at his bedside.

Realizing that Don was failing rapidly, Thurmond decided to use his newly learned skill of anointing with oil as part of his prayer with Don during his daily visits. Thurmond was concerned and wanted to be certain that it was appropriate to anoint with oil. He nervously asked if he was doing it right. I responded, "Yes, of course! What an opportunity for you and Don to share in this beautiful experience." (I often smile that Thurmond was sensitive about the sacredness of anointing prayer. As a true learner, he wanted to be sure he could anoint his friend on a daily basis).

Thurmond's experience as Don's deacon made a deep spiritual impact that I think about often. A regular part of our deacon training meeting was sharing significant experiences that had occurred during the past month. One evening, Thurmond shared about his visitation experiences with Don. He mentioned that, even though Don could not speak because of the breathing machine attached to him, when Thurmond visited him, Don pointed to his forehead, signaling with his hand that he wanted to be anointed with oil. This happened during each of the visits. This anointing grace ministered to Don's heart and gave him immeasurable peace right to the moment of his death.

After the meeting, I affirmed Thurmond that his faithful visits, care, prayer, and anointing with oil prepared Don for his death with hope and God's promise of eternal life. Thurmond looked at me after a thoughtful pause and replied, "Yes, and my experience with Don is preparing me for my death." What an insight! I will never forget his response. Both men were blessed—Don entering heaven prepared to meet his Lord, and Thurmond confident in God's faithfulness to sustain him until the end of his life.

One Hundred and Fifty Years without Discrimination

For the past eleven years, I have been serving as a member of the Orange County advisory board of The Salvation Army (SA). Providentially, one of the members approached me the day of my retirement after serving twenty-eight years at St. Andrew's church, to "come on board." Without hesitation, I knew this was my next call to continued ministry because the organization has an outstanding reputation around the world. I never cease to be amazed at how this historical kingdom work is flourishing as it reaches out to transform lives.

The Salvation Army is a church. While this is not known to many, it all began in the East End of London in 1865 during the Industrial Revolution. William Booth was an ordained itinerant Methodist preacher, who, along with his wife Catherine, had compassion for those abused, in poverty, on the margins of society, and without hope. The conditions during the Industrial Revolution were beyond comprehension. The Booths' passion for the undervalued and poor initiated the "Soup, Soap, and Salvation" movement that is now flourishing in 121 countries around the world. From the beginning, The Salvation Army embraced the biblical gifts of women and men working together to make a difference, lend a hand up, and transform lives. Catherine Booth, along with the Booth's daughter, Evangeline, served together as the ministry reached beyond the borders of the United Kingdom.[3] Evangeline eventually became the first woman general, the chief in command, who gave global oversight to the ministry. Here is their mission statement:

> The Salvation Army, an international movement, is an evangelical part of the universal Christian church. Its message is based on the Bible. Its ministry is motivated by the love of God. Its mission is to preach the gospel of Jesus Christ and to meet human needs in His name without discrimination.[4]

To the majority of people, The Salvation Army is most known for the Christmas Kettle Kick Off. Each year, red kettles are placed in shopping malls and outside grocery stores and other commercial properties, with stationed bell ringers inviting people to give to help those in need in their community. The kettle drive provides food and shelter for the homeless, assistance for those caught in sexual and domestic trafficking, as well as food, clothing, and toys for hundreds and thousands of families in any given community. During the Christmas season, $140 million is raised in the United States to meet these needs by 25,000 bell ringers. One hundred percent of the funds raised with the Red Kettle go directly back into the communities.

In addition, community thrift stores and pickup trucks are visible as they display the red shield and slogan, "Doing the Most Good." All sales in the SA thrift stores go to support the men and women who are committed to recovering from drug and/or alcohol addictions. The recovery program is offered without cost to these women and men.

The depth of the SA ministry work is often unnoticed. Its endless work brings relief and transformation not only to those seeking freedom from substance abuse, but also to the homeless, those ensnared in human trafficking, the hungry, victims of abuse, the unemployed, those in need of transitional housing and disaster relief, and a myriad of others with human needs in all parts of the world.

Behind the scenes is a host of trained men and women working together with astounding dedication to expedite the myriad of outreach ministries and projects. They serve as pastors to officers in the church, administrative leaders, and volunteer lay church members (called Salvationists) around the world. They work endless hours, receive modest pay, live modestly, and have the respect and admiration of scores of citizens

---

3. C. Booth, *Female Ministry*. See also W. Booth, *Darkest England*; Cohen, *The Salvation Army*; Munn, *Theory and Practice*; Watson, *Most Effective Organization*.

4. "The Salvation Army Mission Statement."

worldwide. Eighty-seven percent of every dollar donated to The Salvation Army goes directly to the projects and ministry.

Adult officer training centers are located strategically where young women and men are prepared as cadets and commissioned with equal rank and respect. For officers to serve in lead positions—to be in charge of a command or a corps (church)—they are required to be a married couple. The expansive global work of The Salvation Army could never he accomplished without the combined talents of both women and men engaged in the ministry.

Youth are embraced in their churches, encouraged to participate and serve, and motivated to excel in education, athletics, and music. They are visible playing their instruments in the worship band and leading in praise music during the service. The Salvation Army's youth conferences and athletic and music camps flourish around the world, culminating in preparing the next generation for leadership. It is a family ministry, and all are included!

Captain *Cheryl Kistan* is an officer and serves in Orange County (OC) along with her husband, Captain *Nesan Kistan*. As a family, they were transferred to OC from Sydney, Australia, with their four children. Previous to serving with The Salvation Army, both were employed in the business sector in Australia. Cheryl worked for ten years as a policy writer in Sydney, interpreting important government legislation in the various regions of Australia. After these successful years, she felt called, along with her husband, to give their full time to The Salvation Army. Their early personal stories in South Africa (Nesan's family escaping during apartheid when black teens were assassinated on the streets) and Cheryl's family experience in Australia reflect their deep gratitude for the help they received from The Salvation Amy early in their lives.

Needless to say, their business and life experiences, keen vision, flexibility, and commitment to faith are transforming the mission in our OC territory that is comprised of thirty-four cities. In addition, the primary responsibility of both requires sharing in the managing of their home and the parenting of their four children, ages 6 to 19.

Cheryl's keen insight, her subtly engaging smile, and twinkling eyes have a way of getting right to your heart. Her quick assessment of a person or situation is instant, yet humble, and you have a sense that she intuitively has it right.

Nesan attends to the administrative work of their outreach projects that include homeless shelters, an anti-trafficking safe house, affordable and transitional housing facilities, as well as the new Center of Hope projects being launched in the county.

Cheryl as cocaptain with her husband is involved in the advising process of these ministries. She is also responsible for overseeing the detailed pastoral work of the 300-member church in the thriving community of Tustin Ranch in Orange County. Both Cheryl and her husband give the congregation exposure to their excellent preaching gifts. The sermons are planned one year in advance in six-week biblical series.

Cheryl's spiritual discernment, professional organizational abilities, pastoral grace, and devotional prayer life work together to keep her effective and efficient. Her responsibilities involve giving administrative oversight to the congregation at large, planning and overseeing the Sunday worship services, directing the women's program of the church (including social activities), overseeing fiduciary requirements, visiting the sick, and shepherding the parishioners. And, as Cheryl comments, physical labor is also a part of the job description. In addition, The Salvation Army Women's Auxiliary of Orange County is under Cheryl's leadership, which requires her monthly attendance at meetings and functions that engage women in the greater Orange County territory. For Cheryl, teaching, preaching, and pastoral care are what she loves most and does best!

Pastoral issues and concerns take up many hours of Cheryl's week and, during this past year (2019), there were twenty-five deaths in the church. In addition, both officers are called on to act as liaisons with civic and community officials as they promote the outreach of The Salvation Army.

Having come to the United States for the first time, and assessing the church in wealthy Orange County, Cheryl remarks that wealth is used as a substitute for needing God. She comments that the rich need God more than those disadvantaged and in poverty pockets of the county.

In reflection, she comments with transparency on working side by side with her husband. She feels that the church is still primarily a "man's world," but believes that women cannot shrink back. They need to be confident and use their strong voices with authority. Confidence in the confirmed call to ministry is the work of the Holy Spirit, and that is her freeing source of power, authority, and spiritual confidence.

Cheryl realizes that she cannot do what her husband does. They think differently. She is a realist and looks at the logistics of a situation. Her focus is doing what she does best: filling in the blanks and bringing new ideas. They both come to the table, making decisions based on their unique perspectives and supporting one another without competition. They rely heavily on the Holy Spirit's direction through prayer and bask in celebrating how God works when they "let go and let God." As I conclude this chapter, The Salvation Army is working around the clock as emergency responders meeting the needs of those afflicted by the virus pandemic in 2020.

As I continue to reflect on God's design for his church, witnessing the energy, competence, maturity, and joy in the lives of men and women engaged in their unique and gifted ministries, it is evident—God makes no mistakes!—God has endowed his people, the church, with spiritual gifts to be the greatest force on the earth to fulfill his purpose for all humanity.

The Scriptures clearly inform us, and the history of the church has demonstrated throughout the centuries, that we are truly "God's workmanship, created in Christ Jesus to do good works, which God has prepared in advance for us to do" (Eph 2:10 NIV). When we take seriously the instruction of the Scriptures and train men and women to use their natural and spiritual gifts to minister, the church is stronger, healthier, happier, and a more vibrant and effective witness in the community and the world. Its influence and existence are eternal. What greater call than to train and be trained and connected as cocreators to the eternal Creator of the universe.

References

Booth, Catherine. *Female Ministry: Woman's Right to Preach the Gospel*. New York: The Salvation Army, 1975.

Booth, William. *In Darkest England and the Way Out*. Charleston, SC: BiblioBazaar, 2007.

Bounds, E. M. *The Complete Works of E. M. Bounds on Prayer*. Grand Rapids: Baker, 1990.

Cohen, Susan. *The Salvation Army*. London: Shire, 2013.

Fleming, David L. *What Is Ignatian Spirituality?* Chicago: Loyola, 2008.

Lewis, C. S. *Mere Christianity*. San Francisco: HarperSanFrancisco, 1952.

———. *The Great Divorce*. New York: Simon & Schuster, 1974.

Munn, Janet. *Theory and Practice of Gender Equality in The Salvation Army*. Charleston, SC: CreateSpace, 2015.

Nouwen, Henri J. *Out of Solitude*. Notre Dame, IN: Ave Maria, 1974.

———. *Reaching Out*. Garden City, NY: Doubleday, 1986.

The Salvation Army. "The Salvation Army Mission Statement." https://www.salvationarmyusa.org/usn/. Accessed May 30, 2020.

Stephen Ministries. https://www.stephenministries.org/default.cfm. Accessed May 30, 2020.

Ungerman, Gerard, and Stacey Wear. *Joel & Larry: Two Men, Two Worlds and a Miracle of Hope in Agongo, Kenya*. Vimeo, 11:09. May 23, 2018. https://vimeo.com/271498741.

Watson, Robert A., and Ben Brown. *The Most Effective Organization in the United States: Leadership Secrets of The Salvation Army*. New York: Crown, 2001.

13

Gender Equality in the Church as a Model for the Neighborhood

Ralph A. Kee

As we read about Jesus in the Bible, we see how he lived a God-filled seven-days-a-week life in Galilee. In that culture, he was very visible every day to the neighbors who lived and worked around him. His neighbors saw him as he really was, saw his outside actions, and probably knew his inner thoughts, dreams, and dedications. He lived every day doing God's will for himself personally and for the people around him.

His neighbors, of course, knew his gender. They saw how he related to men and how he related to women. Yes, he was a man, not a woman, in his physical body. But they saw how he related to everybody around him and how he related equally to men and women. This chapter is about gender equality within the Christian community and within the world. Christians for Biblical Equality (CBE) believes that Jesus believed and practiced gender equality. It needs to be seen this way in how Christians live and what Christians do and are called to do in today's world. It needs to be seen this way in the neighborhood and by the neighborhood people where Christians live and where their churches meet on Sundays.

We know that God created a perfect world: perfect in every way. Adam was made perfect, then God made the perfect Eve. Then sin entered, and everything God had made was affected. There were four schisms: (1) Humankind was separated from God. (2) Humankind was separated in some ways from creation itself. Adam and Eve had to leave the Garden of Eden.

Genesis says the weeds started to grow. (3) The human male became separated from the human female in some ways. (4) Then, as humanity began to multiply, separation led to more separation. Their firstborn son Cain killed his brother Abel, premeditated in the first degree.

We are focusing on the third separation, the third schism, in this chapter. Sin infesting the whole creation immediately infected all human relationships, including the male-female relationship, separating the original unity of Adam and Eve. People were now distanced from people as they had not been before sin entered the picture. And the first people to be distanced from each other were the only two people alive. Sin infestation quickly showed itself in the reactions of Adam to Eve, the very one who had been intentionally created to be his absolute equal, Eve, taken from his rib, who was "flesh of his flesh, and bone of his bone."

Adam had been looking for an equal. He had carefully checked out all the animals. (That is why he named them, so he could identify them one from another and as distinct from himself.) Was there an equal to be found, perhaps, in the hippopotamus? "Sorry, Ms. Hippopotamus. My apartment is too small for both of us." Perhaps Ms. Tick? "I'm afraid sooner or later you'd get under my skin." Lovely Ms. Alligator said to Adam, "Let me give you a great big kiss!" "Whoa!" cried Adam, backing away quickly with protective palms in the air. Adam looked and looked, carefully checking out all the animals, but for the life of him, try as he could, he could not find an equal (Gen 2:20b). He was not just looking for a companion; he already had a pet dog and a cat that loved to lie on his lap. He wanted an equal. He finally got so tired of looking that he fell asleep. So, God, in a separate and very intentional act of divine creation, put Adam in a coma and *made* an equal for him. God took Eve out of Adam himself—not out of the elements of the inorganic universe that he had made nor out of the animals, but out of the very essence of Adam, out of the elements of the one human person (Gen 2:21–23). The absolute equality of Eve to Adam was integral to the whole purpose of the Eve-creation. Adam awoke from his sleep, and, wow, his dreams had come true. Upon seeing her he gasped: "Wow! Man, oh, man!" "Wow-man" he called her, then shortened it to *woman*. (An old joke, but a good one, I think.)

And then human sin entered the picture. Immediately, lo and behold, that equality was diminished. The newly arrived sin not only damaged, but it seems nearly destroyed for all subsequent human history that equality that Adam himself had been seeking in equal, opposite-gender, human companionship. "The woman whom You gave to be with me, she gave me (fruit) of the tree, and I ate" (Gen 3:12 Amplified Old Testament). Adam blamed Eve, and male prejudice against the female has been the story of male and female relationships ever since, as in female gender reduction. And the church, ignoring the New Testament big picture about male and female equality in Christian life and ministry, and often confidently quoting from 1 Corinthians 14, Ephesians 5, and 1 Timothy 2 (all three of which texts can be understood in various ways) as the final texts relating to male and female ministry relationship, has failed far too often even in some present-day churches and church plantings to challenge this prejudice adequately. New churches must, from their very beginnings, provide models and voices that celebrate and practice the pre-fall relationship of male and female, coequals in every way, fulfilling each other and complementing each other as absolute equals as per authority, leadership, and ministry.

So new kingdom-of-God churches must incarnate biblical *womanism*. What is womanism? What, more specifically, is biblical womanism? Womanism has been coined to suggest something a little bit different perhaps from *feminism*.[1] Womanism, it seems to me, intentionally stresses male and female mutual respectfulness (which feminism sometimes has seemed not to do) even while concentrating on the female aspect. Womanism respects the male and whatever male distinctiveness there may be. Womanism also holds the nuclear male-and-female family in high regard. An African American term primarily, it clearly energizes full female equality within the African American family and community in a way that does not put down the African American male, but holds him up. Within the church, it seeks full female equality. Any church planter, African American or not, can learn from Christian womanism.

But, as my niece Susan Kee pointed out to me, womanism, as good a term as it is, is still a one-word term that leaves out any male mention (as does the term *feminism*). So, let us come up with a biblically balanced term. How about *wemanism*? "I" human + "you" human = "we human." "I" man + "you" woman = "we" "weman." Let us go with *wemanism*. The Christian Church seeks Christian "wemanism."

What are leadership roles for women in our churches? Can they be a pastor, the senior pastor? Is pointing out that women were the very first people "ordained" by Jesus to go tell the men (preach to the men) that Jesus was raised from the dead a practical way to raise the question, "Can women *really* be pastors"? Jesus did it that way. He ordained women to do

---

1. For example, see Cannon, *Black Womanist Ethics*; Phillips, *The Womanist Reader*. Women writers who have made a positive impact on my theological thinking regarding women are Dorothy Day, Hannah Arendt, and Simone Weil, for instance, Day, *The Long Loneliness; On Pilgrimage*; Arendt, *Responsibility and Judgment*; Weil, *Waiting for God*. Other books which helped me are Jewett, *Paul, Man as Male and Female*; Hardesty and Scanzoni, *All We're Meant to Be*; Arlandson, *Women, Class and Society*.

that. Remember that Mary Magdalene and Mary the mother of James and Salome were looking for the body of the dead Jesus to anoint it. Mary Magdalene asked whom she thought was a custodial worker at the Garden of Gethsemane Cemetery where Jesus was buried. Turned out that "gardener" was in fact the risen Jesus himself (Matt 28:1–10; John 20:11–18). But Jesus is a gardener in that Jesus works with others taking care of God's creation, planet Earth, and cuts down thorns and thistles and weeds that come because sin has overgrown planet Earth. Gardener Jesus told the women to go and tell the men he had risen from the dead. They were to preach the first and greatest sermon ever preached: *He is raised from the dead!* It was preached by the women to the men, preaching it in the first church ever planted, the new church plant right there in Jerusalem.

How can people living in your church's neighborhood see gender equality in your church? How should they see this? Can the church or should the church even advertise this in some ways? Are there special events of the year the secular world features celebrating gender equality in which the church could/should participate? Should we personally push this sometime? I and Judy, my dear wife, who has herself become an ordained pastor, have pushed this. I came to Boston in 1971 as a church planting missionary—I (of course, with others) start churches as a church startup pastor, then someone else becomes the pastor.

One of those church plants, after it had become self-supporting, called Lorraine Anderson, who, with her husband, Bob, were part of that church planting team, to become the full-time pastor. She did, and some of the churches supporting me financially as a missionary dropped me because they saw that as biblically wrong. Christians for Biblical Equality gave Judy and me the Priscilla and Aquila Award for this in 1993, and we thank CBE for that. Over time, some churches changed their thinking and picked me up financially again. But it continues to be an occasional controversial issue, with two supporting churches within the last few years very much questioning me about this, one dropping me financially and one pondering that. (And, if they think I am being unbiblical, they should drop me. No problem. I thank them for the great support they have given, and their prayer. But I have come to see things in the Bible I had not seen some years ago.)

Maybe your church should set certain goals to bring more gender equality into your church if you think that is needed, maybe to suggest to two or three to pray with you about this. Some women and men need to agree as to what should be the percentage of qualified males and qualified females in certain or all leadership committees. Agree the senior pastor could be male or female, and what percentage of Sunday mornings should have the female gender and not just the male gender preaching from the pulpit, probably at least once every two months, if not more. Jim Antal, in his book *Climate Church, Climate World*, suggests once a month something be preached from the pulpit about the critical climate crisis in our world. We need to hear more from pulpits about gender needs right now, too. And it is not just preaching, it is also teaching. Would it be good, reader, for you to develop a six-week Sunday school class focusing on this, and maybe offer the class once every year or so?[2]

As you have read this, I hope this maybe puts one more thought in your mind, one more step to take as to your own personal calling(s), one more thought as to your church being an even better model of gender equality in the neighborhood where it worships on Sunday, an ongoing increasing clarity about this in the neighborhood where you and where I live. Maybe you should start writing down your own growing thoughts. Get together with somebody and further explore it. I thank the Spencers for inviting me to write this chapter for this book. Maybe you should start writing your own book or manual about this. We want people to see the whole Jesus, and seeing gender equality in the people whom Christ inhabits is seeing more fully the whole Jesus as he continues to work through us here on planet Earth.

So, what is our dream for Boston, if you, as Judy and I, live here? Or, what is your dream for where you do live? Certainly, we want the church to reconnect the four original schisms as best we can, but this chapter is focusing on the gender schism that needs to be fixed. In today's Boston, gender equality is seen by more and more people as basic for a better Boston. Probably, wherever you live, more and more people are seeing it this way. And God has always seen it this way.

References

Antal, Jim. *Climate Church, Climate World: How People of Faith Must Work for Change*. Lanham, MD: Rowman & Littlefield, 2018.
Arendt, Hannah, and Jerome Kohn. *Responsibility and Judgment*. New York: Schocken, 2005.
Arlandson, James M. *Women, Class, and Society in Early Christianity: Models from Luke-Acts*. Peabody, MA: Hendrickson, 1997.
Cannon, Katie G. *Black Womanist Ethics*. American Academy of Religion Academy Series. Atlanta: Scholars, 1988.
Day, Dorothy. *The Long Loneliness: The Autobiography of Dorothy Day*. San Francisco: Harper & Row, 1952.

2. Some helpful books on neighborhood outreach are: Powell, James, and Keller, *Together for the City*; Smith and Wilson-Hartgrove, *Slow Church*; Sparks, Soerens, and Friesen, *New Parish*; Nelson, *Economics of Neighborly Love*; Florida, *New Urban Crisis?*; Lupton, *Toxic Charity*.

———. *On Pilgrimage*. Grand Rapids: Eerdmans, 1999.

Florida, Richard. *New Urban Crisis? How Our Cities Are Increasing Inequality, Deepening Segregation, and Failing the Middle Class—What We Can Do About It*. New York: Basic, 2017.

Hardesty, Nancy, and Letha Scanzoni. *All We're Meant to Be: A Biblical Approach to Women's Liberation*. Waco, TX: Word, 1975.

Jewett, Paul King. *Man as Male and Female: A Study in Sexual Relationships from a Theological Point of View*. Grand Rapids: Eerdmans, 1975.

Lupton, Robert D. *Toxic Charity: How Churches and Charities Hurt Those They Help (and How to Reverse It)*. New York: HarperOne, 2011.

Nelson, Tom. *The Economics of Neighborly Love: Investing in Your Community's Compassion and Capacity*. Downers Grove, IL: InterVarsity, 2017.

Phillips, Layli, ed. *The Womanist Reader*. New York: Routledge, 2006.

Powell, Neil, John James, and Timothy Keller. *Together for the City: How Collaborative Church Planting Leads to Citywide Movements*. Downers Grove, IL: InterVarsity, 2019.

Smith, C. Christopher, and Jonathan Wilson-Hartgrove. *Slow Church: Cultivating Community in the Patient Way of Jesus*. Downers Grove, IL: InterVarsity, 2014.

Sparks, Paul, Tim Soerens, and Dwight J. Friesen. *The New Parish: How Neighborhood Churches Are Transforming Mission, Discipleship, and Community*. Downers Grove, IL: InterVarsity, 2014.

Weil, Simone. *Waiting for God*. New York: Harper and Row, 1951.

14

Communal Decision Making and the Fate of Retiring Pastors

Lorraine Cleaves Anderson

THE CELEBRATION WAS OVER-THE-TOP extraordinary. Little kids who had grown up in First Baptist, now serving as deacons, used their tech savvy to put together a kaleidoscope of videos, photos, interviews, community awards, denominational accolades, family testimonies, sermon clips, and more. The hall rocked with music, laughter, tears, exceptional cuisine, speeches, singing, praying, and no shortage of memories. When the chair of the deacons presented her with an all-expenses-paid trip to the Holy Lands, the crowd erupted into cheers of "Hallelujah, Jesus! Praise the Lord!" Then one of the youngest members of the church, two-year-old Martin, wheeled his little red wagon to the front. In it was an ornate, gold-leafed plaque with her name and dates of service that would hang over the prayer chapel in her honor. A chorus of, "Speech! Speech!" engulfed her as she was escorted to the pulpit to deliver teary-eyed words of gratitude and love. What a night—one everyone would cherish for a very long time.

After thirty-seven years as their much-loved pastor, Rev. Maria Greever[1] had now retired. She disappeared for about a year enjoying her vacation to Israel, cleaning out closets, visiting cousins and friends she had not seen in years, sleeping in, reading the newspaper over coffee each morning, volunteering in the neighborhood homeless shelter, and visiting different churches

---

1. All names have been changed.

each Sunday. Just as her assumed year away was up, she received an email from the new pastor asking her not to return to worship, for the sake of the congregation's adjustment to himself as their new pastor.

Five years later, Rev. Greever has not been invited by her successor to a church celebration, special worship, or event. When members question him, their new pastor, Rev. Nicholas Sharp, cites their denomination's Code of Ethics, in which retirees are enjoined to sever all ministerial leadership ties with their former congregation. However, the sign out front, the website, all literature, bumper stickers, and promotional materials emphatically state: "ALL are welcome here!" All.

A New Conversation Is Needed

My attention is directed toward one group of people, often one individual in one place at a time, who is apt to be overlooked and, according to protocol, ignored—the retired pastor. The ramifications of barring any person from the church can be devastating both to the individual and to the congregation, but requiring the retired pastor to live "outside the camp"[2] (Num 12:14, 15) potentially harms both the retiree and the community.

This chapter seeks to spark renewed conversation about holding all involved parties with inclusion, ethics, and love throughout one of life's most dramatic transitions: retiring from pastoral ministry.

We will refer to the policy of one specific denomination, American Baptists in the USA, and critique one portion of their Code of Ethics.[3] We will search for the code's historical context, both societally and ecclesiastically. We will ponder contrasting examples of embracing and not embracing the retired pastor with ethical hospitality, voiced through a small survey of diverse churches, after which we will document one pastor's story. Furthermore, we will sample the scriptural basis, which suggests christocentric ethical relationships. Lastly, we will consider pros and cons of continued retiree connection and offer recommendations for several ways to reframe relationships between the congregation, the retired pastor, and the new pastor.

---

2. All Bible quotations are from the NIV unless otherwise indicated.
3. The Ministers Council, "*Code of Ethics and Guide*," Bullet 10.

Historical Context of the American Baptist Churches in the USA, Code of Ethics

Through a phone call to the American Baptist Historical Society in Atlanta, Georgia, I discovered that a plethora of documents recording the history of the Code of Ethics had just arrived! Although I am keen to discover the code's ecclesial, societal, and cultural roots, such research is well outside the scope of this chapter. Contents of those several boxes will provide excellent scrutiny for an eager historian one day. At this time, none of the material has been processed. What I can offer here, however, is some basic information provided on the website of The Ministers Council, American Baptist Churches USA.

The Code of Ethics contains a statement pertinent to retired pastors, which reads:

> I will, upon my resignation or retirement, sever my ministerial leadership relations with my former constituents, and will not make ministerial contacts in the field of another ministerial leader without their request and/or consent.[4]

Two complementary articles appear. One is entitled, "Learning Guide on the Covenant and Code of Ethics for Ministerial Leaders of American Baptist Churches." The other article falls under the heading, "Commentary," and is called, "The Covenant and Code of Ethics for Ministerial Leaders of American Baptist Churches" by Dave Lundholm, associate executive for professional ministry, American Baptist Churches of Nebraska.[5]

I am eager to learn the historical wording and extenuating pressures within society and the church that have shaped section 10 above.[6] To my Baptist ear, it sounds dogmatic and harsh. This chapter seeks to transfer the choice of whether or not to remain in one's church after retirement to the pastors themselves rather than to a rule; and to the inner consciences of the retiree and the new leader over the external imposition of a creed or code or rule. Should it not be normal to retain longstanding relationships? And why cannot mature leaders do this with an ethical, professional understanding? Have they not been preaching and teaching how human relationships are best patterned after God's love for God and Jesus's sacrificial love for humans? Does it not make sense, therefore, that especially a seasoned, retiring or retired pastor would possess the grace to

---

4. The Ministers Council, "*The Covenant and Code of Ethics*," section 10.

5. The Ministers Council, "*The Covenant and Code of Ethics*," section 10.

6. When a featured article or book is published on the history of the Code of Ethics, we shall all be anxious to read it.

remain with no detriment to the congregation or incoming pastor? At the very least, I contend, the choice is best made by the retiring pastor, the incoming leader, and the congregation, not the code.

A Small Survey of Diverse Churches

Rationale and Method of Survey

In 2017, Massachusetts Baptist Multicultural Ministries issued a call for projects that would reach out to immigrant churches in Metro Boston with hospitality.[7] Several of us wanted to hear their stories and concerns, particularly pertaining to their culture's embrace, or not, of their retired clergy.[8] We specifically were seeking to learn: How do relationally dynamic churches bridge the relationship between their congregation, their retired pastor, and their new pastor? Can the congregation minister *to* the retiring pastor during this brand-new chapter of life, and, after an agreed-upon hiatus, can the retiree slip into a receptive role without undermining the new leadership in any way?

We interviewed fifteen pastors/leaders from sixteen ethnic (for lack of a better term) churches and multicultural churches: African American, African American-Multicultural, Multicultural, Costa Rican, Korean, Haitian, Burmese, and Brazilian.[9] We designed a questionnaire that invited them to share how their church culture back home and in the United States relates to their retired pastor.[10] Their stories and opinions were candid and illuminating, and represent only their individual experiences. In no way are we intimating cultural generalizations.

"Hospitality" is defined as "the cordial and generous reception and entertainment of guests or strangers," the kindness of which can heal and empower those who find themselves outside the community.[11] We agreed that hospitality is grounded in the character of God, shown ultimately in the incarnation of Jesus Christ.[12]

---

7. Imsong, "Embracing Hospitality Project," The Annual Gathering of The American Baptist Churches of Massachusetts.

8. Interviewers: Lorraine Anderson, Maung Maung Htwe, Eric Nelson, and Anonymous.

9. Appendix A, Summary of Survey Interviews.

10. Appendix B, Survey Questionnaire.

11. *Webster's Third New International Dictionary*, Vol. 2, s.v.

12. Anderson, *Under One Steeple*, 151–66.

Summary of Survey

Summary of Relationships between Retiree, New Pastor, and Congregation (2017)

Self-Identified Church Culture	15 Surveys of Leaders & Churches	View toward Retiree	Ongoing Pastoral Support	Relationships between Congregation & Retiree
African American; African American-Multicultural; Multicultural	6	Give retiree wide discretion; mentor & consultant; overlapping transition; few retire	mixed	Ongoing
Costa Rican	1	Few retire	no	Ongoing
Korean	1	Mentor & consultant; usually retiree & new pastor do not work well together		Ongoing
Burmese	3	Should be able to come back for a transitional or longer time		
Brazilian	2	Should leave & not get involved in former church	yes	At invitation of new pastor
Haitian	2	Mentor	yes	At invitation of new pastor

Within this limited survey, African American, African American-Multicultural, and Multicultural churches described an honoring, ancillary relationship with their retired pastor, which ameliorated retiree isolation.[13] Simultaneously, they anticipated and welcomed innovative leadership from their incoming pastor.

In contrast, Costa Rican, Korean, and Brazilian churches noted that incoming pastors usually find it threatening and distracting to have the retired pastor present. One quoted their expression, "There is one sun in the sky."

The Burmese churches we surveyed felt that the wisdom of including their retired pastor into the life of the church was entirely dependent on the relational quality between the two leaders. They allowed, however, the

---

13. See Appendix A.

retiree to make that choice, while giving the new pastor discretion in adjusting boundaries of involvement. According to them, maturity and courage emanating from healthy relationships were key.

The Haitian churches interviewed were open to having the retired pastor continue to participate in the church's life and to preach at the invitation of the new leadership.

Most of our interviewees felt that the incoming pastor determines the extent and quality of ongoing relationships between the congregation, their retired pastor, and themselves.

This was a modest survey, conducted over one academic year, intended to elicit conversation and to expand thinking on a delicate subject. We submit that seminarians, settled pastors, and congregations can learn how to balance this critical life transition in such a way that everyone gains and no one, including the retiree, is left outside their beloved community indefinitely.

One Pastor's Story

In the 1960s, Ralph A. Kee was pastoring a church in upstate New York, where the only African American family in town attended. As the Civil Rights Movement began gaining momentum and Ralph began studying the Old Testament prophets, he felt compelled to investigate ministry in the inner city. He heard about a Black church in Harlem, New York, in need of a pastor, so he applied. The church never got back to him, so he applied elsewhere. During a serendipitous drive home from New York, he discovered that letters between himself and the church had more than crossed in the mail. They had been stolen somewhere between New York City and Boston.

Ralph's plans were in motion by then to join Conservative Baptist Home Mission Society (CBHMS) as an urban church-planting missionary. Most of CBHMS's work was centered in Chicago at the time, but when he was offered a choice of cities, he enthusiastically chose Boston: Harlem's loss, Boston's gain.

With his wife and two young children, he moved into the old South End, a neighborhood pulsing with diversity, poverty, small shops, bars, and missions galore. At first, he worked with Christians for Urban Justice, while partnering with a lively parachurch organization, Emmanuel Gospel Center (EGC). EGC soon asked him to lead their weekly Bible study group through the process of incorporating as a church. The hope and excitement were palpable because EGC and a faithful group of South Enders had been praying for years for more churches to start up in their neighborhood.

With thirteen charter members, Ralph planted South End Neighborhood Church of Emmanuel in 1972. Stories abound of lives transformed, people coming to Christ, bars closing, drug deals shrinking, pimps weakened, neighborhood housing established, and more.

Ralph had an uncanny ability to stimulate gifts and abilities in just about everyone in the church. He was generous about sharing leadership, from preaching to teaching to leading to organizing. According to Ronald Heifetz and Marty Linsky's distinction between a leader and a manager, Ralph Kee was and is definitely a leader, with secondary managerial skills.[14] He brought vision, empathy, respect, and love to this remarkable church. And, not surprisingly, the congregation returned in kind their respect, love, and appreciation to him, for, under his leadership, many felt empowered for the first time to express their gifts and talents in their newfound church home.

Twelve years later, when Ralph, as a church planter, felt called by God to respond to another ministry need in the city, people were devastated. They rose, nonetheless, to the challenge of identifying and calling their next pastor, who would lead them for more than thirty years before he retired. South End Neighborhood of Emmanuel still thrives today with its new, younger pastor, who has invited the recently retired pastor to remain actively involved.

Throughout the years, Ralph stayed involved with South End Neighborhood Church. He planted several other churches and ministries and later began a ministry to support urban church planters. The churches he pastored often joined South End Neighborhood Church for events and outreach. Some South End Church members even loaned themselves to help Ralph with one of the startup congregations. Later, he devoted himself full-time to church planter support and no longer pastors a congregation directly.

He worships in a wide variety of settings throughout the city, but considers South End Neighborhood Church of Emmanuel and one other his two home-base churches. By his own words, he has never felt unwelcomed or barred from either congregation in any way. He attends meetings and gatherings of all types and is able to maintain a supportive, unobtrusive presence.

When I was pastoring, I was always glad to see Ralph in attendance, even though I had been his pastoral colleague and transitional successor. I never felt threatened by Ralph's participation. Instead I was encouraged and energized when he attended.

Ralph A. Kee is a commendable example of a pastor who leaves a congregation and chooses to return later in a nonthreatening, helping capacity.

---

14. Heifetz and Linsky, *Leadership on the Line*, 17.

Scriptural Basis for Including Retired Pastors in Former Congregations

Jesus and his followers left us with examples, gospels, and epistles that promote christocentric, ethical relationships: easy to quote, challenging to apply. Just as Jesus's incarnation was filled with ambiguity, paradox, mystery, inclusion, and love, so are relationships.[15] But Jesus, the quintessential ethicist and relational genius, also left his Spirit to guide us into all truth and galvanize us into mirroring his leadership (John 16:13).

Thus, when the incoming pastor appropriately acknowledges the retiree as a valuable member of the church family, and the retiree champions the incoming pastor as the capable successor, everyone benefits. No one loses. In addition, as previously described in the above story, the two leaders role model an emulative life transition.

Several leaders Jesus enfolded, directly and indirectly, went away transformed more into Jesus's likeness: Zacchaeus the tax collector became an ethical role model for Jesus (Luke 19:1–10), Levi the Zealot and tax collector became Matthew the disciple of Jesus (Matt 9:9–13), and the Roman centurion stationed at Golgotha suddenly realized who Jesus was (Matt 27:54).

If the following Scriptures apply to everyone, then they enfold the retired pastor, too.

- "Love one another" (John 13:34). No exceptions.

- "Live in harmony with each another; do not be haughty . . . do not claim to be wiser than you are" (Rom 12:16).

- "Let mutual love continue. Do not neglect to show hospitality to the stranger (*retired pastor*) for by doing that some have entertained angels without knowing it" (Heb 13:1–2).

- "The body is a unit, though it is made up of many parts; and though all its parts are many, they form one body" (1 Cor 12:12).

- "From him the whole body, joined and held together by every supporting ligament, grows and builds itself up in love, as each part does its work" (Eph 4:16).

- Jesus taught the critical importance of caring for one's elderly parents.[16]

- "Your will be done on earth as it is in heaven" (Matt 6:10).

---

15. Anderson, *Under One Steeple*, 151–166.
16. Mark 7:9–13; Matt 15:1–10.

Isaiah gives us a picture of life in the New Jerusalem, where young and old alike are vibrantly respected,[17] and where wolves and lambs, lions and oxen live together in perfect harmony. Life in heaven is our model, where no one is considered too old or too young, too experienced or too inexperienced to be valued. In response to Jesus's prayer, "Thy will be done on earth as it is in heaven,"[18] can we not likewise promote unity across barriers of age, status, and rank? Can church leaders, young and old, current and retired, not joyfully serve together in God's kingdom on earth? Indeed, love includes harmony and hospitality between retiring and incoming pastors, and a congregation needs both. Caring for retiring pastors is analogous to and a role model for caring for one's aging parents.

Gilbert Bilezikian, in his book *Community 101*, describes what biblical, consensual decision making looks like when a congregation is fully engaged in deciding a course of action. He cites Ephesians 5:21 where Paul enjoins Christians to "submit to one another out of reverence for Christ."[19] Bilezikian reminds church members, whom he calls, "a community of servants,"[20] that they are filled with the Holy Spirit, individually and collectively, and thus can trust that God has led in their final decision. Bilezikian offers biblical support for consensual decision making by citing the apostles' controversy over Gentile inclusion, a dispute between godly women, and more.[21]

Recommendations

The majority of church representatives we interviewed expressed the ideal of a strategically planned, overlapping transition between retiring and incoming pastors, but lamented the reality that incoming pastors generally find it difficult to embrace the retirees with hospitality, giving and receiving from them, and retiring pastors generally find it hard not to interfere.[22] Successors often find it too perplexing to include retirees in their new stage of life.

Could this transform into a "spectrum relationship," allowing for more fluidity and creativity? After a predetermined amount of time, could the retiree return "home" in a new, gentler, quieter role where no interference occurs and where the new pastor is now confident and anchored? Can our immigrant and refugee churches teach us how to do this much better? Can

17. Isa 65:17–25.
18. Matt 6:10
19. Bilezikian, *Community 101*, 139–42.
20. Bilezikian, *Community 101*, 140.
21. Bilezikian, *Community 101*, 140–41.
22. Appendix A.

the retired pastor contribute in ways which are life-giving both for the congregation and the new pastor, as well as for the retiree?

Our study merely posed the question and knocked on the door.

Perhaps the answer is no. Perhaps, as traditionally taught, the danger of retiree interference poses too great a risk.[23] Maybe retirees have to guillotine all previous congregant relationships in order for the next stage of the church's life to flourish.[24] How does a dramatic severance of relationships, then, affect church vitality? Metaphorically, what happens in a relatively loving family when Grampa or Gramma is sent away?

On the other hand, perhaps the answer to the question ("Can both the aging former pastor and the new pastor defer to each other within their new positions, much like the reversal of roles between adult child and aging parent?") is yes.[25] Could the congregation serve the retired pastor? Could long-term relationships be protected and even deepened by an open discussion and clear agreements? Could the church help the retiree discover new fulfilling ways to serve the church? What could the twenty-first century church learn from the insights of a movement like the National Age in Place Council?[26] Could retired pastors age in their home church if they choose? Can ethical principles be taught so that the retiring and incoming pastors provide comfort and strength to each other and their congregation? And, even more critically, could they live out before their public a biblical model for life change that is honoring to God and to each other, accurately self-assessing, loving à la Jesus, deferent, and grateful? *Within the parameters of ethical leadership*, can the church energize, rather than dismiss, the retired pastor?[27] Are we leading the whole church ethically when a formative, godly member is excluded?

---

23. American Baptist Ministers Council Senate, "Learning Guide on the Covenant and Code of Ethics," Section 10.

24. Code of Ethics, bullet 10.

25. "Role Reversal with Our Parents."

26. The National Age in Place Council, "Age in Place," 2018, www.ageinplace.org.

27. Northouse, *Leadership*, 359. In chapter 13, Northouse "suggests that sound ethical leadership is rooted in respect, service, justice, honesty, and community. It is the duty of leaders to treat others with *respect*—to listen to them closely and be tolerant of opposing points of view. Ethical leaders *serve* others by being altruistic, placing others' welfare ahead of their own in an effort to contribute to the common good. *Justice* requires that leaders place fairness at the center of their decision making, including the challenging task of being fair to the individual while simultaneously being fair to the common interests of the community. Good leaders are *honest*. They do not lie, nor do they present truth to others in ways that are destructive or counterproductive. Finally, ethical leaders are committed to building *community*, which includes searching for goals that are compatible with the goals of followers and with society [i.e., church] as a whole. "

In their work on leadership, Heifetz and Linsky insist that "people do not resist change, per se. People resist loss."[28] This is why pastors *must* learn to talk calmly with their people, draw out their concerns and stories, and interact with them often and sincerely. What degree of relationship does the congregation want with their retired pastor and their new one? Can both pastors hear the congregation's reply? Assuming, as Heifetz and Linsky propose, that a pastor's role is to bring hope, empathy, and envisioning in quantities that congregants can absorb, how can both pastoral leaders guide their congregation through this emotionally charged change of leadership? "Leaders," they say, "appear dangerous . . . when they question people's values, beliefs, or habits of a lifetime."[29] Can we be less dogmatic and more empathetic? At the least, can we transition more gradually and more graciously?

Heifetz and Linsky also stress the critical urgency of promoting people's resourcefulness, restraining themselves from giving dogmatic solutions.[30] People need to look to themselves and to each other for solutions, à la democracy, and not to authority figures.[31] The latter can, instead, facilitate that communal brainstorming and collaboration and not jump in with answers, which in the end may destroy the congregation's self-confidence and ability to self-lead.[32] Heifetz and Linsky use terms like, "prickly conversations" and "disturbing people"[33] . . . but slowly, with genuine respect—and I would add, love—to nudge them along to community building and peaceful action. Can the congregation, the retired pastor, and the new pastor commit to allowing the love of God, rather than rules, to lead them? We cannot lead anyone until we actually do love them. We cannot influence for good what we do not love.

In the end, have we made a turbulent ocean out of a trickling stream? What prompted such a section in The American Baptist Code of Ethics in the first place? (Hence our need to study those historical documents!) It all comes down to three imperatives: the relationship we have with ourselves, the relationship we have with God through Jesus, and the relationship we have with one another—all of us striving to have the mind of Christ and the heart of God in living out those relationships.

---

28. Heifetz and Linsky, *Leadership*, 11.
29. Heifetz and Linsky, *Leadership*, 12.
30. Heifetz and Linsky, *Leadership*, 15.
31. Heifetz and Linsky, *Leadership*, 17.
32. Heifetz and Linsky, *Leadership*, 18.
33. Heifetz and Linsky, *Leadership*, 19.

We are currently living through a decade where leadership at the highest democratic levels in church and state is suspect at best.[34] May churches, therefore, be prophetic in modeling a leadership paradigm of peaceful relationships, where honesty and love build one another up for the common good, omitting no one who wishes to participate responsibly, including the retired clergy.

Conclusion

I simply propose that retired pastors, like anyone else, need to be free to choose where and when they will worship, and with what community of believers. Codes and rules and protocol that eliminate that freedom, no matter how well-meaning, need to be revisited. Churches cannot afford to prevent any well-intentioned persons from throwing in their shoulders to build the kingdom of God on earth. Please let us not reject the retired pastors, if they choose to return. Let us instead empower them, as we empower the whole church with them.

I have written two songs pertinent to the topic of appropriately the retired pastor. One is called "Reciprocate." The lyrics suggest a healthy, mature, godly passing of the torch from one leader to the next. It sings easily to the tune of *Amazing Grace*.

Reciprocate[35]

1. With soothing water, towel, and care,

    Friend, may I wash your feet?

    "Mine too are tired; so, Lord, humble me

    To let her reciprocate."

2. With silent words and honest prayer,

    Friend, may I dry your tears?

    "Mine, too, are aflame; so Lord, humble me

    To let him reciprocate."

3. God's love for God—reciprocal.

    Friend, God loves you the same.

---

34. Peters and Chira, "Kavanaugh Borrows from Trump's Playbook."
35. Anderson, *Under One Steeple*, xi.

"Lord, pour in your love and humble me

That I may reciprocate."

4. With gratitude and heav'n-born joy,

Friends, may I step aside?

"They've learned and prayed. Now, Lord, humble me,

As they reciprocate."

The second song is called, "Let No One Be Invisible."[36] It describes a society, including churches, where no one remains unnoticed, nor precluded from entry.

Let No One Be Invisible

1. Let no one be invisible, let no one be outside.

    We can stand beside them, no matter where they hide;

    Listen to the wanderer, and let them be our guide . . .

    Open up the circle, bid them home.

2. Let no one be invisible, let no one be alone,

    Let us not look through them, but look into their soul.

    See God's image in their face and stamped on them as gold . . .

    Open up the circle, bid them home.

    (Bridge)

    The aching and the stranded, those running for their lives,

    Those between the headlines whose stories are denied.

    Why are they outside?

3. Let no one be invisible, let no one be afraid.

    Beckon to the introvert to come out from the shade.

    Look beyond the surface to see the one God made . . .

    Open up the circle, Open up the circle, Open up the circle,

    Welcome HOME!

---

36. Lorraine C. Anderson and Erin Sullivan, unpublished, 2018.

Appendix A: Summary of Survey

We did not approach interviews with prescribed cultural labels. Rather, interviewees themselves were asked to identify their church culturally. Thus, our survey comprised eight cultures, fifteen churches, and fifteen interviewees:

African American	3
African American-Multicultural	1
Multicultural	2
Haitian	2
Brazilian	2
Costa Rican	1
Korean	1
Burmese	3

Summary of Survey Interviews by Lorraine Anderson

African American, African American-Multicultural, and Multicultural Churches

In the African American, African American-Multicultural, and Multicultural churches we interviewed, all of them spoke about esteeming the retired pastor. Assuming the pastor retired amicably, respecting their long-term ministry was universal, even, as Deacon Griffins[37] suggested, vesting them with the title, Pastor Emeritus. There was broad agreement on giving the retiree wide discretion in attending worship and special events. Retirees were expected to serve as mentors and consultants both within their own church and, according to Natalie Adams, within the broader citywide alliance of churches. Retired clergy were encouraged to pursue and learn about their own interests beyond the realm of ministry. Harold Smith stated, "Continued relationships are essential, when initiated by the new pastor. It is incumbent on the new pastor to both enter the retired pastor's world and to ask the retiree, 'What do you want to do in the church now?' Most will both appreciate being asked and will respond, 'Nothing much. Just attend when I can. What can I do to support you?'" Geoffrey Rowens

---

37. Names as they appear in the appendixes have been changed.

emphasized the ideal of an overlapping transition between the retiring pastor and the new pastor, a sentiment, interestingly, expressed by every interviewee of these two cultures.

Harold Smith emphasized that the "retired pastor wants to feel wanted and appreciated, and the new pastor wants to forge their own direction." A healthy relationship between retiring and incoming pastors is the key to a beneficial and respectful transition. Both Geoffrey Rowens and Natalie Adams said a thought-through transition can enable both pastors to learn from the other in a nonadversarial way. Deacon Griffins expanded the sentiment in saying, "The retiring pastor needs to groom an incoming pastor, while expecting the new pastor to go in their own direction."

Harold Smith suggests that the church, as a practical way of honoring and assisting the retiring pastor, encourage the retiree to plan and even start a "new" life well in advance of retirement. Respect and communication, Smith states, are key.

When asked about ongoing pastoral care of the retired pastor, responses were mixed. If the retiree aligns with another congregation or ministry, that church then becomes, as Geoffrey Rowens states, "the responsive church." Interviewees experienced their culture's sense of responsibility toward the retiree's financial needs from no support to lifelong stipend of gratitude.

Lastly, relationships: to maintain or not to maintain, that is the question, and how? Unilaterally, it was felt among these interviewees that relationships do not simply end. But the responsibility of role modeling how church relationships can be nurtured well into an outgoing pastor's retirement lies squarely on the shoulders of the new pastor. Harold Smith thoughtfully summed it up this way: "A relationship with the retired pastor that enables everyone, including congregants and both pastors, to transition well, must be initiated and modeled by the new pastor. Therefore, it all depends on the new pastor's capacity to love." And, I might add, to lead ethically.

Costa Rican Churches

Cristina and Luis DaSilva have pastored in Costa Rica for more than twenty years and know the church culture well. Churches they started in the United States continue to be multicultural Hispanic, though their responses and insights reflect church culture in Costa Rica.

In Cristina's words, "In Costa Rica, the retired pastor always has a green light to maintain relationships, if they are supporting the new pastor. It is unusual for the new pastor to block the retiree from visiting. However, you must understand that few pastors ever actually retire. They continue until they become feeble or die because, if they stop, their income stops. It is customary for tithes to go to the pastor and offerings to church expenses. Upon actual retirement, all income for the pastor is cut off."

Should elderly pastors continue residing near the church, it is assumed that they will attend worship and special events and assist with ceremonies. Interestingly though, no routine pastoral care is offered. The one exception is if or when the church learns of a crisis or emergency, pastoral care will usually be extended.

Generally in their Costa Rican culture, pastors are grown from within. Younger aspiring novices are mentored and sent out to plant churches, but replacement pastors almost always come from the existing congregation. The elderly retiring pastor and the replacement pastor have known each other for many years and have a trusting relationship which has prepared the younger leader for the new role, although it is expected that the new pastor will lead in refreshing new ways.

Korean Churches

The Korean pastor interviewed has returned to his homeland. His responses reflect his hopes for Korean churches in the future, based on what he has experienced in the United States. But the reality of Korean church culture, according to him, is quite opposite to his aspirations.

Chul Kim understands the value of an ongoing relationship between the retiring pastor, the new pastor, and the congregation. The retired pastor has a lifetime of wisdom, experience, and walk with God from which a younger pastor could only benefit. The congregation, too, would value an ongoing relationship between themselves and their longtime pastor, albeit in a deferring, behind-the-scenes role. Chul Kim would like to see Korea embrace a biblical hospitality toward their retirees, built on open communication, trust, prayer, and mutual honor. There is nothing a younger, incoming pastor cannot learn from a tactful, mature, godly retiree. He also envisions some level of ongoing financial support for the retiree as an expression of gratitude and respect.

He concludes his questionnaire by saying, "I cannot speak, of course, for all Korean churches. But [shared, open, nondefensive leadership between the retiring pastor and the new pastor] is what I have experienced [in the US] and is my view too. However, in most Korean churches, the retired pastor and new pastor do not work well together. It depends on personalities and is generally because of authority conflicts. We have an expression in our culture, 'There is one sun in the sky.'"

Summary of Survey Interviews
by Maung Maung Htwe

BURMESE CHURCHES

I am grateful and honored to be part of this research team and to contemplate this matter. I interviewed three Burmese ministers who are serving in three different cities in the United States. I heard their experiences as members, then as incoming ministers of their churches. All of them grew up and actively participated through their young adult years before becoming ordained ministers. I have distilled their responses to two critical factors: a retired minister's church involvement is rooted in relationships and in maturity.

The relationship between the retiring pastor and church members, and the relationship between the retiring and incoming pastor, are crucial. If a pastor decides to retire for personal reasons, having maintained positive relationships with church members and feeling eager to promote their successor, then they should be able attend church at will.

One of the people I interviewed was both a minister and a "PK," pastor's kid. His experience as an incoming minister was very beautiful. The retired pastor walked and worked alongside him for the first few months, introducing and connecting him to individuals and groups within and beyond the church. Then, the retired pastor gradually began worshiping elsewhere.

This same fledgling, incoming pastor further reflected on his own father's retirement experience, when the church members and council honored him as Pastor Emeritus. To every special occasion the church not only invited him, but also arranged transportation. He felt honored and included until he sensed ill feelings from his younger replacement, who, incidentally, used to be his associate pastor. Shortly thereafter, the Pastor Emeritus slipped out of the scene.

When Moses realized he could not carry his task any longer, he appointed Joshua to lead God's people. He blessed Joshua and anointed him as leader, but Moses still taught the people as they crossed the Jordan River and prepared to inherit the Promised Land.

Some pastors, the group of three interviewees reflected, retire from a particular church not for health or age-related reasons, but because of conflicts. The Code of Ethics of the American Baptist Churches, then, can become a hiding place and legitimate reason not to retain any relationships or even nurture the incoming pastor.

On the other hand, as incoming ministers, we must remember that we are called to minister to the whole world, including the retired minister. If we want everyone in the community to be welcomed into the sheepfold, why should we exclude our retired minster if they want to continue worshiping with us? Should they cross the boundary of trying to remain in control, then we exercise the love of God and remind them of their new role. The Lord does not give us a spirit of timidity and cowardice, but of love and power.

In conclusion, ministry is about relationships, and relationships require a lifelong commitment to our own maturity and courage so that we can minister to whomever God brings across our path—including our own retired pastor.

Summary of Survey Interviews
by Eric Nelson

Brazilian Churches

We interviewed two pastors of Brazilian congregations. Neither had the experience of the retired pastor staying in the church he left. They both thought that was a good thing. In one case, the retired pastor, although attending another church, maintained a good relationship with the former church. One pastor cautioned that, if the retired pastor keeps attending the church, he should not get involved with the church administration and politics. He is supposed to honor the new pastor.

While both pastors thought the retired pastor should leave, they both thought the incoming pastor could learn from the retired pastor in the following ways: history of the church, administrative information, and relational dynamics in the congregation. In such conversations, the retired pastor could obtain a new perspective on the church from the incoming pastor. As to the kind of relationship the retired pastor could have with people in the congregation, it was thought the retired pastor should prayerfully decide how he will continue to relate to the congregation, but only at the invitation of the new pastor. This could involve preaching, teaching, and visiting. If he feels he could not be loyal or give support to the new pastor, he should leave peacefully and attend another church.

While the pastoral relationship is severed, both felt the church had a responsibility to continue to care for the retired pastor's spiritual and physical needs, even helping with medical bills or giving help to have a place to live.

Haitian Churches

This is the response of two Haitian pastors. They were open to having the retired pastor continue to attend worship and even preach with permission. They felt the incoming pastor could learn from the retired pastor the history of the church, administrative information, building logistics protocol, and housing issues. The retired pastor could get a new perspective on the church from the new pastor. Both thought the retired pastor could do visits and calling, but, again, with permission.

They also thought the church had a continuing responsibility to care for the retired minister as he dealt with health and financial issues.

African American Churches

We interviewed one pastor, Samuel Rolands. His first reaction is that many pastors in the Black church tradition do not retire. Some cannot afford it, and others have their identity so tied up in pastoring that they do not give it up.

His experience with retired pastors was negative at first. When he arrived at the church, he learned of trouble with his predecessor and his predecessor's predecessor, a retired pastor. The retiree had continued to attend church with the congregation's blessing, and even served on committees. The then-incoming pastor, whose personal struggles surfaced, sharply resented the retiree.

When Rolands became pastor, the retired pastor continued to attend and serve, but this was not a problem. Rolands saw the retired pastor as a source of wisdom and strength. The relationship all depended on the personality and security of the incoming pastor. Rolands saw the retired pastor as a mentor and friend, a walking history of the church, and appreciated his friendship. If the incoming pastor is secure enough, he/she could embrace the retired pastor and learn from them. A real friendship can possibly develop.

The retired pastor could learn from the new pastor about new perspectives on the church and especially use of media and how physical presence is not as important as it used to be. The retired pastor should be able to maintain friendships. There are certain people he has bonded with, and those bonds cannot be broken. The church should continue to esteem and respect the retired pastor, offering personal assistance when needed, company, and maybe even having a Pastor Emeritus Day once a year.

Appendix B: Survey Questionnaire

A group of TABCOM[38] pastors and laypeople has formed to talk about the relationship retired pastors should have with their former churches. We especially want to see what other traditions such as immigrant churches and African American churches have to say on the subject. Would you be willing to meet with me to answer a few questions on the subject of retired pastors? Your answers will form part of a report on the subject which we will present to Massachusetts Baptist Multicultural Ministry. In addition, we will include information from other churches.

1. Have you been part of a church where the pastor retired after many years?

2. Was your experience with the retired pastor after retirement positive, negative, or mixed? Please explain.

3. In your experience, what is the expected role of a retired pastor?

    ( ) Stay away from the church; ( ) attend worship; ( ) serve on a committee; ( ) preach with permission; ( ) other: please be specific.

4. Which aspects might an incoming pastor learn from a retired pastor?

    ( ) history of the church; ( ) administrative information; ( ) routines; ( ) building logistics; ( ) relational dynamics; ( ) protocol; ( ) housing; ( ) giving; ( ) TABCOM info; ( ) other: please explain.

5. What might the retired pastor learn from the incoming pastor?

    ( ) technology; ( ) new perspective on the church; ( ) modern culture; ( ) life experience informing the other's life experience; ( ) other.

6. How does the retired pastor maintain relationships with people in the congregation?

    ( ) Not at all; ( ) visits; ( ) calling; ( ) other: please explain.

7. What, if any, responsibility does the church have to care for the retired pastor?

    ( ) no responsibility; ( ) continued—how? What does that look like?

---

38. The American Baptist Churches of Massachusetts

References

American Baptist Churches USA. "Code of Ethics for The American Baptist Churches in the USA." Bullet 10. Oct. 2004.

———. "Code of Ethics and Guide." The Ministers Council. (Oct. 2004). http://ministerscouncil.com/resources/code-of-ethics-and-guide/.

American Baptist Ministers Council Senate. Professional Effectiveness Committee. "Learning Guide on the Covenant and Code of Ethics." Section 10. Nov. 2006.

Anderson, Lorraine Cleaves. *Under One Steeple*. House of Prisca and Aquila Series. Eugene, OR: Wipf & Stock. 2012.

———. "Under One Steeple: Biblical and Theological Foundations for Sharing Church Space." In *Reaching for the New Jerusalem*, edited by Seong Hyun Park, Aída Besançon Spencer, and William David Spencer, 151–66. Urban Voice. Eugene, OR: Wipf & Stock. 2013.

Bilezikian, Gilbert, *Community 101: Reclaiming the Local Church as Community Oneness*. Grand Rapids: Zondervan. 1997.

Harvey, Michael, and Dee Dee Turlington, eds. "Learning Guide on the Covenant and Code of Ethics for Ministerial Leaders of American Baptist Churches." American Baptist Churches USA. http://ministerscouncil.com/resources/covenant/covenant_english.pdf. Revised Oct. 2004.

Heifetz, Ronald A., and Marty Linsky. *Leadership on the Line: Staying Alive through the Dangers of Leading*. Boston: Harvard Business School. 2002.

Imsong, Mar. "Embracing Hospitality Project: A Proposal from Massachusetts Baptist Multi-Cultural Ministries." The Annual Gathering of The American Baptist Churches of Massachusetts. May 5, 2017.

National Age in Place Council. "Age in Place." http://www.ageinplace.org. Accessed May 31, 2020.

Northouse, Peter G. *Leadership: Theory and Practice*. 6th ed. New Delhi: Sage, 2012.

Peters, Jeremy W., and Susan Chira. "Kavanaugh Borrows from Trump's Playbook on White Male Anger." *The New York Times*: Politics. Sept. 29, 2018. https://www.nytimes.com/2018/09/29/us/politics/brett-kavanaugh-trump-men.html.

Visiting Angels Living Assistance Services website. "Role Reversal with Our Parents." www.visitingangels.com. Accessed May 31, 2020.

Webster's Third New International Dictionary, vol. 2. Manila: G. & C. Merriam, 1976.

15

Egalitarian Leadership in Global Mission

J. Creamer

From the time that Mary Magdalene was commissioned by Jesus to "go and tell my brothers" about the resurrection (Matt 28:10 NRSV), women have proclaimed the good news of the risen Christ. Mary Magdalene and the women with her, sadly, were not well received: "But these words seemed to them an idle tale, and they did not believe them" (Luke 24:11, NRSV). Why did Mary's words seem like an idle tale? Jesus had informed his followers repeatedly that he would be crucified and raised on the third day. Was it because of a low view of women that the apostles were dismissive of Mary's report? Or was it a simple case of unbelief? Nonetheless, as an eyewitness of the resurrection, Mary Magdalene was faithful to deliver the message. Only Peter and John responded (John 20:3–10). From the days of Jesus, women, like Mary Magdalene, have proclaimed the good news in spite of various challenges.

This chapter surveys the legacy of women's leadership in global mission from the mid-1800s to the present, first by exploring the contributions of both Western and Asian women and then by exploring ways that South Asian women today can be empowered for even greater impact. The history of women in mission leadership from the 1860s to the present is a narrative of women who broke social, cultural, and structural barriers in order to serve.

In the mid-nineteenth and early twentieth centuries, many North American women knew the calling of God. They also knew the cultural expectations to marry, stay at home, and manage a household. Mission boards in the early to mid-1800s sent very few single women to international locations. New opportunities emerged, however, when women in North America heard the requests for help from their married missionary sisters in foreign lands. These missionary wives appealed for the help of single women who would be able to devote their time to the work of reaching women in need. The women at home took action. Since the men refused to send single women, the women established and ran their own female mission organizations. The women navigated successfully around patriarchy. The first set of these gender-separate mission boards was founded in the 1860s. The establishment of women's missions agencies set into motion the women's missionary movement, which empowered women for mission up through the 1920s and 1930s. These agencies sent out women who led revivals; planted churches; founded and directed seminaries, schools, and hospitals; rescued children at risk; trained pastors; improved the treatment and status of women; and served in places where men could not—or would not—go. Women have a long history of capable and innovative leadership in mission.

Beginning in the twentieth century, the locus of global Christianity shifted away from the West and toward the nations of the Global South. Philip Jenkins, professor of history at Baylor University, defines the Global South as the regions in the developing world where Christianity is growing most rapidly today: South America, Africa, and Asia.[1] A "West to the rest" mission theory is no longer applicable in many, if not most, cases. National mission and church leaders now shoulder the responsibility of carrying the gospel to places where it has not yet been heard. As most of the regions of the Global South have deeply embedded patriarchal cultures, a need has arisen to find creative ways around the barriers that women in these nations face with respect to serving in leadership roles. Even within organizations that do embrace egalitarianism, female leaders are a minority. A case study, including the examination of three women's stories, will explore some reasons for the disproportionate lack of women in leadership and seek to identify factors that help empower women.

The Women's Missionary Movement

Women today generally have the freedom to follow a missionary calling, regardless of marital status. This has not always been the case. Until the

---

1. Jenkins, *The Next Christendom*, 2–5. Jenkins includes developing Asian nations in his broad definition of the Global South, even though they are not part of the Southern Hemisphere.

1860s, a single woman hoping to serve in foreign missions did not usually have an opportunity unless she could find a missionary husband first.[2] To send a single woman overseas seemed, to the men who directed mission boards, a breach of propriety. The prerequisite of marriage caused some women to rush into matrimony under less than ideal circumstances. A lifetime with an unsuitable partner compounded the difficulties of missionary life. Moreover, once married, most women found that the vast majority of their waking hours were consumed by childrearing, cooking, and cleaning. Little time remained for ministry. Thus, the prohibition of sending unmarried women to the field precipitated the start of the women's missionary movement,[3] which has been considered the first feminist movement in North America.[4] The women's missionary movement gained momentum shortly before the women's rights movement that began in the nineteenth century with the push for a woman's right to vote. North American women wanted equality.

The Women's Union Missionary Society, the first woman's missionary agency in North America, was founded in 1861 by Sarah Doremus. The society welcomed members from many church denominations. Sarah Marston was the first unmarried woman to be sent out by the society. She went to Burma. Within twenty years, more than one hundred unmarried women had been sent out through the Women's Union Missionary Society alone. Many similar organizations were formed, each usually publishing their own missions magazine as well as other books and, of course, sending out single women as missionaries. A focus was women's ministry to other women. No longer was marriage a requirement for women wanting to serve overseas.[5]

Since 1860, female missionaries have been involved in every aspect of ministry, from church planting, to administration, to hospitality, to education, to mercy ministry, and to social work. Women have ministered in dangerous places closed to men. With great momentum, the female mission societies raised funds, educated the church about missions, recruited workers for the foreign field, and sent them out. These activities continued until the years following 1920, when denominational mission boards began to accept applications from unmarried women.

Mabel Francis was one of the women who worked in the midst of dangerous circumstances. She had trained at the Boston Missionary

---

2. Beaver, *American Protestant Women in World Mission*, 49–53.
3. Tucker, *Guardians*, 99.
4. Beaver, *American Protestant Women in World Mission*, 9.
5. Tucker, *Guardians*, 100–01.

Training School.⁶ Mabel left for Japan in 1909, when she was twenty-nine years old. Her ministry spanned an impressive fifty-six years and included church planting, evangelism, and discipleship. Her brother joined her in 1913. Together, they planted twenty churches. Mabel's sister joined her in 1922. Mabel and her sister worked together in Japan for most of the next forty years. Her brother left during World War II due to Japanese suspicions. Mabel, however, refused to leave. She was kept under house arrest during most of the war, but, like the Apostle Paul (Acts 28:16–31), she kept the ministry going by welcoming visitors into her home. Mabel was later interned in a Catholic monastery where she continued to speak about her faith. Mabel and her sister were respected greatly by the Japanese people for their untiring service during and after the war. In 1962, Mabel was awarded, by the emperor of Japan, the highest honor given to a civilian: membership in the Fifth Order of the Sacred Treasure. She was given this award for her service in "the welfare of the Japanese people in their distress and confusion at the time of their defeat."⁷

Another remarkable female missionary is Amy Carmichael. Amy's first mission assignment was also in Japan. She arrived in 1893, having been sent from the United Kingdom.⁸ While in Japan, Amy lacked a clear picture of her calling. Her initial experience with missions was a disappointment. Amy found the Japanese language difficult, the missionary community less than harmonious, and the weather uncomfortable. "The climate is dreadful upon the brain," she opined to her mother.⁹ During her time in Japan, Amy agonized over the matter of her singleness. She eventually reached a point of acceptance:

> On this day many years ago I went away alone to a cave in the mountain called Arima. I had feelings of fear about the future. That was why I went there—to be alone with God. The devil kept on whispering, "It's all right now, but what about afterwards? You are going to be very lonely." And he painted pictures of loneliness—I can see them still. And I turned to my God in a kind of desperation and said, "Lord, what can I do? How can I go on to the end?" And He said, "None of them that trust in Me

---

6. Tucker, *Guardians*, 176. The Boston Missionary Training School, founded by the Rev. Dr. A. J. Gordon in 1889, eventually moved to the North Shore of Massachusetts and became two institutions: Gordon College and Gordon-Conwell Theological Seminary. "History of Gordon."

7. Tucker, *Guardians*, 176–78.

8. Tucker, *From Jerusalem to Irian Jaya*, 239.

9. Tucker, *Guardians*, 131.

shall be desolate." That word has been with me ever since. It has been fulfilled to me.[10]

Amy left Japan after fifteen months of service. She believed that God was calling her to South Asia. After nearly ten years of missionary service, Amy rescued her first child from temple prostitution in southern India. Her calling zoomed into sharp focus. Amy devoted the rest of her life to rescuing, caring for, and educating children who had been trafficked into temple prostitution. Her ministry was difficult: she faced risks, trials, and threats by hostile idol worshipers. Financial challenges also abounded for her children's home which, by 1945, accommodated more than 800 children. Every project was a project of faith. In her book *Meal in a Barrel*, Amy detailed many instances of God answering prayers with miraculous provision. God supplied all that was needed for the construction of multiple facilities, one building project at a time. Amy trained Indian women to do the everyday work of caring for and educating the children. Many of the girls who lived in Amy's children's home stayed on as workers when they grew up. Others went on to do other kinds of Christian work or to marry and raise families. Amy Carmichael lived in India as a single woman for fifty-five years without a furlough and authored thirty-five books, an array of narratives, and devotional literature.

Pandita Ramabai was another exceptional woman of this era. Pandita was a Hindu convert who, as a young widow, worked for the education of girls and needs of the women among her own people in India during the late 1800s and early 1900s. Prior to her conversion, she began a comparative study of Hinduism and Christianity. Pandita observed that there was a great difference between them pertaining to the view of women. Jesus treated women with respect. But the Indian holy writings said that "women of high and low caste, as a class, were bad, very bad, worse than demons, as unholy as untruth, and that they could not get *moksha* [transcendent freedom from the cycle of rebirth] as men."[11] To complicate matters further, the hope of salvation for a Hindu woman was conditional upon the worship of her husband—who was made to be her god. The abuse resulting from such beliefs was horrendous. Pandita wanted to improve the status of women. Her initial thought was to be a reformer within the Hindu world. As she continued to study the Christian Scriptures, however, she found herself drawn to its teachings. She eventually converted to Christianity.

Pandita was a free thinker. She designed her school in accordance with her own ideas rather than following a typical mission school model. Her

---

10. Tucker, *Guardians*, 133–34.
11. Tucker, *Guardians*, 144.

insistence on respecting the caste regulations and customs of her Hindu students was unconventional. For this, she received no little criticism. "I am having a right good time in the storm of public indignation that is raging over my head," she commented.[12] Pandita learned Hebrew and Greek so that she could translate the Bible into a simple form of the Marathi language.[13] She also directed the school she founded, started a famine relief ministry, trained women's evangelism teams (eventually numbering four hundred women), and started a school for boys. Pandita was concerned that her girls have the option to marry suitable Christian men rather than be pushed into incompatible marriages. For this reason, she founded the boys' school. Pandita Ramabai, like Amy Carmichael, ran her finances by faith. But, unlike Amy, she raised her funds entirely from within India. Of Pandita's influence, her biographer summarizes:

> She did more than any other to call attention to the wrongs done to India's women and to create a conscience that demands that these wrongs be righted . . . the debt that India owes to this woman has yet to be realized and acknowledged. She is certainly one of the nation's liberators.[14]

Mukti Mission, the umbrella organization for the schools and ministries that she started, is still in operation today.[15]

The women's missionary movement reached a high point in 1920, when Helen Barrett Montgomery was elected the president of the Northern Baptist Convention. Prior to serving as the president of her denomination, Helen promoted the cause of missions through her teachings and publications. She was the teacher of the Barrett Memorial women's class in Rochester, New York for forty-four years—a class that regularly attracted more than two hundred in attendance, including "some of the most influential women in the city."[16] Among her writings is *Western Women in Eastern Lands* (1910), a history of women in mission, written for the occasion of the fiftieth anniversary of the women's missionary movement. In this book, Helen noted that, in the year 1861, one unmarried woman was sent overseas. By 1909, however, the number of female overseas workers had multiplied to 4,710. Women had started 2,100 schools and 75 hospitals,

---

12. Tucker, *Guardians*, 145.
13. Available online at http://sth-archon.bu.edu/massbibles/bible/items/16.html.
14. MacNicol and Mangalwadi, *What Liberates a Woman?* 196.
15. See https://muktimission.us/.
16. Tucker, *Guardians*, 108.

among other works.[17] *Western Women in Eastern Lands* sold more than a hundred thousand copies. Seven years after publishing her landmark book, Helen helped to establish the encompassing Federation of Woman's Boards of Foreign Missions. She served as the president. Her responsibilities included extensive travel to visit missionary enterprises run by women around the world. Helen was considered the leading organizer and promoter of women's missions in her day. When Helen was elected president of the Northern Baptist Convention in 1920, she became the first woman to lead a major denomination in the United States.[18]

Countless women of this era have stories worth hearing. Mary Slessor cast off the constraints of Western culture in order to embrace a more incarnational approach to missions within the African context. Lottie Moon was regarded as the "best man among our missionaries"[19] in China. Maria Taylor worked closely with her husband, Hudson, also in China. Women have served in missions at tremendous personal cost, whether it be a lifetime of unanticipated singleness, the death of a child or husband, sickness, danger, or poverty. The price was often high, but the results were great. Women not only brought the teachings of Christ to foreign lands, they also helped to elevate the status and treatment of women by addressing basic matters of human rights. They did this by providing education, health care, and many other services that benefited girls and women.

United States women gained the right to vote in 1920. With this breakthrough in women's rights, the landscape began to change for the women's mission societies. The concept of gender-separate spheres for women and men began to feel outdated. At last, women had equality with men, at least when it came to elections. Women had the right to vote in civic, state, and federal matters, but still had no voice when it came to church matters. The women's boards began to be dissolved by men:

> In the name of efficiency and centralization, but with strong sub-texts of theological division and male domination, the very denominations whose recent missionary expansions had been carried by the women began dismantling their women's missionary societies and dividing the remains under various male-dominated church agencies . . . since women typically had no rights to speak or to vote in denominational church councils,

---

17. Montgomery, *Western Women in Eastern Lands*, 243–44.
18. Robert, *Gospel Bearers*, 8–9.
19. Tucker, *Guardians*, 42.

they were powerless to stop the dissolution of women's missionary organizations.[20]

As a precursor to the dismantling of the women's mission societies, the Southern Methodists, at an all-male conference, made a decision to merge the women's home mission and foreign mission boards—without consulting the women. In 1923, the Presbyterian Church USA scrapped its female national mission organization, also without seeking input from the women. One after another, women's mission societies were assimilated into denominational mission boards administrated by men. By the 1930s, there were a few women sitting on the integrated denominational mission boards and councils in the United States. They remained, however, a minority voice.[21] Regarding the end of the women's missionary movement, Dana Robert notes, "Ironically, a movement that had sought empowerment for Christian women around the world found itself disempowered by patriarchal forces within the western churches themselves."[22] Nonetheless, the denominational mission boards were now willing to accept applications from single female candidates.

Women and the Shift to the Global South

Beginning in the 1920s and extending for several decades, a number of circumstances deeply impaired the funding of women's projects on the foreign field. These included the dissolution of the women's organizations, the diversion of missionary funds to other denominational projects, infighting over church doctrine, and reduced donations due to the Great Depression. The onset of World War II in 1939 caused further cuts in missionary finances. Many missionaries were recalled due to a lack of funding. Others were forced to leave their posts when they suddenly found themselves in enemy territory. Missionaries in Southeast Asia and the South Pacific were interned in Japanese concentration camps after the bombing of Pearl Harbor.[23] Further, the rise of nationalist movements in Asian and African countries under colonial rule and the resulting decolonization of nations in the postwar era precipitated the expulsion of numerous foreign missionaries. Even though, in many cases, missionary work predated colonization, missionaries were often construed as being part and parcel

---

20. Robert, *Gospel Bearers*, 9–10.
21. Robert, *Gospel Bearers*, 10–12.
22. Robert, *Gospel Bearers*, 10.
23. Robert, *Gospel Bearers*, 16.

with colonizing forces. This was, in part, because some missions had received assistance from colonial governments. In some African nations, for instance, missions had received government land grants. Leaders of nationalist movements, however, accused missionaries of telling Africans to pray and stealing their land while their eyes were closed. Others accused missionaries of destroying their native culture.[24]

These factors could have dealt a death blow to foreign missions. Instead, something else happened. A seismic shift occurred. The imminent departure of countless missionaries, together with major disruptions in funding, caused plans for the indigenization of overseas missions to be accelerated. Ready or not, ministries were turned over to national leaders. Many of these handovers yielded good results. Other ministries folded, lacking funding or experienced leadership. It was a rocky transition. Nonetheless, the message of Christ began to take on more culturally sensitive expressions around the world.

Christianity began to multiply exponentially in the Southern Hemisphere and in Asia. Christianity was no longer the white person's religion. The Christian faith had resided primarily in Europe and North America for hundreds of years. By the late twentieth century, however, the typical Christian might not be a European or North American male, but "a woman living in a village in Nigeria or in a Brazilian *favela*."[25] The changing landscape of global Christianity is no secret. Philip Jenkins, in his thought-provoking book, *The Next Christendom: The Coming of Global Christianity*, describes the explosion of Christianity in non-Western countries. South Korea, Nigeria, and Brazil are just a few of the nations experiencing unprecedented church growth. As one example, it may be noted that the largest number of Anglicans today reside in Africa, not in the United Kingdom or in North America. China is another example. Communist persecution was unable to stamp out Christianity. In fact, the reverse happened: indigenous Protestants in China grew in number from 700,000 in 1949 to somewhere between twelve and thirty-six million by the year 2000.[26] The majority of Christians around the world now reside in the Global South.

As Christianity takes root in Africa, Latin America, and parts of Asia, we must consider the control that patriarchalism has held over women in these places. What we have in the context of the Global South is, once

---

24. Many of those who joined nationalist movements had learned leadership skills, democratic values, critical thinking, and the importance of the rights of the individual in the missionary schools they had attended. Mission schools, thus, had an impact on decolonization. See Robert, "Shifting Southward," 50–53.

25. Jenkins, *The Next Christendom*, 1–2.

26. Robert, "Shifting Southward," 53.

again, the challenge of how to handle patriarchal attitudes when it comes to women in leadership. There is an additional challenge for those who live in post–colonial nations. Not only are they contending with patriarchy, but also with the residual disempowerment that lingers over nations affected by colonial rule. A sense of disempowerment, stemming from patriarchalism as well as from centuries of imperial domination, often manifests itself in women's lack of confidence and initiative.

The Asian Context Today

The population center of today's world is in Asia. More people now live in Asia than in all of North America, South America, Europe, and Africa. As of 2015, about four billion people lived in Asia. It is estimated that, by the year 2040, that number will swell to about four and a half billion. In contrast, the populations of North America, South America, and Europe will not increase nearly as significantly.[27] Not only are the number of people living in Asia and Africa increasing, but the number of those who claim to adhere to Christianity on these continents is growing at a rate that outpaces that of other continents by a wide margin.[28] Yet, the challenge remains: neither Asian nor African nations are generally known for egalitarian leadership.

For the remainder of this chapter, we turn our attention to egalitarian leadership against the backdrop of the South Asian social and cultural context. The preference for a boy child is so pervasive in India that laws have been passed that make it illegal for a doctor to disclose the gender of a baby in utero. The womb is, indeed, a dangerous place for a girl child. The gender ratio in India is skewed due to sex-selective abortion: despite the laws, there are nine females for every ten males at birth.[29] It has been reported that there are 63 million missing girls and women in India, mostly due to sex-selective abortion, but also due to female infanticide,[30] abuse, and neglect.[31] In other words, the number of missing females in India is higher than the

---

27. Africa's population is also projected for an increase of about half a billion by 2040, according to "World Population Prospects." For more information on global population growth and development, see Rosling, *Factfulness*, 75–100.
28. Jenkins, *The Next Christendom*, 3.
29. "Sex Ratio (Females/1000 Males)."
30. "Female Infanticide."
31. Gowen, "India Has 63 Million 'Missing' Women and 21 Million Unwanted Girls, Government Says."

number of people living in the states of California, Oregon, Washington, Nevada, and Arizona, combined.[32]

Can egalitarian leadership exist in a region that gives preference to males from conception? There are many organizations in which egalitarian leadership does not exist. The following reflections will not focus on organizations that do not permit women to use their gifts. Rather, the discussion will focus on matters related to the empowerment of women within a mission setting that does permit women to lead. Despite women being allowed to lead, there are few national women who actually do so. Why is there such a discrepancy between belief and practice?

Case Study: Mission Location X

As a case study, we will take a look at Mission Location X, which was founded in a city in South Asia in the early 1990s by a group of Western missionaries from Organization Y.[33] Mission Location X trains missionaries for service in various capacities where the needs are the greatest. In the early days of its existence, all programs at Mission Location X were founded and directed by Westerners. Both men and women were represented among the leadership, although a majority of the leaders at that time were women. Lisa,[34] the primary founder, is a North American married to another North American. Lisa and her husband both have decades of experience in South Asia. Lisa provided vision for the growing missionary training enterprise. Her own family was growing, as well. By the mid-1990s, Lisa had two small children. Since Lisa was living in a location where all cooking is from scratch, where it is so dry and dusty that floors must be swept and mopped every single day, and where there was, at that time, no supermarket—the grocery shopping involved a time-consuming process of frequenting separate vendors for fruit, for leafy vegetables, for non-leafy vegetables, for chicken and eggs, for red meat, for fish, for cleaning products, for toiletries, for dry goods and bread, for milk, and so on—she did what any sensible woman enjoying a beneficial exchange rate for the American dollar would do: she employed household help. Every morning, three women would report for duty. One swept, mopped, and dusted the house; the second washed the clothes, hung them on the line, and folded yesterday's laundry; and the third cooked, washed dishes, and supervised

---

32. "US States–Ranked by Population 2019."

33. The names of the mission center and organization are not identified for security reasons.

34. Names have been changed.

the other two workers. This procedure took two hours every day, providing the equivalent of six hours of daily household help. With the most time-consuming of the household chores taken care of by her cook and cleaning ladies, Lisa was able to spend her days overseeing the growth of the mission training center and caring for her young children.

The mission started small, with a handful of Asian students training to be missionaries. In less than ten years, however, the center had relocated several times in order to accommodate the increasing number of students and staff. In the late 1990s, Lisa gathered the staff for a retreat and made an announcement: it was time to purchase property for a campus. Shock waves resounded through the hearts of the program directors. These leaders were struggling to find money to buy rice to feed their students. And here was Lisa, telling them that their vision was too small. Could she possibly be right?

As it turned out, Lisa was right. Through the sacrificial generosity of many individuals and organizations, a campus was purchased outside the city. Things were in full swing by the mid-2000s. Half a dozen or more training programs were being run every year, with most being directed by single, middle-aged women from Western countries. In most cases, these directors made every effort to raise up nationals for leadership positions. A few male nationals were willing to take on leadership positions. But, when national women were asked to lead, few agreed. At one point, Malika, a capable teaching assistant with several years of experience, insisted that someone from "outside" was needed to lead the program when her director left the position. Arguments ensued, but Malika stood her ground. Despite invitations, exhortations, and appeals, no female national at that time was willing to assume a leadership role.[35]

A bump in the road occurred in the late 2000s. All of the international staff families moved out of the country around the same time due to visa complications. Only one or two international single staff remained on the campus. Suddenly, those of the view that they could not lead had no choice. If the training campus were to continue, it would have to be led by a team of national program directors. Today, twelve years later, nearly every leader is a national. There are three primary campus directors; all are male. Of the other decision-making bodies and program directors, there are now a few female leaders, but the majority are males.

---

35. After several years, Malika finally agreed to direct the program, which she did for nearly a decade. She then launched a new enterprise to empower disenfranchised women through vocational training, employment, and discipleship, which she still directs.

Why, in a missionary training center that was started by a woman, are there not more women in leadership? A few explanations follow.[36]

Marriage, Motherhood, and Meal Preparation

Marriage is valued highly in South Asia. Marriage equals status; singleness equals shame—usually. The initial conversation between a Westerner and a new acquaintance almost invariably follows this pattern: "Where are you from?" Then, the second question comes: "Are you married?" If the answer is "No," a, third question comes: "Why not?" One Western woman answered this predictable series of questions recently with a woman she met at a local gym. As they did their exercises, side by side, the Western woman explained that, in her culture, marriage is not a requirement. The Asian woman's eyes grew big. She became quiet. Finally, her face lit up. The thought of having a choice regarding whether or not to marry was remarkable to her. She spoke of how she was never given an option to do anything other than marry and bear children. She left the gym a few minutes later, clad in an oversized black dress and matching burqa—the typical coverings worn by women of the Muslim faith in South Asia. Women are defined by marital status in every race, caste, and creed in South Asia. Not to be married by a certain age (typically age 23 or 24) for a woman, in particular, is often considered an indicator that something is wrong. Something is *very* wrong.

The cultural, social, and family pressures to marry are formidable. And, once the marriage has occurred, there is the next event. The expectation to have a child within the first year of marriage is unequivocal. Most of the staff couples who marry in Mission Location X do have a child very early in their marriage. Once pregnant, a wife is no longer expected to do any outside work. She is a mother. Childcare does not exist as we know it in America. Since the couple may not live in a joint family (who would help with the children), many mothers find themselves too overwhelmed with the needs of young children to assume other responsibilities. Although Lisa, their founding leader, was able to afford household help, not all nationals are able to do so.

Food is also a big part of the culture in South Asia. Whereas, in the Western world, two cold meals and one hot meal are the norm for most families, in South Asia, three hot meals are served each and every day. A sandwich is considered a snack, not a meal. Several women in Mission Location X were

---

36. These explanations have been gleaned, in part, through interviews with the women at Mission Location X.

asked how much time in a day they spend cooking. One woman first replied, "Not much. Only about three and a half hours a day." Upon further reflection, she revised her answer. It actually takes her around five hours a day to produce three hot meals for her family and an after-school snack for her children. Others also prefaced their answers with "not much." "Not much, only two or three hours a day." "Not much. I do very simple cooking. Only about two and a half hours a day." A typical housewife (not involved in ministry) might spend six or more hours a day in her kitchen. Not only does meal preparation consume a large portion of a woman's day, it also involves an early morning shift. Since both breakfast and lunch must be cooked before sending children off to school with packed tiffin boxes including rice, homemade flat breads, and curries, preparations often begin at five a.m. or earlier. Compare this with the relatively small amount of time that North Americans spend cooking. A recent study showed that North Americans spend an average of thirty-seven minutes in the kitchen each day.[37]

Male Culture

It is not uncommon to find in South Asia a man in his thirties who has never swept a floor and has not the faintest idea of how to go about cleaning a toilet. One Western woman was in for a shock once when she realized that she would need to teach a South Asian male, who was more than thirty years old, how to clean a commode. The male approached the job with great drama: after returning with a bandana tied over his face, rubber gloves on his hands, jeans rolled up to his knees, and a brush in his hand, he was ready for war. Male children are often spoiled at home. Boys may be given better food and education than their sisters. Their mothers and sisters usually do most, if not all, household chores. This lack of expectation to participate in household chores leads to entitlement and laziness. Many boys grow up thinking that they do not need to do anything in the house because there are girls and women around who will do everything. Boys reared in such an environment are known commonly as little kings. Girls are, typically, brought up to be housewives, while boys are brought up to prepare for a career. It is no surprise then if males do few household chores after marriage. Typically, a man might do some occasional marketing while his wife or mother does everything else. The *Times of India* ran an article in 2018 commenting on a

---

37 This study concluded that American women spend an average of 51 minutes a day preparing food, serving, and cleaning up afterward. Men average 22 minutes a day for the same tasks. Hamrick, "Americans Spend an Average of 37 Minutes a Day Preparing and Serving Food and Cleaning Up."

study that showed that Indian men spend less than an hour a day on household work, while Indian women spend six hours a day on cooking, cleaning, and household management.[38] There is, however, a new generation of urban professionals who, with both husband and wife holding full-time jobs, come home after work to cook dinner and clean the house together.

Leadership in Mission Location X is often passed on from one leader to the next. When one generation of leaders is male, the next generation often will be, as well. Why is this so? Leaders may look for someone like themselves when searching for a replacement. A preponderance of males in leadership may be the result. Among traits valued in leaders are confidence, initiative, and an ability to argue effectively in meetings. These are three characteristics that South Asian women are not typically encouraged to possess. By cultural dictate, a woman should be demure, submissive, and quiet. It is unlikely, however, that such a soft-spoken individual will be nominated for leadership no matter how exceptional her other qualities may be.

Three South Asian Women in Leadership and How They Do It

Despite the obstacles that can prevent women from participating in leadership, there are several women in Location X who do serve in leadership capacities. Lakshmi, Kavita, and Zara have managed to swim against the tide. Housework and cooking, of course, do not go away on their own. We will take a look at their lives to see how they negotiate family and cultural expectations with calling. Lakshmi and Kavita, the first two women, are married; Zara, the third woman, is single.

Lakshmi

Lakshmi grew up in a small, rural village. Her schooling was discontinued when she was in the eighth grade. Lakshmi's parents separated permanently that year. After the separation, Lakshmi's mother lacked the financial means to care for her and her siblings. Consequently, Lakshmi was shuffled back and forth between relatives' houses for several years. By the time she was seventeen, she took up work as a live-in caretaker. She was never given an opportunity to attend high school. Years later, Lakshmi joined the mission and got married. Lakshmi's husband had attended a one-year Bible course at the mission training center and later completed a Master of Divinity degree

---

38. "Indian Women Do Most Household Work While Men Do Very Little."

at a nearby seminary. Lakshmi's initial training was in classical dance and evangelism but, as the years went by, more and more people encouraged her to enroll in the Bible course. Lakshmi was full of apprehension. With so little education in her background, she was lacking confidence. She was unsure of her ability to pass a college-level course, especially since it was taught in English—which she had learned on her own. After three years of exhortation by the program director, Lakshmi acquiesced. She enrolled in the first term of the Bible course, intending to discontinue before the start of the second term. Time and again, Lakshmi's assignments came back with high grades. The program director found that Lakshmi's student papers were often more insightful than those written by students who had previously attended graduate school. After much prompting, Lakshmi decided to continue with the second quarter of the program. Needless to say, Lakshmi completed the full three-quarter sequence, achieving high grades each term. Later, Lakshmi's husband encouraged her to complete secondary school. Beginning in her early thirties, Lakshmi completed her tenth grade certificate, her twelfth grade diploma, her bachelor's degree, and her master's degree. The entire sequence took about ten years. Along the way, she gave birth to two children and adopted a third. Lakshmi is a hard worker, to be sure, but her academic accomplishments would not have been possible without her husband's ongoing encouragement and substantial participation in parenting and household chores.

Lakshmi and her husband are a fine example of team ministry. Both participate in the work of the ministry and both participate in the work at home. Together, they have established numerous community development projects in local slums and established more than two dozen house fellowships. Recently, Lakshmi has cut back some of her afternoon ministry commitments in order to spend more time with her children when they get home from school. In the mornings, she leads a project that teaches women how to sew and how to start a small tailoring business with microfinance. She plans to expand the ministry soon to a second sewing class in another slum. Lakshmi is also gifted in the areas of hospitality and mentoring. She and her husband have welcomed into their home many individuals who have stayed for extended periods of time and grown into followers of Christ as a result.

Kavita

Kavita has served with the mission for many years, primarily in the capacity of directing discipleship programs. Kavita began directing training programs as a single woman during the late 2000s. She had previously completed a bachelor's degree in theology. As a new leader, Kavita was wavering in confidence, sometimes anxious, and frequently in her own leader's office, asking for advice. Twelve years later, she now gives advice to other new leaders. Kavita was invited to join the leadership team, the primary decision-making body of the campus, about ten years ago. She was the only woman on the leadership team for many years. Of her experience, she recounts: "I kept quiet in the leadership meetings at first. For an entire year, I waited for someone to ask my opinion, but no one ever did. Now I argue like a man in those meetings" (uproarious laughter follows).

Kavita got married in her late thirties. She was already well established as a leader and as an instructor of spiritual formation when she met her husband. She continues to serve in ministry on a full-time basis and to travel as a guest speaker. With the amount of time that household duties take, how can Kavita do this? She and her husband have a clear division of labor. She does all the cooking, which she says she can finish in two hours a day. He does all the cleaning and provides much of the care for their young daughter. Like Lakshmi's husband, Kavita's husband is her greatest champion. One day, he realized that she had not traveled anywhere in quite a while. Soon, Kavita was hearing her husband's exhortations: "Why aren't you doing any guest speaking? You can't stop just because you are married now."

Zara

Zara joined the mission when she was in her mid-thirties, after working as a professional for many years. She had long wanted to be a missionary, but other responsibilities needed to be attended to first. In her own words, her father "quit home" when she was eighteen years old. Zara, the oldest of five children, worked in a job to put herself through college and graduate school. After completing her master's degree, she went to work as an accountant. She put her younger siblings through college. By the time these years were completed, Zara's brother had taken a job in the United States and her three sisters were married. Her brother married a few years later. Only Zara remained single.

Finally, Zara joined the mission. She delighted in her newly found freedom and immersed herself in keeping the campus accounts free from error. Before long, Zara was working closely with Lisa, the founder of Mission Location X. Recognizing Zara's insight and abilities, Lisa appointed her to various leadership positions. Eventually, Zara agreed to be the primary campus director for an interim period of two years. After leaving that post, Zara relocated to her home state so that she could spend more time with her aging mother. But she continued to travel for guest teaching and to lead—by this time, as a regional director overseeing all of the mission's operating locations in two states.

Zara has spearheaded multiple new training programs and ministry locations. She is a pioneer as well as a leader. She is full of vision. Not only does Zara have innovative ideas, but she also has the wherewithal to implement those ideas. Now that she needs to spend more time near her mother, she is turning her attention to ministry in that region. She is currently establishing a new Bible college in her home state.

Reflections

The lives of Lakshmi, Kavita, and Zara illustrate a few ways that South Asian women may be empowered for leadership. In the cases of Lakshmi and Kavita, both have husbands who participate substantially in household affairs. Lakshmi and Kavita's husbands also encourage them to use their gifts in ministry. Lakshmi's husband did not grow up as an entitled male. On the contrary, he was expected from a young age to work hard both in the house and in the fields. Likewise, Kavita's husband, a pastor by training, is no stranger to hard work. Before he married, he spent several years serving in a ministry for street children, a ministry that required many hours of handwashing the children's clothes, cooking, and cleaning each day.[39]

In Zara's case, her singleness has given her the mobility, freedom, and time to devote herself to leadership in multiple capacities, including the empowerment of other leaders. She may not have expected that she would remain single, yet it has been her singleness that has meant she can devote large chunks of time to leadership which, in her case, requires considerable travel. Besides having a gifting in the area of leadership, Zara's life experience of taking responsibility for her younger siblings has, likely, helped to shape in her an ability to provide oversight and care for others.

Another observation is that all three of these women have completed at least one program of higher education. Both Lakshmi and Zara have master's degrees. Kavita has a bachelor's degree. It may be that higher education has helped to empower these women by providing them with skills and increased confidence. Higher education may also help foster an expectation in women to contribute to their communities.

---

39. It may also be noted that physical work is part of the curriculum in Mission Location X. Students participate in the work of running the campus by serving an hour each day in an assigned duty, whether meal preparation, cleaning, or outdoor work. This requirement may help improve attitudes toward physical labor.

These observations, while not comprehensive, point to a few areas for empowerment that could result in more women in leadership. The first has to do with team ministry and parenting. There is a need for more couples to catch a vision for this lifestyle. This could be facilitated through teaching and open discussion. All couples could consider team ministry as a viable option.

The second area is a need for a theology of singleness. Throughout history, God has used single persons, as well as married persons, to accomplish his purposes. Jeremiah, Ezekiel, Daniel, Paul, and Anna the prophet are just a few examples of single persons who had significant ministries in the Bible—not to mention Jesus.[40] Single women have made enormous contributions to mission over the past few centuries. A little encouragement about the value of singleness could go a long way for those experiencing unwanted pressures to marry. Not only do families and society at large elevate the status of the married, but also Protestant church culture often promotes an expectation for marriage. This expectation may be more applicable for single men than for single women. With a ratio of two single women to every one single man in the church worldwide,[41] there is an urgent need for teaching that affirms singleness as a worthwhile option. Not all will find spouses in the church.

A third area that could help empower women in South Asia is access to higher education. Women with university degrees typically have better critical thinking and problem-solving skills than those who have not had the opportunity to study. They may also have greater confidence and a higher expectation to engage in the world outside their own homes. In South Asia, a large percentage of students, both male and female, conclude their education at the end of tenth grade. Women as well as men would benefit from opportunities to continue their education. Numerous distance-learning options exist for those who, like Lakshmi, wish to continue to study, but need encouragement and an accessible option.

There is a need for greater participation in leadership by women in South Asia. This is true not only because better representation is needed for women, but also because the workers are few and the needs are great.

---

40. God commanded Jeremiah to remain single due to the soon-coming fall of Jerusalem (Jer. 16:1–4). Ezekiel prophesied first as a married man, then as a widower after his wife, "the delight of your eyes" was taken from him (Ezek. 24:15–18 NRSV). Daniel prophesied in the royal Babylonian courts as an unmarried man. He may have been a eunuch, but the text is unclear. The Apostle Paul mentions his singleness in 1 Cor 7:7. Anna, the prophet "of a great age" who proclaimed the birth of Christ, had been married for seven years before being widowed (Luke 2:26–38 NRSV).

41. Robert, "World Christianity as a Women's Movement," 182–83.

Without the participation of more women in leadership, there will be fewer workers trained and fewer workers sent. (And, when all this is said, if God gifts women and calls women to go, they should go.)

Conclusion

Barriers to female leadership in the mission have existed for many years and may always exist. Yet, history shows us that women can, and do, find ways around these barriers. When the mission boards of the nineteenth century declined single female applicants out of concern for propriety and decorum, new opportunities emerged when women took initiative to start female missionary societies. The barrier of paternalism was circumvented and the women's missionary movement was birthed. What started with a small number of women being sent overseas in the early 1860s grew into thousands by the time Helen Barrett Montgomery wrote *Western Women in Eastern Lands* in 1910. As the women's missionary societies were shut down, when denominations fought, when finances dried up, when wars broke out, when missionaries had to return to their homelands, the global church not only became established, it flourished. Indigenous expressions of faith proved to be effective. The message of Jesus Christ grew rapidly in the Global South.

The social expectations in South Asia today for women to marry, bear children, and spend their time managing the homes while their husbands go to work, are not far from the social expectations placed on North American and European women in the 1800s to the early 1900s and beyond. Even within egalitarian mission organizations, there may be many more men than women in leadership. But there are also many women who do serve faithfully as leaders. They teach, mentor, make important decisions, and launch new ministries. Even so, many more women need to be trained, empowered, and released into leadership in order to help meet the needs of regions with burgeoning populations and expanding Christian movements. Couples need to be encouraged to consider team parenting and team ministry. A greater affirmation and understanding of singleness, as well as encouragement to continue with higher education, would also help to empower women for leadership in South Asia. The leadership of both women and men, both single and married, is needed in order to reflect more completely the heart of God to a generation in need. We need the whole church to reach the whole world.

References

Beaver, R. Pierce. *American Protestant Women in World Mission: A History of the First Feminist Movement in North America*. Grand Rapids: Eerdmans, 1968.

Carmichael, Amy. *Meal in a Barrel*. Madras: Christian Literature Society, 1929.

"Female Infanticide." BBC Ethics Guide website. http://www.bbc.co.uk/ethics/abortion/medical/infanticide_1.shtml. Accessed Nov. 18, 2019.

Gordon College. "History of Gordon." https://www.gordon.edu/history. Accessed Nov. 19, 2019.

Gowen, Annie. "India Has 63 Million 'Missing' Women and 21 Million Unwanted Girls, Government Says." *Washington Post*. https://www.washingtonpost.com/news/worldviews/wp/2018/01/29/india-has-63-million-missing-women-and-21-million-unwanted-girls-government-says/. Jan. 29, 2018.

Hamrick, Karen. "Americans Spend an Average of 37 Minutes a Day Preparing and Serving Food and Cleaning Up." United States Department of Agriculture Economic Research Service. Nov. 7, 2016. https://www.ers.usda.gov/amber-waves/2016/november/americans-spend-an-average-of-37-minutes-a-day-preparing-and-serving-food-and-cleaning-up/.

"Indian Women Do Most Household Work While Men Do Very Little." *Times of India*. Nov. 1, 2018. https://timesofindia.indiatimes.com/business/indian-women-do-most-household-work-while-men-do-very-little/articleshow/66456334.cms.

Jenkins, Philip. *The Next Christendom: The Coming of Global Christianity*. 3rd ed. New York: Oxford University Press, 2011.

MacNicol, Nicol, and Vishal Mangalwadi. *What Liberates A Woman? The Story of Pandita Ramabai: A Builder of Modern India*. New Delhi: Good Books, 1996.

Montgomery, Helen Barrett. *Western Women in Eastern Lands*. Norwood, MA: Macmillan, 1910.

NITI Aayog, Government of India. "Sex Ratio (Females/1000 Males)." https://niti.gov.in/content/sex-ratio-females-1000-males. Accessed Nov. 4, 2019.

Robert, Dana L., ed. *Gospel Bearers, Gender Barriers: Missionary Women in the Twentieth Century*. Maryknoll, NY: Orbis, 2002.

———. "Shifting Southward." *International Bulletin of Missionary Research* 24 (2000): 50–58.

———. "World Christianity as a Women's Movement." *International Bulletin of Missionary Research* 30 (2006): 180–88.

Rosling, Hans. *Factfulness: Ten Reasons We're Wrong about the World—And Why Things Are Better Than You Think*. London: Scepter, 2018.

Tucker, Ruth. *Guardians of the Great Commission*. Grand Rapids: Zondervan, 1988.

———. *From Jerusalem to Irian Jaya: A Biographical History of Christian Mission*. Grand Rapids: Zondervan, 1983.

United Nations. *World Population Prospects*. 2015. https://population.un.org/wpp/Publications/Files/WPP2015_DataBooklet.pdf.

World Population Review. "US States–Ranked by Population 2019." http://worldpopulationreview.com/states/. Accessed Nov. 4, 2019.

Conclusion

Aída Besançon Spencer

I REMEMBER ONE BRIGHT SUNNY day as a young child (elementary age), I walked a few blocks to see a parade on Máximo Gomez Avenue. I stood at the corner, a little blonde girl in pigtails, as the president and generalissimo of the country passed by on his float. He peered down at me as I gaped up, shocked: Why, that man has white powder all over his face! The dictator Rafael Leonidas Trujillo Molina was the epitome of the ruler who overpowered and tyrannized his people (Mark 10:42). Trujillo's aspiration was to be taken for a higher-class person than he was. He wanted to look European, like those of the class to which he aspired, so he put white powder on his own face and began to drive out or execute Haitians and Dominicans of dark color.

He wanted to be perceived as wealthy, so one day he declared all the cattle in the country were his. My mother was extending her father's inter-island business of selling burlap sacks and scrap metal from Puerto Rico to the Dominican Republic. Somehow, Trujillo found out that my mother had sold but not delivered yet a shipment of metal. He demanded it for his own use. When she refused to cancel her completed sale and sell it to him, Trujillo had my father incarcerated as a hostage until she changed her mind. Foreigners, such as my Dutch father, were normally not attacked by Trujillo, but when the painter E. Scott complained, he disappeared. His paintings still grace our walls in memory of him.

Countries like the United States who wanted to curry Trujillo's favor (not wanting another Cuba) gave him presents, such as instruments of power, like his own state-of-the-art electric chair, where he could enjoy electrocuting victims. Today's 200 pesos bill celebrates the three Maribal sisters (Patria, Minerva, and Maria Teresa) known in the underground as the Butterflies, who were sexually and physically assaulted and murdered after their protests.

Trujillo's aspirations were self-centered and hierarchical, a self-glorifying patriarchy that were simply wrong. He already had power automatically invested in his position as president and general over the police, so he did not have to bully the nation and terrify it with his police force to get more power, control, and status. (At that time, he stationed police on every corner!) Trujillo perpetuated the system started by the conquistadores who enslaved the Taino Indians, stole their land, and assigned it to the invaders, many of whom were criminals, drawn from the prisons in Europe.[1] This classist heritage was historically there, and Trujillo augmented it.

I realized when I grew up in this environment how very evil such dictatorial actions were, and, thus, I became an adamant advocate for egalitarian principles.

That is the kind of misuse of power we do *not* want in our nations, our institutions, our churches, or our families. Instead, we want to use our power as Jesus did—to serve others in a sacrificial way. What is "success" anyway? Is not authentic success receiving the approval of Jesus, God incarnate? As humans, we can choose to be aggressively competitive or humbly loving.

We have learned in this book what is entailed in the hierarchical tyranny of the Gentiles and Christian egalitarian servant leadership, as we see the tension exhibited in the New Testament, Old Testament, and ancient philosophy. Leadership styles affect the relationships of women and men, minority and majority cultures and ethnic groups, and those in different life stages: wife and husband, children and parents, girl and boy, lay and clergy, neighborhood and church, retiree and church, and, finally, national and foreigner.

What is Gentile tyranny? I saw it modeled to me by dictator Trujillo;[2] Jesus saw it in his disciples James and John, sons of Zebedee (Mark 10:35–45). Pagan rulers jockey for power, seek to be the greatest by lording it over others, ask for and seek places of privilege. Such rulership may rest on aggressive assault or accepted innate authority and permanent rank by virtue of blood, gender, birthright, race, wealth, that results in an attitude of arrogance and haughtiness and entitlement. Power is concentrated in hierarchical leaders while underlings do all the work. One self-appointed bully

---

1. Further, see W. Spencer, "God of Power," *Global God*, 43–48.
2. Trujillo was assassinated, and since then the Dominican Republic is a democracy.

makes the decisions for all, with no input from the persons affected. He (or she) has a one-way command and control. One rules; the other is ruled. Fear and violence may epitomize this mode of authority. Self-centered, self-seeking, self-glorifying, dominating power and prestige often result in the harmful use of power and greed. They leave the people they rule as infants, stunted in growth and, therefore, subject to deceitful teaching. Their gifts are not fully used. As a result, marginal persons (often women, minorities, wives, children, girls, laity, outsiders, retirees, nationals) are often ignored, silenced, restricted, excluded, harassed, abused, and even killed. Stereotypes arise that perpetuate the unjust system, such as the marginal person labeled as not logical or reasonable, but, rather, emotional, illogical, passive, inferior, not able to command, and not fully created in God's image. There is a permanent inequality because the marginal person is said to be incomplete, impotent, imperfect, unworthy, less important, insignificant, even stupid. They are, however, "the least of these [Jesus's] brothers and sisters," they are even Jesus himself (Matt 25:40–45).

Are these qualities aspects of "strong" leadership? Is this the way to guide, direct, advise, command, or show the way to others? No, says Jesus and his authentic disciples!

In contrast, what is Christian egalitarian servant leadership? It is gentle, not "Gentile," in style. Although Jesus uses the concept of Gentile rulers in a negative way, he was not negative against all Gentiles. Gentile overpowering and tyrannical rulership can be exhibited by Jews and half-Jews, including Herod the elder and his son Archelaus, but not by the other son, Herod Philip (Matt 2:1–23; 14:3; Luke 3:1). *Christian leadership* is modeled on Christ's character and actions, enabled by God-the-Trinity, and intended to honor Christ. Christ sacrificed himself for others and was others-oriented. Although God, he lived, not entitled, but, rather, humbly. He is the epitome of love and thankfulness for all good. The good news, according to the Scriptures (our authority), promotes such a type of leadership.

Therefore, *Christian egalitarian leadership* is mutual service or submission between partners in ministry for Christ's sake. Christian egalitarian leadership is an intrinsic aspect of *servant* leadership. *Servant leadership* is sacrificial service for others in Christ's behalf. It is others-oriented power, humble, gentle, thankful, loving, Christ honoring and promoting, and not abusive, harmful, self-centered, self-seeking, or entitled. *Egalitarian leadership* entails equality between the genders, races, economic and social classes, differing ages, differing power, honor, and education, married and single, differently gifted. There is no innate or permanent hierarchy of rank, status, or authority. Rather, there is mutual submission, interdependence, service out of love, cooperative partnership, shared power and decision making, and mutual respect, deference, and honor. Christian egalitarian leadership is characterized by a communal, interdependent, and cooperative effort of love, caring service, skill, education, intercession, confession, and forgiveness to cause the body of believers to grow into Christ and to worship God. All humans are equal in worth, rights, and status, but are not the same in gifts, skills, function, age, sex, ethnic background, wealth, or education. People are unique and variety is good. However, resources and gifts must be shared. Any ranking should be by service. Decisions are impartial. The whole church is encouraged and empowered.

Such a leadership style may be explained by the model of able and faithful leaders such as Deborah and Barak, Phoebe and Paul, the many model Christians mentioned in Romans 16, and by contemporary examples, but also by biblical concepts, such as servant leadership, mutual submission, "weak" leadership, Christ's body, hospitality, equality, impartiality, spiritual gifts, the priesthood of all believers, the new covenant, and communal authority. Salvation *and* leadership are open to all: men and women, father and mother, Jews and Gentiles, rich and poor, free and slave, the powerful and the less powerful, the old and the young. Jesus explained: "All of you are equal as brothers and sisters" (Matt 23:8 NLT) and "Since I, your Lord and Teacher, have washed your feet, you ought to wash each other's feet. I have given you an example to follow. Do as I have done to you" (John 13:14–15 NLT). Jesus used his own power and authority for sacrificial humble service for others. Servant leadership is costly and hard work. It must be learned, developed, and nurtured.

Sometimes, we confuse genuine functional or active egalitarianism with theoretical egalitarianism. The difference is the presence or lack of humility. Functional egalitarianism sees itself as only one part of a whole where everyone's contribution is needed. Words are then reflected in actions. Genuine egalitarianism must be communal and interdependent. All are created and recreated in God's image. All proclaim the gospel. All have access to the Father through the Spirit because of the Son's sacrifice. All are filled by the Spirit. All are dependent on God. All can learn from others because all people are God's masterpieces.

This book is not a repetition of the many excellent studies showing how the Bible supports women in ministry. These books have been referenced throughout the chapters for further reading. Rather, our goal is to advance to the next stage. How does egalitarian leadership affect all the marginalized in the church? We have not exhausted this topic. The ramifications are endless. How does Christian egalitarian leadership affect all the structures of society and all people groups?

In the writing of the book we attempted to model egalitarian principles. Although I (Aída) coordinated the venture, with Bill's consultation in scholarship and grammatical acumen, we sought leaders to research and write on different topics from the basis of their own strengths and concerns. We were honored to find women and men, with different cultures, ethnic, and economic backgrounds to write. Bill and Aída especially appreciated the participation of many long-term members of the editorial team of the House of Prisca and Aquila series (partnering with Wipf and Stock since 2006). The team project is in gratitude to them, as we all begin to reflect on what it means not to lead in Gentile tyranny, but to lead according to Jesus's sacrificial love.

Reference

Spencer, William David. "God of Power versus God of Love: The United States of America." In *The Global God: Multicultural Evangelical Views of God*, edited by Aída Besançon Spencer and William David Spencer, 37–62. Grand Rapids: Baker, 1998.

Subject Index

Abel, 234
Abraham, 11, 158
Adam, and Eve, 38–39, 42, 69, 72–80, 104, 108–9, 167–68, 208, 211–12, 233–35. *See also teshuqah*
adolescence, 194, 198, 200–214, 217–21. *See also* children
Alexander, the Great, 90, 97
American Baptist Churches, 240–44, 249
Amit, Yairah, 52n22
Amonde, Joel, 224
Ananias, and Sapphira, 22
Anderson, Lorraine, 236
Andrew, 131–32
Andronicus, and Junia, 9, 11, 45, 112
Anna, 16–17, 278
Antal, Jim, 237
Apollos, 132–33
apostle(s), 5, 9, 11–12, 14, 32, 34, 39, 55–56
apostropheē ("turning"), 76–79. *See also teshuqah*
Aristotle, 83–84, 90–98, 100–101, 105–10, 112. *See also* marriage, women
Artemis, 68n29
artist(s), 123–24
astheneō ("weak"), 8–9. *See also* leadership

Athenagoras, 62
Atkins, Robert A., 18n49
Audrey, 221
Augustine, 4, 98–100, 106–9
authority, xxv, 19–21, 26–33, 37, 40, 49, 54, 80, 207–9, 283; defined, 19. *See also* authority-submission structure
authority-submission structure, 60, 66–67
autism, 173–76

Bagster, Samuel, 76, 79
Barak, 47, 49–52, 55, 284
Barnabas, 20–21
Baylis, Candy, 224
Belleville, Linda, 36
Biebel, David, 192
Bigg, Charles, 61–62
Bilezikian, Gilbert, 21, 209, 247
Bonhoeffer, Dietrich, 141–43
Boone, Pat, and Shirley, 121–22
Booth, Catherine, 228–29
Booth, Evangeline, 229
Booth, William, 228–29
Brock, Tom, 224
Bruce, F. F., 30
Buechner, Frederick, 50

Cain, 77, 79, 234

canon, 28, 31
Carmichael, Amy, 263–65
Castelli, James, 143
Cerinthus, 71–72
Chapman, Linda, 124
children; childrearing, 7, 87–89, 108, 111, 125, 149, 152–54, 157–63, 174–76, 180–93, 195–98, 203–5, 218, 262, 264, 272, 275, 279
Christians for Biblical Equality (CBE), 33, 35, 233, 236
Clement, of Alexandria, 62
Code of Ethics, 240–41, 249–50
Cohen, Shaye, 156–57
community, xxi, xxv, 18n49, 21, 35, 88, 120, 128, 131, 142, 148–49, 154, 157–63, 197, 219, 240, 242, 247–49, 275, 284. *See also* Ubuntu philosophy
Cornelius, 11, 18, 130
Corral, Michelle, 122–23
Council on Biblical Manhood and Womanhood (CBMW), 35, 107, 110. *See also* Danvers Statement
covenant, new, 3, 5, 16, 18, 284
Crossan, John Dominic, 37

Daane, J., 29–30
Daniel, 278
Daniels, David D., 145–46
Danvers Statement on Biblical Manhood and Womanhood, 35, 107–10, 112. *See also* Council on Biblical Manhood and Womanhood (CBMW)
David, 27, 52, 158
Davis, Billy, 122
Davis, Julia, 125–27
De Toqueville, Alexis, 148
deacon, 226–28, 239
Deborah, 20, 42, 47–53, 55, 58, 112, 284
demuth ("likeness"), 69. *See also* image, of God
Denault, Leigh, 87
DeSouza, Herbert, 121
diakonos; doulos ("service-oriented"), 4, 43–45
Diere, Jack, 33

denomination(s), 31–32, 34–35, 145–46, 149, 217, 262, 266–67, 279
doctrinal distinctives, 32–33
Dishpande, Omker, xxiii
domestic violence (DV), 95, 98, 110–12, 196, 200–203, 204–7, 210–14. *See also* sex
Don, 227–28
Doremus, Sarah, 262
Dowdy, Naomi, 53–58

Eber, Charlene, 122–23
egalitarianism, 13, 22, 35–37, 40, 107, 117, 153, 199, 208, 261, 282, 284–85; functional, 9, 13–15, 22, 284. *See also* equality; leadership; marriage
Ehud, 49
Eikenberry, Jeris, and Joyce, 220–21
Eisen, Ute E., 45
elder(s), 20, 226–27. *See also* leader(s)
elohim ("God"), 69–70, 72
English Language Learner(s) (ELL), 126–27
Epaenetus, 9
Epaphras, 43
equality (*isotēs*) xxii-xxiii, xxv, 3–6, 10–11, 18, 23, 38–40, 86, 102–3, 105, 167, 184–86, 199, 210, 214, 233–37, 266, 284. *See also* egalitarianism; hierarchy; leadership
Erickson, Millard, 29
Esther, 112
eudaimonia ("happiness"), 91. *See also* happiness, pursuit of
Eunice, 152, 154–55, 157, 162
evangelist(s), 12, 17, 56
Evans, Anthony, 137–39
Eve. *See* Adam, and Eve
Ezekiel, 278

faith genealogy, 152, 154, 158, 161
Fee, Gordon, 28, 36
Feldman, Marcus, xxiii
Fisher, Albert Franklin, 141
Francis, Mabel, 262–63
Fung, Benjamin, 168–79

Fung, Scarlet Tsao, 168–79
Fung, Theodora, 173–76

Gaarder, Jostein, 95
Gallup, George, 143
Gentile(s) (*ethnos*), 11, 13, 18, 21, 32, 64, 89, 124, 130–36, 157, 282–83, 285
Gesenius, William, 69
Gideon, 51–52
gifts, spiritual, 3, 12–16, 19, 22, 32–33, 56, 109, 174, 177, 184–85, 212, 219, 231–32, 283–84
Glahn, Sandra, 51
Global South, 267–69, 278–79; defined, 261
Gorospe, Athena, 42–48, 52–53
Grady, Lee, 35
grandmother hypothesis, 155–57, 160–61, 163
Gray, Peter, xxii–xxiii
Greer, Lindred, xxi, xxv
"Greever, Maria," 239–40

happiness, pursuit of, 147–49, 167. *See also eudaimonia*
Hawley, Patricia H., xvii
Heifetz, Ronald. 245, 249
Herod, Archelaus, 283
Herod, elder, 283
Herod Philip, 283
Hess, Bartlett, 219
hierarchy, xii, 4–5, 7, 9, 12, 14, 16, 18, 23, 61–63, 67, 72, 81, 87, 92–93, 101, 107, 196–99, 203, 281–82. *See also* leadership; patriarchy
honor, mutual, 13–15, 23
hospitality, xxv, 13, 51, 240, 242, 246–47, 254, 262, 275, 284
House of Prisca and Aquila (HPA), 35–36, 117–19, 123, 125, 127, 285
Hudson, Nancy, 46–47, 55, 58
Hudson, Rock, 121–22
huiothesia ("adoption"), 18n49
Huldah, 49n11, 112
Hull, Gretchen Gaebelein, 38–39
hupakouō ("obey"), 7

hupotassō ("submit"), 7–8. *See also* submission, mutual

image, of God, 61, 73–74, 102–3, 195, 208, 211–12, 283–84
impartiality, 3, 11. *See also* equality
inerrancy, 29–32, 36, 40
International Fellowship of Christian Assemblies, 30, 34
Irenaeus, 71
Isaac, 158

Jael, wife of Heber, 51–53, 55
James, 1, 21, 282
James, Carolyn Custis, 33
Jenkins, Philip, 261, 268
Jeremiah, 278
Jerusalem, xxiv, 17–18, 21, 27, 236, 278n40; new, 10, 247
Jesus, model, 5–7, 9–12, 17, 22, 130–31, 158, 177–78, 182–84, 199–200, 207–10, 214, 233, 235–36, 246–47, 264, 278, 283–85; teachings, 26–27, 31; teachings on equality, xxiv–xxv, 4–7, 10, 19, 21, 80, 134, 185–86, 195–96, 284; uniqueness, 21, 31
Jesus Movement, 220
Jethro, 20
Joel, 18
"John," 210, 212
John, apostle, 4, 9, 32, 65–66, 69, 71–72, 127, 131, 260, 282
John the Baptist, 184
Josiah, 184
Jubin, King, 48–49
judge(s) (*shophetim*), 48–52
Junia. *See* Andronicus, and Junia
Justin Martyr, 64–65, 68

"Kavita," 274–77
Kee, Judy, 236
Kee, Ralph, 244–45
Kee, Susan, 235
Keener, Craig, 27, 35–37, 45, 154
kenodoxia ("empty glory"), 6
kephalē ("head"), 7, 12, 28, 208, 212
Kern, Ally, 204–5, 211

king(s), 20–21, 73, 80. *See also* rule
King, John, 31
King, Martin Luther, 118, 129, 134
Kistan, Cheryl, 230–31
Kistan, Nesan, 230–31
Kumpler, Karol, 212
kurieuō; katakurieuō ("lord it over"), xxiv, 73, 79–81

"Lakshmi," 274–78
Larrits, Bryan, 141
Larry, 222–25
lay sponsor(s). *See* laypeople.
laypeople, 218–28, 232
leader(s), 16, 245, 249; defined, 3, 12, 22, 207; plural, 19–21, 55
leadership, Christian, 13–14, 16, 22, 161–63, 217, 282–84; egalitarian, xxi-xxvi, 3–4, 9, 13, 19, 22, 60, 75, 78–81, 133, 153–55, 211, 250, 269–79; defined, 3n1, 12, 23, 283; hierarchical, xxi-xxv, 8; multicultural, 132, 139, 144–46; servant, 3–4, 6, 9, 21n60, 143, 162, 181–82, 185, 191, 207, 209, 247, 284; defined, 22–23, 283. *See also* egalitarianism, hierarchy, multiculturalism
Levi, Matthew, 246
Lewis, C. S., 190, 220
Linsky, Marty, 245, 249
"Lisa," 270–72, 276
Lois, 152, 154–55, 157, 162
Luther, Martin, 18n45, 73n33

Macaulay, Susan Schaeffer, 192
MacLeod, Gavin, and Patti, 121, 124
"Malika," 271
Mandela, Nelson, 198
Mangena, Philip, 47
Manicheanism, 98
Mann, Aaron (Ezra), 124
marriage, 7, 67–68, 92, 99, 102, 104–5, 107, 109, 111, 156, 166–79, 185, 197–98, 205–6, 208, 210–11, 260–62, 270–80. *See also* submission; women

Marston, Sarah, 262
Mary, 5, 9, 45, 131, 236
Mary Magdalene, 236, 260
"Maryanne," 205–6, 210–12
Mathews, Alice, 208
matope ("waste"), 224
matrilineal principle, 155, 157. *See also* grandmother hypothesis
McCann, J. Clinton, 49
McCoo, Marilyn, 122
Metzger, Paul Louis, 147
Mike, 222–23
Miriam, 49n11, 53
mission(s), 260–79
Montgomery, Helen Barrett, 44n2, 265–66, 279
Moo, Douglas, 32
Moon, Lottie, 266
Moses, 19–20, 26–27, 48, 51–53, 126, 255
Moss, Otis, 137
multiculturalism, 36, 118–24, 126–27, 129–49, 242–44, 282, 285. *See also* leadership
multiethnicity. *See* multiculturalism

Naaman's servant, 184
Nathaniel, 131
Neoplatonism, 98–99. *See also* Plato
Northouse, Peter G., 3
Nouwen, Henri, 220
Novak, Mel, 119–21
Nwadiokwu, C. N., 159

Ogden, Greg, 18n45
O'Neal, Yvonnette, 118–19
Onesimus, 11
Origen, 62, 68

pastor(s), 12, 21–22, 46–47, 54, 56. *See also* women, ministry
patriarchy, 83, 97, 108, 110, 153, 157, 160–61, 196–98, 202–3, 261, 267, 269, 279, 282
Paul, model, 132, 152, 155, 162–63, 263, 278, 284; teachings on equality, 6–16, 42, 45, 133, 155, 197, 203, 207–9, 211, 246

Pendergrass, Lee Ann, 124
Perictione, 86
Perkins, John, 148
Peter, 10–12, 20–21, 27, 29, 31–32, 39, 131, 133, 260
Peter, Jonathan, 47
Petronella, Joanne, 122–23
Philip, 39, 131–32
Philip, of Macedon, 86
Philo, 62, 65–66
Phoebe, 9, 11, 42–47, 58, 284
Pilate, Pontius, 4
Plato; Platonist(s), 61–64, 66–68, 72, 83–91, 99–100, 106–10, 112. See also Neoplatonist(s)
Pliny, 45
Pollock, Jozy, 119–21
Polycarp, 71
Powell, Adam Clayton, 141–42
power, 5–6, 11, 19, 22–23, 282–83
preachers survey, 136–37
priest(s), 48. See also priesthood, of all believers
priesthood, of all believers, 3, 16–19, 284
Prisca (Priscilla), and Aquila, 9, 37, 45, 112
prophet(s), 12, 14–18, 20, 48–51, 53, 56
prostatis ("leader"), 43
Ptolemy II Philadelphus, 79
Pythagorus, 62

Rah, Soong Chan, 141
Ramabai, Pandita, 264–65
Rebecca, 158
retired pastor(s), 239–59
revelation, God's, 3, 27, 29, 36. See also Scripture(s)
Rieth, Bob, 122
Ringma, Charles, 47–48
Robeck, Cecil M., 144
Robert, Dana, 267
Rogers, Deborah, xxiii-xxiv
rule (*arxeis*), 79–81, 198, 207–9, 211, 283. See also king(s)
Ruth, 49

Samson, 51–52
Samuel, 20, 48, 52, 77–78, 184
Schell, Adam, xxii
Scott, E., 281
Scripture(s) (Bible), 29–31, 38, 119, 163, 186–87, 205. See also inerrancy
Septuagint (LXX), 76, 78–79
Serpell, Robert, 160
service, mutual. See submission, mutual
sex; sexual misconduct, 54, 101, 202–3, 269, 282. See also domestic violence
Seymour, William, 144
Shamgar, 50
Sharp, Nicholas, 240
Shenandoah, April, 122
Sisera, 49, 51, 53
skandalizō ("to stumble"), 196
slave(s); slavery, 4–8, 11, 17–18, 92–93, 102, 112, 284
Slesser, Mary, 266
Smith, Hannah, 180, 183, 185, 188, 191–92
Smith, Jonathan, 180–81, 185, 188, 92
Smith, Sara, 180–81, 183, 185, 188, 192
Socrates, 62, 84–86
Soler, Olga, 124
spectrum relationship(s), 247
Spencer, Aída Besançon, 37–40, 79, 212, 237
Spencer, William David, 38, 127–28, 237
Spirit, Holy, xxv, 14, 18, 20–22, 29, 32–33, 39, 62, 64–65, 67, 69, 70–72, 108, 117–25, 127, 169–70, 177, 186, 202–3, 208–10, 212, 220, 231, 246–47, 284
Stafford, Susan, 121–22, 124
Stephana(s), household, 8
Stephen Ministry, 225–26
story, 180, 187, 189, 219–20. See also children
Stuart, Doug, 28
submission, mutual, 3–4, 6–9, 12–13, 16, 22–23, 207–9, 213–14, 247, 285–84
Sue Ann, 223

Swan, Monte, 192
Sweeney, Terry, 121

T., Nancy, 225
T., Tom, 225–26
tapeinoō ("bring low"), 196
Taylor, Maria, 266
teacher(s), 12, 14, 56
temple, 16–18, 130, 184, 203
Teresa, of Calcutta, 121
teshuqah ("desire"), 75–77
The Salvation Army, 228–31
Thomas, Aquinas, 100–109, 112, 145
Thurmond, 227–28
Timothy, 20, 43, 51, 56, 104, 132, 52–57, 162–63, 184, 186
Titus, 11, 56, 132
Tracy, Steven, 111
Trinity, 21n60, 22, 60–62, 64, 66–73, 80, 199
Trophimus, 130
Trueblood, Elton, 220
Trujillo, Rafael Leonidas, 281–82
Trypho, 64
Tychicus, 43

Ubuntu philosophy, 158–62
upbringing. *See* children; childrearing

Van Bunderen, Lisonne, xxi
virtue, 86, 91

Vuolanto, Ville, 155–56

Walsh, Dylan, xxi
Ware, Bruce, 60–61, 66–68, 75n33
Wenger, Gemma, 120–21
West, Ralph Douglas, 137
white evangelicalism, 135–49
Wilder, Almanzo, 190
Williams, Reggie L., 142
Winter, Miriam Therese, 37
Wisdom, 64–65, 67
Withun, David, 99
womanism, 235
women, general, 63–64, 84–85, 87–96, 100–112; ministry, 33–35, 37, 44–46, 56–58, 112, 127, 202–3, 210–12, 217–19, 228–31, 235–37, 262–66, 274–79; single, 261–67, 276–78, 279. *See also* marriage
Woolery, Chuck, 121
Word, 64–66, 69, 71–72

Xanthippe, 85–86

Yeo, Dominic, 54
YHWH ("the Lord"), 70

Zacchaeus, 246
"Zara," 274, 276–77
Zuckor, Patti, 124

Scripture Index

Old Testament

Genesis

1	61–62, 70, 167
1:1	71
1:2	72
1:2–3	69
1:17	211
1:26–27	33, 66, 69–70, 72, 195
1:26–28	38, 75, 78
1:27	73, 206, 208
1:28	74
1:31	167, 206
2	167
2:16–18	109, 167
2:18–25	78, 157
2:20–23	234
2:21–22	167
2:21–24	109, 166
3:1–13	109
3:6	39
3:12	234
3:16	72, 75–79, 109
4:7	77, 79

Exodus

3:18	19
12:12	70
14:15–31	53
14:24	50
15:1–18	53
15:20–21	49, 53
16:18–20	10
18:13	48
18:21–22	20
19:6	17
19:8	19

Leviticus

14:1–32	27

Numbers

1:50–51	16
1:53	16
3:7–9	16
4:3	16
6:24–26	190
11:11–15	20
11:16–17	20
11:26	20
11:29	20
12:14–15	240

Deuteronomy

4:2	31
5:22–27	19
6:4	70
6:6–9	187
8:3	38
10:17–18	11
18:15	27
18:18	27
22:1	77
24:1–4	26
25:4	27
25:5–6	27
27:9–26	48
28:1–14	48
31:18	77
32:2	126
33:25	176

Judges

1:16	52
2:18	52
3:9	52
3:15	52
3:21–22	49
3:31	50
4	47, 48, 53, 112
4:4–5	48
4:6–8	49
4:9–10	49
4:11	52
4:12	50
4:14	51
4:15	50
4:16	51
4:17–19	51
4:22	51
5	47, 48, 53, 112
5:1	51
5:7	52
5:20–21	50
5:24–30	53
19	197
19:30	197
20	197
21:25	48

Ruth

1:16	49

1 Samuel

3	184
7:16	48
7:17	77, 78
8:5	20
8:7	20
8:9–18	20

2 Kings

5:2–3	184
22:1–2	184
22:14	49
22:14–20	112

2 Chronicles

34:22–33	112

Nehemiah

6:14	49

Psalms

8:2	184
16:8–11	27
19:14	125
110:1	27
121:1–2	224
133:1	127
139	211

Proverbs

4:23	188
8	65, 67
8:21	189
8:22–31	64
17:1	126
18:2	125

18:24	125
22:6	125
31	105

Ecclesiastes

7:29	74

Isaiah

5:16	18
5:19–20	18
8:3	49
40:31	225
61:6	17
62:1	49
65:17–25	247

Jeremiah

5:6	77, 78
6:19	77
8:5	77
9:23–24	11
16:1–4	278
18:11–12	77
31:31–34	18

Ezekiel

16:53	77
24:15–18	278
33:11	77

Daniel

10:6	49
11:32	187

Joel

2:28–29	18
2:32	18

Micah

2:12	77–78

Zechariah

12:6	49

Malachi

2:7	17

New Testament

Matthew

1:21	208
1:23	208
2:1–23	283
4:4	30–31, 38
4:7	31
4:10	31
5:17	31
5:5	148
6:6	205
6:10	246
6:33	169
8:5–13	130
8:10	130
8:26	130
8:28–34	130
9:9–13	246
11:29	8
14:3	283
14:13–21	184
15:1–20	26
16:18	27
18	185
18:4–6	195
18:4–14	196
18:6	183
18:7–14	213
18:15–20	21
19:14	195
19:16–22	172
20:1–16	10
22:16	5

Matthew (continued)

22:24–28	27
23:5–12	6
23:8	284
23:11	6
25:40–45	283
27:54	246
28	134
28:1–10	236
28:16–20	130
28:18–20	28, 55

Mark

1:4	5
1:7	5
1:15	5
1:22	5
2:15–17	5
3:14–15	5
3:33–34	5
5:1–20	130–31
5:38–42	184
6:7–13	5, 20
6:35–43	5
7:1–23	26
7:7	26
8:1–9	5
10:13–16	182
10:35–45	9, 282
10:37–45	4
10:40	4
10:41	xxiv
10:42	xxiv, 281
10:42–44	4
10:45	4
11:17	130
12:14	5
12:29–30	6
12:31	125
12:38–44	5
13:10	130
14:22–24	5

Luke

1:5–9	16
1:41	184
2:26–38	278
2:37–38	17
3:1	283
4:17–19	17
6:13	55
7:1–10	130
8:17	203
8:26–39	130–31
10:1	20
10:38–42	5
14:26–27	8
19:1–10	246
22:24	xxiv
22:25–26	xxiv, 73, 80
24:11	260

John

1:1–3	65, 71–72
1:1–4	70
1:1–14	69
1:3	64, 72
1:7	72
1:9	72
1:14	65, 72, 121, 177
1:16	72
1:41	131
1:46	131
2:4	131
2:16–18	19
3:16	39, 190
3:31–35	5
4:24	177
4:39	131
4:46–54	130
5:18	10, 199
7:6	131
12	131
12:22–23	131
13:13–15	xxiv, 5
13:14–15	284
13:34	246
14:6	31, 39
16:13	246

17	213	15:28	21
17:4	209	16:1	132, 152, 154
17:6	209	16:3	154
17:11–12	210	16:14–15	44
17:15	210	17:11	28, 127
17:17	210	18:2–3	20
17:19–20	210	18:24	133
17:20–23	34, 127, 139	18:26	37
20:3–10	260	18:27–28	133
20:11–18	236	20:17	20
		20:28	20, 27–28
		21:9	39

Acts

		21:28–29	130
		21:37–38	132
		22:28	132
1:8	39	28:16–31	263
1:12–14	28, 34, 39		
1:21–22	14		
2:1–4	20, 28, 34, 39		

Romans

2:16–18	39		
2:17–18	18		
2:21	39	3:23	39
2:25–28	27	5:12	39
2:34–35	27	8:17	207
2:42–44	xxv	8:29	29, 203
2:42–47	126	10:13	39
2:45	xxv	12:1	15
2:46	xxv	12:3–8	14–15, 21
2:47	xxv	12:5	14
3:22	27	12:7	15
4	138	12:8	15, 16, 43
4:12	31, 39	12:9–10	14–15
4:23–31	34	12:9–21	15, 29
5:1–4	22	12:11	15
5:5	22	12:12	16
5:7–9	22	12:14	16
5:10	22	12:16	14, 16, 246
9	138	13:1–4	16, 19
10:9–16	17	13:5	16
10:9–33	11	14:12	203
10:34–35	11, 17	16	284
11:5–18	17	16:1–3	9, 11, 19, 42–46
12:12	44	16:3–5	9, 37, 44–45
13	138	16:6	9
13:2	20	16:7	9, 11, 112
15:2–6	21	16:9	9
15:7–12	21	16:12–13	9, 45
15:13–18	21	16:15	45
15:22–32	21		

1 Corinthians

1:10	34
1:11	44
1:12	34
1:19–31	11
1:31	11
2:2	8
2:10	71
3:1–9	133
3:4	34, 118
3:6–7	181
4:6	31
5:1–15	54
6:13–20	27–28, 203
7:4	19, 197
7:7	278
7:21	7
9:9	27
11:2–16	35
11:5	39
11:7–9	109
11:10	19
11:20–22	14
11:29–34	14
12	13, 39
12:4–6	21
12:4–27	202
12:7	13
12:11	33
12:12	246
12:14–20	13
12:21	13
12:22–24	13
12:25–26	13, 197
12:28	14, 56
12:29–30	14
12:31–13:13	13
13	209
13:6–7	9
13:11	186
14	235
14:3	51
15:3–4	3
15:22	39
16:15	8
16:16	8, 209
16:18	8
16:19	37

2 Corinthians

3:3–17	21
7:6–7	132
7:13	132
8:12–14	10
8:13–15	10, 13
8:23	132
10:1	8
11:7–33	6
11:20–21	4, 8
11:21–33	9
12:9	52

Galatians

2:3	11, 132
2:12	10
2:14	11
3:27	11
3:28	11, 28, 35, 112
3:29	11
6:2	20

Ephesians

1:4	190, 208
1:22	28, 208
2:10	211, 232
2:14	28
2:17–22	18
4	13
4:6–16	12, 21, 56
4:12–13	217
4:14	12, 31
4:15–16	12, 126, 211, 246
4:21–24	213
4:22–5:2	29
4:24	73
5	235
5:2–6	6
5:7–17	6
5:10	7, 104
5:17	7
5:18–21	6–7

5:21	8, 109, 195, 200, 207–9, 212, 247
5:21–24	7
5:21–33	68, 211
5:22	104
5:23	7, 28
5:25–28	197
5:27	7
5:31	7
5:33	7
6	186, 190
6:2	7
6:4	7, 186
6:5–9	7
6:10–13	8
6:18–19	8
6:21	43

Philippians

1:1	20
1:6	190
2:2–4	6, 34
2:5–6	6, 200
2:6–8	10
2:7–11	6
3:4–8	132

Colossians

1:7	43
1:9	18
1:12	11
1:16	69
1:18	28
3:5–14	29
3:10	73
3:11	28
3:11–16	17
3:13	126
4:7	43
4:15	44

1 Thessalonians

5:12	43

1 Timothy

1:2	155
1:3–7	154
2	235
2:1–4	155
2:5–6	31, 39, 207
2:9–15	36, 155
2:11–15	35, 36
2:12	19, 104
2:14	39
3	155
3:8–13	226
3:12	43
3:14	43
4:6	43
4:15	51
5	154
5:17	43

2 Timothy

1:5	152–54, 161
2:2	20
2:15	28, 112
3:15	154, 184, 186
3:16–17	29–30, 37

Titus

3:8	132

Philemon

2	44
10–18	11

Hebrews

1:3	73
8:5	17
8:8–11	18
9:27	xxii
10:10–25	17
11:32	51
11:34	51–52
12:1–2	52

Hebrews (continued)

13:1–2	246
13:5	190
13:10	17

James

1:19	125
2:1	11
2:9	11
4:8	184
5:14	20

1 Peter

1:18–19	28
1:20–21	29–30
2:9	17
3:15–16	31
4	13
4:3–7	13
4:9–11	12–13
5:5	209

1 John

2:2	39
3:1–2	74, 190
4:8	11
4:16	11

Revelation

2:1–7	155
7:9	28
12:11	123
21:16	10
22:18–19	31

Apocrypha

Sirach

18:24	77
41:21	77

3 Maccabees

2:10	77

www.ingramcontent.com/pod-product-compliance
Lightning Source LLC
Chambersburg PA
CBHW050618300426
44112CB00012B/1559